INTERNATIONAL BUSINESS

T0313292

INTERNATIONAL BUSINESS

A Course on the Essentials

THIRD EDITION

RIAD A. AJAMI AND G. JASON GODDARD

Routledge
Taylor & Francis Group

LONDON AND NEW YORK

This book is dedicated to Ali R. Charles Ajami, Alya Ajami,
and Leila Goddard, and to our students.

First published 2014 by M.E. Sharpe

Published 2015 by Routledge

2 Park Square, Milton Park, Abingdon, Oxon OX14 4RN
711 Third Avenue, New York, NY 10017, USA

Routledge is an imprint of the Taylor & Francis Group, an informa business

Library of Congress Cataloging-in-Publication Data

Ajami, Riad A.
 International business : a course on the essentials / by Riad A. Ajami, G. Jason Goddard.—
Third edition.
     pages cm.
 Revised edition of: International business : theory and practice / Riad A. Ajami . . . [et al.],
2nd edition, published in 2006.
 Includes bibliographical references and index.
 ISBN 978-0-7656-3134-3 (pbk. : alk. paper)
1. International trade. I. Title.

HF1379.K43 2013
658′.049—dc23   2013009454

ISBN 13: 9780765631343 (pbk)

Detailed Contents

Preface

In the wake of the recent financial crisis, some of the pillars of international business specifically, and globalization generally, were no longer universally cheered by all market participants. The European Union's sovereign debt crisis, the subprime mortgage crisis, and the inability to complete the World Trade Organization's Doha trade agenda all pointed to market participant fears that free trade and global capitalism had gone too far prior to the financial crisis. We do not believe this to be the case, and telling this story is the purpose for this third edition of *International Business: A Course on the Essentials*. We think that rather than focusing on the few problems of regional economic integration and global market integration, the time is ripe for a renewed discussion of the solid strengths of international business in light of recent market declines.

International business and multinational corporate activities have grown significantly during the past few decades. The rapid and continuous growth of cross-border economic linkages has contributed to the importance of the study of international business. Furthermore, the mandates by the international Assembly of the Collegiate Schools of Business regarding the globalization of the business curricula added to the relevance and importance of international business teaching. The objective of this text is to present an overview of international business teaching as a balance between international business environments from both an academic and practical perspective. The book also contains an analysis of issues of importance in today's global economy, such as the partnership between multinational corporations and commercial banks in the facilitation of international trade, and the continued importance of world energy markets. Moreover, the timelessness of the case studies with their cross-regional geographic focus presents a bridge between globalization, corporate strategies, and environmental and social concerns.

This third edition is a more compact version of the second edition, allowing all chapters to be covered in a traditional semester. The first two chapters deal with the scope of international business and the multinational corporation and present the institutional framework of economic theories and global strategies. The first three chapters contain updated global economic statistics such as world foreign direct investment (FDI) flows and the growth of world trade, and in-depth discussions of specific leading multinational firms. Chapter 3 includes discussion of both classical theories of economic development by such noted scholars as Adam Smith and David Ricardo, as well as modern theories by economists such as Albert Hirschman, John Kenneth Galbraith, and Amartya Sen. Chapters 4 through 6 discuss the functioning of the international monetary system, the foreign exchange markets, and supranational organizations such as the World Trade Organization, the International Monetary Fund, and the World Bank. Chapter 4 contains new discussion of special drawing rights, which will become more important in a world of major market currency declines, and coverage of the EU sovereign debt crisis. Chapter 4 also includes expanded coverage of the US balance of payments, including a table that compares performance from 1960 until the present day. This will allow students to identify trends over time that affect the competitiveness of the United States in the global economy. Chapter 5 on foreign exchange truly differentiates our text from others, given the depth of coverage which is typically not found in competing texts. In this new edition, coverage is further expanded to include tax havens and transfer pricing, reinforcing the blend of theory and practice. An interesting new feature for Chapter 6 is the illustration of the creation of regional trade agreements, with discussion of the explosion of such agreements since the forming of the WTO. Chapters 7 through 10 evaluate the environmental constraints in international business as they are applied to international business operations. In particular, those chapters focus on analyzing national economies, market demand forecasting, international law, intellectual property rights, and sociocultural factors in international business, as well as the researching of risk in foreign investment. Chapter 9 discusses corporate diversity initiatives and includes the illustration of the identity wheel, neither of which is discussed in competing texts. Finally, the textbook covers social and ethical issues, as well as the future of international business. Chapter 11 discusses emerging environmental concerns, the responses to those concerns by multinational firms, and the social responsibility and sustainability of business in the modern world. Chapter 11 includes updated statistics on the environmental impact of international business and new coverage of declining fish stocks worldwide. This chapter also includes discussion of the green paradox, which questions whether the best-laid plans of national governments are in the best interest of environmental protection in the final analysis. The last chapter provides a thought-provoking discussion concerning future trends affecting international business and the impacts of those trends on the multinational firm. Our final chapter includes a best-in-class discussion of letters of credit in international trade and identifies key strategic variables to be considered for the future of international business. The importance of sovereign wealth funds is also highlighted in Chapter 12.

Many colleagues have given the authors invaluable assistance in the preparation of this book. Our appreciation goes to the many who are too numerous to mention individually by name. However, our deepest gratitude goes to the following academic colleagues: Kamel Abdallah of the American University, Beirut; James T. Goode, Osaka International University, Japan; Hanne Norreklit, Aarhus School of Business, Denmark; Frederic

Herlin, Center for Creative Leadership, Brussels, Austria, and Greensboro; Karel Cool, INSEAD, Fontainebleau, France; M'hamed Merdji, Audencia, School of Management, France; Ram Baliga and Bill Marcum, Wake Forest University, North Carolina; Gerhard Raab, University of Applied Sciences, Ludwigshafen, Germany; and Mary Lynn Davis-Ajami, University of Maryland, Baltimore. On the practitioner side, the authors would like to thank Mrs. Salim Tyan for his assistance with the letters of credit discussion in Chapter 12, and Mrs. Leila Goddard for providing thoughtful comments concerning the revised manuscript.

The authors are also indebted to our support team of James Madder, Kendra Newman, Lindsey Lambert, Basmah Aljabr, Rachel M. White, Michelle L. Hatton, and Joseph R. Lavigne at the Center for Global Business and Education at Wright State University.

Finally, the authors wish to note that the primary motivation for this third edition was our students. May they continue to learn and appreciate the vastness of international business and the benefits of a globally integrated world.

Prologue:
Ode to the Yes Era

In Aldous Huxley's *Brave New World*,[1] the past was not looked upon favorably. In fact, the leadership believed that *"ending is better than mending"* and that *"we have no use for old things here."* So is often the case with international business markets. When times are good, market participants have the confidence of a brighter future, a future that is often much brighter than results previously experienced. As global markets struggle to recover from the recent financial crisis, the authors would like to offer summary comments about how things looked from the top of the hill, so that we may learn from the follies of the past.

The following chart summarizes the results of the University of Michigan Consumer Sentiment Survey[2] from January 2002 until June 2012. By most accounts, the beginning of the financial excesses that ended in 2008 began sometime during 2002 or 2003. The chart shows that the peak of the consumer sentiment results during this period came in January 2004 with a value of 103.8. This was the highest score for the survey since the end of the twentieth century and the euphoria of the dot-com bubble. The trough in consumer sentiment for the period 2002–2008 came in November 2008 at 55.3. Those were indeed dark days, with the collapse of Lehman Brothers and the uncertainties surrounding the future of the global economy hanging in the balance.

We refer to the period 2002–2007 as the "Yes Era." Everyone was a winner, everyone got a trophy, and everyone, it seems, got a loan. The last consumer sentiment score of at least 90 was in July 2007. If we travel back in time to that date and review some of the basic tenets of market activity conducted during this time, we may be able to shed some light on what pathways future economic activity should take so that the excesses of the past do not return to us in a slightly different, probably more toxic form.

Figure P.1   **University of Michigan: Consumer Sentiment**

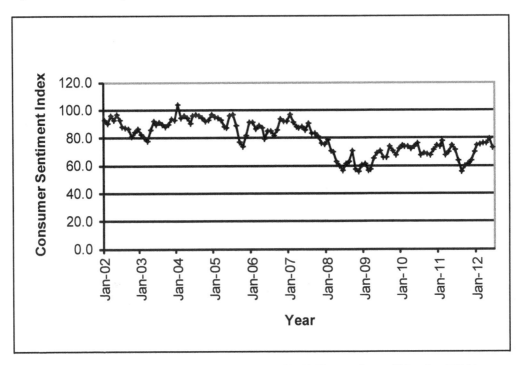

Source: University of Michigan: Consumer Sentiment (UMCSENT), Thomson Reuters/University of Michigan, http://research.stlouisfed.org/fred2/series/UMCSENT/downloaddata?cid=98.

WE WANT TO BELIEVE

Few people wish economic calamities on anyone. There are always a few bears who, like Chicken Little, make their fame by continually claiming that the sky is falling. These prognosticators are similar to broken clocks in that eventually the constant message meets up with the appropriate time. For the most part, market participants desire well-functioning markets that foster environments of stability and growth. Sometimes the desire for well-functioning markets goes beyond reasonable levels, which was palpably the case during the Yes Era. Some economists believe that tinkering with the prevailing interest rates in an economy will guide the behavior of market participants away from excess speculation. This tinkering invariably does work to much effect during normal times, but the Yes Era was hardly a normal period. For example, the Federal Reserve increased interest rates seventeen consecutive times from June 2004 to July 2006, but this had a negligible effect on curtailing the speculative fervor created by markets of high confidence and low past due loans. While the prime rate was increased from 4.00 percent to 8.25 percent during this time, bank lending did not slow as banks typically curtail lending when past dues increase rather than simply when the lending rates increase.

"What goes up must come down" thus became "what goes up will stay up forever." As is typical of any market expansion environment, the most speculative projects with the highest risk were consummated just before the end of the market expansion. The good times brought stellar results, and the longer the expansion lasted, the farther in the past any problems seemed. This activity reminds us of the basic message in any personal investment: *the past is not necessarily an indicator of future results*.

THE TORTOISE AND THE HARE

What lessons have we learned from the fall of the Yes Era? Like the Aesop fable whose name graces the title of this section, there are two pathways of travel. One is a quantity-focused, volume-driven pathway that favors short-term reward over long-term gain. Businesses that follow this pathway often pursue speculative projects or enter markets without performing proper due diligence analysis. The other pathway follows a more organic growth model, where businesses are rewarded based on the quality of their international expansion plans and the return on investment provided to the shareholder.

If the business cycle is seen in the long view, businesses and shareholders alike benefit from growth models based on asset quality and financial soundness.

As Yogi Berra said, "You can see a lot just by observing." None of us enjoyed the fall of the Yes Era, but we have certainly learned its many lessons. We will end this prologue as we began with a quote from Aldous Huxley:

> Knee deep he goes where, penny-wiser
> Than all his kind who steal and hoard
> Year after year, some sylvan miser
> His copper wealth has stored.[3]

NOTES

1. Huxley, *Brave New World*.
2. St. Louis Federal Reserve, University of Michigan Consumer Sentiment Survey, 2013.
3. Huxley, *Those Barren Leaves*.

BIBLIOGRAPHY

Huxley, Aldous. *Brave New World*. New York: Harper, 2006 (1932).
———. *Those Barren Leaves*. Champaign, IL: Dalkey Archive Press, 2010 (1925).
St. Louis Federal Reserve. University of Michigan Consumer Sentiment Survey, 2013. http://research.stlouisfed.org/fred2/data/UMCSENT.txt.

Maps

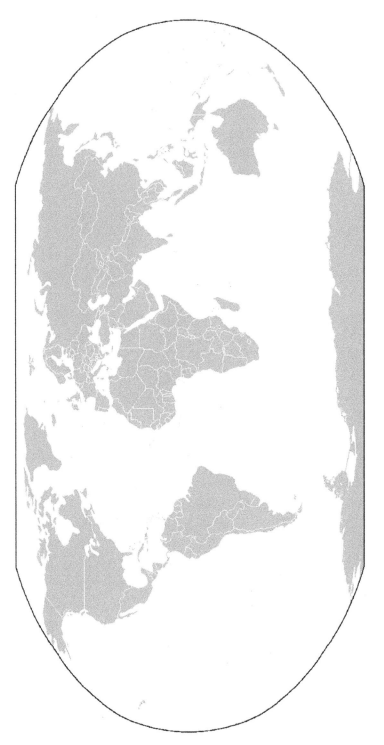

WORLD MAP

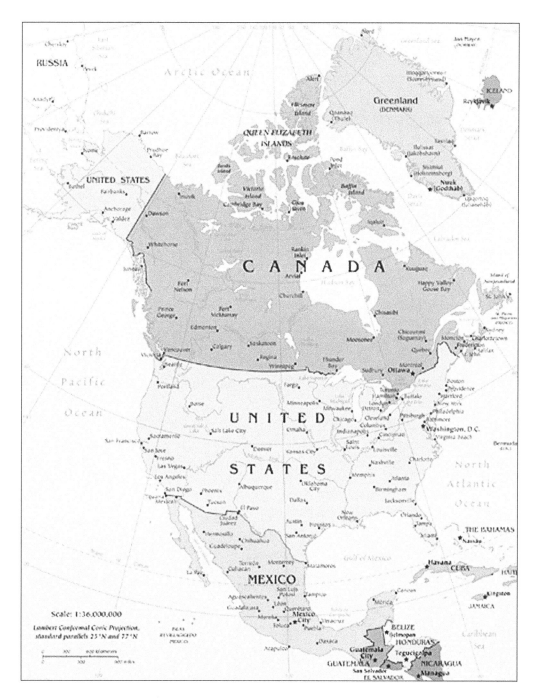

POLITICAL NORTH AMERICA

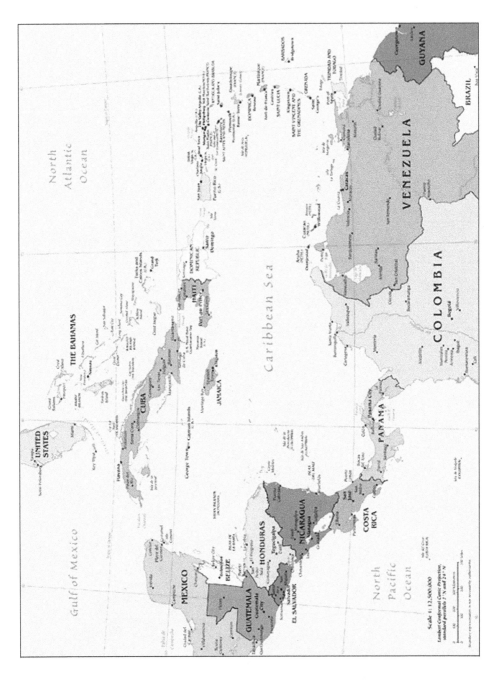

POLITICAL CENTRAL AMERICA AND THE CARIBBEAN

POLITICAL SOUTH AMERICA

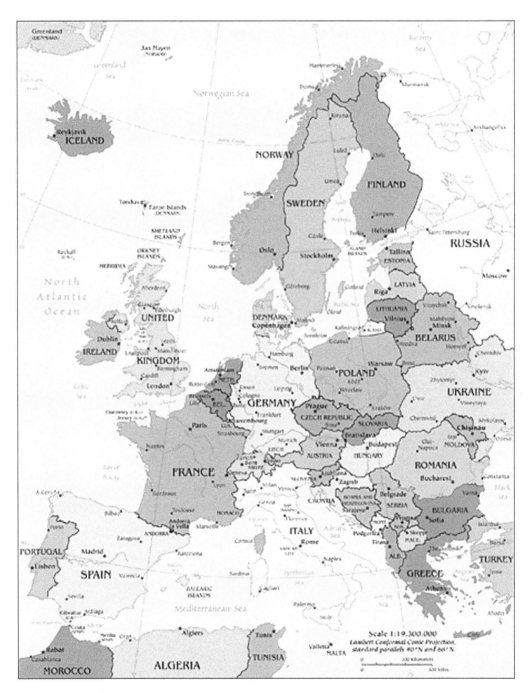

POLITICAL EUROPE

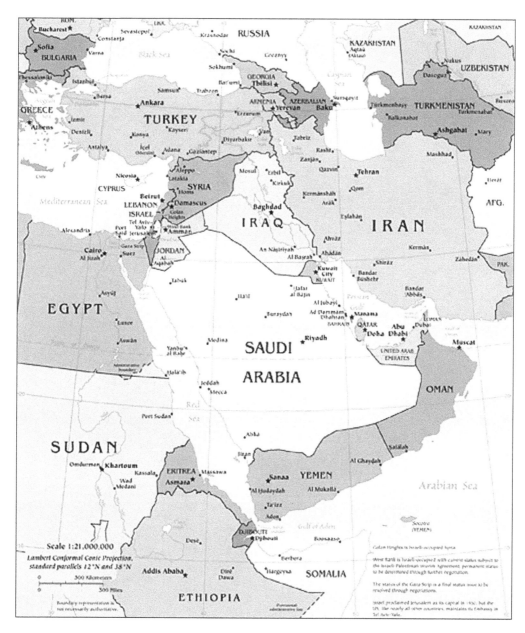

POLITICAL MIDDLE EAST

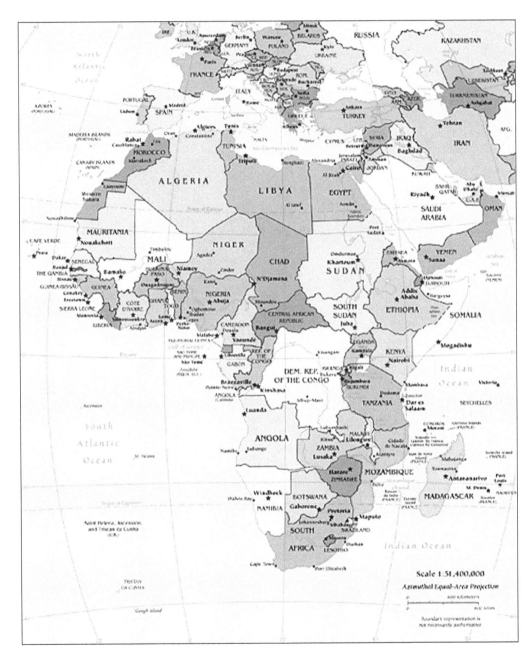

POLITICAL AFRICA

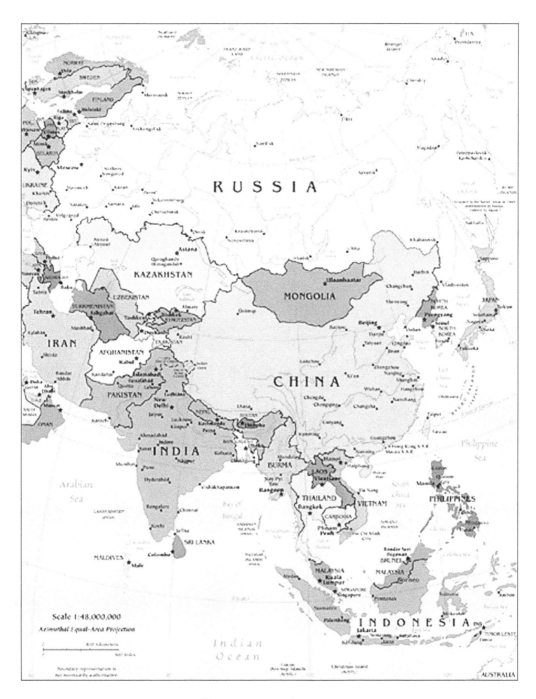

POLITICAL ASIA

POLITICAL OCEANIA

INTERNATIONAL
BUSINESS

CHAPTER 1

An Introduction to International Business and Multinational Corporations

"The first thing to understand is that you do not understand."
—Søren Kierkegaard

CHAPTER OBJECTIVES

This chapter will:

- Present the historical context of international business and establish the role of multinational corporations in the current business environment
- Describe the various operating advantages and disadvantages facing the multinational corporation

---

The quote above by the Danish philosopher Kierkegaard was intended for a philosophical interpretation, but the quote could just as easily apply to international business. Countless businesses have failed in their international expansion effort because they did not heed these words. For students as well as for business professionals, the successful entry into foreign markets must come with the realization that everything is not necessarily the same as in the domestic market. This first chapter will provide examples of some companies that have been successful by learning how to successfully compete in today's global marketplace. But first, the subject of international business must be discussed in its historical context.

3

CURRENT SCOPE AND HISTORICAL ANTECEDENTS

In the world of business in the twenty-first century, vast business interrelationships span the globe. Far more than ever before, products, capital, and personnel are becoming intertwined as business entities increasingly consider their market areas as global rather than simply domestic or even foreign. More and more companies, some of which have annual sales levels larger than the gross national product of some countries, consider every corner of the globe a feasible source of raw materials and labor or a new market possibility.

As business has expanded across national borders, it has been followed by banks and financial institutions to meet the need for capital for investment and operations around the world. Financial markets have also become intricately linked, and movements and changes in the US stock market have a direct impact on equity markets in other parts of the world.

Today, only a naive businessperson would believe that an enterprise can grow and prosper entirely within the confines of its domestic market borders. The phenomenon of global expansion is not only for large corporations, as evidenced by the success of Germany's **Mittelstand**. These are medium-sized, family-owned businesses that have experienced much success in exporting in recent years. Domestic business must at least be aware of international sources of competition, because they are an ever-present and growing threat as international business relationships become increasingly intricate and complex. The source of these changes in the dynamics of world markets and economies is international business activity being pursued around the globe.

WHAT IS INTERNATIONAL BUSINESS?

In its purest definition, international business is described as any business activity that crosses national boundaries. The entities involved in business can be private, governmental, or a mixture of the two. International business can be broken down into four types: foreign trade, trade in services, portfolio investments, and direct investments.

In foreign trade visible physical goods or commodities move between countries as exports or imports. Exports consist of merchandise that leaves a country. Imports are those items brought across national borders into a country. Exporting and importing constitute the most fundamental, and usually the largest, international business activity in most countries.

In addition to tangible goods, countries also trade in services, such as insurance, banking, hotels, consulting, and travel and transportation. The international firm is paid for services it renders in another country. The earnings can be in the form of fees or royalties. Fees are generated through the satisfaction of specific performance and can be earned through long- or short-term contractual agreements, such as management or consulting contracts. Royalties accrue from the use of one company's process, name, trademark, or patent by someone else.

Figure 1.1 **World FDI Inflows, 1998–2010**

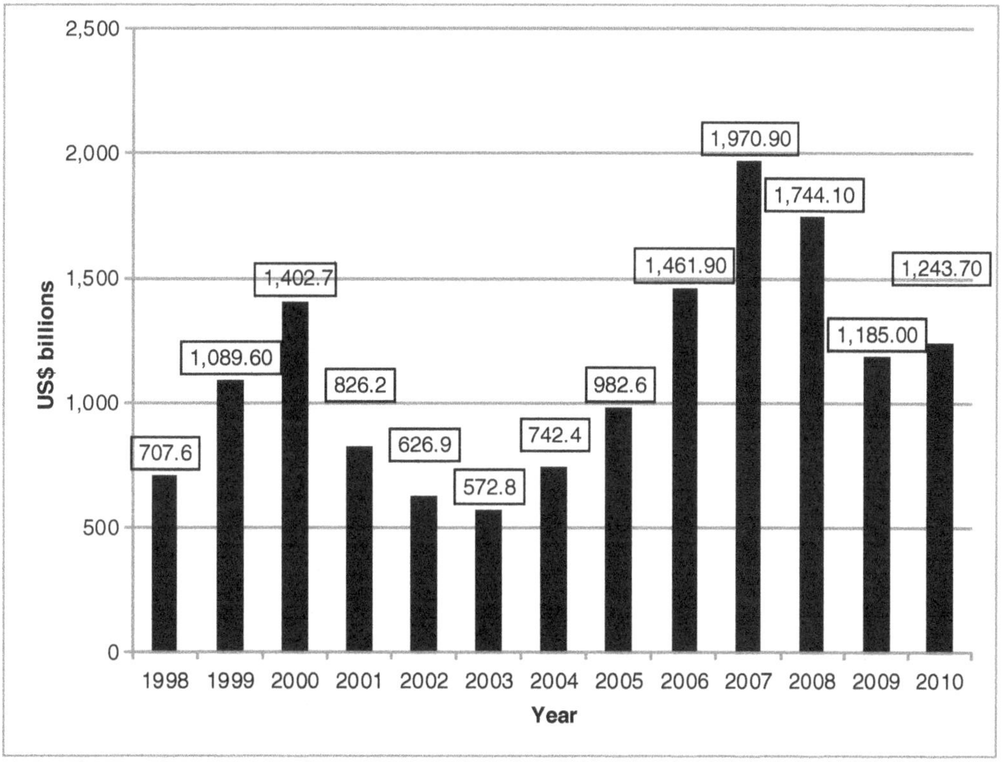

One example of a fee situation is the **turnkey operation**, in which a foreign government or enterprise hires the expertise appropriate to starting a new concern, plant, or operation. The turnkey manager goes into the foreign environment and gets an operation up and running by designing the plant, setting up equipment, and training personnel to take over. The foreign firm then takes over the reins of management and continues operating the facility. Alternatively, a firm can earn royalties from abroad by licensing the use of its technology, processes, or information to another firm or by selling its franchise in overseas markets.

Portfolio investments are financial investments made in foreign countries. The investor purchases debt or equity in the expectation of nothing more than a financial return on the investment. Resources such as equipment, time, or personnel are not contributed to the overseas venture. **Direct investments** are differentiated by much greater levels of control over the project or enterprise by the investor. The level of control can vary from full control, when a firm owns a foreign subsidiary entirely, to partial control, as in arrangements such as joint ventures with other domestic or foreign firms or a foreign government. The methods of conducting international business will be discussed more thoroughly in subsequent chapters. As is illustrated in Figure 1.1, the level of foreign

6

Figure 1.2 **FDI Inflows Developed vs. Developing and Transition**

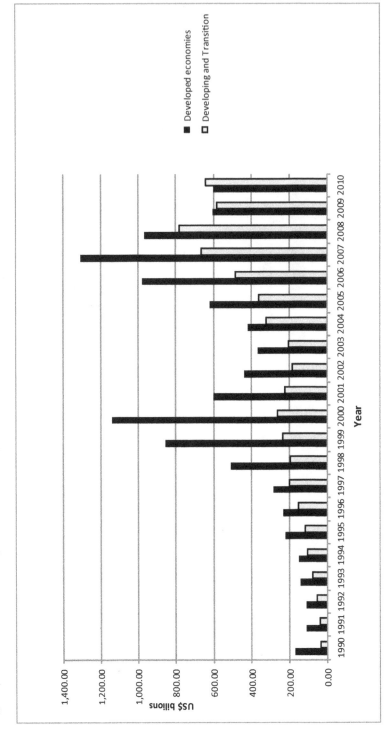

Source: Inward and outward foreign direct investment flows, annual, 1990–2010, UNCTAD Stat, http://unctadstat.unctad.org/ReportFolders/reportFolders.aspx.

direct investment (FDI) peaked at $1.970 trillion in 2007, the year of the global economic downturn. Since 2007, FDI growth has slowed the most in developed economies. While the developed economies in Europe were the leading destination of FDI prior to the 2007 financial crisis, FDI has decreased from $895 billion in 2007 to $313 billion in 2010. Combined developing and transitioning economies' FDI peaked in 2008 at $778.9 billion, while developed economies FDI slowed to $965 billion. As illustrated in Figure 1.2, more FDI is now flowing to developing and transition economies than flowing to developed economies.[1]

BRIEF HISTORY OF INTERNATIONAL BUSINESS

International business is not new, having been practiced around the world for thousands of years, although its forms, methods, and importance are constantly evolving. In ancient times, the Phoenicians, Mesopotamians, and Greeks traded along routes established in the Mediterranean. Commerce continued to grow throughout history as sophisticated business techniques emerged, facilitating the flow of goods, resources, and funds between countries. Some of these business methods included the establishment of credit for exchange, banking, and pooling of resources in joint stock ventures during the Renaissance period. This growth was further stimulated by colonization activities in the seventeenth and eighteenth centuries, which provided the maritime nations with rich resources of raw materials as well as enormous potential markets in the new worlds.

The Industrial Revolution further encouraged the growth of international business by providing methods of production for mass markets and more efficient methods of utilizing raw materials. As industrialization increased, greater and greater demand was created for supplies, raw materials, labor, and transportation. The flow and mobility of capital also increased as higher production provided surplus income, which was, in turn, reinvested in further production domestically or in the colonies. The technological developments and inventions resulting from the Industrial Revolution accelerated and smoothed the flow of goods, services, and capital between countries.

By the 1880s the Industrial Revolution was in full swing in Europe and the United States, and production grew to unprecedented levels, abetted by scientific inventions, the development of new sources of energy, efficiencies achieved in production, and new forms of transportation, such as domestic and international railroad systems. Growth continued in an upward spiral as mass production met and surpassed domestic demand, pushing manufacturers to seek enlarged, foreign markets for their products. It led ultimately to the emergence of the multinational corporation (MNC) as a new organizational entity in the international business world.

In more modern times, the creation of the internet as an electronic commerce platform and the ever-expanding capacity of telecommunications and technology have contributed to an increased expectation for product and service quality and availability throughout the world. As global markets become increasingly interconnected, the benefits of integration have become more obvious, as have the pitfalls of the increased speed of transactions.

The current form of international business is a continuation of globalization that began long ago, with no end in sight for its future march of progress.

THE MULTINATIONAL CORPORATION

During its early stages, international business was conducted in the form of enterprises that were owned singly or in partnerships. As the size of organizations grew with industrialization and need for capital by companies increased, corporations began to displace privately held firms. These corporations had the distinct advantage of being entities with a separate legal identity, consequently limiting the liability of the principals or owners. At the same time, by issuing shares of stock, the corporation could tap an enormous pool of excess funds held by potential individual investors.

With the emergence of the multinational enterprise in the late 1800s and early part of the twentieth century, the corporation underwent yet another modification.[2] Some early multinational enterprises were those that sought resources and supplies abroad, such as oil in Mexico (Standard Oil), precious minerals in North America (Amalgamated Copper, International Nickel, Kennecot), fruit in the Caribbean (United Fruit), or rubber in Sumatra (U.S. Rubber). Other firms entered foreign markets in a search for markets to absorb their excess domestic production or to obtain economies of scale in production. Some of these early market seekers from the United States were Singer, National Cash Register Company, International Harvester (now Navistar International), and Remington, who sought to use their advantages of superior metal production skills against European producers.

These early entrants were quickly followed by companies with other areas of expertise, such as Cable Telephone (now Norvado), Eastman Kodak, and Westinghouse. All of these early US multinational firms marketed their products primarily in the neighboring countries of Canada and Mexico and in European markets.

DEFINITION OF A MULTINATIONAL CORPORATION

There is no formal definition of a multinational corporation, although various definitions have been proposed using different criteria. Some believe that a multinational firm is one that is structured so that business is conducted or ownership is held across a number of countries or one that is organized into global product divisions. Others look to specific ratios of foreign business activities or assets to total firm activities or assets. Under these criteria, a multinational firm is one in which a certain percentage of its earnings, assets, sales, or personnel come from or are deployed in foreign locations. A third definition is based on the perspective of the corporation, that is, its behavior and its thinking. According to this definition, if the management of a corporation holds the perception and the attitude that the parameters of its sphere of operations and markets are multinational, then the firm is indeed a multinational corporation.

In his study of the topic, Howard V. Perlmutter[3] looked at the attitude held by the decision-makers of an organization and differentiated between ethnocentric, polycentric, and geocentric organizational types. **Ethnocentric** organizations are those that are focused in a home or domestic environment and therefore exclude MNCs. **Polycentric** organizations have investments, operations, or markets in several countries, but do not integrate the management of these international functions. **Geocentric** organizations, on the other hand, are integrated and have a world perspective regarding the breadth and reach of possible organizational operations. Some students of international business (and sticklers for linguistic accuracy) dispute the use of the terms "global" or "world" corporation in reference to MNCs. They argue that a truly global corporation or enterprise looks to every market in the world as a potential market and allocates resources without regard for the location of its home country. Under this definition, for example, an international corporation with subsidiaries and markets in Europe and South America would not be considered a global enterprise. As the globalization of international markets has continued, more firms have realized that the key to their future success depends upon increasing their business activities in other parts of the world (including China, India, and Southeast Asian nations).

The existence of different definitions for multinational corporations is not surprising. There are many different types of multinational corporations and most definitions characterize only a particular type. Because there are so many possible ways in which a corporation can be organized and transact business across national borders, it is indeed very difficult for any one definition to adequately describe all forms of multinational corporations.

Another problem in standardizing the definition of a multinational corporation is the gradual evolution of purely domestic companies to multinational status. In this process, the point at which a company becomes a multinational cannot be clearly demarcated. Such demarcations, if at all possible, also cannot explain or describe adequately the wide differences in the extent to which corporations have gone international.

The United Nations does not use the terms "multinational corporations" or "multinational enterprises." Instead, it calls them "transnational corporations," but this term is not used widely. This text will use the terms "multinational corporation" (MNC) and "multinational enterprise" (MNE) interchangeably to identify a firm that conducts international business from a multitude of locations in different countries.

MULTINATIONAL CORPORATIONS COME OF AGE

The multinational corporation began to flourish in the decade following World War II, primarily in the United States. It was spurred by reconstruction efforts in Europe and an inflow of US dollars geared to take advantage of new opportunities as countries of the ravaged continent attempted to rebuild their economies. US corporations, having prospered through wartime demand, channeled investments into other countries, notably in Europe and Canada. During the period from 1950 to 1970, the book value of US direct foreign investments skyrocketed from $11.8 billion to $78.1 billion.[4]

Table 1.1   **The World's Biggest Public Companies, April 2012** (US$ billions)

Rank	Company	Revenue	Home
1	Walmart Stores	$469.20	USA
2	Royal Dutch Shell	$467.20	Netherlands
3	Exxon Mobile	$420.70	USA
4	Sinopec China Petroleum	$411.70	China
5	BP	$370.90	UK
6	Petro China	$308.90	China
7	Volkswagen	$254.00	Germany
8	Total	$240.50	France
9	Toyota Motor	$224.50	Japan
10	Chevron	$222.60	USA
11	Glencore International	$214.40	Switz
12	Samsung Electronics	$187.80	Korea
13	E.ON	$174.20	Germany
14	Phillips 66	$166.10	USA
15	Apple	$164.70	USA
16	ENI	$163.70	Italy
17	Berkshire Hathaway	$162.50	USA
18	General Motors	$152.30	USA
19	Daimler	$150.80	Germany
20	AXA Group	$147.50	France

Source: Forbes, "The World's Biggest Public Companies," 2012.

As the European economy strengthened during this period, the motives of US companies doing business there switched from an aggressive market and profit-seeking stance to a defensive position of protecting their European market share and domestic US markets from encroachments by increasingly strong European competitors. In the 1960s, US firms also began to take advantage of the availability of new capital and debt markets: the **Eurodollar** and **Eurobond** markets emerging in that part of the world. During this period, the orientation of US MNCs also began to change, from seeking raw materials and being involved in the extractive industries to focusing more on overseas manufacturing industries.

By the 1970s the United States had lost its nearly complete dominance of multinational industry, partially because of the reemergence of strong European concerns, but also due to Japan and the other emerging giants of the East. As Table 1.1 shows, as of April 2012, only seven of the top twenty companies were from the United States, while Europe had eight of the top twenty companies. The rest of the top twenty companies were from Asia and South America. Brazil, South Korea, and China are now represented in the world's top twenty companies.

Walmart is now the world's largest company from a revenue perspective. Walmart is still the world's largest retailer, with stores in the United States, Argentina, Brazil, Canada,

Germany, Korea, Mexico, Puerto Rico, and the United Kingdom. The fact that Walmart is the largest retailing company in the world without yet completely penetrating the European market shows just how successful this company has been in North America. As an interesting side note, of the top twenty companies in the world, thirteen of them are either in the oil or automobile industry. Royal Dutch/Shell Group, Exxon Mobil, Sinopec China Petroleum, BP, Petro China, Total, Chevron, Phillips 66, and ENI are all in the oil industry, while Volkswagen, Toyota, General Motors, and Daimler are in the automobile industry. Except for AXA Group of France, financial services have dropped out of the top twenty, allowing for a more diverse group of companies to enter, such as Apple, Samsung Electronics, E. On, Glencore International, and Berkshire Hathaway.

A Look at Present-Day Multinationals

In order to understand the complexities of operations pursued by multinational firms, it is helpful to look at the structure and operations of three multinational business organizations. In this way, the student of international business can envision the enormous size and complexity of operations for a global bank, a multinational manufacturing company, and an international conglomerate: Citigroup, Sony, and Nestlé.

Citigroup (USA)

Citigroup is a prime example of a truly global corporation. Indeed, the company calls itself a global financial services company and attempts to provide a full range of banking services in all parts of the world. The bank achieved revenue levels of $94.71 billion in 2003, as well as net profits of $17.85 billion. Citigroup derived 64 percent of its revenues from North America, and global business accounted for 32 percent of its revenue (with 10 percent coming from Asia).[5] By 2011, Citigroup's revenues decreased by more than $30 billion with revenues of $64.6 billion, with only 36 percent derived from North America, 24 percent from Asia, 21 percent from Latin America, and the remaining 19 percent from Europe, the Middle East, and Africa. The 2011 revenue was diversified in the following manner: global consumer banking (50 percent), global transaction services (16 percent), and securities and banking (34 percent) (see Figure 1.3). By year-end of 2011, Citicorp held total assets of $1.874 trillion, employed 266,000 people, and managed 200 million customer accounts in more than 160 countries on six continents.[6]

The Citicorp segment consists of global consumer banking businesses, and the Institutional Clients Group acquired the Sears and Home Depot credit card portfolios in 2003, making it the leading private label provider in the United States. Citigroup also became the first international bank in Russia to launch credit cards to consumers. In 2004, Citigroup acquired Washington Mutual's consumer finance business, which helped to increase the bank's position as the leading community-based lender in the United States. In 2003, Citigold Wealth Management programs were launched in the Czech Republic, Egypt, France, Hungary, Poland, Russia, Turkey, and the United Arab Emirates. Citigroup

Figure 1.3 **Citicorp Revenues** (2011 revenues: $64.6 billion)

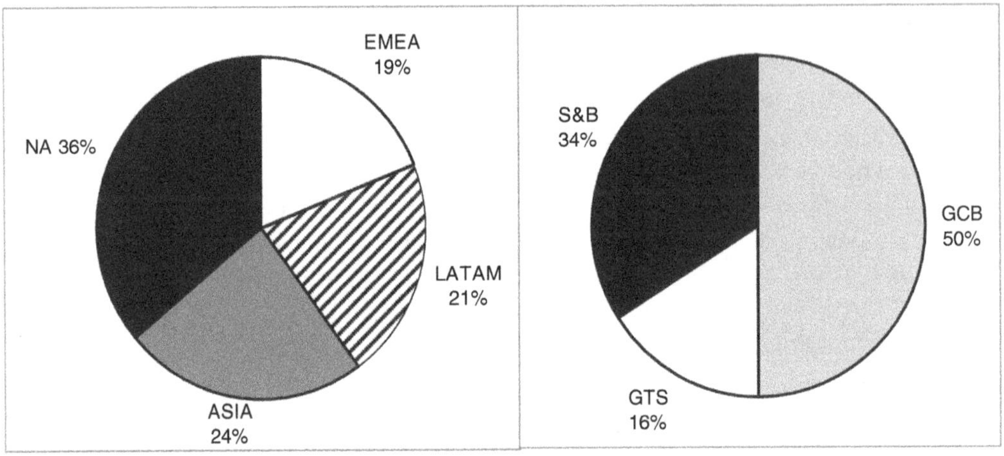

Source: Citigroup Annual Report, 2011, p. 7.

NA—North America
EMEA—Europe, Middle East, and Africa
LATAM—Latin America

GCB—Global Consumer Banking
S&B—Securities and Banking
GTS—Global Transaction Services

also launched the Banamex Tricolor card, which makes it easier and more affordable for people in Mexico to receive funds from their friends and relatives in the United States. Citigroup continues to rely on growth in the international regions. In 2011, about half of Citicorp's net income came from Asia and Latin America.

The Citi Holdings segment consists of the Brokerage and Asset Management, Local Consumer Lending, and Special Asset Pool business units. The Citi Holdings segment's assets are slowly being shifted to the Citibank segment. Local Consumer Lending in 2011 was the segment's largest asset.

Clearly, Citigroup is an organization with a global approach that has been very successful by finding ways to cater to various markets in the world. In recent years, the company's advertising campaign has centered on the slogan "Live Richly," which has been communicated in English, Chinese, Spanish, and many other languages throughout the world.

Sony Corporation (Japan)

Sony Corporation, based in Tokyo, Japan, is a major world manufacturer of televisions, DVD players, gaming systems, and semiconductors. While Sony's reach is not as wide as Citicorp's in terms of international scope, product line, or diversity, the company's success since its incorporation in 1946 is still remarkable. Since the 1940s, Sony has constantly continued its growth and development in the electronics and telecommunica-

Figure 1.4   **Sony Sales by Area, Year Ending March 31, 2011**

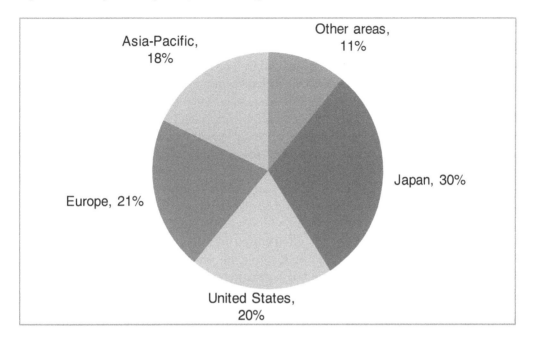

tions fields, producing in Japan in 1950 the first tape recorder and magnetic tape. This accomplishment was followed by the production of transistors in 1954, the technology of which was applied to radios, televisions, and tape recorders. This period was followed by growth in the 1960s, culminating with the production of the Trinitron color television tube in 1968. Advances followed in video equipment that led to the introduction of the Betamax videocassette recorder in 1975 and the subsequent introduction of the Walkman personal cassette tape player and radio.

Sony's enormous growth was evidenced in a quintupling of sales in the decade from 1972 to 1981. Further demonstrating Sony's pace of growth, revenues increased from $5 billion in FY1985 to $67 billion in FY2003 and $84.8 billion in FY2010.[7] Total assets reached ¥12,866,114 million/$152 billion at the end of FY2010. For FY2010, 47 percent of Sony's revenues came from the consumer, professional, and devices segment. This segment includes televisions, digital imaging, audio and video, and semiconductors. Some 21 percent of Sony's revenues come from the networked products and services segment, which includes the game, personal computer, and other networked businesses. This primarily includes the Sony Playstation Two (PS2) video game consoles and software. Sony also achieves revenue from the music segment (8 percent of total revenues), the picture segment (6 percent of total revenues), and the financial services segment (11 percent of total revenues).[8]

Sony's financial success lies in its enormous research and development strengths, its international revenue diversity (see Figure 1.4), and its ability to find successful partnerships and methods of increasing the breadth of its sales to a given consumer. Sony's R&D strategy is based upon creating an environment of freedom and open-mindedness in which its researchers and developers can use their imaginations freely, while also efficiently focusing management resources in strategic fields. Most of Sony's production facilities are in Asia, but the company does have a presence in both Europe and North America as well.

In order to continue its success in today's global marketplace, Sony focuses on four key areas for growth. The networked products and services will focus on entertainment devices for delivering content to consumers, such as the Sony tablet and networked televisions and home theater systems. Sony desires to be an industry leader through its 3D world initiative, bringing 3D hardware-compatible devices and entertainment into the market-place, both in the theater and the home. Continued development of the semiconductors that are the core of its electronics product line will allow Sony to focus on its third key area, which is competitive advantage through differentiated technologies. The "Exmor R" semiconductor sensor allows Sony to offer a product that differentiates its camcorder and photography products from the competition by offering superior light-capturing technology. The final key area for growth is to focus on emerging markets, particularly the BRIC (Brazil, Russia, India, and China) markets, where Sony expects GDP growth to outpace the global average.

Nestlé SA (Switzerland)

Nestlé, the world's leading food processor, is, like Citigroup, a truly global corporation. Based in Vevey, Switzerland, the company operates 511 factories in 86 countries around the world.

Nestlé originated in Switzerland with the founding by chemist Henri Nestlé of a condensed milk factory in the mid-1800s and a factory to manufacture a milk-based baby food. In the early part of the 1900s, these two factories merged and rapidly expanded their operations and manufacturing facilities to all of Europe, the United States, and Latin America.

In the 1930s the firm's fortunes were abetted by its move into the instant drink market with one of its major products, Nescafé instant coffee, which was introduced in 1938. Since then, the company has continued to grow because of its strategies of diversification, market expansion, and product development. At present, Nestlé's product line includes instant drinks; dairy products; culinary products, such as bouillon, soups, spices, and dehydrated sauces; chocolate and candy; frozen foods and ice cream; infant and dietetic products; and liquid drinks. In addition, the company manufactures pharmaceutical products, such as instruments and medicines, owns and runs restaurants and hotels in the United States and Europe, and has a minority share in L'Oréal, a producer of cosmetics, perfumes, and beauty products.[9]

In 2011, Nestlé achieved annual revenues of CH 83.642 billion (see Figure 1.5). Six worldwide brands, Nestlé, Nescafé, Nestea, Maggi, Buitoni, and Purina, account for about 70 percent of the company's sales.

Figure 1.5

Nestlé Sales by Product Group, 2011   **Nestlé Sales by Management Area, 2011**

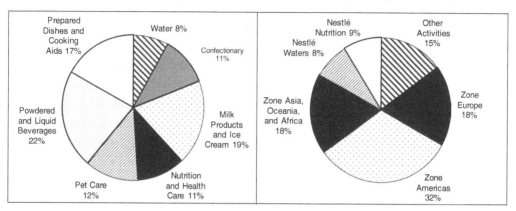

Nestlé products are sold in more than 140 countries around the world, and the company has manufacturing centers in 86 different countries. Nestlé manufacturing plants produce such familiar products as Ovaltine, Stouffer's frozen foods, Poland Spring bottled water, Libby vegetables and other canned foods, Beechnut baby food, and Taster's Choice coffee. In addition, the company produces cheese and other dairy products, chocolates, candies, cookies, and its own cans for fruit and vegetable packing. Nestlé also produces Friskies and Alpo pet foods.

Nestlé's desire to produce healthy, nutritious products is shown in its current advertising slogan, "Good Food, Good Life." The company is seeking to transform itself from the world's leading food company to the world's leading food, beverage, nutrition, health, and wellness company. Many R&D efforts are currently focusing on producing more healthy and nutritious products. By adding the pharmaceutical product line to the company, Nestlé has tried to strengthen its credibility in the medical community. An example of the company's focus on health is evident in its effort to create products that blur the line between pharmaceuticals and food. A new company, Nestlé Health Science, was created in January 2011 within Nestlé to innovate and bring these new products to market.[10]

OPERATING ADVANTAGES AND DISADVANTAGES OF MULTINATIONALS

Multinational firms experience unique advantages and disadvantages in their operations that make them quite different from purely domestically oriented companies. The international success of the MNCs is due primarily to their ability to overcome the disadvantages and capitalize on their advantages. Both advantages and disadvantages depend to a large extent upon the nature of individual corporations themselves and on each of their types of business. Studies of MNCs, however, show that a pattern of common characteristics exists across the broad spectrum of different corporations operating around the globe.

Advantages Gained by MNCs

Superior Technical Know-How

Perhaps the most important advantage that MNCs enjoy is patented technical know-how, which enables them to compete internationally. Most large MNCs have access to advanced levels of technology that was either developed or acquired by the corporation. Such technology is patented and held quite closely. It can be in the areas of production, management, services, or processes. Widespread application of such technology gives the MNC a strong competitive advantage in the international market, because it results in the production of efficient, hi-tech, and low-priced products and services that command a large international market following. The Banamex Tricolor card technology developed by Citigroup is an example of how an MNC can obtain a competitive advantage by developing, patenting, and then exploiting advanced technology.[11] Apple and Microsoft Corporation in computers, Boeing in aviation, and BASF in chemicals are further examples.

Large Size and Economies of Scale

Most MNCs tend to be large. Some of them, such as Walmart or Exxon Mobil, have sales that are larger than the gross national products of many countries. The large size confers significant advantages of economies of scale to MNCs. The high volume of production lowers per-unit fixed costs for the company's products, which is reflected in lower final costs. Competitors who produce smaller volumes of goods must price them higher in order to recover higher fixed costs. This situation is especially true in such capital-intensive industries as steel, petrochemicals, and automobiles, in which the fixed costs form a substantial proportion of total costs. Thus, an MNC such as Nippon Steel & Sumitomo Metal Corporation of Japan can sell its products at much cheaper prices than those of companies with smaller plants.

Lower Input Costs Due to Large Size

The large production levels of multinationals necessitate the purchase of inputs in commensurately large volumes. Bulk purchases of inputs enable MNCs to bargain for lower input costs, and they are able to obtain substantial volume discounts. The lowered input costs imply less expensive and, therefore, more competitive finished products. Nestlé, which buys huge quantities of coffee on the market, can command much lower prices than smaller buyers. Walmart is able to sell its products at low prices relative to its competition due to both its bulk purchasing and effective inventory control. By understanding which products are selling effectively, Walmart combines low-cost purchasing with the effective movement of inventory to achieve competitive advantage in the retail consumer products market.

Ability to Access Raw Materials Overseas

Many MNCs lower input and production costs by accessing raw materials in foreign countries. In many of these cases, MNCs supply the technology to extract and/or refine the raw materials. In addition to lowering costs, such access can give them monopolistic control over the raw materials because they often supply technology only in exchange for such monopolistic control. This control allows them to manipulate the supply of the raw materials or even to deny access to their competitors.

Ability to Shift Production Overseas

The ability to shift production overseas is another advantage enjoyed by MNCs. In order to increase their international competitiveness, MNCs relocate their production facilities overseas to take advantage of lower costs for labor, raw materials, and other inputs, and, often, incentives offered by host countries. The reduced costs achieved at these locations are exploited by exporting lower-cost goods to foreign markets. Several major MNCs have set up factories in such low-cost locations as China, India, and Mexico, to name only a few. This advantage is unique to MNCs, and it gives them a distinct edge over purely domestic corporations.[12]

Scale Economies in Shipment, Distribution, and Promotion

Scale economies allow MNCs to achieve lower costs in shipment expenses. The large volumes of freight they ship across nations permit them to negotiate lower rates with the shippers. Some of the very large corporations, especially the oil giants, have operations that are large enough to justify the purchase of their own ships, which is an even more effective way to reduce costs.

Distribution and promotion costs are also lowered for MNCs because of their high volumes of production. The distributors in different countries charge lower commissions to move the products because they are able to make substantial profits on their high volumes. A similar lowering of costs accrues with promotional expenses. MNCs have large advertising budgets and are valuable clients for advertising agencies and the media. Consequently, they are able to obtain cheaper rates. More importantly, MNCs are often able to standardize a promotional message and use it in different countries (e.g., the Marlboro cigarette advertisements or several Coca-Cola promotions that have been released in different countries using standardized messages).

Brand Image and Goodwill Advantage

Many of the MNCs possess product lines that have established a good reputation for quality, performance, value, and service. This reputation spreads abroad through exports and promotion, adding to the arsenal of potent weapons of the MNC in the form of brand image or goodwill, which it is able to use to differentiate its own products from others in its genre. The MNC is able to leverage this goodwill or brand image by standardizing its product line in different countries and achieving economies of scale. For example, Sony Playstations do not have any special modifications for different countries (except for voltage) and the home-based plant churns out standardized products for the world market. Similarly, Levi Strauss & Company is able to market its standard denim jeans around the globe even though clothing fashions vary widely within different cultures. Moreover, goodwill and brand names allow the company to charge premium prices for its products (e.g., Sony) because the customers are convinced that the products are good values even at premium prices.

Access to Low-Cost Financing

As a result of their size, MNCs require large amounts of financing, and generally, they are excellent credit risks. Therefore, they are the favored customers of the financial institutions that lend to them at their best rates. The lower cost of financing for the MNCs adds to their competitive strength. MNCs also have the additional advantage of access to different financial markets, which allows them to borrow from the source offering the best deal; the funds are then transferred internally to required locations. This access enables MNCs to avoid credit rationing in some countries and to obtain financing at costs lower than those available to their domestic-oriented competitors.

Financial Flexibility

MNCs also have an advantage in being able to manipulate their profits and shift them to lower tax locations. This greater financial leverage can be used to artificially lower prices to enter new markets or increase market shares in existing ones. The manipulation of profits to save taxes is generally accomplished through transfer pricing, where the overseas subsidiaries are charged artificially higher prices for products supplied to them by the parent company. There are also several financial mechanisms with the objectives of shifting profits and manipulating taxes.

Information Advantages

Multinationals have a global market view and are able to collect, process, analyze, and exploit their in-depth knowledge of worldwide markets. They use this knowledge to create new openings for their existing products or create new products for potential market niches. Their special knowledge is used to diversify and expand the market coverage of their products and to design strategies to counter the marketing efforts of their competitors. Moreover, excess production can be sold off, as the company can quickly find new markets through its global search and marketing mechanism.

The information-gathering abilities of an MNC are an advantage not only in marketing, but also in all other aspects of its operation. The MNC is able to gather commercial intelligence, forecast government controls, and assess political and other risks through its information network. The network also provides valuable information about changing market and economic conditions, demographics, social and cultural changes, and many other variables that affect the business of MNEs in different countries. Access to this information provides the MNE with the opportunity to position itself appropriately to respond to any contingencies and exploit any opportunities.

Managerial Experience and Expertise

Because MNCs function simultaneously in a large number of very different countries, they are able to assimilate a wealth of valuable managerial experience. This experience provides insights into dealing with different business situations and problems around the globe. The MNC also acquires expertise in different ways of approaching business problems and can effectively apply this knowledge to its other locations. For example, a multinational located in Japan can acquire in-depth knowledge of Japanese management methods and apply them successfully elsewhere. MNCs also develop expertise in multi-country operations management as their executives gather experience working in different countries on their way to senior management positions.

Diversification of Risks

The simultaneous presence of MNCs in different countries allows them to more effectively bear the risk of cyclic economic declines. Generally these cycles are not the same in different countries. Thus, if operations in one country suffer losses, these losses can be offset by gains in other countries. Simultaneous operations also provide considerable flexibility, enabling MNCs to diversify the political, economic, and other risks that they face in different countries. Thus, if an MNC is not able to keep up production levels in one country, it can still retain its market share by serving the market with products from a factory located in a different country. In another instance, if raw material supply is stopped from one source, the global presence of the MNC assures supplies from alternative sources. In the oil market, for example, if a Russian pipeline is shut down unexpectedly, nations such as Saudi Arabia have the necessary spare capacity to temporarily increase the supply of oil on the world markets in an effort to stabilize prices over the short term.

Disadvantages Faced by MNCs

Business Risks

MNCs have to bear several serious risks that are not borne by companies whose operations are purely domestic in nature. Since MNCs do business outside the borders of their own countries, they deal with the currencies of other countries, which render them vulnerable to fluctuations in exchange rates. Violent movements in exchange rates can wipe out the entire profit of a particular business activity. Over the long run, MNCs have to live with this risk because it is extremely difficult to eliminate it. Over the short run, however, there are market mechanisms such as currency swaps and forward contracts that allow an MNC to minimize the movement of exchange rates for a particular business transaction. Companies that engage in these forms of financial contracts understand that they are not in the currency-risk business and that it makes sense to minimize this risk when at all possible.

Host-Country Regulations

Operating in different countries subjects MNCs to a myriad of host-country regulations that vary from country to country and, in most cases, are quite different from those of the home country. The MNC has the difficult task of familiarizing itself with these regulations and modifying its operations to ensure that it does not overstep them. Regulations are often changed, and such changes can have adverse implications for MNCs. For example, a country may ban the import of a certain raw material or restrict the availability of bank credit. Such constraints can have serious effects on production levels. In many developing countries national controls are quite pervasive and almost every facet of private business activity is subject to government approval. The MNCs of developed countries are not used to such controls, and their methods of doing business are not geared to work in this type of environment.

Different Legal Systems

MNCs must operate under the different legal systems of different countries. In some countries the legislative and judicial processes are extremely cumbersome and contain many nuances that are not easily understood by outsiders. Some legislation can also prohibit the type of business activity the MNC would regard as normal in its home country.

Political Risks

Host countries are sovereign entities and their actions normally do not admit any appeals. There is little that an MNC can do if a host country is determined to take actions that are inimical to its interest. This political risk, as it is known, increases in countries whose governments are unstable and tend to change frequently.

Operational Difficulties

Multinational firms work in wide varieties of business environments which create substantial operational difficulties. Unwritten business practices and market conventions often prevail in host countries. MNCs that lack familiarity with such conventions will find it difficult to conduct business in accordance with them. Often the normal methods of operation of an MNC can be quite contrary to a country's business practices. A typical example is informal credit. In many countries retailers agree to stock goods of a manufacturing company only if they are offered a market-determined period of credit that is not covered by a written document. The accounting and sales policies of an MNC may not permit such arrangements. On the other hand, doing business in a certain country may not be at all possible without such arrangements. The multinational must therefore adjust its business practices or lose business entirely.

Cultural Differences

Cultural differences often lead to major problems for MNCs. Many find that their expatriate executives are not able to turn in optimal performance because they are not able to adjust to the local culture, both personally as well as professionally. On the other hand, local managers of MNCs often have difficulties in dealing with the home office of an MNC because of culturally based mutual communication and understanding problems. Inability to understand and respond appropriately to local cultures has often led MNC products to fail. Misunderstanding of local cultures, work ethics, and social norms often leads to problems between MNCs and their local customers, business associates, government officials, and even their own employees.

Many of the problems and challenges of doing international business involve overcoming disadvantages and capitalizing on advantages that arise when corporations go international. These problems and challenges will be discussed in detail in subsequent chapters.

RECENT TRENDS IN WORLD TRADE

EXPANDING VOLUME

The sheer volume of trade between nations has grown enormously since World War II. In 1948 world trade was only $51 billion. It rose to $331.72 billion in 1970, $7.865 trillion in 2000, and peaked at $19.622 trillion in 2008 (see Figure 1.6). Due to the financial crisis of 2008, world traded decreased to $15.582 trillion in 2009 before rebounding to $18.589 trillion in 2010. Trade in merchandise constitutes the largest part of global trade; however, trade in services continues to grow as an overall proportion of world trade. The international trade arena continues to be dominated by the world's high-income or industrialized countries, which account for as much as 68 percent of world trade.[13] Major changes are occurring in the trading patterns in the high-income and the newly developing BRIC (Brazil, Russia, India, and China) nations. For example, the BRIC nations in 2000 represented 6.1 percent of world trade volume. By 2010, their share of world trade had increased to 15.1 percent. As a part of the BRIC nations, China alone increased its share of world trade volume from 3.3 percent in 2000 to 9.3 percent in 2010. By way of comparison, the European Union has been able to maintain its share of world trade volume while the United States' share has been steadily decreasing, from 16.1 percent in 2000 to 11.9 percent in 2010 (see Figure 1.7). These trends have very important implications for international business. It is clear that the world trading environment is now truly international, in the sense that it is no longer dominated by any one country. There has, in fact, been a reversal of roles for some countries, most significantly, the United States, which incurred huge trade deficits in the 1980s and has moved from being the world's largest creditor to being the world's largest debtor. There are many reasons for this dramatic change. During the 1990s, the US budget did return to a surplus result, only

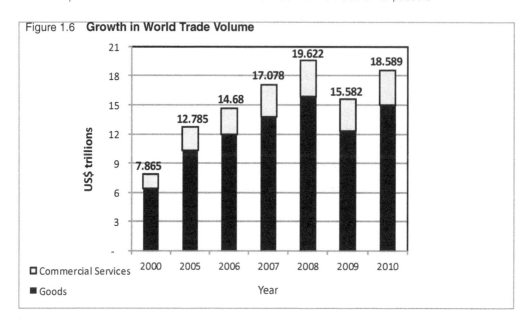

Figure 1.6   **Growth in World Trade Volume**

Source: World Trade Organization, "World Trade in the 21st Century: The 1st Decade," *WTO Stat Talk 6* (December 2011), www.wto.org/english/res_e/statis_e/stattalk_dec11_e.pdf.

Note: World total trade is calculated as the average of world exports and imports of goods and commercial services.

to fall back into deficits in the last few years. The trade deficits that began in the 1980s still persist, however.

The United States faces intense competition in its home market as well as in foreign markets from several countries, especially Germany, Japan, and the BRIC countries. The BRIC nations have been increasing their share of world trade, while Europe and North America have reduced their imports and increased their exports (see Figure 1.8). The high-income countries, categorized by the World Trade Organization (WTO) as having a 2010 gross national income (GNI) per capita greater than $12,276, represented 81 percent of world trade volume in 2000 and then fell to 68 percent by 2010. However, the middle-income countries, categorized by the WTO as having a 2010 GNI per capita of between $1,006 and $12,276, increased their portion of world trade volume from 19 percent in 2000 to 31 percent in 2010. The low-income countries, categorized by the WTO as having a 2010 GNI per capita income of less than $1,006, represent less than 1 percent of world trade. The trade patterns are likely to further change as the impacts of the 2008 financial crisis in the United States and Europe change consumption patterns. Furthermore, the long-term impact in the shifting of FDI trends from the developed countries to the developing countries will continue to affect the trend of the middle-income countries representing a larger proportion of world trade volume.

Figure 1.7 **World Trade, 2010**

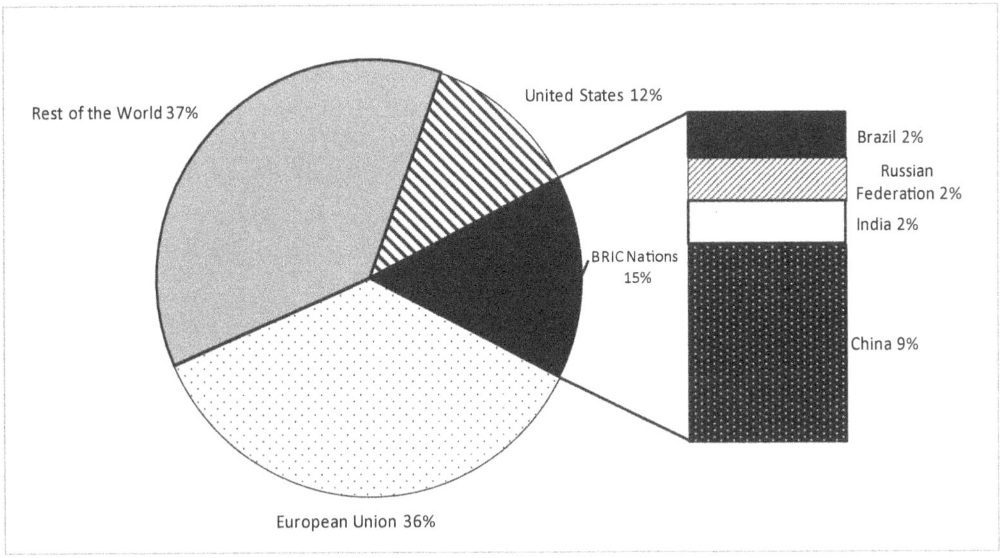

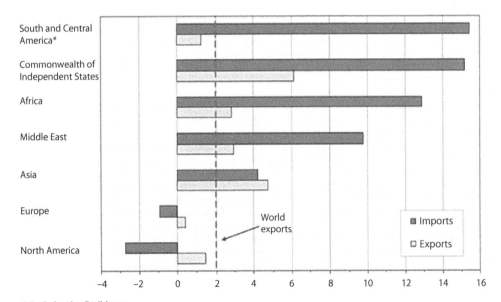

Source: World Bank, "World Development Indicators," April 2012, http://data.worldbank.org/data-catalog/world-development-indicators.

Figure 1.8 **Real Merchandise Trade Growth by Region, 2008**

* Includes the Caribbean.
Source: WTO Secretariat.

INCREASED COMPETITION

Competition on the international trade front is likely to intensify. The emergence of the European Union in 1992, the further strengthening of Asian exporting capabilities, and the continuing increase in Chinese exports are likely to put further pressures on the United States. To respond to these pressures, the United States will have to take a more active and positive approach to international business. The realization that we live in a globalized world must become more deeply rooted as a necessary component in the quest to maintain a competitive advantage. Increased attention to international business is therefore not only likely, but also necessary.

INCREASING COMPLEXITY

The nature of international business also continues to grow more complex. As more and more nations industrialize, they offer both opportunities as well as threats in the field of international business. Many developing countries, such as Mexico, China, and India, have large corporations that are now competing for export markets as well as foreign direct investment opportunities in other countries. Most of the ex-socialistic bloc countries are opening, selectively, their economies for trade with the rest of the world. There is also increasing emphasis on boosting the trade participation of the heavily indebted countries of Latin America and sub-Saharan Africa. Many developing countries, disappointed by the performance of commodities trade, which had been their mainstay, are shifting their emphasis to the production and export of manufactured goods. This shift opens new opportunities for relocating production facilities, thereby establishing manufacturing and trading arrangements. As these economies mature, they are better able to offer infrastructural facilities that provide electricity, transportation, communications, and labor and that can support large-scale manufacturing facilities. Low labor costs and government incentives are attracting overseas investments on a large scale to such countries. While foreign direct investment grew during the 1980s and 1990s in support of such activities, global inflows of foreign direct investment declined in 2003 for the third consecutive year. This was again due to a fall in FDI flows to developed countries, before rebounding in 2004, reaching its most recent peak in 2007. Worldwide, 111 countries saw a rise in flows, and 82 a decline. In the United States, FDI was at a high of $314 billion in 2000 before falling to $53 billion in 2003 and then rebounding to a recent high of $306 billion in 2008. One trend that is not expected to reverse is the movement to services. In 1990 inward services FDI flows accounted for 49 percent of the total FDI; in 2002, services accounted for 60 percent of inward FDI flows. Figure 1.6 (page 22) demonstrates the growth in commercial services as a proportion of overall trade. Prospects for growth post 2010 are promising due to an increase in cross-border mergers and acquisitions, improved economic growth, and improved corporate profitability, which should lead to a better result. However, the failure of Europe and the United States to manage their national debt has the potential to lead to a stagflation since the overall national debt puts a drag on the overall economic recovery in the countries dealing with a high debt to GDP ratio. The countries of eastern Europe, Latin America, and Asia that have either transformed their economies from a planned economy or faced debt crises of their own will be less prone in the future to become overleveraged. These countries will have a competitive advantage in the future due to their lower debt structure, stabilized economies, and lower cost of doing business.

TRADE IN SERVICES

As just mentioned, trade in services is also growing rapidly. The revolution in communications ushered in by the use of computer satellite-based networks has enabled almost instantaneous transmission of information from any part of the world. This development has resulted in an enormous expansion of services industries—banking, travel and tourism, and consulting—all of which have expanded rapidly across the world, integrating trade in services more than ever into a global business framework.

THE FIELD OF INTERNATIONAL BUSINESS STUDIES

The large volumes of trade, the existence of huge multinational business entities, and the rapidly changing international business environment merely emphasize the fundamental interrelationships of business firms, governments, economies, and markets in the world today. Thus, the study of international business and the knowledge of the forces operating in the world have direct implications for everyone in the modern world: for consumers, who are presented with an increasing array of foreign product choices; for political leaders, who find more and more that political concerns are directly tied to economic and international trade concerns; and, naturally, for business managers, who face increasing competition not only from domestic but also from foreign producers of goods and services, who, despite many disadvantages, have many factors working in their favor.

The study of international business also provides the modern business manager with a greater awareness of wider business opportunities than those within local borders, which, in strategic management terms, means that the parameters of the manager's external environment, as well as the possible configuration of that external environment, have expanded for the modern and progressive firm.

The study of international business, however, does not merely expand the parameters of the external environment of the modern business firm. It stimulates a more basic, attitudinal change in doing business in this widened environment. The business manager is exposed to the problems that inward-looking attitudes, such as ethnocentrism and parochialism, can and do create for international business. The business manager is encouraged to become aware of these constraints and to overcome them by seeking practical solutions in the real world. Companies must promote awareness in their employees that people and cultures do differ around the globe and that these differences are sometimes crucial to the conduct of international business. This awareness is the starting point for developing attitudinal changes that move business managers to flexibility and adaptability in dealing with the varied situations that arise in the conduct of international business.

These developments in the past fifty years provide a fascinating area of study for the student of international business because it was a time of unparalleled growth and activity. The trend is likely to continue upward, with increases in the flow of goods, capital, investments, and labor across national borders, plus the growth of truly global industries and corporations.

DISCUSSION QUESTIONS

1. Why has international business become so important in today's environment?
2. What are some of the reasons that corporations choose to develop international operations?
3. What differentiates the modern multinational corporation from the import-export firm?
4. What factors makes international business more complex than conducting domestic businesses?
5. Obtain the annual report of a large multinational corporation and identify the scope of its international operations and the countries in which it currently operates.
6. What are some of the conflicts that may occur between a multinational corporation and the local government hosting the multinational?
7. How can increases in world trade affect the owners of small businesses in your hometown?
8. How can studying international business increase your understanding of the world around you?

NOTES

1. United Nations Conference on Trade and Development, Statistics Database, 2011.
2. Wilkins, *Emergence of the Multinational Enterprise*.
3. Perlmutter, "Tortuous Evolution of the MNC."
4. US Department of Commerce, Bureau of International Commerce, *Trends in Direct Investment Abroad by U.S. Multinational Corporations*, 1975.
5. Citigroup, *Citigroup 2003 Annual Report*, 2003.
6. Citigroup, *Citigroup 2011 Annual Report*, 2011.
7. Sony, *Annual Report 2003*, 2003.
8. Sony, *Annual Report 2011*, 2011.
9. Nestlé, "General Information," *Management Report 2003*, 2003.
10. Nestle, Annual Report 2011, 2011.
11. Some texts use the term "proprietary technology" for technology that has been patented by a firm.
12. World Bank, "World Development Indicators," 2012.
13. United Nations Conference on Trade and Development, *World Investment Report, 2004*.

BIBLIOGRAPHY

Citigroup. Annual Reports. 2003, 2004, 2011. www.citigroup.com/citi/investor/quarterly/2012/ar11c_en.pdf?ieNocache=625.

Economist. "Foreign Direct Investment." September 23, 2004.

Forbes. "The World's Biggest Public Companies." June 2012.

Nestlé. "General Information." Management Report 2003, 2011. www.nestle.com/asset-library/Documents/Library/Documents/Annual_Reports/2003-Management-Report-EN.pdf.

———. "Indonesia: Bottled Water Joint Venture between Nestlé and Coca-Cola." Press release, July 20, 2004.

Perlmutter, Howard. 1969. "The Tortuous Evolution of the MNC." *Columbia Journal of World Business* (January/February): 9–18.

Sony. Annual Reports. 2003, 2011. www.sony.net/SonyInfo/IR/financial/ar/qfhh7c000000g7z4-att/e_ar2003.pdf.

Stopford, John M. *The World Directory of Multinational Enterprises, 1982–83*. Detroit: Gale Research Company, 1984.

United Nations Conference on Trade and Development. *World Investment Report, 2004*. New York: United Nations, 2004.

———. Statistics Database. 2011. http://unctad.org/en/Docs/wir2004_en.pdf.

US Department of Commerce. *Survey of Current Business* (published quarterly). Washington, DC: Government Printing Office.

US Department of Commerce, Bureau of International Commerce. *Trends in Direct Investment Abroad by U.S. Multinational Corporations*. Washington, DC: Government Printing Office, 1975.

Whiteside, David E., Otis Port, and Larry Armstrong. 1988. "Sony Isn't Mourning the 'Death' of Beta-max." *Business Week*, January 25, 1988, 37.

Wilkins, Mira. *The Emergence of the Multinational Enterprise: American Business Abroad from the Colonial Era to 1914*. Cambridge, MA: Harvard University Press, 1970.

World Bank. "World Development Indicators." April 2012. http://data.worldbank.org/data-catalog/world-development-indicators.

World Trade Organization. "World Trade in the 21st Century: The 1st Decade." *WTO Stat Talk* 6 (December 2011), www.wto.org/english/res_e/statis_e/stattalk_dec11_e.pdf.

———. *World Trade Report, 2004*. Geneva: WTO, 2004. Appendix, Table 1A.1, p. 20.

World Trade Organization Secretariat. www.wto.org/english/news_e/pres09_e/pr554_e.htm.

GLOBALIZATION AT THE CROSSROADS: GERMANY'S MITTELSTAND AND COMPETITIVE ADVANTAGE

It seems that the great job hollowing out myth was vastly overblown. The idea that Western developed economies would no longer be able to compete with the low cost manufacturing prowess of Asia has indeed led to developed world manufacturing job losses, but there are some success stories. The continued importance of the United States as a key manufacturer of large capital intensive products is well documented. Another example involves the small to medium sized family owned companies of Germany, known collectively as the "Mittelstand." These "midsized" firms typically have revenues less than $1 billion, are based in rural German communities, and have been in business for over fifty years. These firms are well integrated into the fabric of German society, receiving funding from Germany's state owned banks (Landesbanken) or smaller savings banks (Sparkassen). Germany has proven that an export orientation with a focus on quality can reap rewards in today's global economy. Much of the success of the Mittelstand centers on the strength of Germany's research and development efforts, and on their focus on production of (often *unglamorous) innovative, high value products. Mittelstand firms often seek market niches and partner with universities in their research and development efforts. These private firms often spend a higher percentage of their total revenues on research and development than their larger public competitors, and use this investment to compete globally based on superior value. The example of the Mittelstand illustrates that innovative, high quality production can lead to global competitive advantage while at the same time keeping well-paying manufacturing jobs in the developed world.*

QUESTIONS FOR DISCUSSION

1. *Research successful Mittelstand firms to better understand the products they produce and the markets that they serve.*
2. *What lessons can other developed nations learn from the success of the Mittelstand?*
3. *What lessons can small businesses everywhere learn from this example?*
4. *What does this success say about the future of academics in general?*

CASE STUDY 1.1

TRANSWORLD MINERALS INC.

John Wright reclined fully his first-class seat and pulled a sleeping mask over his eyes; he wanted to relax, he told the flight attendant, and would not have dinner for the next two or three hours. Wright was, however, anything but relaxed. A senior vice president in charge of international investment planning with Transworld Minerals Inc., a large multinational corporation based in Dallas, Texas, he was returning from a business trip to Salaysia, a small mineral-rich country in Asia. His company was considering a major investment there in a new coal-mining project, using Transworld's recently developed advanced technology that highly automated all operations. Wright had just finished a preliminary evaluation of the prospects.

On the face of it, it looked like a great investment that would generate substantial revenues in the long run. Salaysia had enormous deposits of coal in the northeastern parts of the country, located principally in Nebong Province. Most of these deposits had been recently discovered, as a result of a sustained geological exploration undertaken by Salaysia with the help of a large exploration firm from Australia. Most of the deposits were of high-quality anthracite coal, which was in considerable demand in steel manufacturing plants in China, Japan, and other newly industrializing economies of Southeast Asia.

The government seemed encouraging, primarily because it did not have the technology to exploit these reserves and was badly in need of additional export revenues to meet the deficits in its balance of payments. That meant, however, that much of the project would have to be financed by Transworld.

Transworld had substantial financial resources. Its net working capital had been expanding steadily over the past five years, and it had been on schedule in repayment of all its loans from leading international banks in four countries: the United States, United Kingdom, Japan, and China (via Hong Kong). It had an excellent credit standing, and two years ago, it had floated a successful bond issue in the UK market that raised 150 million pounds to finance a major project in Zambia. It had good working relationships with banks in Singapore and Hong Kong, two leading financial centers in the region. Wright also had had discussions with the local branches of three multinational banks in Salaysia, and they appeared to be interested, at least on a preliminary consideration basis.

Transworld was the world leader in advanced coal mining technology: its latest processes resulted in high-speed extraction; that is, the stacking and loading of coal from depths that had not been accessible to most of the existing mining techniques. Because the technology was highly automated, there were substantial economies because of saved labor costs. Most of the operations would be optimized by Transworld by using its sophisticated, computer-based optimization models that would generate the best possible sequencing, timing, and coordination of different operations, which would be at least 20 percent more efficient than the technology currently in use in Salaysia.

The company had substantial marketing strength. It ran coal-mining operations in several countries in Asia and Africa and had other mineral extraction operations in Latin America. Most of the products were sold to industrial consumers in Japan, Italy, and France. Transworld had strong business relationships with major shipping lines and considerable strength at the bargaining table while negotiating pricing for shipping its products. The world market for coal was expected to remain strong, and Transworld could reasonably expect to make at least an average level of profit on the exports of Salaysian coal.

There were, however, a few problems. Salaysia's local coal mining company was exerting substantial pressure on the home government to allow it to run the new project. It argued that it could access a similar level of technology by entering into a joint venture with Intermetals, an Australian mining company from which it could obtain the technical know-how, while the local implementation of the entire project would be in its hands. This venture would mean that Salaysia would only be buying the technical know-how from Australia, and the entire mining, extraction,

(continued)

Case Study 1.1 *(continued)*

processing, shipping, and marketing operations would be carried out by the Salaysian Coal Mining Company. The company had access to relatively dated machinery and extraction processes, but it had considerable financial strength and good relations with the labor force. Although it was relatively unknown abroad, the company was a major force in Salaysia's domestic mining industry. The management of the Salaysian Coal Mining Company also had good relations with the current minister of industries and was attempting to convince him that placing the entire project into the hands of multinational Transworld would be detrimental to the national interest and could lead to foreign domination of the domestic coal mining industry.

The Industries Ministry was weighing the two alternatives and had called for additional details before the proposals could be submitted to the Industrial Approvals Board of the Salaysian government for a final decision. John Wright indeed had much to think about as the plane headed back to Dallas.

DISCUSSION QUESTIONS

1. What additional incentives should Wright suggest to improve the attractiveness of Transworld's proposal to the Industries Ministry?
2. What strategy should Transworld adopt to offset the political advantage enjoyed by the Salaysian Coal Mining Company?

CHAPTER 2

The Nature of International Business

"The individual serves the industrial system not by supplying it with savings and the resulting capital; he serves it by consuming its products."
—John Kenneth Galbraith

CHAPTER OBJECTIVES

This chapter will:

- Explain the difference between the domestic and international contexts of business
- Introduce the various entry methods a corporation may use to establish international business
- Describe the changes in world trade patterns in terms of countries, products, and direct investment
- Discuss the role of central governments in establishing trade policy and providing environments that support or restrict international trade

DOMESTIC VERSUS INTERNATIONAL BUSINESS

The student of business is certainly familiar with the nature of doing business in a domestic market-based economy. A firm needs to identify its potential market, locate adequate and available sources of supplies of raw materials and labor, raise initial amounts of capital, hire personnel, develop a marketing plan, establish channels of distribution, and identify retail outlets. As an overlay upon this comprehensive system, the firm must also establish management controls and feedback systems, as well as accounting, finance, and personnel functions.

Not only must the novice international businesspeople contend with establishing an international component to add to domestic operations, but also they must contend with the fact that international business activities are conducted in environments and arenas that differ from their own in all aspects: in economies, cultures, government, and political systems. The differences range along a continuum. For example, economies can range from being market-oriented to centrally planned, and political systems from democracies to autocracies. The nations of Zimbabwe and North Korea would be considered centrally planned, autocratic governments. Countries are widely divergent in cultural parameters such as ethnic varieties, religious beliefs, social habits, and customs. The problems and difficulties these differences generate are exacerbated by problems of distance, which complicate the firm's ability to communicate clearly, transmit data and documents, and even find compatible business hours, because of the differences in time zones around the world. A US firm with a subsidiary operation in the Far East faces a fifteen-hour time difference. Consequently, US standard hours of 9 AM to 5 PM would be the equivalent of midnight to 8 AM overseas.

Business activities require vast investments of time, energy, and personnel on the domestic level. Adding an international component merely intensifies the number of steps necessary and the length and breadth of the firm's reach of effort and activity. Imagine establishing international components for all business functions as separate and discrete units. The prospective commitment is staggering and is generally avoided by many domestic businesses.

It is more likely that domestic firms enter foreign markets in a progressive way, beginning with exporting, which involves the least amount of resources and risk, before moving to a full-scale commitment in the form of establishing wholly owned overseas subsidiaries. A company must take many factors into consideration before deciding whether or not to move overseas. It must evaluate its own resources: personnel, assets, experience in overseas markets, and the suitability of its products or organization for transplantation overseas. It is also crucial that a firm decide on the minimum and optimum levels of return it wishes to receive, as well as the amount of risk it is willing to bear. A firm must also evaluate the level of control necessary to manage the overseas operation. These factors must be critiqued in light of competition expected in markets abroad and the potential business opportunities that are to be created by the international operation.

All of these factors must be weighted in terms of the overall short-term and long-term strategic goals and objectives of the firm. For example, a firm may have a long-term goal to build a production facility abroad to serve a foreign market within ten years. Consequently, it would be unwise to enter into a licensing agreement that would hold up its use of its rights for a long period of time.

Methods of Going International

Exporting

Exporting requires the least amount of involvement by a firm in terms of resources required and allocated to serving an overseas market. Basically, the company uses existing domestic capacity for production, distribution, and administration and designates a certain portion of its home production to a market abroad. It makes the goods locally and sends them by air, ship, rail, truck, or even pipeline across its nation's borders into another country's market.

Entrance into an export market frequently begins casually, with the placement of an order by a customer overseas. At other times, an enterprise sees a market opportunity and actively decides to take its products or services abroad. A firm can be either a direct or indirect exporter. As a direct exporter, it sees to all phases of the sale and transmittal of the merchandise. In indirect exporting, the exporter hires the expertise of someone else to facilitate the exchange. This intermediary is, of course, happy to oblige for a fee. There are several types of intermediaries: manufacturers' export agents who sell the company's product overseas; manufacturers' representatives who sell the products of a number of exporting firms in overseas markets; export commission agents who act as buyers for overseas markets; export commission agents who act as buyers for overseas customers; and export merchants who buy and sell on their own for a variety of markets.

Sales contacts within the foreign market are made through personal meetings, targeted mailings, telephone calls, or international trade fairs. Some of these trade expositions take unusual forms. For example, in an attempt to promote the sale of US products in Japanese markets, the Japanese government established a traveling trade show on a train. In the initial stages, the objective of the exporter is to develop an awareness of outstanding features of the firm's products, such as competitiveness against local products, innovation, durability, or reasonable prices.

The mechanics of exporting require obtaining appropriate permission from domestic governments (e.g., for food products and some technology and products considered crucial for national security); securing reliable transportation and transit insurance; and fulfilling requirements imposed by the importing nation, such as payment of appropriate duties, declarations, and inspections. Prior to the completion of the transaction, terms must be worked out for payment. The parties must establish the terms of the sale and whether the buyer will be extended credit, must open a letter of credit, pay in advance, or pay cash on delivery. In addition, the participants in the sale must also determine which currency will be used in the exchange. The currency used is especially crucial in light of fluctuations in exchange rates between countries. Sometimes the facilitation of an international transaction is difficult if the two currencies involved (of the buyer and the seller) are not actively traded on the world markets. One method of completing the transaction is to use the US dollar as an intermediary currency (the buyers convert their home currency into dollars and pay the sellers in dollars; then the sellers convert the dollars into their own domestic currency). Thus the US dollar has become a very important currency in international business today.

Advantages of Exporting

The prime advantage of exporting is that it involves very little risk and low allocation of resources for the exporter, who is able to use domestic production toward foreign markets and thus increase sales and reduce inventories. The exporter is not involved in the problems inherent in the foreign operating environment; the most that could be lost is the value of the exported products or an opportunity if the venture fails to establish the identity or characteristics of the product.

Exporting also provides an easy way to identify market potential and establish recognition of a name brand. If the enterprise proves unprofitable, the company can merely stop the practice with no diminution of operations in other spheres and no long-term losses of capital investments.

Disadvantages of Exporting

Exporting can be more expensive than other methods of overseas involvement on a per-unit basis because of mistakes and the costs of fees, or commissions, export duties, taxes, and transportation. In addition, exporting could lead to less than optimal market penetration because of improper packaging or promotion. Exported goods could also be lacking features appropriate to specific overseas market. Relying on exporting alone, a firm may have trouble maintaining market share and contacts over long distances. Additional market share could be lost if local competition copies the products or services offered by the exporter. The exporting firm also could face restrictions against its products from the host country.

While some of these problems can be addressed by establishing direct exporting capability through the establishment of a sales company within the foreign market to handle the technical aspects of export trading and keep abreast of market developments, demand, and competition, many firms choose instead to expand their operations in foreign spheres to include other forms of investments.

LICENSING

Through **licensing**, a firm (licensor) grants a foreign entity (licensee) some type of intangible rights, such as the rights to a process, a patent, a program, a trademark, a copyright, or expertise. In essence, the licensee is buying the assets of another firm in the form of know-how or research and development. The licensor can grant these rights exclusively to one licensee or nonexclusively to several licensees.

Advantages of Licensing

Licensing provides advantages to both parties. The licensor receives profits in addition to those generated from operations in domestic markets. These profits may be additional revenues from a single process or method used at home that the manufacturer is unable to utilize abroad. The method or process could have the beneficial effect of extending the life cycle of the firm's product beyond that which it would experience in local markets.

Additional revenues could also represent a return on a product or process that is ancillary to the strategic core of the firm in its domestic market; that is, the firm could have developed a method of production that is marketable as a separate product under a licensing agreement. In addition, by licensing, the firm often realizes increased sales by providing replacement parts abroad. In addition, it protects itself against piracy by having an agent in the licensed user who watches for copyright or patent infringement.

The licensee benefits by acquiring the rights to a process and state-of-the-art technology while avoiding the research and development costs.

Disadvantages of Licensing

The prime disadvantage of licensing to the licensor is that it limits future profit opportunities associated with the property by tying up its rights for an extended period of time. Additionally, by licensing these rights to another, the firm loses control over the quality of its products and processes, the use or misuse of the assets, and even the protection of its corporate reputation.

To protect against such problems, the licensing agreement should clearly delineate the appropriate uses of the process, method, or name, as well as the allowable market and reexport parameters for the licensee. The contract should also stipulate contingencies and recourse, should the licensor fail to comply with its terms.

FRANCHISING

Franchising is similar to licensing, except that in addition to granting the franchisee permission to use a name, process, method, or trademark, the firm assists the franchisee with the operations of the franchise and/or supplies raw materials. The franchiser generally also has a larger degree of control over the quality of the product than under licensing. Payment is similar to licensing in that the franchiser pays an initial fee and a proportion of its sales or revenues to the franchising firm.

The prime examples of US franchising companies are service industries and restaurants, particularly fast-food concerns, soft-drink bottlers, and home and auto maintenance companies (e.g., McDonald's, Kentucky Fried Chicken, Holiday Inn, Hilton, and Disney in Japan).[1] Only companies with models that have been successful in the domestic markets should consider franchising internationally. If the franchisor has not had success in the domestic market, it would not be wise to consider an international franchising program.

Advantages and Disadvantages of Franchising

The advantages accruing to the franchiser are increased revenues and expansion of its name brand identification and market reach. The greatest disadvantage, as with licensing, is coping with the problems of assuring quality control and operating standards.

Franchise contracts should be written carefully and provide recourse for the franchising firm, should the franchiser not comply with the terms of the agreement. Other difficulties with franchises come with the need to make slight adjustments or adaptations in the standardized product or service. For example, some ingredients in restaurant franchises may need to be adapted to suit the tastes of local clientele, which may differ from those of the original customers.

MANAGEMENT CONTRACTS

Management contracts are those in which a firm basically rents its expertise or know-how to a government or company in the form of personnel who go into the foreign environment and run the concern. This method of involvement in foreign markets is often used with a new facility, after **expropriation** of a concern by a national government, or when an operation is in trouble.

Management contracts are frequently used in concert with **turnkey operations**. Under these agreements, firms provide the service of overseeing all details in the startup of facilities, including design, construction, and operation. These are usually large-scale projects, such as production plants or utility constructions. The problem faced in turnkey operations is often the time length of the contract, which yields long payout schedules and carries greater risk in currency markets. Other problems can arise in the form of an increase in potential competition in the future as overseas capacity is increased by the new facilities. Turnkey operations also face all the problems of operating in remote locations.

CONTRACT MANUFACTURING

Contract manufacturing is another method for firms to enter the foreign arena. Here the MNE contracts with a local firm to provide manufacturing services. This arrangement is akin to vertical integration, except that instead of establishing its own production locations, the MNE subcontracts the production, which it does in two ways. In one case it enters into a full production contract with the local plant producing goods to be sold under the name of the original manufacturer. The other way is to enter into contracts with another firm to provide partial manufacturing services, such as assembly work or parts production.

Contract manufacturing has the advantage of expanding the supply or production expertise of the contracting firm at minimum cost. It is as if it can diversify vertically without a full-scale commitment of resources and personnel. By the same token, however, the firm also forgoes some degree of control over the production supply timetable when it contracts with a local firm to provide specific services. These problems are, however, no more substantial than operating normal raw material supplier contracts.

DIRECT INVESTMENT

When a company invests directly within foreign shores, it is making a very real commitment of its capital, personnel, and assets beyond domestic borders. While this commitment of resources increases the profit potential of an MNC dramatically by providing greater control over costs and operations of the foreign firm, it is also accompanied by an increase in the risks involved in operating in a foreign country and environment.

As with other forms of international activity, direct investment runs a continuum from joint ventures where risk is shared (but so are returns) to wholly owned subsidiaries where MNEs have the opportunity to reap the rewards, but also must shoulder the lion's share of the risk. Multinationals decide to make direct investments for two main reasons. The first is to gain access to enlarged markets. The second reason is to take advantage of cost differentials in overseas markets that arise from closer production resources, available economies of scale, and prospects for developing operating efficiencies. Both reasons lead to the enjoyment of enhanced profitability. Alternatively, a firm enters a foreign market for defensive reasons to counter strategic moves by its competitors or to follow a market leader into new markets.

STRATEGIC ALLIANCES

Strategic alliances (or **joint ventures**) are business arrangements in which two or more firms or entities join together to establish some sort of operation. Strategic alliances may be formed by two MNEs, an MNE and a government, or an MNE and local businesspersons. If there are more than two participants in the deal, it is also called a consortium operation.

Each party to these ventures contributes capital, equity, or assets. Ownership of the joint venture need not be a 50–50 arrangement and, indeed, it ranges according to the proportionate amounts contributed by each party to the enterprise. Some strategic alliances may be for only a short period of time, while others can endure for longer periods. Often the successful alliances are those whereby all parties stand to gain from the new alliance. Some countries stipulate the relative amount of ownership allowable to foreign firms in joint ventures. Vietnam is an example of a country that has historically had foreign ownership limits with regard to joint ventures. In July 2001, the United States and Vietnam signed a bilateral trade agreement. The agreement restricted United States citizens' ownership in joint ventures to 49 percent for three years. After six years, this requirement was lessened in the majority of industries, allowing US persons to own 51 percent of the joint venture. In some industries, such as hotels, restaurants, and travel agencies, the US will have no equity-limit restrictions after five years.[2]

Advantages of Strategic Alliances

Strategic alliances provide many advantages for both local and international participants. By entering a local market with a local partner, the MNE finds an opportunity to increase its growth and access to new markets while avoiding excessive tariffs and taxes associated with the entry of products. At the same time, joining forces with local businesses often neutralizes local existing and potential competition and protects the firm against the risk of expropriation because local nationals have a stake in the success of the operations of the firm. It is also frequently easier to raise capital in local markets when host-country nationals are involved in the operation. In some cases, host governments provide tax benefits as incentives to increase the participation of foreign firms in joint enterprises with local businesspersons.

Disadvantages of Strategic Alliances

The involvement of local ownership can also lead to major disadvantages for overseas partners in strategic alliances. Some of the problems faced by the MNE partners are limits on profit repatriation to the parent office; successful operations becoming an inviting target for **nationalization** or expropriation by the host government; and problems of control and decision-making. For example, different partners might have different objectives for the joint ventures. An MNE might have a goal of achieving profitability on a shorter timetable than its local partner, who might be more concerned about long-term profitability and maintaining local employment levels. It is a necessity, therefore, that firms establish guidelines regarding the objectives, control, and decision-making structures of joint ventures before entering into agreements.

Joint ventures tend to be relatively low-risk operations because the risks are shared by individual partners. Nevertheless, not having full control of the operation remains a predominant problem for the overseas participants in these ventures. A firm can achieve full control over operations, decision-making, and profits only when it establishes its own wholly owned subsidiary on foreign soil.

WHOLLY OWNED SUBSIDIARIES

By establishing its own foreign arm, a firm retains total control over marketing, pricing, and production decisions and maintains greater security over its technological assets. In return, it is entitled to 100 percent of the profits generated by the enterprise. Although it faces no problems with minority shareholders, the firm bears the entire risk involved in operating the facility. These risks are the same as those customarily encountered in domestic operations, but with an additional layer of special risks associated with international operations, such as expropriation, limits on profits being repatriated, and local operating laws and regulations, including the requirement to employ local labor and management personnel. In these cases, the MNCs do not have the benefit of local shareholders to run interference for them with local governments.

In establishing a subsidiary, a firm must choose either of two routes: acquire an ongoing operation or start from scratch and build its own plant. Buying a firm (also known as the **brownfield strategy**) has the advantage of avoiding startup costs of capital and a time lag. It is a faster process that is often easier to capitalize at local levels and generally cheaper than building. Buying also has the advantages of not adding to a country's existing capacity levels and of improving goodwill with host-country nationals. Downsides for the brownfield strategy are that any existing labor issues at the acquired site will remain after acquisition and that the purchased facility may no longer be state-of-the-art in use and design.

A company may decide to build a new plant (also known as the **greenfield strategy**) if no suitable facilities exist for acquisition or if it has special requirements for design or equipment. Although building a plant may avoid acquiring the problems of an existing physical plant, the firm may face difficulties in obtaining adequate financing from local capital markets and may generate ill-will among local citizenry.[3]

GLOBALIZED OPERATIONS

Some theorists believe that consumers around the world are becoming increasingly alike in their goals and requirements for products and product attributes.[4] As a result, the world is becoming a global market in which products would be standardized across all cultures, enabling corporations to manufacture and sell low-cost reliable products around the world. Such firms would be characterized by globalized operations, as distinct from multinational operations. A firm that has globalized operations would be able to take advantage of business opportunities occurring anywhere in the world and would not be constrained to specific sectors. Indeed, some firms have been able to achieve substantial globalization of operations as their products cross national borders without being adapted to individual country preferences. Prime examples include Levi-Strauss & Company, PepsiCo, Coca-Cola, and several other companies ranging from consumer goods to fast food.

PORTFOLIO INVESTMENTS

Portfolio investments do not require the physical presence of a firm's personnel or products on foreign shores. These investments can be made in the form of marketable securities in foreign markets, such as notes, bonds, commercial paper, certificates of deposit, and non-controlling shares of stock. They can also be investments in foreign bank accounts or foreign loans. Investors make decisions to acquire securities or invest money abroad for several reasons, primarily to diversify their portfolios among markets and locations, to achieve higher rates of return, to avoid political risks by taking their investments out of the country, or to speculate in foreign exchange markets.

Portfolio investments can be made either by individuals or through special investment funds. These investment funds pool local resources for investment in overseas stock and financial markets. Many mutual fund companies, such as Fidelity and Vanguard, have funds with an international focus. These funds invest in companies in a specific region of the world for investors in the United States. This allows both individuals as well as institutional investors to diversify their investments geographically. The Vanguard Global

Figure 2.1 **Global Diversification**

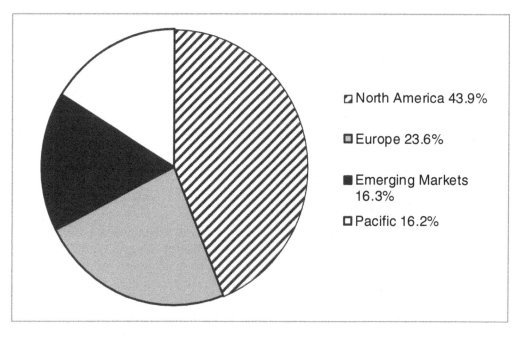

Source: Vanguard Group, *Vanguard Global Equity Fund: Annual Report, September 30, 2011* (Valley Forge, PA: Vanguard Group), www.vanguard.com/funds/reports/q1290.pdf. © The Vanguard Group, used with permission.

Equity Fund, for example, as of its annual report of September 30, 2011, invests in a total of 897 companies worldwide and has net assets of $3.329 billion. Figure 2.1 shows how this fund is geographically disbursed in terms of its portfolio of investments.[5]

Over the last few years, some emerging economies have reformed the rules and regulations to encourage foreign investment.[6] Most developed countries allow free access to their stock markets to overseas investors. Other developing economies allow less access to their stock markets. Overall, the developing world ranges from being less restrictive than it has been in the past to operating an open market system.

There are several factors that determine the degree to which a particular country will be able to attract portfolio investments. Political stability and economic growth are the most basic factors. The size, liquidity, and stability of stock markets, the level of interest rates and government taxes, and the nature of government regulation are also important determinants. The degree of restrictions on repatriation of income and capital invested are other major variables that affect the attractiveness of a country to overseas portfolio investors. Historically, most of international portfolio investment has been concentrated in the industrialized countries; the United States, Japan, France, the United Kingdom, Switzerland, the Netherlands, and Canada receive substantial amounts of portfolio investments in their markets. In recent years, some emerging stock markets, such as China,

Figure 2.2 **Portfolio Investment Inflows**

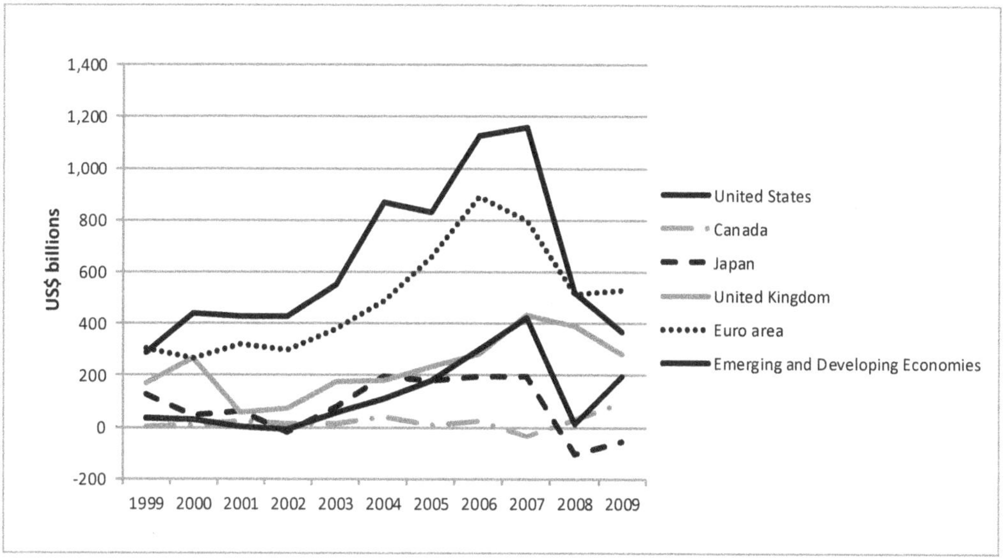

Source: International Monetary Fund, *Global Financial Stability Report: Statistical Appendix* (October 2010), www.imf.org/external/pubs/ft/gfsr/2010/02/pdf/statappx.pdf.

India, Malaysia, Indonesia, and Taiwan, have been able to attract significant amounts of foreign portfolio investment. Between 1999 and 2007, portfolio investments increased in the United States, reaching a peak of $1,156.6 billion, before falling to $520.1 billion in 2008 and $366.7 billion in 2009. Similarly, in the United Kingdom, portfolio investment peaked in 2007 at $435.9 billion in 2007 before falling to $389.2 billion in 2008 and $284.1 billion in 2009. The Euro area reached a peak of portfolio investment in 2006 at $890.5 billion before declining over the following three years. In contrast, in the emerging markets and developing countries of the world, portfolio investment dramatically increased between 2002 and 2007, reaching a peak of $421.1 billion, and then dropping to $12.7 billion as a result of the global financial crisis. The fluctuations of portfolio investments are illustrated in Figure 2.2.[7]

RECENT TRADE PATTERNS AND CHANGES IN GLOBAL TRADE

As the world has become more and more industrialized and as markets have become global entities, trade has increased proportionately and grown tremendously both in volume and dollar terms. Concomitantly, patterns in trade have also changed, as new nations enter the world-trading arena. In 1948 world trade totaled $60 billion. This figure rose to $323 billion in 1970 and $2,440 billion in 1980. As the world opened up to trade following economic and political reforms in eastern Europe and Asia, the volume of world trade

Figure 2.3 **Growth in World Trade**

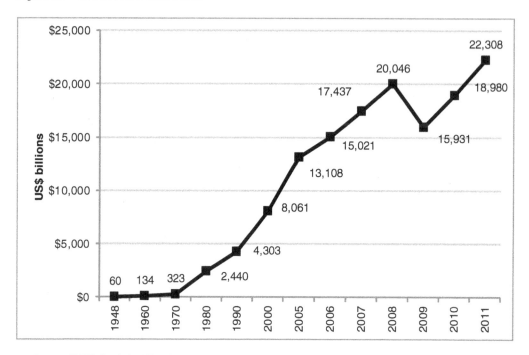

Source: WTO Statistical Database.

has increased 366 percent from $4,303 billion in 1990 to $20,045 billion in 2008.[8] As a result of the global financial crisis, world trade volume fell by more than 20 percent between 2008 and 2009, before rebounding to $22,307 billion in 2011.[9] Total world trade volume is the aggregate of each country's average trade volume, which is the average of a country's merchandise exports and imports plus the average of the country's commercial services exports and imports, calculated in current dollars. This increase in world trade volume can be best illustrated by the chart in Figure 2.3.[10]

Most of the world's trade is carried out between the industrialized countries and traded within the region where the goods are produced. Less-developed countries tend to be exporters of commodities and importers of finished goods. In 2011, China was the world's biggest exporter of goods and services, followed by the United States, at 9.3 percent and 9.2 percent respectively, as a percentage of the world's global exports (see Table 2.1). Trade flows tend to be intraregional, with a great amount of trade remaining in the region in which it was produced.[11] For example, in 2011, the European Union exported $7,790 billion worth of goods and services; 37.5 percent was exported outside of the region, while 62.5 percent remained within the European Union. In 2010, Western Europe, North America, and Japan accounted for 56.3 percent of merchandise exports sent to other countries and received 61.3 percent of all merchandise imports.[12] In 2010,

Table 2.1 **World's Leading Exporters, 2011**

		Percent of world exports		
	Country	Goods	Services	Total
1	China	10.4	4.4	9.30
2	United States	8.1	13.9	9.20
3	Germany	8.1	6.1	7.72
4	Japan	4.5	3.4	4.32
5	Netherlands	3.6	3.1	3.53
6	France	3.3	3.9	3.39
7	United Kingdom	2.6	6.6	3.34
8	Korea, Republic of	3.0	2.3	2.90
9	Italy	2.9	2.6	2.81
10	Hong Kong, China	2.5	2.9	2.58

Source: World Trade Organization (WTO), "Statistical Database," 2012, www.wto.org.

Table 2.2 **OPEC's Share of the World Market, 2010** (in percent)

	Crude oil	Natural gas
Reserves	81.3	49
Production	41.8	18

Source: Organization of the Petroleum Exporting Countries (OPEC), *OPEC Annual Statistical Bulletin, 2010/2011.*

China accounted for 10.6 percent of the world's merchandise exports and 9.3 percent of the world's merchandise imports.[13] The United States is the biggest exporter and importer of commercial services. The top four exporters and importers of commercial services in 2010 were the United States, Germany, China, and the United Kingdom, which in aggregate, exported 31 percent and imported 27.7 percent of global commercial services.

OPEC's participation in world trade declined in the second half of the 1980s because prices and demand for oil have fallen since the early 1970s. Given the recent upswing in the demand for oil (due to the expansion of the Chinese economy and the continued demand of the United States) and the price per barrel of oil, OPEC retains a major proportion of the share of developing countries' exports in world trade (see Table 2.2). OPEC nations[14] represented 7 percent ($1,077 billion) of world merchandise trade in 2010. Of that total, energy exports accounted for $745.066 billion. Without the contribution of OPEC, the share of the remaining developing countries exports in world trade is only 28 percent.[15]

This pattern of trade is changing, however, as the fortunes of nations change in different trading regions. While high-income developed countries continue to hold the lion's share of world trade, greater portions of activity are being taken over by new entrants into the world market. The most notable, historically, is Japan, which completely reversed its fortunes, prospects, and future since its reconstruction and growth after World War II.

In 1950 Japan had merchandise exports of $820 million and imports of $974 million; by 1970 this level had risen to exports of $19.318 billion and imports of $8.881 billion. By 2003 Japan was exporting $542 billion worth of products and services in world markets and importing products and services valued at $493 billion.[16]

Japan is being joined by other countries that are nipping at the heels of the wealthy, industrialized world by rapidly increasing their levels of industrialization, production, and exports. Increased competition from other Asian countries that follow the export model for growth has reduced some of Japan's export growth. China has taken the world by surprise in its rapid growth in exports since the turn of the millennium. The value of Chinese exports of goods and services rose from $483 billion in 2003 to more than $2.080 trillion in 2011, while its imports had a value of $467 billion in 2003, rising to over $1.979 trillion in 2011. Given China's strong projected GDP growth over the next decade, this trend is sure to continue. Instead of Japan being the dominant Asian economy, China has now taken over that role. Other challengers to China and Japan include the so-called **newly industrialized countries (NICs)** of South Korea, Taiwan, Singapore, and Hong Kong, along with the developing nations of Vietnam, the Philippines, and Indonesia. Trade activity by these nations is slowly moving the focus of international trade patterns away from traditional *north-north* routes between developed countries to increased trade between *north and south*—that is, between developed and developing nations. Similarly, the growth in trade by less-developed countries is increasing, as economic development and increases in standards of living provide citizens of those nations with higher incomes and surplus resources to spend on goods other than basic necessities.

These trends in trade patterns indicate a reduction of US and European dominance in the world trade arena. On the other hand, the Asian and Middle Eastern countries are increasing their participation in world trade, because of their rapid industrialization and the importance of petroleum and petroleum products. US trade with these countries has also been increasing significantly, marking a departure from its traditional trading pattern that relied to a very large extent on trade with European trading partners. Furthermore, changes in the international political climate, especially the thawing of relations with formerly centrally planned economy countries as they move toward market economies, have led to marked increases of US trade with Russia and the former Soviet bloc countries and the People's Republic of China. Rapid and far-reaching technological developments have also affected trade patterns; for example, monopolies in raw materials such as rubber and metals have been shattered by high-tech substitutes, such as synthetic products. Countries that were major exporters of such raw materials have had to look for other products to export, and export market shares in these commodities have shifted dramatically.

PRODUCT GROUPS

In world trade, the major product categories of goods are exports of manufactured goods, machinery, and fuels, which account for 80 percent of all world commodity trade. The remaining 20 percent of commodity types are crude commodities, agricultural products, and chemicals. Until 1972 manufactured goods continued to increase in relative importance in world trade. After that, they began to decline in importance because of the increase in oil prices and the worldwide recession that followed. The developed countries account for the largest proportion of goods traded in world markets. The Euro Area emerged as the world's leading exporter, but China was the largest single-country exporter of goods. The United States is the world's leading exporter of services.

Lesser-developed countries have increased their relative shares of world trade. Non-Middle-Eastern Asian countries have slightly increased their exports from the period of 1980 to 2003 (to roughly 9 percent of world commodity exports), as compared to an overall decline in total Middle East exports over the same period. The regions of Africa and Central and South America stayed relatively constant over the last two decades, with each accounting for less than 3 percent of the world's commodity exports. China's portion of world commodity exports rose by 35 percent from 2002 to 2003, and it now accounts for 6.0 percent, while China's imports rose in the same time period by 40 percent and now account for 5.5 percent of world totals.

PATTERNS OF DIRECT INVESTMENT

As trading patterns in merchandise continue to change, so do the patterns of countries investing in resources abroad. Many believe that direct investment activity is a natural adjunct to trading activities in different locations; that is, investment funds follow trade activity. Direct investment can be measured according to the source country of funds or ownership. Generally, foreign direct investment of capital is differentiated from portfolio investments according to levels of managerial involvement and control by owners. Some countries distinguish effective control according to a level of percentage ownership. The United States, for example, has used a level of 10 percent as a criterion.

World foreign direct investment inflow levels were $1,243 billion by the end of 2010 (see Figure 2.4). These figures are misleading, however, because they reflect the book value of the investments, which is the value at which they were acquired; these are historical figures that do not account for appreciation in value over time or for inflation. According to recent studies, the bulk of world direct investment is within the industrialized countries of the world. The United States, France, and the United Kingdom in 2003 together accounted for about 43 percent of the world total foreign direct investment outflow, while they received 20 percent of the world foreign direct investment inflow.[17] By 2010, the United States, France, and the United Kingdom accounted for 32 percent of the foreign direct investment outflow and received 25 percent of the foreign direct investment inflows. China is also a major source of foreign direct investment outflows and recipient of inflows. In 2010, China was the source of 10.9 percent of the world foreign direct investment outflows and the recipient of 14 percent of the world foreign direct investment inflows. Foreign direct investments are generally made according to two patterns: geographically between countries in close proximity to each other, and

Figure 2.4 **World FDI Level**

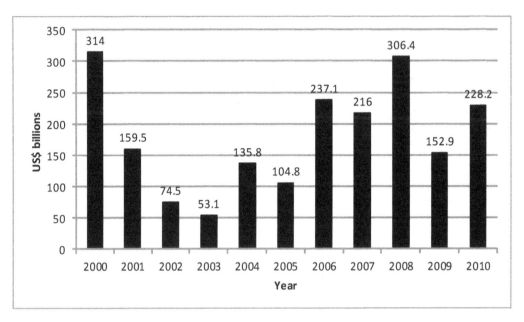

Source: UNCTADstat.

along traditional lines based on the strength of historical or political alliances or the ties between countries and their former colonies. While foreign direct investment into the United States has been trending downward over the last few years, as was discussed in Chapter 1, this was due primarily to a worldwide recession and historically low interest rate levels in the United States (see Figure 2.4). Another explanation is that with the arrival of China and India on the world stage, there are now many other destinations for foreign direct investment. While the portion of the US share of foreign direct investment inflows is decreasing, foreign direct investment is flowing to developing countries at an increasing rate, which was impacted by the beginning of the 2007 financial crisis, peaking at $1,907 billion (see Figure 2.5).

Investments, in general, are made by very large firms and have seen the highest growth in the areas of manufacturing, petroleum, and industries that require high levels of capital assets. The investments are made primarily in industrial countries with the lowest level of risk and the largest possible markets.

GOVERNMENT INVOLVEMENT IN TRADE RESTRICTIONS AND INCENTIVES

All governments attempt to restrict or support international trade or transfers of resources. This intervention can take the form of controlling the flow of trade and transfer of goods,

Figure 2.5 **FDI into the United States**

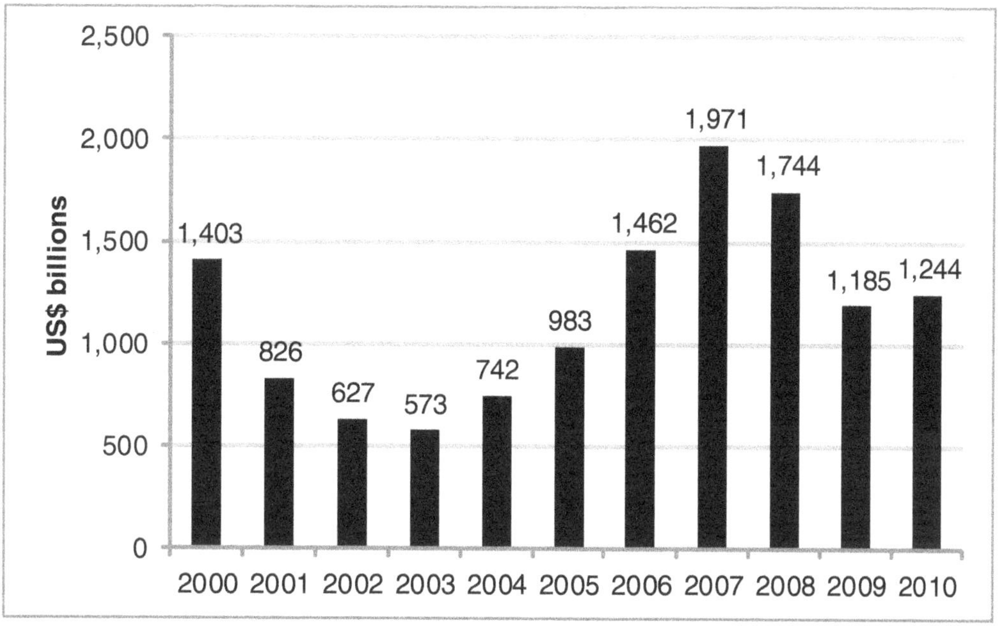

Source: UNCTADstat.

controlling the transfer of capital flows, or controlling the movement of personnel and technology. Rationales for intervention vary but fall into several patterns, all of which are based on the notion that the governmental actions will promote the best interests of the nation.

Governments may be motivated by economic goals, such as increasing revenues or the supply of hard currency in the country. They also may have economic or monetary considerations in equalizing balances of trade or keeping inflation to a minimum. They may cite country objectives, such as maintaining self-sufficiency, economic independence, and national security. There may be specific concerns in the country regarding the welfare of the populace, such as health and safety considerations or full employment goals. Political objectives also play a major role in establishing trade policy by governments.

PROTECTIONISM

Protectionism refers to government intervention in trade markets to protect specific industries in its economy. Impetus for protecting industries comes from special-interest groups within different sectors of the economy who plead their case for protecting domestic capacity and production facilities. Many believe that calls for protectionism should be interpreted as a need for the country to make structural changes in its industrial base in order to increase its competitiveness in foreign markets, rather than have the government intervene in order to support inefficient industries.

One rationale promulgated for protecting industry is to ensure full employment. This argument holds that the substitution of imports for domestic products causes jobs to be lost at home and that protecting industries is necessary for a strong domestic employment base.

A second rationale is protecting **infant industries**, which is especially true in less-developed and developing countries. The infant-industry justification holds that newly established industries cannot compete effectively at first against established giants from industrialized nations. Consequently, the industry is protected (theoretically) until such time as it can grow to achieve economies of scale and operational efficiencies matching those of its major competitors. Under this scenario, difficulties occur when the time comes to withdraw such protection, which by then has become institutionalized and is vociferously defended by industry participants. This argument was first made by Alexander Hamilton, the first US secretary of the Treasury, in 1792. Hamilton wanted to protect the fledgling industries of the new nation from European competition (he also advocated the idea of not recognizing foreign patents and copyrights for similar competitive reasons).

A third rationale for protecting specific industries is that the industrialization objectives of a country justify a promotion of specific sectors of the economy in order to diversify the economic structure. Thus, protection and incentives are given to those industries that are expected to grow quickly, bring in investment dollars, and yield high marginal returns. For this reason, many developing countries attempt to promote the growth of industries that provide high value-added materials and emphasize the use of agricultural or locally available primary raw materials.

The ultimate rationale for protectionism is more accurately based in emotionalism than in sound economic arguments, and its cost is high. Protectionism leads to higher prices for consumers for imported products and components. It may lead to retaliation by importing countries, which may reduce the home country's exports abroad and employment in local markets. Protectionism also may increase opportunity costs by allocating the resources of a country inappropriately and at the expense of other sectors of the industrial base of the economy.

Governmental intervention in markets takes several different forms. The primary and most direct method is through the application of tariffs to exports or imports. A less direct method is the application of nontariff barriers.

TARIFFS

Tariffs or **duties** are a basic method of intervention that may be used to protect industries by raising the price of imports, to bring import prices even with domestic prices, or to generate revenues. Tariffs may be placed on goods leaving the country as export duties or on goods entering the country as import duties. They are the most typical controls on imports. Tariffs are assessed in three different ways:

1. **Ad valorem duties** are assessed on the value of the goods and are levied as a percentage of that value.
2. **Specific duties** are assessed according to a physical unit of measurement, such as per ton, per bushel, or per meter, and are stipulated at a specific monetary value.
3. **Compound tariffs** are a combination of ad valorem and specific duties.

Determining Tariffs

Tariffs have an advantage as a tool for government intervention in international markets because they can be varied and applied on a selective basis according to commodity or country of origin. Some countries can be assessed higher duties on their imports than others. These duties are prescribed according to tariff schedules. Single-column schedules are those in which the duties on products and commodities are the same for everyone. Multicolumn schedules list tariffs rates for different products and different countries accorded to trade agreements between the two countries.

Some countries that are treated separately are those that have most-favored-nation (MFN) status accorded to them. These countries have entered into agreements under which all the signatories are accorded the same preferential tariff status. Countries enter into these agreements to facilitate entry of their own exports and for political and other economic reasons. There are many groups of trading partners in the world, the largest and most important of which was the General Agreement on Tariffs and Trade (GATT), which was established soon after World War II with an original membership of nineteen countries. GATT was replaced by the World Trade Organization (WTO) in 1995. The WTO was expanded to include discussions on services (in addition to merchandise exports) and now includes 155 member nations and 29 observer nations.[18]

WORLD TRADE ORGANIZATION

The purpose of the WTO is to establish an umbrella under which its signatory members can meet to establish reciprocal reductions in tariffs and the liberalization of trade in a mutual and nondiscriminatory manner. A major objective of the body is to extend tariff accords and most-favored-nation status to all members. Under the WTO, methods and rules of trade liberalization are established with provisions for monitoring trade activity, enforcement, and the settling of disputes. WTO rules allow for certain exceptions to reduce trade barriers, such as allowing countries to continue to provide support for domestic agriculture and for developing countries to protect infant industries.

Reductions in trade barriers are achieved through the meeting of the signatories in negotiating sessions, or trade rounds. These meetings are held periodically to discuss the further lowering of barriers to trade. In recent rounds, WTO members have attempted to deal with nontariff problems and other current issues, such as trade in agriculture and services, technology transfer, and nonmonetary barriers put up by countries to discourage free trade.

REGIONAL TRADE GROUPS

Trade groups organized along regional or political lines are less pervasive and influential. Two major regional trading groups are the European Union (EU), which is composed of twenty-eight European countries, and the North American Free Trade Agreement (NAFTA), which consists of the United States, Canada, and Mexico.

Traditionally, trade groups have also been organized according to specific commodity types and agreements that allow for monitoring and/or controlling the supply of those commodities. Ten such basic commodities have been identified by the United Nations: coffee, cocoa, tea, sugar, cotton, rubber, jute, sisal, copper, and tin. Some of these commodities are traded on open and free markets, where their prices fluctuate to a great degree. Sales of other commodities—such as sugar, rubber, tin, cocoa, and coffee—have historically come under the aegis of international commodity agreements that promote use of import and export quotas and a system of buffer stocks. In today's marketplace, prices are subject to market pressure, so these types of groups are less meaningful than they have been in the past. Other trade groups are organized among producers, consumers, or both.

Generally, under these agreements prices are allowed to move up and down within a certain range, but if the price moves above or below that range, an outside collective agency is authorized to buy or sell the commodity to support its price. Similarly, a commodity agreement may provide for quotas on exports from individual supply countries to limit supplies of the commodities on world markets, thus shoring up prices.

CARTELS

Another form of a commodity agreement group is the **cartel**, in which a group of commodity-producing countries join forces to bargain as a single entity in world markets. A cartel can be formed only when there is a relatively small group of producers who hold an oligopoly position—that is, they control the bulk of the commodity supply. The most notable cartel in recent years has been the **Organization of Petroleum Exporting Countries (OPEC)**, which has a membership of twelve oil-producing nations. It is composed of six Middle Eastern countries—and six other oil-producing countries in the world.[19]

In the early 1970s, OPEC was able to raise the price of crude oil from $3.64 per barrel to $11.65 per barrel within a single year. It was able to do so because it had a great deal of leverage in the world marketplace; its members controlled more than half of the world production of oil in 1973. World demand for oil was very high and the top oil-consuming countries were not able to meet the demand with domestic supplies.[20] There were few suitable energy substitutes being utilized around the world. The cartel was also successful because its members adhered to their production and pricing agreements.

Frequently, cartels fail because members violate their agreements by dropping prices or raising production and forcing the other members back into a competitive position. Although this did not occur with OPEC, the cartel's hold on world markets began to slip in the mid-1970s as a worldwide recession, conservation, and the use of energy substitutes reduced the demand for oil. In addition, non-OPEC producers increased their production to take advantage of price escalations in world markets. Political turmoil, the emergence of the Chinese economy, and an insatiable demand for oil by the United States led to an increase in the price of oil to more than $50 per barrel in 2003, peaking to $140 per barrel in 2008. In 2011, world oil demand was 87.79 million barrels per day. Non-OPEC countries produced 52.390 million barrels per day, and OPEC produced 29.942 million barrels per day, totaling 82.332 million barrels per day. North America (led by the United States) accounted for 23.37 million barrels a day or 26.67 percent of the total demand, but only 15.52 million barrels a day or 19 percent of world oil supply. China, demonstrating its significant growth, now contributes 5 percent to the world oil supply but is responsible for 11.17 percent of world oil demand.[21]

Nontariff Barriers to Merchandise Trade

Nontariff barriers have become a controversial topic in trade activity over the past decade. They are a matter of concern because they are not traditional methods of discouraging imports through the application of duties. Instead, they work to slow the flow of goods into a country by increasing the physical and administrative difficulties involved in importing.

Nontariff barriers can take a number of forms that provide effective restraints on trade.

- Government discrimination against foreign suppliers in bidding procedures
- Highly involved and rigorous customs and country-entry procedures
- Excessively severe inspection and standards requirements
- Detailed safety specifications and domestic testing requirements
- Required percentages of domestic content material

Some nations regulate the consumption of certain products that they deem harmful to their citizens. Canada, for example, has strict entry requirements for individuals and companies that are bringing tobacco products into the country. Other countries attempt to control the amount of a certain product being imported by returning entire shipments of goods just because one sample failed to meet the acceptable standards. In the aftermath of the Canadian mad cow disease scare in May 2003, Japanese officials discussed the possibility of requiring that all imported Canadian beef products had to be inspected, rather than following the typical sampling procedures. Rather than incurring the cost of such inspections, the government of Japan decided to ban future shipments of Canadian beef until any problem in Canada could be resolved.

Some countries have restrictions on services, such as prohibiting transportation carriers from serving specific destinations or only allowing advertising that features models of that country's nationality.

QUOTAS

The most widely used method of restricting quantity, volume, or value-based imports are the imposition of quotas upon imports into a country. These quotas may be unilateral according to commodity and stipulate that only a certain aggregate amount of the import from any source may enter a country. Alternatively, they can be selective on a country or regional basis. A type of quota is an **embargo**, which prohibits all trade between countries. Another type, encountered only in recent trade history, is the voluntary entry restriction, in which foreign countries that agree to restrict their exports to a country are actually forced into compliance through the use of direct or subtle political pressure by major trading partners.

While the imposition of quotas may impede the flow of imports into a country, it does little to help that country find a level of readjustment; that is, it does nothing in the way of leading to lowered domestic prices. It often leads to higher import prices.

The imposition of quotas also causes serious administrative problems for the authorities of both the importing and exporting countries. Once quotas are imposed, the amount of goods to be sent from the exporting country is not determined by market demand but by an arbitrary ceiling. The quantity of goods allowed to be exported under the quota ceilings are often much lower than the normal export levels, which implies that all exporters of the affected country cannot export at their previous levels. The new levels have to be determined by the authorities, which for large, widespread export industries is an expensive and cumbersome process. Problems arise for the importing country because the imported quantities under the quota rules are not adequate to meet market demand, so the government has to take over the role of the market in allocating the available goods imported under quota rules. Apart from the expense and delays of the administrative process that is required to accomplish nonmarket distribution of imported goods, there is also the danger of creating inequities, because it is often difficult to verify genuine needs and claims.

NONTARIFF PRICE BARRIERS

Nontariff and competitive barriers can also be implemented as adjustments in prices. For example, some countries use **subsidies** to enhance the competitiveness of their exports in international markets. In a well-known WTO dispute, the United States insisted that Canada had subsidized its soft wood lumber industry, a charge that Canada denied. The subsidized industry would have then been able to sell its product in the United States at a much reduced cost, thereby gaining a competitive advantage. The WTO decided in favor of Canada in July 2004, although the result was disputed by the United States. Some subsidized services, such as export promotion, are permissible according to trade conventions. Others, such as special tax incentives or government provisions of fundamental research, are contested by trading nations as being against free trade. Other governmental intervention strategies such as "buy domestic" campaigns are less subtle attempts to influence purchases in favor of domestic producers.

Some countries raise the effective costs of exporting by assessing special fees for importing, requiring customs deposits, or establishing minimum sales prices in foreign markets, thereby making it less profitable for exporters to send goods to their markets. Similarly, the manipulation of exchange rates can affect the position of a country's goods in overseas markets because undervaluing one's currency exchange rate will make that country's goods more competitive abroad.

Another type of nontariff price barrier is erected by valuing imports at customs under the ad valorem method of assessing tariffs. Countries can vary their valuation criteria and value goods at their own country's retail prices rather than at the wholesale/invoice prices being paid by the importer.

In determining the appropriate pricing levels for tariffs in the event of disputes, one would first use the invoice price, then the price of identical goods, then similar goods. A particular problem arises when goods are entering a market-based economy from a centrally planned or nonmarket economy where there is no established pricing structure or valuation procedure. An example of this recently has been the Chinese furniture industry. Many US manufacturers have accused China of **dumping**[22] its furniture in the US market in an effort to unfairly gain market share. A similar case occurred when nonmarket economies tried to bring chemical fertilizers into the United States at below market prices, which was achieved by undervaluing the costs of crucial inputs such as natural gas.

GOVERNMENT RESTRICTION OF EXPORTS

In addition to controlling or taxing national imports, governments often have laws and regulations that limit certain types of exports generally or to specific countries. Governments apply these limits to maintain domestic supply and price levels of goods, to keep world prices high, or to meet national defense, political, or environmental goals. In the United States, under the Export Administration Act of 1969 and its amendments of 1979, US export licenses could be limited to promote foreign policy objectives, to protect the economy from a drain of limited or scarce resources, or to prevent military use by the recipient nations. Licenses are required for the export of items on the US-controlled commodity list and for the export of any product to communist countries. The administration of these licenses is overseen by the US Department of Commerce in tandem with the Departments of State and Defense.

SUMMARY

International business requires the same basic functional and operational activities as domestic business activities. As international business crosses borders, however, it encounters different economies, cultures, legal systems, governments, and languages, which must be integrated into business policies and practices. Entry into international business varies along a continuum from the simplest form, exporting, through other entry methods, including licensing, franchising, contract manufacturing, direct investment, joint ventures, wholly owned subsidiaries, globalized operations, and portfolio investments.

Recent changes in global trade patterns reveal a reduction in the dominance of the United States and Europe, while Asian (especially China and Japan) and Middle Eastern countries are increasing their levels of output. Direct investment, 32 percent originated in United States, France, and the United Kingdom in 2010, is generally located in the industrialized countries, where risks are lowest and potential returns are high.

The governments of host countries play an important role in either restricting or supporting international trade. Often, international trade policies are determined in order to achieve economic or monetary goals; maintain national security; improve health, safety, and employment levels; or support specific political objectives. Protectionism, tariffs, nontariff barriers, and government restrictions on exports are direct and indirect methods of restricting international trade.

DISCUSSION QUESTIONS

1. Which factors should a firm consider before it decides to conduct business internationally?
2. Which method of going international would you use if you were

   - an automobile manufacturer?
   - a software developer?
   - an oil exploration and production company?
   - an electrical power plant builder?
   - a farmer with large surplus of wheat?
   - a restaurant operator with a new barbecue rib recipe?

Discuss the reasons that determined your decision.

3. When might a corporation go international using a joint venture approach rather than a wholly owned subsidiary approach? Give an example.
4. What type of business transaction generally uses a turnkey operation approach?
5. Identify the top five leading exporting countries.
6. What are the differences between foreign direct investment stock, portfolio investment, and foreign direct investment inflows and outflows?
7. Which country is the leading provider of services in the world?
8. Give a recent example in which China invested directly in the United States.
9. How might multinational direct investment help or hurt the country receiving the investment?
10. Discuss the methods governments use to protect their domestic business environments.

NOTES

1. D.A. Bell, *Business America*, 1986.
2. U.S.–Vietnam Trade Council, "Vietnam Trade Agreement: Summary of Key Provisions."
3. Kitching, "Winning and Losing with European Acquisition," 81.
4. Levitt, "Globalization of Markets."
5. Vanguard Group, *Vanguard Global Equity Fund*.
6. International Finance Corporation, *Emerging Stock Markets Fact Book,* 2004.
7. International Monetary Fund, *Global Financial Stability Report*.
8. World Trade Organization, "Statistical Database," May 2012.
9. World Trade Organization, "Statistical Database."
10. World Trade Organization, "Statistical Database."
11. World Trade Organization. *World Trade Organization International Trade Statistics 2012.*
12. World Trade Organization, *World Trade Report 2004*, Appendix, Table 1A.1.
13. World Trade Organization, International Trade Statistics.
14. OPEC members include Algeria, Angola, Ecuador, Iran, Iraq, Kuwait, Libya, Nigeria, Qatar, Saudi Arabia, United Arab Emirates, and Venezuela.
15. OPEC *Annual Statistical Bulletin*, 2003; OPEC *Annual Statistical Bulletin*, 2011; World Trade Organization, "Statistical Database."
16. United Nations Conference on Trade and Development, World Trade Report, 2004.
17. United Nations Conference on Trade and Development, Country Fact Sheets, 2004.
18. www.wto.org/english/thewto_e/whatis_e/tif_e/org6_e.htm.
19. www.opec.org/opec_web/en/about_us/25.htm.
20. Daniels and Radebaugh, "The Middle East Squeeze on Oil Grants," 56.
21. OPEC, *Monthly Oil Market Report*, July 2012, p. 20.
22. In international trade, dumping is defined as one country selling a product in another country at a price that is less than the cost of production of that same product in the destination country.

BIBLIOGRAPHY

Belassa, Bela, ed. *Changing Patterns in Foreign Trade and Payments*, 3rd ed. New York: Norton, 1978.

Bell, David A. Business America. 1986. http://www.econbiz.de/en/search/detailed-view/doc/all/business-america-the-magazine-of-international-trade/10000361067/?no_cache=1.

Czinkota, Michael R. "International Trade and Business in the Late 1980s: An Integrated U.S. Perspective." *Journal of International Business Studies* (Spring 1986): 127–134.

Daniels, John, and Lee Radebaugh. "The Middle East Squeeze on Oil Grants." *Business Week*, July 29, 1972, 56.

International Finance Corporation. *Emerging Stock Markets Fact Book*. Washington, DC: International Finance Corporation, 2004.

International Monetary Fund. *Global Financial Stability Report*, October 2010.

Kitching, John. "Winning and Losing with European Acquisition." *Harvard Business Review* (March/April 1974): 81.

Levitt, Theodore. "Globalization of Markets." *Harvard Business Review* (May/June 1983): 92–102.

Mirus, Rolf, and Bernard Yeung. "Economic Incentives for Countertrade." *Journal of International Business Studies* (Fall 1986): 27–39.

OPEC. *Annual Statistical Bulletin, 2010/2011*. Vienna: OPEC.

———. Monthly Oil Market Report. July 2012. www.opec.org/opec_web/en/17.htm.

Schoening, Niles C. "A Slow Leak: Effects of the U.S. Shifts in International Investment." *Survey of Business* (Spring 1988): 21–26.

Suzuki, Katshiko. "Choice Between International Capital and Labor Mobility of Diversified Economies." *Journal of International Economics* (November 1989): 347–361.

United Nations. *Statistical Yearbook*. New York: United Nations, 2004.

United Nations Conference on Trade and Development. Country Fact Sheets. 2004.

———. World Trade Report. 2004.

US Department of Commerce. *Survey of Current Business*. Washington, DC: Government Printing Office, 2004.

U.S.–Vietnam Trade Council. "Vietnam Trade Agreement: Summary of Key Provisions." July 13, 2005, www.usvtc.org/BTA/BTA_Rueters.htm.

Vanguard Group. *Vanguard Global Equity Fund: Annual Report, September 30, 2011*. Valley Forge, PA: Vanguard Group. www.vanguard.com/funds/reports/q1290.pdf.

World Bank. *World Development Report, 2004*. New York: Oxford University Press, 2004.

World Trade Organization, *World Trade Report 2004*, Appendix, Table 1A.1.

World, Trade Organization. *World Trade Organization International Trade Statistics 2012*. [S.l.]: Bernan, 2012.

World Trade Organization. "Statistical Database." 2012. www.wto.org.

GLOBALIZATION AT THE CROSSROADS: IS SECURITIZATION THE ENEMY?

In the wake of the "Yes Era" (i.e., the start of the recent global recession) there were many comments in the financial press that probable cause for the economic calamity lay at the feet of bankers who created securitization products which package mortgages together for sale to investors. Securitization comes in many forms but typically involves the packaging of residential or commercial mortgages, or other loans such as automobiles and student loans, into bonds sold to the public. As many securitized pools of residential and commercial mortgages contained loans of dubious quality, securitization itself was seen as the enemy of continued global progress. If economies such as Iceland, Ireland, and Spain could be placed on the brink of economic calamity from purchasing highly risky pools of mortgages, something is awry in the securitization model itself; or at least so it seems. Residential mortgage backed securities (RMBS) and commercial mortgage backed securities (CMBS) came crashing down in 2009 from the heights just a few years before. Lost in the blame game was the fact that covered bonds in Europe, which represent pools of bank approved mortgages held on the balance sheets of financial institutions, had not experienced a default in over 200 years. A basic difference between the covered bond model (known as pfandbriefe in Germany) and the stateside version of mortgage backed securities was that the government legislation in Europe allows for the banks to remove poorly performing assets from the covered bond pools, while such laws do not yet exist in the RMBS and CMBS models. The securitization of mortgage and other debt allows for banks to free up their balance sheets so that they can continue to lend. This added liquidity in the market has the effect of lowering the cost of lending for everyone. The question for debate is whether securitization is the enemy or if the benefits outweigh the costs.

QUESTIONS FOR DISCUSSION

1. *Research the current state of the securitization industry. Has the industry made a comeback?*
2. *Based on your research, is the securitization model inherently flawed?*
3. *Why was mortgage securitization seen as the culprit in the recent financial crisis?*
4. *What role does regulation play in both the blame game and the recovery of the market?*

CASE STUDY 2.1

ELECTRONICS INTERNATIONAL LTD.

Electronics International Ltd. is a large consumer electronics manufacturer based in Southampton, England. Its product line consists of compact disk players, DVD players, home entertainment systems, and so on. Annual sales in 2012 were $186 million, 44 percent of which came from overseas sales. Most of the company's exports go to developing countries in Asia and Africa, with a small percentage of its products going to Turkey and Greece. Its most important export market is Zempa, a relatively prosperous developing country in the western part of Africa. Exports to Zempa total nearly 26 percent of all export revenues and have been showing an upward trend for the past six years.

Total sales to Zempa in 2012 were $140 million, up from $120 million in 2011 and $110 million in 2010. The company controls approximately 20 percent of the audio products market in Zempa, with the rest taken up by other competitors, all of whom are overseas corporations. Zempa has no audio products manufacturing industry, so all domestic requirements are met through imports. Electronics International is the third biggest player in the Zempa market, with the top two slots occupied by a German company and a Japanese company, respectively. Electronics International's products are well-established and enjoy considerable customer loyalty.

Recently, the government of Zempa has become increasingly concerned about the relatively backward state of its manufacturing industry and wants to rapidly industrialize the economy by attracting overseas investment in key sectors. One of the important priorities for the Zempan government in this connection is the consumer electronics industry. As part of its policy to develop the local economy by

(continued)

Case Study 2.1 *(continued)*

stimulating domestic manufacturing activity, the Zempan government queries each of the major exporters of consumer electronics products about setting up domestic production facilities in Zempa. The managing director of Electronics International receives a letter from the Zempa government, inviting the company to set up a manufacturing facility in Zempa and promising considerable official assistance should the company decide to do so.

Electronics International is asked to evaluate this offer and to reply within three months. The government also acknowledges that the other leading suppliers are also considering setting up local manufacturing establishments in Zempa.

The idea of setting up a manufacturing operation in Zempa does not appeal initially to the managing director. The company is doing well in Zempa as an exporter: sales have been increasing each year. There have been no difficulties in shipping its products; most of the goods are transported by sea and costs are acceptable. True, there are some problems with the local customs authorities, but they are not insurmountable. The distributors are good, reliable people who are pushing sales hard and meeting their contractual obligations to the company without any major problems. The Zempan government's regulations regarding remittance of payments for imports/exports are tedious and at times a little frustrating, but with the help of the company's local agents, most of the issues regarding repatriation of exchange proceeds are resolved in reasonable time. Therefore, why should the company think of setting up manufacturing operations in Zempa? The infrastructure for industry in Zempa is relatively undeveloped. The electricity supply is especially unreliable. There is little trained manpower, and the production of electronic products requires workers who are adept at carrying out the delicate assembling tasks. On the verge of dictating a letter thanking the Zempan government for its invitation to set up a factory but conveying the company's decision to stay on only as an exporter, the managing director decides to consult Bill McLowan, the strategic planning director at Electronics International. A couple of days later, McLowan presents a seven-page executive memo that differs from the thoughts of the managing director. The memo raises five main points:

1. Zempa is a valuable market for Electronics International, and as the economy of the country develops, the market size is likely to continue to grow rapidly. What is therefore needed is an increase not only in sales volume, but also an increase in market share. The memo points out that although the sales of Electronics International's products have risen steadily over the past six years, its market share has stagnated while those of its main competitors have increased.

2. The Zempan government has not only invited Electronics International to set up manufacturing facilities, but also solicited investments from its two major competitors. If both competitors accept the invitation and set up local manufacturing operations, they could outprice Electronics International from the Zempa market because the costs of local production are bound to be lower, given the lower wage rates and other input costs.

3. Zempa is under increasing domestic and external economic pressure. There is considerable inflation, primarily because of a substantial federal budget deficit (the government has not been able to raise required levels of revenues). Although the external balance position has been comfortable in the past five years because of firm commodity prices (commodities are the main exports of Zempa, generating 95 percent of export revenues), indicators of a weakening are already evident. In the event of a balance-of-payments crisis, the government is likely to limit imports, and one of the first items to be put on the banned list would be consumer electronics, because they would be deemed nonessential in the face of competing demands from such imports as defense equipment.

4. Although there are some impediments to the establishment of manufacturing operations, at this stage the government has assured the company of all assistance. If Electronics International goes in now and the other competitors do not, it would gain considerable leverage with the home government, which could be used to attack the dominance of the competition.

5. There are certain risks—the local currency might depreciate and the lack of training of local workers and the state of local infrastructural facilities might impair the efficiency of the plant. There may be other constraints imposed later on the manufacturing operation. Given the emerging scenario, however, these risks are worth taking, and the company should at least in principle accept the invitation from the government of Zempa and prepare for further negotiations.

Given the difference of opinion presented by McLowan, the managing director had quite a dilemma to resolve.

DISCUSSION QUESTIONS

1. Assume that you are the managing director in this case. What strategy should Electronics International adopt in this situation? Should the company continue exporting or make direct investment?
2. Are there any other alternatives open for Electronics International?

CHAPTER 3

Theories of Trade and Economic Development

"An unjust world is inherently unsustainable."
—Mahbub ul Haq

CHAPTER OBJECTIVES

This chapter will:

- Present the major trade and economic theories that attempt to explain international trade
- Describe the continuum of political economic development within the global community of nations and differentiate between the high-income, middle-income, and low-income nations
- Discuss current economic development theory
- Briefly discuss the recent dynamic changes occurring in the global economy

---

INTRODUCTION TO INTERNATIONAL TRADE THEORIES

Theories of international trade attempt to provide explanations of trade motives, underlying trade patterns, and the ultimate benefits that come from trade. An understanding of these basic factors enables individuals, private interests, and governments to better determine how to act for their own benefit within the trading systems. The major questions to be answered through such an examination of trade are the following:

Why does trade occur? Is it because of price differentials, supply differentials, or differences in individual tastes? What is traded and what are the prices or terms agreed upon in these trading actions? Do trade flows relate to specific economic and social characteristics of a country? What are the gains from trade and who realizes these gains? What are the effects of restrictions put on trading activity? The theories discussed in this chapter answer some of these questions. Although no theory by itself offers all the answers, the different theories do contribute significantly to our understanding.

Theories of trade have evolved over time, beginning with the emergence of strong nation-states and the organization of systematic exchanges of goods between these nations. The theories are associated with discrete time periods, and the earliest of these periods was the era of mercantilism.

MERCANTILISM

Mercantilism, which became popular in the late seventeenth and early eighteenth centuries in Western Europe, was based on the notion that governments (not individuals, who were deemed untrustworthy) should become involved in the transfer of goods between nations in order to increase the wealth of each national entity. Wealth was defined as an accumulation of precious metals, especially gold.

Consequently, the aim of the governments was to facilitate and support all exports while limiting imports, which was accomplished through the conduct of trade by government monopolies and intervention in the market through the subsidization of domestic exporting industries and the allocation of trading rights. Additionally, nations imposed duties or quotas upon imports to limit their volume. During this period, nations acquired colonies to provide sources of raw materials or precious metals. Trade opportunities with the colonies were exploited, and local manufacturing was repressed in those offshore locations. The colonials were often required to buy their goods from their mother countries.

The concept of mercantilism incorporates three fallacies. The first was the incorrect belief that gold or precious metals have intrinsic value, when actually they cannot be used for either production or consumption. Thus, nations subscribing to the mercantilist notion exchanged the products of their manufacturing or agricultural capacity for this nonproductive wealth. The second fallacy is that the theory of mercantilism ignores the concept of production efficiency through specialization. Instead of emphasizing cost-effective production of goods, mercantilism emphasizes sheer volumes of exports and imports and equates the amassing of wealth with acquisition of power. The third fallacy of mercantilism concerned the overall goal of the system. If the goal was to maximize wealth from the sale of exports, and if every participating nation had the same aim, the system itself did not promote trade, since all nations cannot maximize exports (and thus gold accumulation) simultaneously.[1]

Neomercantilism corrected the first fallacy by looking at the overall favorable or unfavorable balance of trade in all commodities; that is, nations attempted to have a positive balance of trade in all goods produced so that all exports exceeded imports. The term "balance of trade" continues in popular use today as nations attempt to correct their trade deficit positions by increasing exports or reducing imports so that outflow of goods balances the inflow.

The second fallacy, a disregard for the concept of efficient production, was addressed in subsequent theories, notably the classical theory of trade, which rests on the doctrine of comparative advantage. Subsequent theories also attempted to address the third fallacy as well.

CLASSICAL THEORY

What is now called the classical theory of trade superseded the theory of mercantilism at the beginning of the nineteenth century and coincided with three economic and political revolutions: the Industrial Revolution, the American Revolution, and the French Revolution. This theory was based in the economic theory of free trade and enterprise that was evolving at the time. In 1776, in *The Wealth of Nations*,[2] Adam Smith rejected as foolish the concept that gold was synonymous with wealth. Instead, Smith insisted that nations benefited the most when they acquired through trade those goods they could not produce efficiently and produced only those goods that they could manufacture with maximum efficiency. The crux of the argument was that the costs of production should dictate what should be produced by each nation or trading partner.

Under this concept of **absolute advantage**, a nation would produce only those goods that made the best use of its available natural and acquired resources and its climatic advantages. Acquired resources include available pools of appropriately trained and skilled labor, capital resources, technological advances, and even a tradition of entrepreneurship.

The use of such absolute advantage is the simplest explanation of trading behavior. For example, take two trading nations, Greece and Sweden, which both have the capacity to produce olives and martini glasses. In Greece, 500 crates of green olives require 100 units of resources (i.e., workers) to produce, from cultivation and harvesting to processing and packaging. Because of the lack of manufacturing facilities and machinery in that country, however, 100 crates of martini glasses (an equivalent value to 500 crates of olives) take 500 resource units to produce because each glass must be hand-blown. This contrasts with the situation in Sweden, where production of 100 crates of martini glasses can be easily mechanized using only 300 resource units. Because of Sweden's northern climate, however, olives can only be grown in greenhouses under artificial environmental conditions, a very expensive process requiring 600 units to produce 500 crates. Comparison of these figures leads to a clear conclusion as to how trade should be conducted to provide the citizens of Greece and Sweden with the perfect cocktail. Olives should be grown in Greece and traded for glasses produced in Swedish glass factories, because of the number of resource units required for each country to produce olives and glasses:

Country	Olives	Martini Glasses
	(500 crates)	(100 crates)
Greece	100 units	500 units
Sweden	600 units	300 units

If Sweden concentrates on the production of martini glasses and Greece on the production of olives, production costs are minimized for both products at 100 resource units/500 crates of olives and 300 resource units/100 crates of martini glasses, for a total of 400 resource units.

This conclusion, of course, posits that each country should produce the good that it can manufacture at minimum cost. What if, however, a country could produce both or several goods or commodities at costs lower than the other country? Do both nations still have impetus to trade?

COMPARATIVE ADVANTAGE

This question was considered by David Ricardo,[3] who in 1817 developed the important concept of **comparative advantage** in considering a nation's relative production efficiencies as they apply to international trade. In Ricardo's view, the exporting country should look at the relative efficiencies of production for both commodities and make only those goods it could produce most efficiently.

Suppose, for example, that Greece developed an efficient manufacturing capacity so that martini glasses could be produced by machine rather than being hand-blown. In fact, since the development of the productive capacity and capital plants were newer than those in Sweden, Greece could produce 100 crates of martini glasses using only 200 resource units as opposed to the 300 units required by Sweden. Thus, Greece's comparative costs would fall below those of Sweden for both products and its comparative advantage vis-à-vis those products would be higher. Therefore, the resource units required to produce olives and glasses would now be as follows:

Country	Olives	Martini Glasses
	(500 crates)	(100 crates)
Greece	100 units	200 units
Sweden	600 units	300 units

Logically, Greece should be the producer of both olives and martini glasses, and Sweden's capital and labor used in making these happy-hour supplies should be directed to Greece, so that maximum production efficiencies are achieved. Neither capital nor labor is entirely mobile, however, so each country should specialize: Greece in olives at 100 resource units per 500 crates, and Sweden in glass production at 300 resource units per 100 crates. Greece is still better off at maximizing its efficiencies in olive production. By doing so, it produces twice as many goods for export with the same amount of resources than if it allocated production to glassmaking, even at the new, more efficient production level.

While Sweden's production costs for glasses are still higher than those of Greece at 300 units, the resources of Sweden are better allocated to this production than to expensive olive-growing. In this way, Sweden minimizes its inefficiencies and Greece maximizes its efficiencies. The point is not that a country should produce all the goods it can more cheaply, but only those it can make cheapest. Such trading activity leads to maximum resource efficiency.

The concepts of absolute advantage and comparative advantage were used in a subsequent theory development by John Stuart Mill,[4] who in 1848 looked at the question of determining the value of export goods and developed the concept of **terms of trade**. Under this concept, export value is determined according to how much of a domestic commodity each country must exchange to obtain an equivalent amount of an imported commodity. Thus, the value of the product to be obtained in the exchange was stated in terms of the amount of products produced domestically that would be given up in exchange. For example, Sweden's terms with Greece would be exporting of 100 crates of glasses for an equivalent 500 crates of olives.

WEAKNESSES OF EARLY THEORIES

While the work of Smith, Ricardo, and Mill went far in describing the flow of trade between nations, classical theory was not without its flaws. For example, the theory incorrectly assumed

- the existence of perfect knowledge regarding international markets and opportunities
- full mobility of labor and production factors throughout each country
- full labor employment within each country

The theory also assumed that each country had, as its objective, full production efficiency. It neglected such other motives as traditional employment and production history, self-sufficiency, or political objectives.

In addition, the theory is overly simplistic in that it deals only with two commodities and two countries. In reality, given the full range of production by many countries and interplay of many motives and factors, the trade situation is actually an ongoing dynamic process in which there is interplay of forces and products.

The largest area of weakness in classical theory is that while we considered all resource units used in production, the only costs considered by classical economists were those associated with labor. The theorists did not account for other resources used in the production of commodities or manufactured goods for export, such as transportation costs, the use of land, and capital. This failing was addressed by subsequent trade theorists, who, in modern theory, include all factors of production in looking at theories of comparative advantage.

MORE RECENT THEORIES

FACTOR ENDOWMENT THEORY

The Eli Heckscher and Bertil Ohlin theory of factor endowment addressed the question of the basis of cost differentials in the production of trading nations. They posited that each country allocates its production according to the relative proportions of all its **production factor endowments**: land, labor, and capital on a basic level, and, on a more complex level, such factors as management and technological skills, specialized production facilities, and established distribution networks.

Thus, the range of products made or grown for export would depend on the relative availability of different factors in each country. For example, agricultural production or cattle grazing would be emphasized in such countries as Canada and Australia, which are generously endowed with land. Conversely, in small-land-mass countries with high populations, export products would center on labor-intensive articles. Similarly, rich nations might center their export base on capital-intensive production.

In this way, countries would be expected to produce goods that require large amounts of the factors they hold in relative abundance. Because of the availability and low costs of these factors, each country should also be able to sell its products in foreign markets at less than international price levels. Although this theory holds in general, it does not explain export production that arises from taste differences rather than factor differentials. For example, luxury imported goods, such as Italian leather products, deluxe automobiles, and French wine, are valued for their quality, prestige, or panache. Like classical theory, the Heckscher-Olin theory does not account for transportation costs in its computation, nor does it account for differences among nations in the availability of technology.

Economist Paul Samuelson extended the factor endowment theory to look at the effect of trade upon national welfare and the prices of production factors. Samuelson posited that the effect of free trade among nations would be to increase overall welfare by equalizing not only the prices of the goods exchanged in trade, but also of all involved factors. Thus, according to his theory, the returns generated by use of the factors would be the same in all countries.[5]

THE LEONTIEF PARADOX

An exception to the Heckscher-Ohlin theory was examined by W.W. Leontief in the 1950s. Leontief found that US exports were less capital-intensive than imports, although the presumption according to the Heckscher-Ohlin theory would have been that capital-intensive rather than labor-intensive export goods would have been more common, because the proportion of capital endowments at that time was higher than labor in the United States. The answer, as outlined by Leontief, was that these factor endowments are not homogeneous, and they differ along parameters other than relative abundance.[6] Labor pools, for example, can range from being unskilled to highly skilled. Similarly, production methods can be more technically sophisticated or advanced in different locations within a nation. Thus, it made sense at the time that US exported products were made through the efforts of highly skilled labor and imported products were produced through the efforts of less skilled workers in other countries.

Thus, Leontief attempted to answer his own paradox by stating that since US workers were more efficient, US imports appeared to be more capital-intensive than US exports. This result could also have been owing to protection of labor-intensive industries or to not expanding the research into other factors of production (to also include land, human capital, and technology).

CRITICISMS

Although these more recent theories seem to go far in explaining why nations trade, they have nonetheless come under the following criticisms as being only partial explanations for the exchange of goods and services between nations:

- The theories assume that nations trade, when in reality trade between nations is initiated and conducted by individuals or individual firms within those nations.
- They are limited in looking at either the transfer of goods or of direct investments. No theories explain the comprehensive, dynamic flow of trade in goods, services, and financial flows.
- They do not recognize the importance of technology and expertise in the areas of marketing and management.

Consequently, some scholars have looked separately at the reasons why firms enter into trade or foreign investment. One of these theories is the international product life cycle, which looks at the path a product takes as it departs domestic shores and enters foreign markets.

MODERN THEORIES

INTERNATIONAL PRODUCT LIFE CYCLE THEORY

The international product life cycle theory puts forth a different explanation for the fundamental motivations for trade between and among nations.[7] It relies primarily on the traditional marketing theory regarding the development, progress, and life span of products in markets. This theory looks at the potential export possibilities of a product in four discrete stages in its life cycle. In the first stage, innovation, a new product is manufactured in the domestic arena of the innovating country and sold primarily in that domestic market. Any overseas sales are generally achieved through exports to other markets, often those of industrial countries. In this stage, the company generally has little competition in its markets abroad.

In the second stage, the growth of the product, sales tend to increase. Unfortunately, so does competition as other firms enter the arena and the product becomes increasingly standardized. At this point, the firm begins some production abroad to maximize the service of foreign markets and to meet the activity of the competition.

As the product enters the third stage, maturity, exports from the home country decrease because of increased production in overseas locations. Foreign manufacturing facilities are put in place to counter increasing competition and to maximize profits from higher sales levels in foreign markets. At this point, price becomes a crucial determinant of competitiveness. Consequently, minimizing costs becomes an important objective of the manufacturing firm. The site of production also frequently shifts from within foreign industrial markets to less costly lesser-developed countries to take advantage of cheaper production factors, especially low labor costs. At this point the innovator country may even decide to discontinue all domestic production, produce only in third-world countries, and re-export the product back to the home country and to other markets.

In the final stage of the product life cycle, the product enters a period of decline, often because new competitors have achieved levels of production high enough to effect scale economies in the production that are equivalent to those of the original manufacturing country. Often, the product has become a commodity in the marketplace.

The international product life cycle theory has been found to hold primarily for such products as consumer durables, synthetic fabrics, and electronic equipment; that is, those products that have long lives in terms of the time span from innovation to eventual high consumer demand. The theory does not hold for products with a rapid time span of innovation, development, and obsolescence.

The theory holds less often these days because of the growth of multinational global enterprises that often introduce products simultaneously in several markets of the world. Similarly, multinational firms no longer necessarily first introduce a product at home. Instead, they might launch an innovation from a foreign source in the domestic markets to test production methods and the market itself, without incurring the high initial production costs of the domestic environment.

OTHER MODERN INVESTMENT THEORIES

Other theorists explain investing overseas by firms as a response to the availability of opportunities not shared by their competitors; that is, they take advantage of imperfections in markets and enter foreign spheres of production only when their competitive advantages outweigh the costs of going overseas. These advantages may be production, brand awareness, product identification, economies of scale, or access to favorable capital markets. These firms may make horizontal investments, producing the same goods abroad as they do at home, or they may make vertical investment, in order to take advantage of sources of supplies or inputs.

Going a step further, some believe that firms within an oligopoly enter foreign markets merely as a competitive response to the actions of an industry leader and to equalize relative advantages. **Oligopolies** are those market situations in which there are few sellers of a product that is usually mass merchandised. Two examples are the automobile and steel industries. In these situations, no firm can profit by cutting prices because competitors quickly respond in kind. Consequently, prices for oligopolistic products are practically identical and are set through industry agreement (either openly or tacitly).

Thus, firms within an oligopoly must be keenly aware of the actions, market reach, and activities of their competitors. Unless their response to the actions of competitors is to follow the leader, they will yield precious competitive edges to their competitors. Therefore, it follows that when a market leader in an oligopoly establishes a foreign production facility abroad, its competitors rush to follow suit.

Thus, the impetus for a firm to go abroad may come from a wish to expand for internal reasons: to use existing competitive advantages in additional spheres of operations, to take advantage of technology, or to use raw materials available in other locations. Alternatively, the motive might arise from external forces, such as competitive actions, customer requests, or government incentives. The final determinant, however, is based in a cost-benefit analysis. The firm will move abroad if it can use its own particular advantages to provide benefits that outweigh the costs of exporting or production abroad and provide a profit.

Michael Porter of Harvard University authored the "National Competitive Advantage Theory" in 1991. It brings in many of the elements already discussed in this chapter. Porter believes that successful international trade comes from the interaction of four country- and firm-specific elements:

- factor conditions
- demand conditions
- related and supporting industries
- firm strategy, structure, and rivalry

Factor conditions include land, labor, and capital, as mentioned by others. Porter also includes the education of the workforce and the quality of a country's infrastructure as important factor conditions. Demand conditions relate to the need for strong domestic consumption to spur the innovation of products and services. As mentioned previously, successful international expansion requires a successful product in the domestic market (that has been sufficiently challenged at home). A successful domestic industry will stimulate local supplier activity. Having numerous local suppliers will tend to lower prices, raise quality, and increase the usage of technology. Thus, the rivalry of domestic industries will improve the quality of the product or service, which will improve the company's performance. Successful companies will then attempt to expand their products or services internationally. Porter's last dimension is company strategy. As mentioned in Chapter 1, a firm can chose between having an ethnocentric, geocentric, or polycentric strategy. Additionally, there should be some consistency in strategy at home and abroad; this topic will be discussed in subsequent chapters.

THEORIES OF ECONOMIC DEVELOPMENT

Beyond merely examining what types of economic systems exist in the world, people involved in international business must place notions about methods of allocating resources within a country in a theoretical framework. How do basically agrarian national economies become producers of sophisticated manufactured goods? How does economic development come about?

Classical economic theory, put forth by economists Adam Smith, Thomas Malthus, David Ricardo, and John Stuart Mill in the late 1700s and early 1800s, held little hope for a nation to sustain its economic growth. This dismal forecast was due to the substantial weakness in the theory (as evidenced by subsequent historical events), which assumed that no developments would be achieved in technology or production methods. Instead, these economists, Malthus foremost among them, predicted that the finite availability of land would limit any nation's development and that the natural equilibrium in labor wages would hover at subsistence levels because of the interaction of labor supply, agricultural production, and wage systems. For example, they believed that if labor supplies were low, wages would rise and would motivate workers to increase their number. Increases in the size of the population and labor pool would then put stress on finite supplies of food, increase the costs of nourishment, and ultimately lead to decreases in wages because of increased competition for such employment.

In a nutshell, classical theory holds that expanding the labor pool leads to declines in the accumulation of capital per worker, lower worker productivity, and lower income per person, eventually causing stagnation or economic decline. Naturally, this theory was proven incorrect by numerous scientific and technological discoveries, which provided for greater efficiencies in production and greater returns on inputs of land, capital, and labor. It was also knocked awry by the growing acceptance of birth control as a means of limiting population size.

ROSTOW'S STAGES OF ECONOMIC GROWTH

A more recent and applicable theory of economic development was provided in the 1960s by Walter W. Rostow, who attempted to outline the various stages of a nation's economic growth and based his theory on the notion that shifts in economic development coincided with abrupt changes within the nations themselves.[8] He identified five different economic stages for a country: traditional society, preconditions for takeoff, takeoff, the drive to maturity, and the age of high mass consumption.

Stage 1: Traditional Society

Rostow saw traditional society as a static economy, which he likened to the pre-1700s attitudes and technology experienced by the world's current economically developed countries. He believed that the turning point for these countries came with the work of Sir Isaac Newton, when people began to believe that the world was subject to a set of physical laws but was malleable within these laws. In other words, people could effect change within the system of descriptive laws as developed by Newton.

Stage 2: Preconditions for Takeoff

Rostow identified the preconditions for economic takeoff as growth or radical changes in three specific, nonindustrial sectors that provided the basis for economic development:

- *Increased investment in transportation*, which enlarged prospective markets and increased product specialization capacity
- *Agricultural developments* providing for the feeding and nourishing of larger, primarily urban populations
- An *expansion of imports* into the country

These preconditioning changes were to be experienced in concert with an increasing national emphasis on education and entrepreneurship.

Stage 3: Takeoff

The takeoff stage of growth occurs, according to Rostow, over a period of twenty to thirty years and is marked by major transformations that stimulate the economy. These transformations could include widespread technological developments, the effective functioning of an efficient distribution system, and even political revolutions. During this period, barriers to growth are eliminated within the country and, indeed, the concept of economic growth as a national objective becomes the norm. To achieve the takeoff, Rostow believes that three conditions must be met:

- Net investment as a percentage of net national product must increase sharply.
- At least one substantial manufacturing sector must grow rapidly. This rapid growth and larger output trickles down as growth in ancillary and supplier industries.
- A supportive framework for growth must emerge on political, social, and institutional fronts. For example, banks, capital markets, and tax systems should develop and entrepreneurship should be considered a norm.

Stage 4: The Drive to Maturity

Within Rostow's scheme, this stage is characterized as one where growth becomes self-sustaining and a widespread expectation within the country. During this period, Rostow believes that the labor pool becomes more skilled and more urban and that technology reaches heights of advancement.

Stage 5: The Age of Mass Consumption

The last stage of development, as Rostow sees it, is an age of mass consumption, when there is a shift to consumer durables in all sectors and when the populace achieves a high standard of living, as evidenced through the ownership of such sophisticated goods as automobiles, televisions, and appliances.

Since its introduction in the 1960s, Rostow's framework has been criticized as being overly ambitious in attempting to describe the economic paths of many nations. Also, history has not proved the framework to be true. For example, many lesser-developed countries exhibit dualism; that is, state-of-the-art technology is used in certain industries and primitive production methods are retained in others. Similarly, empirical data have shown that there is no twenty- to thirty-year growth period. Such countries as the United Kingdom, Germany, Sweden, and Japan are more characterized by slow, steady growth patterns than by abrupt takeoff periods.

THE BIG PUSH: BALANCED VERSUS UNBALANCED GROWTH

While Rostow was attempting to place economic development within a sequential framework, the debate during the 1950s and 1960s centered on whether development efforts should center on specific economic sectors within countries or should be made in all major sectors of the economy: manufacturing, agriculture, and service.

Economist Ragnar Nurske advocated that development efforts should consist of a synchronized use of capital to develop wide ranges of industries in nations. He believed that only a concerted overall effort would propel developing nations beyond the vicious circle of poverty, which perpetuates itself because of the limited supply of capital caused by low savings rates.

The advocates of channeling capital to all sectors in a balanced approach also support the big push thesis and believe that these investments cannot be made gradually. They must be made all at once for the positive impetus to be sufficient to overcome significant barriers to development, such as the lack of an adequate infrastructure.

The theory of balanced development has been criticized because it ignores the economic notion of overall benefits accruing from specialization in development and production. It has also been criticized for being unrealistic; that is, if a country had enough resources to invest in all sectors of the economy at once, it would, in fact, not be undeveloped. The theory also assumes that all nations would be starting from the same zero point, when, in reality, their economies may have some historical strengths or investment capacity. The theory has been discredited, to a very significant extent, by the actual progress of less-developed countries in the 1960s and 1970s. These countries experienced a great deal of growth without any attempts to synchronize simultaneous investments in all sectors, as recommended by proponents of balanced growth theory, but most remain comparatively undeveloped.

HIRSCHMAN'S STRATEGY OF UNBALANCE

Some theorists have advocated a strategy of selective investment as the engine of growth in developing countries. Albert O. Hirschman promulgated the idea of making unbalanced investments in economic sectors to complement the imbalances that already exist within the economy of a nation. Hirschman argued that the less-developed countries do not have access to adequate resources to mount a balanced, big-push investment strategy. Investments should be made instead in strategically selected economic areas, in order to provide growth in other sectors through backward and forward linkages. Backward linkages spur new investments in input industries, while forward linkages do so in those sectors purchasing the output of the selected industry. Thus, in Hirschman's scheme, the situation of each country must be carefully analyzed to determine what investment constitutes the best means to reach an ultimate balance among all investment sectors.

Pakistani economist Mahbub ul Haq increased the focus of the strategy of unbalance by describing the failed attempts to generate economic development by ill-targeted Western aid to developing nations. In the seminal work *The Poverty Curtain* (1976), Haq blamed both the developed country providers and the developing country recipients for the failures of Western aid to affect materially the lives of the citizens of the developing world. These thoughts echo earlier critiques by Hirschman on the subject.

GALBRAITH'S EQUILIBRIUM OF POVERTY

Many of the theories discussed thus far have illuminated how a developing country can improve its overall standing in the world economy via increasing income levels and exports. While these are commendable aims by themselves, the theories discussed so far have not explained how a country can create a climate for such growth. Examples of newly industrialized countries such as Singapore and South Korea have been cited as a useful framework to implement in countries throughout the world. While these economies have been very successful, they have also had the levels of political stability and entrepreneurship incentives necessary to create economic expansion. John Kenneth Galbraith was one of the first economists to discuss the mind-set of individuals in developing countries, using a term he coined: the "equilibrium of poverty."[9] Rather than assuming that every developing country had a historical precedent for economic success or merely needed new technologies, Galbraith considered what would happen if neither of these options were available. If there is not an escape from poverty and there has not been such an escape for generations, many people will simply not be motivated to change their situation. Thus resignation settles in. Galbraith stated that in order to break the contentment there needs to be education as well as traumas (famines, droughts, etc.) that cause the desire for change. Globalization itself often contributes to showing people in developing countries a better way of life (via radio and television ads). Galbraith then offered the following framework necessary to successfully industrialize a poor economy:

- Adequate security against expropriation of property, physical threats, or very high taxation
- Reliable infrastructure system of roads, ports, electrical power supplies, and communications
- Adequate supply of capital from private investment and public borrowers and an intelligent system for passing on loans
- State-supported industries initially as they have more means in developing countries than individual firms
- Training and specialized education in order to obtain a workforce capable of doing the required tasks of employment

Galbraith's theory thus combined the efforts of Rostow, Hirschman, and Haq in a framework of economic development. In the "chicken and the egg" world of economic development frameworks, the order in which the various steps for improvement are followed depends on the context of the particular country, region, and the general economic climate.[10]

SEN'S DEVELOPMENT AS FREEDOM

Amartya Sen, recipient of the 1998 Nobel Prize in Economics, further improved the framework for development that Galbraith and others had started. Sen asked the question, *Is the measure of GDP growth the best way to compare the living standards of the world's people?* He considers the measurement of GDP an aggregate measure of the wealth produced within a country, but it does not necessarily account for the quality of life. Sen gained Nobel distinction for his work in welfare economics. He has also questioned the viability of the concept of the "poverty line"[11] and has offered a similar line of reasoning for why this measure, like GDP, is unsuitable for developing countries. The concepts of the poverty line and GDP do not consider the amount of political participation and dissent allowed within a given country. These factors are essential characteristics of freedom and thus the ability to improve the quality of life of a society. Sen would rather frame the argument in terms of an individual's "capabilities," which are influenced by quality-of-life issues such as being adequately nourished, being in good health, avoiding escapable morbidity and premature mortality, being happy, having self-respect, and taking part in the community as a whole.

Give these elements, Sen offers a framework for development as follows:

- Political freedom
- Economic facilities
- Social opportunities
- Transparency guarantees
- Protective security

Sen views **political freedom** as having opportunities to determine who should govern and on what principles. It also includes the ability to scrutinize and criticize authorities, freedom of political expression, and an uncensored press. **Economic facilities** consist of opportunities to utilize economic resources for the purpose of consumption, production, or exchange. This includes the access to credit for large and small companies. **Social opportunities** consist of arrangements that society makes for education and health care, which allow improvement in the ability to live better lives. Things such as illiteracy, high fertility rates, and morbidity are diminished via these freedoms. Sen's framework for development also contains **transparency guarantees**. These involve the need for openness and the freedom to deal with each other under guarantees of trust. Transparency helps to prevent corruption, financial irresponsibility, and underhanded dealings. While

Sen's framework mainly applies to developing countries, developed nations could also improve in this area, given the recent corporate scandals (and sovereign debt crises) that have been in the news in the United States, Canada, and Europe. The final area of Sen's development framework is **protective security**. This is a social safety net for preventing the affected population from being reduced to abject poverty and misery. This includes unemployment benefits, statutory income supplements to the indigent, and emergency public employment to generate income for the destitute (this is similar to the New Deal program for public employment implemented in the United States during the Great Depression).

The key to Sen's philosophy is that these freedoms are required prior to development. While it would appear that having a reasonable health-care system in a developing country is unrealistic, many of these services are labor-intensive, so lesser resources would be required to provide these basic services in low-wage countries. Sen argues that guaranteed health care and education can achieve remarkable results in length and quality of life improvements. Literacy and numeracy help the participation of the masses in the process of economic expansion. This, in turn, improves the productive capabilities of the nation as a whole.

THE GLOBAL CONTINUUM: WHERE NATIONS FALL TODAY

All trading nations of the world fall within the descriptive continuum of political structures, forms of economic organization, and levels of development. The existence of these three descriptive parameters provides for enormous variation in categorizing world trading nations.

THE POLITICAL CONTINUUM

Political systems constitute the methods by which societies organize in order to function smoothly, and political orientation provides one such classification continuum. Certainly the student of international business is cognizant of the two extremes of political organization in the global political arena of the twenty-first century. At one extreme are societies in which all members have significant power in the decision-making process surrounding the activities, policies, and objectives of their government. These systems are often pluralistic (incorporating a number of different views), use the concept of majority rule in deciding major issues, and often employ a system of representative democracy, where officials are elected to represent their regional constituencies. These nations generally afford all of their citizens some degree of liberty and equality.

At the other end of the political spectrum is the totalitarian state, which is identified by a singular lack of decision-making power among the country's individual citizens. In such a political system, decisions regarding policies, objectives, and the direction of the nation are controlled by a select few individuals who generally operate under the auspices of the government. In these states, the activities and liberties of citizens are often restricted.

All nations in the world fall somewhere along this continuum and take various forms within its parameters, from being highly democratized to being nearly entirely totalitarian. In the past, the two world powers, the United States and the Soviet Union, represented the two extremes in the modern political world. Some modern-day examples of central planning–oriented economies are Cuba and North Korea. Some nations, such as Afghanistan, are in the process of attempting to move toward democracy after many years of tyranny. Other countries, such as the People's Republic of China, are finding new ways of blending a central planning structure with market-based reforms.

THE ECONOMIC CONTINUUM

The political orientation of a country can also be placed within the scope of its economic structure, which, similarly, runs along a continuum. Economic orientations vary according to two separate dimensions: the degree of private versus public (state) ownership of property; and the level of governmental versus individual control over the resources of the nation.

At one extreme is capitalism, which relies on the forces of the marketplace in the allocation of resources. In this free-enterprise system, the market, in the form of consumer sovereignty, defines the relationship between prices for goods and services, quantities produced domestically, and overall supply and demand. For example, if supplies of a product are low and public demand is high, its price will rise as consumers compete to acquire this scarce resource. Similarly, if there is little or no demand for products, manufacturers will have no motivation to produce them.

In free-market economies, the creation of profit is generally considered the operational motive of business, and profitability tends to be the test of success. Capitalist economies also promote the ownership of private property by individuals and theoretically attempt to limit public (state) ownership of property.

In modern free-market countries, however, governments still intervene at some level and own some property. They set legal and regulatory requirements to provide for the general safety and welfare of the populace and levy taxes in order to provide services, such as the national defense or a network of highways. They own resource reserves, land, national parks, and large amounts of capital assets. Indeed, governments often provide the largest single market for manufacturers in many capitalist countries.

The appropriate level of government involvement in the play of market forces continues to be the subject of much debate among economists, politicians, and political parties in many countries. This debate is perhaps best exemplified by the policies put in place by President Ronald Reagan and Prime Minister Margaret Thatcher of the United Kingdom during the 1980s, when significant efforts were made to reduce the role of the central government and promote deregulation of many industries.

At the other end of the economic spectrum are the centrally planned or nonmarket economies. Within this economic form, the government decides what is to be produced, when and where it will be made, and to whom it will be sold. The state controls the sources and means of production, raw materials, and the distribution systems. In addition, the state frequently owns many of the basic and integral industries of the country, which are run in the form of state monopolies and include large-scale power-generating facilities, manufacturing industries, and entire transportation systems. In addition to these production and manufacturing monopolies, all trade with the outside world is financed and conducted by a state trading monopoly.

This centrally planned type of economic structure is based on the belief that a single central agency can coordinate economic activity to provide harmony in the interrelationship of all sectors of the economy. Before 1989, the world's centrally planned or nonmarket economies were most strongly represented by the communist nations of the world, which included the Soviet Union, Poland, Romania, Czechoslovakia, the People's Republic of China, Cuba, Vietnam, and North Korea, among others. Since then, the Soviet Union has been disbanded (in 1991), and most of its former members have become more oriented toward a free-market system.

The nonmarket form of economic organization is not without its problems. The most significant of these are the difficulties arising from attempts to coordinate all factors of production. Frequently, governments attempt to reach their objective of harmonious economic activity by developing complex and extensive goals in the form of long-term (five-year or more) plans for the nation. They attempt to affect production and outcome by setting manufacturing quotas, but these can lead to high costs. For example, production may be geared toward reaching quota levels, not toward achieving efficiencies, which can result in high production costs.

In addition, nonmarket economies also experience problems further down the line, especially with the procurement of raw materials for production. There are either insufficient supplies of raw materials or mismatches of the timing of supply deliveries. Another problem is insufficient long-term planning, especially at the local production facility level. Manufacturing operators have incentives to reach only their production goals for the season or the year; future, long-term production capacity or technological developments are less relevant. Nonmarket economies also face the problem of determining appropriate prices for goods and services produced within their borders. These valuation problems stem from the absence of external criteria of worth, as supplied through consumer demand for products or prices paid for input resources and raw materials. Thus, in these economies prices are set primarily according to the amount of labor involved in their production and are often as much a product of politics and ideology as of actual production costs.

Between these two extremes are mixed economic systems, which combine features of both market and nonmarket systems. These nations combine public and private ownership in varying amounts. Their intention is to provide economic security for the country as a whole, by having some amount of public resource ownership and/or government involvement in decision-making. In these systems, public involvement often takes the form of state ownership of utilities or energy sources. The welfare state and heavy involvement of government in the economic planning of the nation are also basic features of mixed economies. An example of this kind of system exists in modern-day Canada, where the government (public sector) administers a national health-care system for all of its citizens, while the benefits of a free-market system (private sector) are seen in many other industries that are represented on the Toronto Stock Exchange.

To a lesser extent, Japan is also a mixed economy. While there is less government ownership of resources, the state, through its Ministry of International Trade and Industry and Ministry of Finance, is intimately involved in business decisions regarding investments, disinvestments, production, and markets. The government is also intricately involved in conducting basic research and development and deciding long-term and short-term future direction. The government does this by organizing major companies into research consortia, which join together to conduct applied research on new technology. When that research bears fruit in the form of marketable applications, the consortium disbands and each company takes the technology back to its own labs to use in product development.

Integrating Both Continua

The two ranges of political and economic organization of nations can be put together in a general framework. Overall, democratic societies tend to be oriented toward a free-market, capitalist perspective. Supply and demand in production are determined to a degree by consumers in the marketplace; sources of supply and the means of production are owned by private interests or individuals. In contrast, totalitarian societies are characterized by the government's allocation of resources and by state ownership of the means of production. Zimbabwe is an example of a totalitarian economy. The result of this sort of governmental structure has not been good, as is exhibited by Zimbabwe's drop in GDP for much of the last decade.[12]

It appears, however, that as nations of the world become more and more interdependent, the boundaries begin to blur between political and economic descriptions. More and more governments are moving toward a mixture of both public and private ownership of property and allocation of resources. This convergence can perhaps be accounted for by the increasingly apparent knowledge that none of the existing systems provides equitably for all segments of society.

The place each country holds in both the economic and the political continuum is an important consideration for foreign firms that are considering whether or not to do business there. The decision-maker must take into account, for example, whether the political structures of the home and host country are complementary, whether the tendency is toward private or public ownership of resource allocation and production, and to what degree the state controls the daily operations of business firms.

Patterns of World Development
Background: The Role of GNI

Traditionally, countries of the world have been divided into three separate categories known as the first world (high income), second world (middle income), and third world

Table 3.1 **Average GNI per Capita, 2010**

Income level	Atlas method US$	PPP international $
High income	$39,783	$38,637
Medium income	$4,121	$7,215
Low income	$567	$1,375
World average	$9,488	$11,574

Source: World Bank, "GNI per Capita—Atlas and Purchasing Power Parity," http://web.worldbank.org.

(low income). Their assigned categorizations are based on specific economic criteria, such as the gross national income (GNI) per capita. **GNI per capita**[13] is a benchmark used in determining levels of development, because it represents a measure of production relative to population that can be compared across nations. GNI is determined by totaling the dollar value of the goods and services a country produced in, for example, one year and dividing that number by its population, thereby providing a measure of a country's economic activity level as a per person value. In addition to GNI per capita, determinations of development level include assessments of annual export levels, relative growth over time, energy consumption per capita, and the relative percentage of agriculture in total production and employment.

According to the World Bank, the average gross national income per capita in the developed countries was $39,783 (using the Atlas method) and $29,450 (using purchasing power parity) in 2011. The World Bank Atlas method accounts for exchange rate fluctuations by averaging them out over a three-year period and calculates the gross national income using the US dollar as a reference currency. In comparison, the purchasing power parity method attempts to accurately measure the relative price of goods in the economy by comparing the referenced economies' economic output relative to the equivalent purchasing power of the income in the US economy. Based on the World Bank Atlas method, low income is estimated to be $1,025 or less; middle income is estimated to be between $1,026 and $12,475; high income is estimated to be $12,476 or greater. The World Bank further subcategorizes the middle-income countries as lower-middle-income ($1,026 to $4,035) and upper-middle-income ($4,036 to $12,475). The average gross national incomes based on both the World Bank Atlas method and the purchasing power parity methods are displayed in Table 3.1.

In addition, development levels are ascertained according to social criteria, such as life expectancies, infant mortality levels, the availability of health and educational facilities, literacy rates, demographic and population trends, and standards of housing and nutrition. This is where Amartya Sen's human capabilities focus comes into play, as we have earlier discussed.

As Figures 3.1 and 3.2 indicate, there is a wide disparity between where the world's people live and where the majority of the world's income is produced. The low-income countries are the areas where population growth is highest, while their proportion of the

Figure 3.1 **World GDP, 2001–2010**

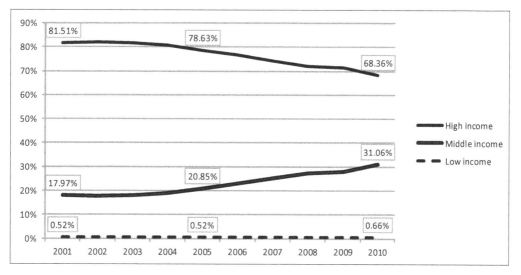

Source: World Bank, 2012.

world's income is not changing. The population is increasing, but their share of world income is not growing. In the middle- and high-income countries, the opposite effect is happening. High-income countries are producing a smaller proportion of the world's GDP, while the percentage of the population is decreasing. The middle-income area is showing both population growth and a growing proportion of the world's production of GDP.

THE DEVELOPED COUNTRIES

The industrialized or developed countries are commonly referred to as the **first world** (or high-income countries). These nations, which generally have economies based in industrial manufacturing, are the wealthiest in the world in terms of incomes and standards of living and are members of the Organization for Economic Cooperation and Development (OECD). The industrialized countries are largely in the Northern Hemisphere. They are the United States and Canada in North America and the nations of Western Europe. Beyond these two geographic areas, only New Zealand, Australia, Japan, and perhaps the Republic of South Africa represent the East or the Southern Hemisphere in this group.

In addition to high production capacity per person, each of these countries has a level of adult literacy reported in the 90th percentile, large values of exported products, low infant mortality figures, and low citizen per physician ratios.

Figure 3.2 **World Population, 1960–2010**

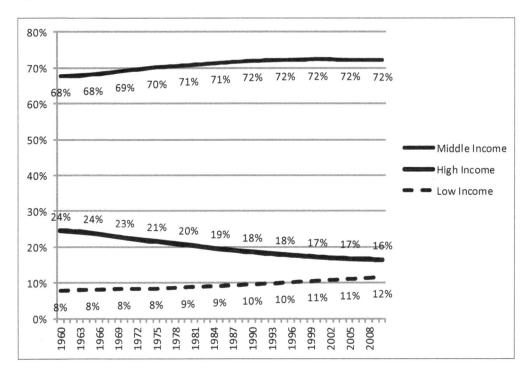

Source: World Bank, 2012.

UPPER-MIDDLE-INCOME COUNTRIES

The middle-income countries can also be described as emerging economies—countries such as China, Turkey, much of the Middle East, Indonesia, and nations of South America and central Europe. Based on the countries just mentioned, there is a wide variety of cultural and economic factors at play within this segment. Some countries, such as China, have moved up in the world economic standings rather quickly, while others, such as many South American nations, have seen stagnant economic growth levels over the last twenty years due in large part to government overregulation in the economy.[14] As shown in Table 3.1, there is also a large gap in GNI per capita between the high-income and middle-income nations. There are also large economic gaps within some middle-income nations. For example, in China, the east coast is rapidly industrializing and experiencing fast growth in incomes, while the interior is slow to be developed. This hasty economic change is creating major shifts in population from the interior to the coast and leaving China with an increasing gap between the wealthy and poor; however, it also has created a middle class equivalent to the population of the United States.

LOW-INCOME AND LOWER-MIDDLE-INCOME COUNTRIES

The low-income and lower-middle-income countries are more commonly referred to as the "third world," which is generally considered to include the less-developed and underdeveloped countries. The poorest nations of the world are generally found on the continents of Asia, Africa, and in parts of Central America. Their poverty is evidenced by inadequate diets, primitive housing, limited schooling, and minimal medical facilities. The common features of most less-developed countries (LDCs) are low per capita GNI and the division into two very disparate classes: a very rich upper class and a very poor lower class. There is hardly any middle class to act as buffer between them. The richer elements have more access to, and are affected by, the westernization of ideas and values, whereas the lower classes, with less education and awareness of externalities, tend to cling to traditional values. The result is inherent conflict between the two.

Lower-middle-income countries have widely varying political systems, which run the gamut from former communist countries, such as Ukraine, Albania, and Kosovo, to emerging democracies, such as Georgia, Mongolia, and India. They also have a number of problems in common, which essentially center on the difficulties of achieving greater industrialization in light of increasing levels of population growth and limited resources.

The low-income countries that have income under $1,025 can be exemplified by Haiti, which has been prone to natural disasters while lacking national resources to provide for its population. Another group comprises countries of central Asia that are rich in resources but lack developed governmental institutions, such as Nepal, the Kyrgyz Republic, and Bangladesh. The last group that falls into the low-income category includes central African countries such as Ethiopia, Uganda, and Liberia, which have experienced ongoing civil conflicts that prevent them from building the governmental institutions needed for economic development.

A major problem in LDCs is that their populations are growing rapidly, as compared to the rate of growth per year in the industrialized countries (see Figure 3.2). This growth forces LDCs to continue allocating scarce resources for providing the basic necessities of food, clothing, and shelter for their populace. As a result, few resources remain within these countries for increasing development, income levels, education, and training. Consequently, these nations frequently face unemployment, underemployment, and a relatively unproductive labor force.

Similarly, most of the economies of LDCs are dependent on agriculture, which often suffers from low productivity but employs the major portion of the workforce. This dependency is often coupled with limited or scarce natural resources, as well as severely limited capital bases to fund ongoing development efforts. Thus, exports are often limited to a very few, basic, low-value-added products that are vulnerable to the violent fluctuations of world commodity prices. This problem is exacerbated by the agricultural protectionism that persists in much of the developed world.

Thus, the situation in LDCs is a continuous vicious cycle. As populations increase, economic activity continues to focus on limited and low-profit agricultural and natural resource production. There is not enough capital available because of low savings. More improvements in the labor pool and diversification of the export base are extremely difficult. Added to these problems, LDCs frequently have undeveloped banking systems, high levels of bureaucratic graft, political instability, serious international debt, severe hard currency needs, and high levels of inflation.

THE SUBTERRANEAN ECONOMIES

While the United Nations and the World Bank consistently use the identification of gross national product per person to evaluate the relative wealth of a nation vis-à-vis its neighbors and trading partners, this figure may not fully represent the actual production of a nation because in many countries, including the United States, there exists an underground economy whose transactions do not enter official records and are not, therefore, shown in the overall figures of the nation's GNP. Unofficial sales and purchases of goods and services are commonly known as black-market transactions, and they make the official GNP figure somewhat lower than it actually is.

Alternately, goods can be traded in barter systems, in which no money changes hands but an economic exchange has been made, or transfers are made in exchange rates between currencies that differ from officially cited rates. These systems also lead to a distortion of aggregate economic data and tax evasion by the participants. Ubiquitous in third world nations, these systems are called shadow, second, or submerged economies, or *travail au noir* (black work), as the underground economy is called in France.

The Peruvian economist Hernando DeSoto[15] refers to one of the causes for the lack of economic growth in the third world as the amount of "dead capital" in the system. "Dead capital" refers to the lack of a legal system of private land ownership in much of the third world. DeSoto has identified a large underground economy in many lower-income countries, but the poor citizens cannot transfer the real property as an asset or use it as collateral for bank financing. Thus, many small companies are unable to obtain the necessary working capital required to finance their business development efforts. Figure 3.3 illustrates the percentage of dead capital in some four low-income countries. The percentages represent the amount of real estate that is not individually owned and is thus unable to be borrowed against for the growth of any prospective small business owners in the third world.

In his book, DeSoto states that this system of legal apartheid must be ended before many third world nations are able to improve their economies. The only solution to this problem, he argues, is to do what was done in the United States in the nineteenth century: that is, simplify the methods for obtaining legally owned land and legalize the claims of those in place now.

PARALLEL TRACKS: THE CONTINUED DIVERSITY OF THE WORLD ECONOMY

Since the 1960s, the world has seen dramatic changes in the patterns of world trade and, indeed, in the relative importance of groups of trading nations and historical trade lead-

Figure 3.3 **How Much Dead Capital?**

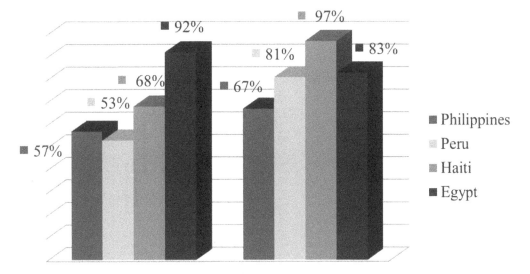

Source: DeSoto, 2003.

ers. The past twenty years or more have seen a shift in trading patterns away from the industrialized countries and toward greater involvement of the less-developed countries and the rising stars in the world. Even more recently, the world economy has seen the rise of India, Brazil, and China as well. In every category, except perhaps agriculture, where the benefits of the latest in technological development and the use of high-yield fertilizer products are being realized, the developed countries of the world have lost market share primarily to LDCs and to the newly industrialized countries (NICs). The Chinese market share is especially remarkable in this scheme, as it shows increases in technology-intensive manufacturing and the transportation trade, while labor-intensive clothing and textile products and land-intensive agricultural production have also increased.

The Chinese economy has grown annually at 8 percent, while the Indian economy has been growing at an average of over 6 percent over the last decade. This is very high compared with countries such as the United States, which has seen growth over the same period at less than 3 percent (based on chained 2005 dollars). Since the economic crisis of 2008, economic growth in the United States has slowed further, averaging less than 0.2 percent from 2008 to 2011; indeed, in 2009, the US economy contracted by 3.5 percent.[16]

The trend of increasing competition to the preeminence of the United States is likely to continue in the foreseeable future, but with increased competition in the global marketplace. With the increasing globalization of the world economy, the number of participants in the world economy will continue to increase. As the developing markets continue to liberalize their trade policies and economies, their participation in world trade is expected to continue the upward trend that it has shown since the 1980s.

Figure 3.4 **GDP and Trade Versus FDI Net Inflows**

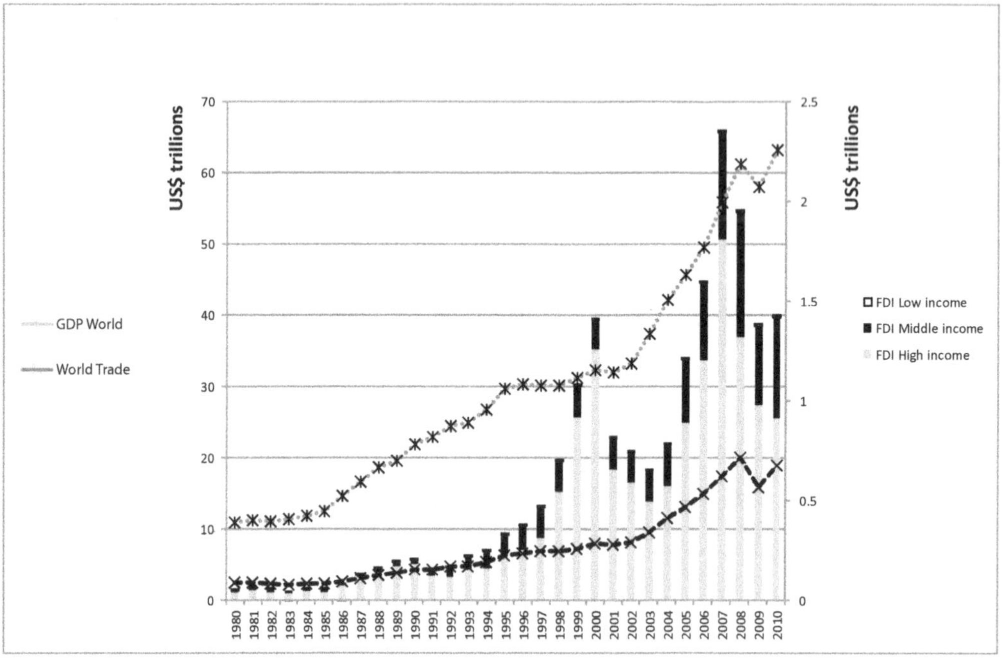

Source: World Bank, 2012.

As demonstrated in Figure 3.4, global world trade peaked in 2007, fell in 2008 and 2009, and recovered somewhat in 2010. Clearly in view are the continued increases in foreign direct investment for middle-income countries at the expense of high-income countries.

SUMMARY

International trade theories attempt to explain motives for trade, underlying trade patterns, and the ultimate benefits of trade. According to the Western European notion of mercantilism, nations, not individuals, should be involved in the transfer of goods between countries in order to increase the wealth of home countries, specifically through the accumulation of gold. The classical theories of absolute and comparative advantage looked at cost efficiencies of production as motivators of trade. Weaknesses in their basic assumptions led to the development of the factor endowment theory, which explains trade among nations on the basis of factors, or inputs, used in production, such as land, labor, capital, technology, facilities, and distribution networks.

Recent theorists have found that individuals, rather than nations, initiate and conduct trade. These theories consider the importance of technology and marketing and management skills, which traditional theories ignored. The international life cycle theory offers different motivations for trade based on the four stages of a product: innovation, growth, maturity, and decline. Other modern theories explain foreign investment as natural competitive responses by which firms seek to optimize market opportunities offering production advantages, economies of scale, and favorable capital markets; firms also react to investment decisions of competitors by following the leader.

Economic development theories attempt to explain the transition from an undeveloped economy to a developed, manufacturing-oriented economy. The classical economic theory limited a nation's development and economic growth to its supply of land and labor and discounted any effects of technology improvements that might create greater efficiencies. Rostow's theory of economic growth attempts to relate economic development to changes within society and identified five stages: traditional society, preconditions for takeoff, takeoff, the drive to maturity, and the age of high mass consumption. The big push theories argued that only synchronized uses of capital to develop wide ranges of industries in combination with an overall popular effort would propel developing nations into more developed stages. Alternatively, Hirschman's strategy of unbalance advocated selective investment in developing countries to create backward and forward linkages. Economists such as John Kenneth Galbraith and Amartya Sen also have contributed to the understanding of developmental economics; Sen devised a framework for development which is useful when deciding on governmental policies in the developing world.

Political and economic systems run along a continuum that has a democratic, free-market economy on one extreme and a totalitarian, centrally planned economy on the other.

Nations have historically been divided into three categories—the first, second, and third worlds—based principally on gross national product per capita criteria. A fourth, or shadow, world exists whose many transactions are not included in official GNI figures, thereby significantly understating real national wealth. Various social criteria, such as life expectancy, infant mortality levels, literacy rates, and health and education standards, also influence categorization.

Trading patterns have shifted away from industrialized countries toward lesser-developed and newly industrialized countries. Increasing competition from countries such as Brazil, Russia, China, and India, is challenging the preeminence of the United States.

DISCUSSION QUESTIONS

1. What are the fallacies of the theory of mercantilism?
2. Briefly describe the differences between the theories of absolute and comparative advantage. What are the shortcomings of these theories?
3. Discuss the various stages of the international product life cycle. Give an example of a product that was introduced to various countries under this theory.
4. Discuss the differences between a free-market economy and a centrally planned economy. What type of economy exists in Japan?
5. Select a country from the first world and the third world and compare the following elements:

- GNP per capita
- Annual export levels
- Life expectancy
- Literacy rates
- Energy consumption levels
- GNP growth rates

What do you find similar/different?

6. What problems or concerns may exist when GNP per capita is used as an indicator to evaluate national economies and potential business opportunities? What other factors could be used?
7. How would you characterize China, India, and Brazil using Rostow's stages of economic growth? Can Sen's framework for development shed some light on differences between these three economies?

NOTES

1. Galbraith, *Economics in Perspective: A Critical History*.
2. Smith, *Wealth of Nations*.
3. Ricardo, *Principles of Political Economy and Taxation*.
4. Mill, *Principles of Political Economy*.
5. Samuelson, "International Factor Price Equalization, Once Again" and "International Trade and the Equalization of Factor Prices."
6. Leontief, "Domestic Production and Foreign Trade."
7. Vernon, "International Investment and International Trade in the Product Life Cycle."
8. Rostow, *Stages of Economic Growth*.
9. Galbraith, *Nature of Mass Poverty*.
10. Rodrick, *One Economics, Many Recipes*.
11. This discussion is taken primarily from three books by Amartya Sen: *Poverty and Famines* (1981), *Inequality Re-examined* (1992), and *Development as Freedom* (1999).
12. *CIA World Fact Book*.
13. In 1993 the World Bank changed the name from "gross domestic product" (GDP) to "gross national income" because the new term reflects goods and services, as well as investment income. This text will use the terms GNI and GDP interchangeably.
14. For more on this point, refer to DeSoto, *Mystery of Capital*.
15. DeSoto, *Mystery of Capital*.
16. US Department of Commerce, Bureau of Economic Analysis, "National Economic Accounts."

BIBLIOGRAPHY

Becker, Gary S., and Robert J. Barro. "A Reformulation of the Economic Theory of Fertility." *Quarterly Journal of Economics* (February 1988): 1–25.
CIA World Fact Book. 2004, www.cia.gov/library/publications/download/download-2004/index.html.
DeSoto, Hernando. *The Mystery of Capital*. New York: Basic Books, 2003.
Fardoust, Shahroukh, and Ashwaith Dhareshwar. *Long-Term Outlook for the World Economy: Issues and Projections for the 1990s*. Edison, NJ: World Bank, 1990.
Galbraith, John Kenneth. *Economics in Perspective: A Critical History*. Boston: Houghton Mifflin, 1987.
———. *The Nature of Mass Poverty*. Cambridge: Harvard University Press, 1979.

Gultekin, Mustafa N., N. Bulent Gultekin, and Allesandro Penati. "Capital Controls and International Capital Market Segmentation: The Evidence from the Japanese and American Stock Markets." *Journal of Finance* (September 1989): 849–869.

Haq, Mahbub. *The Poverty Curtain: Choices for the Third World.* New York: Columbia University Press, 1976.

Heckscher, Eli. "The Effects of Foreign Trade on Distribution of Income." *Economics Tidskrift* (1919): 497–512.

Heller, H. Robert. *International Trade: Theory and Empirical Evidence.* 2nd ed. Englewood Cliffs, NJ: Prentice-Hall, 1973.

Hirschman, Albert O. The Strategy of Economic Development. New York: W.W. Norton, 1980.

Leontief, Wassily W. "Domestic Production and Foreign Trade: The American Capital Position Re-examined." *Economia Internationale* (February 1954): 3–32.

McCarthy, F. Desmond. *Problems of Developing Countries in the 1990s.* Edison, NJ: World Bank, 1990.

Mill, John Stuart. *Principles of Political Economy.* New York: D. Appleton, 1848.

Mundell, Robert. "International Trade and Factor Mobility." *American Economic Review* (June 1957): 321–335.

Nurske, Ragnar. *Problems of Capital Formation in Underdeveloped Countries.* Oxford: Oxford University Press, 1962.

Officer, Laurence H., ed. *International Economics.* Boston: Kluwer, 1987.

Ohlin, Bertil. *Inter-regional and International Trade.* Cambridge, MA: Harvard University Press, 1933.

Pralahad, Coimbatore Krishnarao. *The Fortune at the Bottom of the Pyramid: Eradicating Poverty through Profits.* Upper Saddle River, NJ: Prentice Hall, 2005.

Ricardo, David. *The Principles of Political Economy and Taxation.* New York: E.P. Dutton, 1948. Originally published 1817.

Rodrick, Dani. *One Economics, Many Recipes: Globalization, Institutions, and Economic Growth.* Princeton, NJ: Princeton University Press, 2007.

Rostow, Walt W. *The Stages of Economic Growth: A Non-Communist Manifesto.* New York: Cambridge University Press, 1961.

Samuelson, Paul A. "International Factor Price Equalization, Once Again." *Economic Journal* (June 1949): 121–197.

———. "International Trade and the Equalization of Factor Prices." *Economic Journal* (June 1948): 163–184.

Sen, Amartya. *Development as Freedom.* New York: Anchor, 2000.

Smith, Adam. *The Wealth of Nations.* New York: Modern Library, 1994. Originally published 1776.

U.S. Department of Commerce, Bureau of Economic Analysis. "National Economic Accounts." www.bea.gov/national/index.htm.

Vernon, Raymond. "International Investment and International Trade in the Product Life Cycle." *Quarterly Journal of Economics* (May 1966): 190–207.

World Bank. "Classification of Economies." www.worldbank.org/data/countryclass.

World Bank. "Statistical Talks." www.worldbank.org/indicator.

GLOBALIZATION AT THE CROSSROADS: THE FORTUNE AT THE BOTTOM OF THE PYRAMID

Much of the cost advantages for multinational firms achieved via off-shoring of manufacturing and service positions into emerging markets have already been experienced. This is not to say that the process of outsourcing jobs to foreign markets will not continue, but multinational firms now find themselves ready to capitalize on what economist C.K. Pralahad has called "the fortune at the bottom of the pyramid" for sales of goods and services. As the world population approaches 7 billion, some 4 billion of those people are classified as having low income. While businesses have typically not sought to serve these individuals, the sheer volume of lower income citizens of the world have received the attention of multinational firms seeking global revenue growth at the "bottom of the pyramid." If the benefits of lower cost production can be combined with effective distribution networks, it is possible for profits to increase for multinational firms seeking this strategy. In order for this to be achieved, global firms must decide which product features are crucial to the success of the product, as in order to lower costs of production only the true value added features of a product (or packaging) should be included in mass production. Local entrepreneurs should also be utilized in order to bring the products or services to the target market. As globalization continues to expand, the process of including more of the world's citizens in the production process is well known. In the coming years, sales efforts aimed at these same individuals may prove to be the source of success and frustration for multinational firms. We will be able to understand whether the rising tide of globalization truly does lift all boats.

QUESTIONS FOR DISCUSSION

1. *Research some success stories of companies and products that have catered to the "Bottom of the Pyramid."*
2. *What are some pitfalls of catering to this market?*
3. *There has been some objection to the BOP approach. Research such claims and elaborate on whether they have credence.*
4. *Research the efforts of microfinance organizations in serving this market. What products and services have these organizations provided and how successful have they been in the wake of the recent financial crisis?*

CASE STUDY 3.1

EUROMANAGÉ INC.

Euromanagé Inc. was established in Lyons, France, in 1987 by the Picard brothers, Alain and Michel, as a manufacturer of high-quality baked products that were sold to gourmet shops throughout France, especially in the major cities. As the company grew in strength financially, it expanded its product line to include soft drinks (both bottled and powdered), snack foods, and breakfast cereals. By 2010 the company was a leading processed-food and soft drink manufacturer in France and had established its presence in Switzerland, Germany, Austria, and the Netherlands.

Having gained considerable international experience in Europe, the company makes the decision to expand into Latin America, starting with Massilia, one of the largest countries in Latin America. Massilia has a per capita income of US$6,800 a year, nearly the highest among all countries of the region. Although under considerable Spanish and Portuguese influence because of its heritage, Massilia has a large middle-class population that is increasingly open to international products of different categories. Premarketing research shows that there is a substantial market for the high-quality, upper-end soft drinks and processed-cheese products of Euromanagé. Estimated sales for the first year are US$40 million.

Massilia has a mixed retail system for soft drinks and processed foods. Soft drinks are sold primarily through individually owned small stores that also sell other types of groceries. Large supermarkets in the major cities are also a major source of soft drink sales (about 15 percent). The balance is sold through a variety of outlets, including automatic vending machines (11 percent), restaurants (6 percent), and miscellaneous outlets (8 percent). The large international soft drink manufacturers dominate the market: they have established their own bottling plants in four key regions and set up a comprehensive distribution system operated through local distributors, who have signed agreements with the franchisees.

Euromanagé considers several strategies to break into the market and reaches the conclusion that it could achieve maximum penetration by attacking the high end of the market and carving a niche in the mineral water, fruit juice, and energy drink markets. Much of this market is concentrated in the urban areas, where the professional class is located. With a well-designed marketing plan, Euromanagé hopes to put forth an image of the aesthetic social superiority of its products that would appeal instantly to the upwardly mobile and ambitious sections of Massilia's middle class.

It is also evident that the initial marketing arrangement will be made with the large supermarkets, where most of the higher-income, middle-class customers in urban areas do their shopping. Although in some areas there are high-end, individually owned stores, the supermarkets control as much as 70 percent of the middle- to higher-income retail market in the cities. The supermarkets stock a wide variety of imported foods, so they could also carry Euromanagé processed-cheese products. Further, at some point in the future, the supermarkets could carry more items from the Euromanagé product line. Initial surveys show that customers at the major supermarkets welcome the availability of high-quality French soft drinks and cheeses.

Although this issue is settled fairly quickly, the international marketing strategy for Massilia becomes bogged down in indecision over a choice of a distribution system. Massilia is located on a different continent, where the company's experience in establishing distribution networks in Europe cannot be easily duplicated.

(continued)

Case Study 3.1 *(continued)*

Considerable effort, including on-the-spot studies of the distribution system in Massilia, enable the company to narrow down the options to two. The first is to establish a company distribution office in Mardoe, the major port city and capital of Massilia. Under this arrangement, an executive of Euromanagé would be placed in overall charge of the Massilia distribution operation and would be assisted by a small locally recruited staff. The office would maintain direct contact with all the supermarkets selling Euromanagé products and would coordinate imports and local transportation to various supermarket locations. Letters of credit for imports would be opened by the distribution office on receipt of the supermarket purchase orders. The local office would also be in charge of collections and assist the supermarkets in efficient inventory control of Euromanagé products.

The proposal seems to offer many advantages. Euromanagé is entering into a fairly competitive market with well-entrenched competition. Pricing is a key factor and the existence of an in-house distribution arrangement would save considerably on the middleman's commission. The distribution office could keep in close touch with the supermarkets and offer the company excellent feedback on the market response to Euromanagé products. Further, the executive in charge of the distribution center could actively follow up the promotion of Euromanagé in the new markets.

The second distribution option is to appoint a local agent in Mardoe as the company's sole distributor of soft drinks and processed-cheese products. The distributor would import the products after receiving and consolidating orders from the supermarkets. All transportation, collection, and other arrangements would be made by the distributor, who would also provide periodic market feedback to Euromanagé. At the same time, Euromanagé would be free to talk directly to supermarkets on such issues as the market response to new products, needed changes in product quality and varieties, the nature of store-level promotions, and so on. The distributor would charge a commission on a graduated scale, depending on the level of sales achieved each year, over a given base. There would, however, be a minimum fixed amount of commission payable to the distributor to cover fixed costs.

There are considerable advantages in this proposal, too. The wholesaler would obviously have a better knowledge of the local market and arrive at arrangements with the local supermarkets more easily than would be possible for Euromanagé to accomplish directly. Further, with local experience, the wholesale distributor would be able to smooth out routine problems with the supermarkets more effectively. Because letters of credit would be opened for the account of the wholesaler, Euromanagé would be safe from the credit risk involved in collecting payments from the supermarket outlets. At the same time, the company would also be relieved of the difficult job of handling collections in a foreign country. The wholesaler would already have an office and the necessary facilities in Massilia and would not need additional investments. Moreover, the distributor would have considerable experience and business contacts within the local distribution system and would easily be able to route Euromanagé products to the supermarkets.

Pierre Goulet, vice president of international marketing for Euromanagé, is perplexed. Both options seem to have great advantages, but each also has several disadvantages, and what works in Europe might not work in Latin America. Goulet sends an email to his marketing manager of the Western Hemisphere, Guy Lassalles, asking him to evaluate the difficulties and risks in each alternative from the long-term perspectives of the company, before the executive committee has to make a decision the following week.

DISCUSSION QUESTIONS

1. Assume you are Guy Lassalles. Write a response email providing the analysis sought by Pierre Goulet.
2. What other issues might arise given the firm's intended expansion into Latin America?

CHAPTER 4

International Monetary System and the Balance of Payments

"While money can't buy happiness, it certainly lets you choose your own form of misery."
—Groucho Marx

CHAPTER OBJECTIVES

This chapter will:

- Define the important terms and concepts of the international monetary system
- Provide a brief history of the development of the monetary system, from the gold standard to the establishment of the International Monetary Fund
- Introduce the objectives, roles, and structure of the International Monetary Fund
- Describe the origins, uses, and valuation methodology of the special drawing right
- Explain the problems affecting the Bretton Woods system that resulted in development of the managed, or dirty, float
- Identify areas of reform facing the international monetary system

---

The US dollar has fallen relative to the **euro** (and relative to the currency of many other countries) recently, a drop that has improved the relative pricing of US exports abroad. It has also made foreign imports into the United States relatively more expensive. Thus, in terms of purchasing power, having a weaker currency (as will be described in this chapter) helps domestic manufacturers at home and abroad.

INTERNATIONAL MONETARY TERMINOLOGY

To conduct international business or international trade, a well-organized and internationally accepted system must exist to settle the financial transactions that arise out of trade payments. Moreover, this system has to be in step with the nature of the financial transactions that occur in international business and trade and must be flexible enough to accommodate the constant changes in the patterns, directions, volumes, and nature of the financial flows. This mechanism is broadly termed the **international monetary system (IMS)**. Although international trade dates back thousands of years, the use of money as a medium of settlement is relatively recent. Initially, barter was the primary trading mechanism. It was replaced by more formalized systems that relied on the use of gold as the basis for the settling of international transactions.

The settlement of transactions can be relatively easy when trade is carried on domestically, within the borders of individual countries, because the currency of the country is acceptable to all involved parties. Once more than one currency is involved, however, a need arises to develop an internationally acceptable basis to settle transactions.

HARD CURRENCIES

The first requirement for setting up an IMS is to arrive at an international agreement establishing the basis on which to settle transactions. Arriving at this basis is not easy, because it involves valuing the currency of one country against the currency of one or more other countries. Thus, if a currency forms the basis of the settlement, it has to be accepted by everyone involved.

Currencies of certain countries have a fairly wide acceptance for the settlement of international obligations and are used as a medium in international transactions. These currencies are known as **hard currencies**. The US dollar, British pound, Japanese yen, and euro are examples of hard currencies. Hard currencies can be used by two countries in settling their transactions even if that particular currency is not the home currency of either country. For example, trade transactions between Canada and Mexico can be settled in US dollars, a currency acceptable to both countries even though it is not the home currency of either country. Another important feature of hard currencies is that there is usually a free and active market for them. In other words, if necessary, these currencies can be easily acquired and disposed of internationally in large quantities. There are also usually very few restrictions on the transfer of such currencies in and out of their home countries. Hard currencies, therefore, are an important basis on which to construct an international monetary system.

SOFT CURRENCIES

Soft currencies, on the other hand, are not widely accepted as a medium for settling international financial transactions. Usually there is no free market or foreign exchange for them. Thus, they are not easy to acquire, and disposal is even more difficult. Many soft currencies are subject to restrictions by monetary or governmental authorities on their transfer in and out of their countries. Examples of soft currencies are the Zimbabwe dollar, North Korean won, and Cuban peso.

CONVERTIBILITY

A **convertible currency** is a currency that can be freely converted into another currency. Some countries impose restrictions on currencies so that they cannot be freely converted into the currencies of other countries. These restrictions usually exist in countries that have centrally controlled economies and where transactions outside the country can be made only with official approval. Convertibility implies the availability of a free and active market for a currency. While a currency may be unrestricted by governmental regulations for conversion into other currencies, there may not be adequate demand for that currency by persons outside the country. Such currencies are also said to be lacking in convertibility. Therefore, hard currencies possess the characteristic of convertibility, while soft currencies do not.

When full convertibility of a currency is restricted, a black market that operates outside the control of the government often arises. Essentially, the black market is a free market that parallels the official market and provides full conversion into the local currency, but at a substantial premium over the official rate. The black market in developing countries often operates around parks, international hotels, or transportation stations. As an example of an inconvertible currency, the Zimbabwe dollar has an official exchange rate, but the actual rate in the market place is much higher relative to the foreign currency.

EXCHANGE RATE

When the currency of any one country is used as a medium of settlement for an international transaction, its value has to be fixed vis-à-vis the currency of the other country, either directly or in terms of a third currency. This fixing of a price or value of one currency in terms of another currency is known as the determination of the **exchange rate**. The exchange rate essentially indicates how many units of one currency can be exchanged for one unit of the other currency or vice versa. Exchange rates are not usually fixed permanently. The values of a currency may change upward or downward because of a variety of factors. The frequency with which the currency values change also depends on the type of exchange-rate arrangement of a currency. More fundamentally, however, it has to be understood that the movement of the value of a currency can be either up or down.

APPRECIATION

When the value of a currency is revised or changes upward, it is said to have appreciated.[1] Appreciation of a currency implies that it has become more expensive in terms of other currencies; that is, more units of other currencies will be needed to purchase the same amount of this currency, or fewer units of the appreciated currency will buy the same amount of the other currency. For example, assume that the exchange rate of the pound sterling and the US dollar is £1 = US$2. If, for example, the pound sterling appreciates by 50 percent, then £1 will be equal to US$3. More US dollars can be purchased by the same amount of currency (i.e., £1). Alternatively, in this example, before appreciation US$2 could buy £1. After appreciation, US$3 will be needed to buy the same amount of the foreign currency; that is, £1.

DEPRECIATION

When the price of a currency is changed downward, it is said to have undergone **depreciation.** A currency, upon depreciation, becomes less expensive in terms of another currency. Fewer units of the other currency can be purchased with the same amount of the currency after its devaluation. Alternatively, more units of the depreciated currency are needed to purchase the same amount of foreign currency.

For example, assume that the current exchange rate of the US dollar and the Danish krone is US$1 = DKr6. After a hypothetical depreciation of the dollar, US$1 becomes equal to DKr4. In effect, after depreciation, US$1 now can buy only DKr4. Alternatively it would take US$1.50 to buy DKr6 instead of only US$1, as was the case before depreciation.

A BRIEF HISTORY OF THE INTERNATIONAL MONETARY SYSTEM

The first form of an international monetary system emerged toward the latter half of the nineteenth century. In 1865 four European countries founded the Latin Monetary Union. Its monetary system rested on the use of bimetallic currencies that had international acceptability within member countries of the union. **Bimetallism** refers to the period in monetary history during which two metals (gold and silver) were used to determine the values of different currencies.

THE GOLD STANDARD (1880–1914)

The gold standard, which replaced the bimetallic standard as a system with wide international acceptance, lasted from its introduction in 1880 until the outbreak of World War I in 1914. The central feature of the gold standard was that exchange rates of different countries were fixed, and the parities, or values, were set in relation to gold.

Thus, gold served as the common basis for the determination of individual currency values. Each country adhering to the gold standard specified that one unit of its currency would be equal to a certain amount of gold. Thus, if country A's currency equaled two units of gold and country B's currency equaled four units of gold, the exchange rate of country A's currency against country B's currency would be one to two.

THE GOLD SPECIE STANDARD

The gold specie standard was a pure gold standard. The primary role of gold was as an internationally accepted means of settlement through an arrangement of corresponding debits and credits between different nations. At the same time, gold was in the form of coins, the primary means of settling domestic transactions. Therefore, the gold specie standard required that gold should be available through the monetary authorities in unlimited quantities at fixed prices. There could be no restraints on the import or export of gold, and anyone who possessed the requisite amount of gold could have coins struck at the mint. In effect, this system meant that the face value of gold coins was the same as their exact intrinsic value. The amount of coins, and therefore currency, that a country could issue would be limited to the amount of gold in the possession of a country or its citizens.

THE GOLD BULLION STANDARD

Under the gold bullion standard, the direct link between gold in possession and currency that a country could issue was eliminated. Currency could be in the form of either gold or paper, but the issuing authority of the currency would give a standing guarantee to redeem the currency it had issued in gold on demand at the announced price, which would be fixed. Gold was thus backing the issue, but the requirement to maintain exact proportions between the amount of gold in a country's possession and the amount of currency was eliminated, because the authority could reasonably expect that not all the paper currency that it had issued would come up for redemption at the same time. There was, however, a clear need to maintain a link between the amount of a currency in use and the amount of gold available in the depository of the issuing authority, because a certain proportion of gold backup had to be maintained to honor the estimated requested redemption.

The gold bullion standard was widely adopted in the late nineteenth century. Under the gold bullion standard, international transactions could be settled fairly easily, because each country had defined the value of its currency in terms of gold. Thus, a person with US dollars could trade in those dollars for gold with the US authorities and then use the gold to obtain British pounds in England.

On a country level, the gold standard proved an effective mechanism to settle overall international transactions. A country with a balance of payments deficit faced a situation in which it had to lose some of its gold to pay its debts to the country with the surplus. This led to a reduction in money supply (that was partially backed by gold) and a reduction in prices, which increased the country's export competitiveness and made imports costly. As a result, the balance of payments tended to move away from the deficit toward an equilibrium position because of increasing exports and declining imports. The effect was the opposite on the country with the surplus, which moved away from its surplus position to a position of overall balance of payments equilibrium.

A flaw of the gold standard was that it tended to exacerbate economic conditions between successful countries and those not so successful. For example, if Britain purchased goods from France, then gold would leave Britain and go to France under the gold standard. The continual outflow of gold led to fewer reserves, an increase of interest rates, a contraction of loans, a weakening of prices, and eventually cutbacks in output and employment. In France, the continual influx of gold would raise reserves, which would lead to more loans, higher prices, and higher employment. If these flows continued, depression would occur in Britain, and speculation in France.[2]

Exchange rates were fixed under the gold standard and could not fluctuate beyond upper and lower limits, known as the upper and lower gold points. This slight fluctuation was possible because of the costs involved in the physical movement of equilibrating gold flows from the deficit to the surplus country. If exchange rates went beyond the gold points, the physical transfer of gold would become more remunerative and push the price back within the gold points.

The gold standard worked fairly well during the period from 1880 to 1914. The supply of gold was reasonably steady, and the world economy continued to grow steadily, free from any major international financial crisis. The British Empire was at its zenith, and London was the center of international trade and finance. The central role played by the United Kingdom in general and the Bank of England in particular inspired confidence in the system, which became widely accepted.

The outbreak of World War I, however, radically changed the scenario for the gold standard. Pressures on the United Kingdom's finances because of war expenditures and the resultant gold outflows shook popular confidence in the system. During the war years, no universal system prevailed, most major currencies were in effect floating freely, and the war effort was financed by the creation of large amounts of money that was not backed by gold.

THE INTERWAR YEARS (1918–1939)

At the end of World War I, the IMS was in a state of disarray. Most currencies had undergone wide fluctuations, and the economies of several European countries were severely damaged by the war. Several attempts were made, primarily motivated by Great Britain, to return to the gold standard in the years immediately following the end of World War I. For Great Britain, perhaps, this was an attempt to restore its preeminent prewar position in the international monetary arena. Great Britain therefore announced a prewar exchange parity linked to gold. This was not a realistic exchange rate, however; it was actually grossly overvalued, given the external balance situation at that time. As a result,

Great Britain was forced to redeem substantial amounts of its currency in gold, which led to further outflows of gold and increased pressure on the UK monetary situation.

While Great Britain tried to maintain a strong currency, redeemable in gold, several other countries, eager to improve their international competitive position, began a rush of currency devaluations without any formal agreement with other countries on what a desirable and internationally acceptable value of their currencies should be vis-à-vis other currencies. Apart from the fact that most economies were damaged by war, different countries witnessed different rates of inflation, which upset their international competitive positions at their current level of exchange rates. In an effort to become more competitive, most countries ended up creating a devaluation race, with no formal boundaries or agreed-upon set of rules. The position was clearly a non-system, in which the values of the currencies were determined by the arbitrary decisions of national authorities and the play of market forces.

The difficulties caused by the Great Depression, the problems Germany faced in financing its war reparations, the collapse of the Austrian banking system, and the introduction of exchange controls (restrictions on convertibility of currencies) were symptomatic of the chaos that afflicted the international monetary framework in the 1930s. The United States, having become the world's leading economic power as well as the major creditor, added to the general monetary difficulties by continuing to maintain a relatively undervalued exchange rate, despite having huge balance of payments surpluses.[3] Moreover, by acquiring substantial quantities of gold, which it financed by its balance of payment surpluses, the United States exerted further pressure on the economically beleaguered nations of Europe. Some countries, such as Great Britain and France, established strict exchange controls to ensure the availability of foreign exchange to meet essential imports. Currency blocs were also formed (e.g., the Dollar Area Bloc and the Sterling Area Bloc). In each currency bloc, there were several member countries that had no exchange controls, but all collectively exercised exchange controls with countries outside the bloc.

THE BRETTON WOODS SYSTEM (1944–1973)

During World War II there was a general and increasing recognition of the futility of the arbitrary and antagonistic exchange-rate and monetary policies that had been followed by the major industrialized countries during the 1920s and 1930s.

It was realized that these policies had been largely counterproductive and had resulted in lower trade and employment levels in most countries. It was also found that these formal arrangements had led to a worldwide misallocation of resources that had retarded the efficiency of their utilization. As a result, in 1943 the United States and Great Britain took the initiative toward creating a stable and internationally acceptable monetary system. At the United Nations Monetary and Financial Conference at Bretton Woods, New Hampshire, in 1944, delegates of forty-four countries, after considerable negotiations, agreed to create a new international monetary arrangement.

The Bretton Woods Agreement adopted a **gold exchange standard**, primarily along the proposals made by the US delegation, which was led by Harry Dexter White. The gold exchange standard got its basic logic from the gold standard because it sought to bring gold back into a position of international monetary preeminence and, at the same time, to revive the system of fixed exchange rates. The new system recognized the difficulties inherent in completely rigid exchange rates and made some provisions for flexibility.

Under the Bretton Woods system, participants agreed to stipulate a par value for their respective currencies, either directly in terms of gold or indirectly by linking the currency's par value to the gold content of the US dollar. The exchange rates could fluctuate to the extent of 1 percent of the par value on either side. The par values themselves could not be changed except with the concurrence of the International Monetary Fund (IMF), an institution set up by the Bretton Woods Agreement.[4] Usually, the fund would not object to changes of up to 10 percent in par values.

Thus, the US dollar had a central role in the arrangement. The US government guaranteed that it would be ready to buy or sell unlimited quantities of gold at US$35 per ounce in redemptions of the dollar. To maintain its par value in terms of the US dollar, each participant in the system agreed to buy or sell its currency in requisite amounts against the US dollar.

The dollar's convertibility into gold gave it the primary position in the system because member countries could hold either dollars or gold as their reserves. Many preferred to hold US dollars, which had the advantage of interest income accruing on the reserves, which was not true of reserves held in the form of gold. Moreover, many **central banks** used the dollar as their **intervention currency** (i.e., the currency they bought or sold to maintain the values of their own currencies within the par-value limits prescribed by the Bretton Woods arrangements). The dollar, being the reserve currency, also became the predominant currency for settlement of international trade and financial transactions.

THE INTERNATIONAL MONETARY FUND

AIMS

The Bretton Woods Conference created the International Monetary Fund to administer the exchange-rate arrangements and to secure orderly monetary conditions. More specifically, as laid out in its articles, the IMF had five aims:

1. Promote international cooperation through consultation and collaboration by member countries on international monetary issues
2. Facilitate the expansion and balanced growth of international trade
3. Promote exchange-rate stability and orderly exchange-rate arrangements
4. Foster a multilateral system of international payments and seek elimination of exchange restrictions that hinder the growth of world trade
5. Try to reduce both the duration and the magnitude of imbalances in international payments by making its resources available (with adequate safeguards)

The IMF was asked to deal with three of these goals as a first priority. It was to administer the exchange-rate arrangements agreed on by the member countries, to provide member countries with financial resources to correct temporary payments imbalances, and to provide a forum in which the members could consult and collaborate on international monetary issues of common concern.

MEMBERSHIP

Initially the IMF had 44 member countries; it now has more than 185. Growth in membership was particularly rapid in the 1960s, as newly independent nations of Asia and Africa became members. Most countries of the world are now members of the IMF. Some isolationist nations such as North Korea and Cuba have not yet joined the membership roll of this organization.

Membership in the fund is based on subscription to its resources in the form of a quota. A member's quota, being equal to its subscription to the fund, determines the member's voting power, as well as, to a considerable extent, its access to the fund's resources. Members' quotas are periodically adjusted to reflect changes in the underlying criteria that were used to establish them initially. Quota sizes are determined by a set formula that takes into account factors such as national income, gold and dollar balances, average imports, and variability of exports. The method of computation has undergone several refinements and changes since its inception. There is now a greater emphasis on trade and trade variability as criteria for determining a country's quotas rather than on such criteria as GDP.

STRUCTURE

The highest decision-making body of the IMF is the board of governors, which consists of one governor appointed by each member of the fund. Generally, they are the ministers of finance or governors of central banks of the member countries. Day-to-day operations are overseen by the executive board, which consists of executive directors appointed by the countries with the largest quotas; in addition, groups of countries with smaller quotas jointly elect one executive director each. In 2012 there were twenty-four executive directors, five appointed by the largest quota holders[5] and nineteen elected by the other members in groups of different countries.

The United States has the largest quota. Other large quota holders are Germany, France, Japan, the United Kingdom, and Saudi Arabia. Because major decisions require an 85 percent majority, the United States has an effective veto power over major decisions.

Operation of the fund is headed by a managing director, who is elected by the executive board for an initial term of five years. The managing director reports to the board of governors and participates in the deliberations of major committees of the fund. Traditionally, the managing director has been from one of the European member countries of the fund.

Forms of IMF Assistance

The IMF offers assistance to its member countries by making financial resources available to them through a wide range of sources. The primary purpose of IMF loans is to correct balance of payments imbalances.[6] The basic facility known as a credit tranche drawing permits a member country to borrow from the fund in four tranches (French for "slices" or "stages") of funds equaling its total subscription to the fund or its quota. Each tranche constitutes 25 percent of the member country's quota. Loans under this facility are short-term and are repayable in eight quarterly installments, the last of which has to be within five years of the drawing. Credit tranche drawings were the most utilized facility during the initial years of the fund. Since 1980, funds borrowed through other special facilities have exceeded those made under the basic credit tranche facility.

Extended Fund Facility

The extended fund facility was established in 1974 to provide member countries with financial resources for periods long enough to allow them to take corrective measures with respect to their balance of payments difficulties. The basic rationale of this facility is to allow the countries time to correct structural and policy distortions in their economies without having to bear the shocks of too rapid a transition. Moreover, the resources provided under the facility help the member countries tide over temporary balance of payments deficits that may occur in the course of corrective action. Assistance is provided on the basis of specific corrective programs proposed by the borrowing countries. These programs are usually spread over a period of three years. Borrowing up to 200 percent of the quota is permitted under the facility, subject to the upper limit of 600 percent of the quota not being exceeded on a cumulative basis. Repayments are to be made on a longer schedule than in the credit tranche facility; the first installment begins after four and a half years, and the last is made ten years after the funds are borrowed. Some countries that have benefited from this financing are Ukraine, Colombia, Pakistan, and Argentina.

Structural Adjustment Facilities

Structural adjustment facilities and enhanced structural adjustment facilities are relatively new facilities designed by the IMF to provide financial assistance to member countries that are undertaking specific programs of structural adjustment within their economies.

Structural adjustment programs are essentially a set of policy measures designed to improve the overall efficiency and productive capacity of the economy, as well as to remove existing distortions or other operational deficiencies. Repayments under the facilities are spread over a longer term than are those of other facilities, and the borrower has to agree to a specific policy-change program, which it must treat as its own and not as one imposed by the IMF. Several countries of Africa, Asia, and Latin America have benefited from these new facilities.

IMF CONDITIONALITY

Conditionality is the technical term used to denote the policies that member countries who receive financial assistance from the IMF are expected to follow within their own economies in order to remedy their balance of payments problems. The basic rationale provided by the IMF for requiring conditionality to accompany its lending is the need to address the root causes of the problems and generate in the borrower the capacity to meet its own balance of payments shortfalls and to be able to repay the fund loans. Conditionality is, of course, different for different countries, because the reasons for balance of payments problems differ in varying situations.

There are, however, four conditions that are found in nearly all IMF lending programs:

1. The achievement of a realistic exchange rate that would improve the external competitiveness of the economy; this most often means a substantial devaluation of the currency for many countries
2. The elimination of subsidies and controls within the domestic economy in order to achieve a more efficient allocation of resources and to remove the impediments to enhancing the productivity of the economy
3. Reductions of tariff, trade, and exchange restrictions, thereby creating a relatively more open external sector
4. A reduction of public sector and government spending, which is intended to eliminate excess demand and its impact on the balance of payments

As the balance of payments problems have become increasingly difficult in both magnitude and complexity, the conditionality of the IMF has tended to allow a longer time frame in which borrower countries can make the necessary policy adjustments. Moreover, IMF conditionality has tended to shift from an almost exclusive focus on demand-side measures to policies that are aimed at stabilizing the supply conditions in borrowers' economies. Some of the policies that IMF conditionality requires in the area of supply-side stabilization are increases in real interest rates, economic pricing of public services, and tax reforms, intended to expand manufacturing output and employment.

While providing financial assistance to member countries, the IMF receives from the borrowers specific policy program instructions that are to be followed during the period the member country is in receipt of assistance. These programs include specific targets for certain economic benchmarks, such as bank credit, budgetary deficits, and external borrowings. The programs also contain official commitments not to increase restrictions on exchange rates. The IMF uses these targets as well as assurances as basic criteria to assess the performance of borrower countries. The performance of the borrowers in terms of their criteria is taken into account by the IMF while releasing further tranches of assistance. This practice allows the IMF to monitor and to some extent influence the policies of the countries utilizing its resources. Detailed guidelines have been laid down by the executive board of the IMF, under which the performance criteria are used to phase and control the financial assistance of the IMF to member countries.

In some cases there has been considerable resentment against the imposition of conditionality, both on grounds of its not being appropriate for the conditions prevalent in several borrower countries and on grounds that it is an infringement of a country's sovereign right to determine its economic policy. In some countries IMF conditionality has been blamed for causing considerable problems for the poorest sections of society and for taking a heavy social toll by its economic prescriptions. These fears, as well as some even less-founded ones, were the impetus for protests at annual IMF meetings in Seattle in 1999 and again in Washington, DC, in 2002. In the aftermath of the recent global financial crisis, protests against IMF conditionality took place in Iceland, Greece, and various other EU nations. Counterarguments hold that the IMF is often a scapegoat for economic ills that originated well before its establishment. Moreover, some politicians in the borrowing countries have found it convenient to pass on to the IMF the blame and responsibility for tough economic measures.

IMF conditionality, although basically remaining the same, has thus tended to be modified to take into account the realities in the borrowing countries and now stresses the role of the borrower countries in taking the primary responsibility for carrying out adjustment programs as a part of their own official policy and not as an outside prescription.

SPECIAL DRAWING RIGHTS

USING SPECIAL DRAWING RIGHTS

Special drawing rights (SDRs) were created as a reserve asset by the IMF in 1970. SDRs are essentially book entries that represent the right of the country holding them to access resources of equivalent value. SDRs owe their origin to the crisis in the international monetary system that began to emerge during the 1960s, when the volume of trade expanded much faster than the production of gold. Under the Bretton Woods arrangements, countries could hold reserves in the form of either gold or US dollars. Reserves of US dollars with other countries meant that the United States had to run ever-larger balance of payments deficits. It was feared that a serious liquidity crisis could result if the United States was not able to sustain and manage large deficits or if the deficits themselves increased to a point at which they threatened the stability of the external balance of the United States. SDRs were therefore created as an additional reserve asset to complement existing reserves of US dollars and gold.

Apart from being an international reserve asset, SDRs are the unit of accounting for all transactions between the IMF and its member countries. In addition, SDRs are used to settle international transactions between central banks of IMF member countries. SDRs are not, however, a privately used or traded international currency for commercial or other purposes. Certain international organizations, such as the Asian Development Bank, the Arab Monetary Fund, and the World Bank, have been permitted to hold SDRs.

SDRs are allocated to member countries by the IMF board of governors. Allocations of SDRs are made on the same basis as ordinary quotas to the funds of member countries. Holdings of SDRs constitute a part of the countries' international reserves in addition to gold, foreign exchange, and reserve assets with the IMF. Holding an SDR gives the bearer the option to acquire foreign exchange from the monetary authorities of another IMF member. In fact, the IMF intends the SDR to become the principal reserve asset of the international monetary system. In order for this to occur, a higher volume of trading of SDRs is required in the marketplace.

VALUATION OF SDRS

Originally, the value of the SDR was fixed in terms of gold, with 1 SDR being equivalent to 0.888671 grams of gold or 35 SDRs being equal to 1 troy ounce of gold. In 1974, this basis of SDR valuation was replaced by a system that utilized a weighted average of sixteen currencies, called a basket. Under this arrangement, which lasted from 1974 to 1980, the value of the SDR was determined on a daily basis. The currencies in this basket were those of IMF member countries whose shares in world exports of goods and services exceeded 1 percent each during the years from 1967 to 1972. While this arrangement lasted, there were some changes made in the basket composition that were meant to reflect the changing proportions of world trade being handled by different countries whose currencies were in the basket and by those whose share increased over time, even though their currencies were not in the basket.

Despite the changes made to reflect the changing positions of the shares of different countries in the world's exports of goods and services, this arrangement continued to suffer from certain problems. For one, many of the currencies in the basket were not actively traded internationally, at least in the forward market, which made actual weighting extremely difficult. To remedy this situation and to simplify the calculation procedure, a new SDR basket was introduced in 2000 that comprised the currencies of the countries and areas that had the largest share in world exports of goods and services. The currency composition of the new SDR basket was as follows:

US dollar	45 percent
Euro	29 percent
Japanese yen	15 percent
Pound sterling	11 percent

The value of the SDR is determined by the prevailing market value of the currencies adjusted according to their basket weights. Since the introduction of the euro in 2000, this currency has replaced the German mark and French franc in the basket. Overall, since the 1980 valuation, the respective shares of the US dollar and the Japanese yen have increased at the expense of the others in the basket.

Although SDRs are meant as reserve assets and are to be used only to settle official transactions between the IMF and its members and between the members themselves, there have been commercial uses of SDRs. The commercial utility of SDRs derives from the relatively stable nature that comes from their basket composition, which evens out the wide fluctuations that are the bane of all major international currencies. As a result, many international borrowers have denominated their bonds and other borrowing instruments in SDRs. SDRs have also been used to denominate trade invoicing, even though settlement is ultimately made in one of the traditional currencies. Other users of SDRs in the past have included the International Air Transport Association, for fixing international airfares, and the Republic of Egypt, for denominating tolls for transit through the Suez Canal.

A major controversy surrounding SDRs is their use as a mechanism to create aid financing to meet the requirements of less-developed countries (LDCs). LDCs hold that SDRs should be linked not to quotas but to the actual needs of IMF member countries. Several industrialized countries, however, including the United States, feel that this instrument is primarily meant for creating international reserves and liquidity and that its use as an aid-financing mechanism would distort the original intentions and result in excess liquidity in the international economy. It has also been argued that aid would be extremely difficult to monitor from the utilization point of view if it were channeled through the SDR mechanism.

Although it is intended to be a major reserve asset, the SDR comprises much less than 10 percent of the world's international resources. A greater role for the SDR, however, would be in the interest of both developed and developing countries.

DIFFICULTIES IN THE BRETTON WOODS SYSTEM

Because the US dollar was a key international reserve currency under the Bretton Woods system, the deficit in the US balance of payments was essential if the liquidity requirements of the IMS were to be fully met. If the US dollar deficits grew larger and larger, however, the holders of dollars would tend to lose confidence in the currency as a reserve and in the capacity of the United States to honor its obligations. The economist Robert Triffin noted this problem of relying too heavily on the US dollar. The **Triffin Paradox** states the more that foreigners relied on the US dollar to expand trade, the less confidence they had in the United States being able to honor its commitment of redeeming dollars for gold.

Signs of a future crisis became apparent in the late 1950s, when the United States started running extremely large balance of payments deficits. US expansion and investment overseas, aid under the **Marshall Plan**, and a strong economic recovery by Europe were some of the factors that went into making the US trade account one of almost constant deficit. By the 1960s it was clear that many European and other countries were growing increasingly uncomfortable with their holdings of US dollars as reserves; many of these nations wanted to redeem the dollars for gold at the officially announced price. Moreover, given the central role of the US dollar in the system, it could not be devalued to improve the competitive position of the United States versus other countries.

The crisis of confidence was reflected in a run on gold, which pushed its market price well above the announced official price of US$35 per ounce. The central banks of various countries did manage to stabilize the price of gold, at least at the official level, by forming a gold pool and undertaking open-market operations. As a result, however, the gold market was split in two: the official and the unofficial, with US authorities ready to redeem in gold US dollars received only from official sources. Moreover, the US government exerted pressure on European and other holders of dollar reserves not to press for redemptions into gold.

Another inherent defect in the system was that it passed on the effects of US domestic monetary policies to other countries. If the United States followed expansionary policies, other countries were forced to follow a reverse policy to maintain exchange parity. Moreover, the US rates of inflation continued to be higher than those of European countries. Further, the inability to neutralize the inflationary effects of US dollar holdings irked many countries, which felt that they were losing control over their domestic monetary policies. Due to this problem, the German mark and Dutch guilder had to be revalued, and in 1968 the pound was substantially devalued.

By 1970 US gold reserves had fallen to US$11 billion, while short-term official holdings of US dollars were more than double this amount. The crisis came to a head in 1970 with a decline in US interest rates that sparked a massive outflow of capital from the United States to Europe. The pressure on the value of the US dollar continued unabated despite central bank support from many European countries. As a result, in May 1971, Switzerland and Austria revalued their currencies, and Germany and the Netherlands allowed the prices of their currencies to be determined by the market. Continued flight from the US dollar strengthened doubts about the ability of the US dollar to maintain convertibility into gold.

These doubts were confirmed on August 15, 1971, when President Richard Nixon announced the suspension of the convertibility of the US dollar into gold. With the abandonment of dollar convertibility into gold, the underlying basis of the fixed exchange-rate arrangements of the Bretton Woods system collapsed, and many other countries stopped fixing their exchange rates according to official parities, allowing them to be determined instead by the market.

An attempt was made to return to fixed parities in 1971 through the **Smithsonian Agreement**, under which the United States raised the official price of gold to US$38 per ounce, marking a 7.9 percent devaluation of the dollar. The bands within which currencies could fluctuate against each other were widened to a range of 2.25 percent on each side of the fixed rate, but the dollar was not made convertible into gold. Moreover, the movement of capital across countries continued to put pressure on exchange-rate parities. Faced with either heavy outflows or heavy inflows of foreign currencies, several countries were forced to abandon the freshly fixed parities and allow their currencies to float freely on the international markets. Despite raising the price of gold for a second time, to US$42.20 per ounce, the United States was not able to stem the outflow of dollars, and it became extremely difficult for European countries to maintain the value of their currencies against the US dollar. By the end of the first quarter of 1973, most of the European countries had withdrawn from their participation in the system of parities established under the Smithsonian Agreement.

THE FLOATING-RATE ERA: 1973 TO THE PRESENT

The transition to a system of **floating exchange rates** was not the result of any formal agreement, such as the one that had created the system of fixed exchange rates. It occurred primarily because the earlier system broke down and there was no agreed-on formal arrangement to replace it. In fact, at this stage there was no universal agreement on an appropriate exchange-rate arrangement. Universal agreement continues to elude the international monetary community and a variety of exchange-rate arrangements are followed by different groups of countries. The most important types of exchange-rate arrangements are different types of floating rates, pegging, crawling pegs, basket of currencies, and fixed rates.

PURE FLOATING RATES

Under the pure-floating-rate arrangement, the exchange rate of a country's currency is determined entirely by such market considerations as demand and supply. The government or the monetary authorities make no efforts to either fix or manipulate the exchange rate. Although many industrialized countries officially state that they follow a policy of floating for their exchange rates, most of them do intervene to influence the direction of the movement of their exchange rates.

MANAGED, OR DIRTY, FLOATING RATES

An important feature of the **managed float** system is the necessity for the central bank or the monetary authorities to maintain a certain level of foreign exchange reserves. Foreign exchange reserves are needed because the authorities are required to buy or sell foreign currencies in the market to influence exchange-rate movements. On the other hand, under a free-floating-rate arrangement, these reserves are not necessary, because the exchange market is cleared by a free play of the forces of supply and demand, which fix a particular exchange rate that is the equilibrium rate at any given point of time.

PEGGING

Under a **pegging** arrangement, a country links the value of its currency to that of another currency, which is usually that of its major trading partner. Pegging to a particular currency implies that the value of the pegged currency moves along with the currency to which it is pegged and does not really fluctuate. It does fluctuate, however, against all other currencies to the same extent as the currency to which it is pegged (e.g., the currency of the Republic of Gabon, the CFA franc, has been pegged to the euro since 1999).[7]

CRAWLING PEGS

Under a **crawling peg** arrangement, a country makes small periodic changes in the value of its currency with the intent to move it to a particular value over a period of time. The system, however, can be taken advantage of by currency speculators, who can make substantial profits by buying or selling the currency just before its revaluation or devaluation. The advantage of this system is that it enables a country to spread its exchange-rate adjustment over a longer period than pegging does, thereby avoiding the shocks that can be caused to the economy by sudden and steep revaluations or devaluations. The Mexican peso utilized a crawling-peg regime relative to the US dollar during the 1990s in order to allow the peso to slowly devalue toward a more appropriate exchange rate.

BASKET OF CURRENCIES

Many countries, particularly LDCs, are increasingly fixing the rates of their currencies in terms of a basket of currencies. The arrangement is similar to that used for valuation of SDRs. The basic advantage of the system is that it imparts a degree of stability to the currency of a country as the movements in currencies that comprise the basket counterbalance one another. The selection of the currencies that are to be included in the basket is generally determined by their importance in financing the trade of a particular country. In most currency baskets, different currencies are assigned different weights, in accordance with their relative importance to the country. The actual method of computation of the exchange rate from the basket is relatively similar worldwide but may have individual variations. Some countries, although fixing their exchange rate in terms of a basket of currencies, may choose to conduct most of their official transactions in one or two currencies, which are known as the intervention currencies.

FIXED RATES

Under a fixed rate arrangement, a country announces a specific exchange rate for its currency and maintains this rate by agreeing to buy or sell foreign exchange in unlimited quantities at this rate. At present, however, there are hardly any countries that still follow a completely rigid system of exchange rates. Some of the countries of the former socialist bloc had fixed exchange rates that were announced from time to time and that were used for all official transactions, particularly with countries with which they had bilateral trade arrangements. Today, fixed exchange rates are typically employed by small countries relative to the currency of a larger nation. For example, the Lebanese pound and the Hong Kong dollar are fixed relative to the US dollar, and the Danish krone is fixed relative to the euro.

EUROPEAN MONETARY SYSTEM

Several European countries that were members of the **European Economic Community (EEC)**, concerned by the collapse of the Bretton Woods arrangements, decided in 1979 to enter into an exchange-rate arrangement that would regulate movements in their currencies with respect to one another. The currencies of these countries, with respect to the US dollar, were to float jointly. Limits for variations of currencies within the member-country group were fixed at a 2.5 percent range, while as a group the currencies would vary within a range of 4.5 percent against the US dollar. These arrangements were also a part of the general scheme to achieve significant economic and monetary integration among the member countries of the EEC. One way of achieving greater monetary integration was to reduce the level of fluctuation from their parity values of currencies of different countries within the EEC. The lower range of 2.5 percent prescribed for intra-community fluctuation was termed the "snake," while the broader range of 4.5 percent fluctuation as a group against the US dollar was called the "tunnel."

International monetary cooperation was, however, not so easy to come by in practice, because different member countries were subject to their own individual constraints and found that keeping up with the limits imposed by the snake arrangements did not serve their best economic interests. As a result, France, Great Britain, and Italy withdrew their participation from this arrangement within two years of its inception.

Violent fluctuations in exchange rates in the international markets and renewed interest in achieving greater economic and monetary integration within the members of the EEC prompted efforts to reconsider the establishment of a system of fixed parities, with a limited amount of flexibility, for the exchange rates of member countries. In pursuit of these objectives, the **European Monetary System (EMS)** was established by nine member countries of the EEC in 1979. In some ways, it was a successor to the erstwhile snake arrangement and reflected the experience gained with that system. This system was later replaced with the **European Monetary Union (EMU)** in 1992.

DIFFICULTIES IN THE FLOATING-RATE ERA

Exchange rates in the floating-rate era have been marked by violent fluctuations that have been prompted by a variety of factors. There were periodic crises in the international monetary system, which were reflected in the extreme fluctuations of exchange rates.

The first major crisis to affect the IMS after the breakdown of the Bretton Woods arrangements was the oil crisis that began in 1973, when OPEC placed an embargo on its members' oil exports, which by 1974 resulted in a fourfold increase in oil prices. For some nations, such as the United States and Japan, this meant a sudden and substantial increase in the volume of their import payments, which put pressure on their balance of payments. The industrialized countries were able to meet this crisis by adjusting their economies to a lower level of oil consumption and more aggressive export policies that increased foreign exchange earnings. The oil-exporting countries, on the other hand, accumulated substantial balance of payments surpluses, which were denominated in US dollars. In 1974 the United States lifted capital controls on the international movements of dollars, making them freely transferable across the globe. As long as the dollar remained the primary currency for holding and recycling the dollars held by OPEC countries (also known as **petrodollars**), the value of the dollar would continue to be strong, despite a virtually continuous trade deficit.

The continuous trade deficits, however, and policies that encouraged capital outflows, caused confidence in the dollar to weaken, leading to a sharp fall in its price in 1978. Further, this decline of confidence in the dollar was exacerbated by the difficulties the United States faced in Iran because of its revolution, as well as the problems created by the second oil crisis, of 1979, when the OPEC countries indulged in yet another round of dramatic price increases. The attractiveness of the dollar was enhanced yet again, very quickly, as US authorities decided on a monetary policy that would result in higher US interest rates, which in turn would attract overseas demand for the dollar and raise the exchange rate.

The changed monetary policy also helped to maintain international confidence in the US dollar in the face of the second oil shock as well as the unsettled conditions in Iran, especially in light of the general freeze on Iranian assets held in the United States. A major factor in this new confidence was the expectation that inflation would remain at a lower level in the United States than in other countries. Therefore, investments made in the United States seemed attractive. To invest in the United States meant that the overseas investors had to acquire US dollars, which increased the demand and strengthened the exchange rate of the currency. Although the United States ran huge balance of payments deficits from 1981 to 1985, the dollar's value continued to appreciate. Apart from the high interest rates and low inflation, US investments were attractive because of the strong performance of the US economy, which continued to enjoy a virtually uninterrupted expansion. Moreover, the United States seemed to be the safest haven for investors as political crises affected many parts of the world and threatened to spread further. Other factors that strengthened the US dollar in this period were the decline in the price of oil, the reinvestment of funds by major commercial banks in the US market, and speculative actions of investors in the foreign exchange markets, who kept pushing the value of the dollar even higher by making speculative purchases and increasing demand.

FLUCTUATIONS IN THE US DOLLAR: THE PLAZA AND LOUVRE ACCORDS

By early 1985, continued appreciation of the dollar had caused enough economic problems for the United States to precipitate government action to arrest this trend. The high price of the dollar had made US exports expensive and imports cheap, which led to a decline in the former and a steep rise in the latter, creating a huge deficit in the US trade account. Moreover, most of this deficit was financed not by internal resources but by external borrowings. As a result, the United States decided to follow policies that would reduce the attractiveness of overseas investments in dollar assets and improve the budgetary and trade deficit position. The most important of these policies were an attempt to reduce US interest rates, a reduction of the budget deficit, and coordinated action to

Table 4.1 **European Union Membership**

The EU 15		Subsequent EU additions	
Austria	Italy	Bulgaria	Lithuania
Belgium	Luxembourg	Croatia	Malta
Denmark	Netherlands	Cyprus	Poland
Finland	Portugal	Czech	Republic Romania
France	Spain	Estonia	Slovakia
Germany	Sweden	Hungary	Slovenia
Greece	United Kingdom	Latvia	
Ireland			

bring down the value of the dollar, an action to be taken by the monetary authorities of the major industrialized countries.

The third policy was initiated in September 1985, when finance ministers of the United States, Japan, France, West Germany, and the United Kingdom, as well as their central bank governors, met at the Plaza Hotel in New York City and reached an agreement on coordinated action to be taken to bring down the value of the US dollar. The agreement, known as the **Plaza Accord**, prompted a dramatic decline in the already depreciating dollar, which continued to fall steadily over the next year and a half. By the end of the first quarter of 1987, the value of the dollar had fallen so much that it was considered too weak. Therefore, in 1987 the group of six industrialized countries (the United States, the United Kingdom, West Germany, France, Canada, and Italy) agreed during their annual summit, held that year in Paris, to arrest the decline in the value of the dollar. The agreement, known as the **Louvre Accord**, did not have such a dramatic and immediate impact in achieving its objective as the Plaza Accord, because the dollar continued to decline for a while. By 1988, however, the dollar had recovered some of its strength.

The Plaza Accord was successful primarily because it was in a relatively better position to achieve its objectives, with the dollar already on a downward path. On the other hand, the Louvre Accord had a much more difficult agenda: to reverse the trend in the international foreign exchange markets. Moreover, the Louvre Accord required a relatively consistent and long-term policy-coordination effort that was not so likely to come to pass, given the individual economic imperatives and policies of signatories.

European Monetary Union

In keeping with the goal of achieving greater monetary integration in Europe, the European Monetary Union came into effect in 1992. This agreement was part of the general agreement concerning the European Union, which also came into effect that year. The European Union originally consisted of fifteen member nations; the membership was expanded by ten countries in May 2004, by two countries in 2008, and finally by one country (Croatia) in July 2013 (see Table 4.1).

The primary focus of the European Union was to create one marketplace throughout the continent of Europe to compete with that of the United States. The European Union was created as an economic union with the primary aim of full integration of the afore-mentioned national economies into one united Europe. The European Union eliminated internal trade barriers among member nations, adopted common external trade policies, abolished restrictions on the mobility of the factors of production, and began to coordinate economic activities, such as monetary, fiscal, taxation, and social welfare programs, in an attempt to blend the nations into a single economic entity.

On January 1, 2002, the euro was launched in the twelve member states that opted into the EMU. Of the original fifteen EU member states, all but three adopted the euro as the single currency.8 Denmark, Sweden, and the United Kingdom opted to either not join or delay joining the EMU. Establishment of the new currency was not an isolated event, however. The European Union had to change thousands of national laws, product standards, and regulations to ensure that they were harmonized throughout the member nations. These changes were necessary to create a unified system that would permit the free flow of goods, services, labor, capital, and technology in Europe.

MAASTRICHT TREATY

The Maastricht Treaty went into effect in November 1993. Its purpose was to lay the frame-work for the economic and political integration of the European Union. The treaty, named for the city in the Netherlands where it was signed into law, rests on three pillars:

- A common foreign and defense policy
- Cooperation on police, judicial, and public safety matters
- New provisions to create an economic and monetary union among the member states

The final bullet point is the focus of the discussion here, and it consists of the creation of certain **convergence criteria** that the government of each member state theoretically must adhere to in order to qualify for participation in the common European currency. These rules were necessary because for an economic union among multiple sovereign nations to work, the member states must maintain similar monetary and fiscal policies (and results).

The convergence criteria for the European Union are itemized below:

- Government deficit must not exceed 3 percent of GDP
- Government debt must not exceed 60 percent of GDP
- Inflation and long-term interest rates must not exceed the rates of the three lowest EU member states by more than 2 percent
- Foreign exchange rate of currency must float within a range of 15 percent of those of the other member countries for a period of two years prior to the adoption of the euro

As you can see from the bullet points above, there is a combination of both fiscal and monetary policy requirements necessary for a country to qualify for inclusion in the EMU. Of the twelve original members of the EMU, all qualified for the single currency prior to its launch in January 2002. Italy and Greece had to make the biggest improvements (primarily in their inflation levels) in order to qualify. These same criteria were used in order to phase in the ten member states that joined the European Union (and thus the EMU) in May 2004, and for subsequent members.

Denmark's Challenge to Monetary Union

While the success of the euro since its issue has exceeded initial expectations, three of the original fifteen EU member states do not currently participate in the single currency. The first to buck the trend was Denmark. In the 1990s and again on September 28, 2000, the citizens of Denmark voted to not participate in the euro, instead opting to keep the Danish krone intact. The "Euro-skeptics," or individuals who feared the spread of the European Union in the continent, twice defeated national referendums on adopting the euro. The Danes feared infringement on their national sovereignty due to the country's relative size. The European Parliament, which will eventually become the European Union's primary legislative body, has representation from each member nation according to the population of each country. Under the current arrangement, Denmark has only thirteen members of European Parliament out of a total parliamentary body of 754. Thus, it is easy to see the fears of a small nation concerning its ability to manage its own internal affairs without having to encounter undue influence from the rest of Europe via the European Union's Brussels headquarters.

While Denmark does not participate in the euro, the small nation has opted to allow the krone to float against the euro within a range of 2.5 percent. This policy has worked so far due to the relative strength of the Danish economy, the country's current account surpluses, low unemployment relative to EU averages, sound public finances, and marginally higher interest rates relative to the **European Central Bank** (ECB).[9] The ECB is essentially the central bank of the European Union and is responsible for implementing its monetary policy.

While Denmark's economy prospers, the country clearly benefits from having its currency fixed to the euro without having the political intrusion into its internal affairs that, so far, its citizens have voted against in public referendums. It will be interesting to see what happens should the economy falter in the future.

Asian Financial Crisis

The 1997–1998 **Asian financial crisis** provides another example of how problems can occur in the current international monetary system. The original cause of the problem was thought to be the unpegging of the Thai baht to the US dollar. The Thailand economy had grown by 9 percent from 1985 to 1995, and massive speculation had ensued in the economy. Once the

Thai government decided to allow the baht to float, the currency plummeted in value, losing more than 50 percent of its value in 1997.[10] Further, the Thai stock market crashed by 75 percent. Other countries, including the Philippines, South Korea, Malaysia, and Indonesia, all experienced currency attacks as investors attempted to sell the Thai baht on the world currency market. In Hong Kong, the Hang Seng stock market index fell by more than 23 percent in October, while the government raised interest rates from 8 percent to 23 percent over the period in an attempt to keep the currency pegged to the US dollar.

While it is tempting to assign blame to currency failures for this financial episode, this crisis was merely a symptom and not the root cause of the problem. If currency was at the heart of the problem, you would expect to find budgets at high deficit levels, and high levels of inflation throughout Southeast Asia. While some of the affected countries had some of these symptoms, they were certainly not pervasive throughout the region. If there had been budget deficits, central banks would have printed money in an attempt to balance the budget, which would cause inflation and the desire to sell the inflated currency in favor of a more stable one.[11] Additionally interest rates were not excessively high throughout the region either. Pegging an exchange rate to another currency (the US dollar) requires raising interest rates in order to stop the flight of capital and propping up the value of the domestic currency by buying it (and selling US dollars).

Root Cause of the Asian Financial Crisis

The primary problem was speculative bank lending due to government-guaranteed loans. Thailand's economy, as well as that of South Korea, had large amounts of nonperforming loans on the balance sheets of the nations' banks. Since the governments in the region had provided guarantees for loans, **moral hazard** was the result. Moral hazard ensues when there is no punishment for banks if loans are defaulted on, which creates an incentive for the banks to over-lend. Once the first speculative loans go bad, the government has to step in to bail out the domestic banks. The bailout of the first bank creates a panic for the other banks, and the downward spiral begins. The banks of Southeast Asia were not regulated with regard to quantifying the risk of their loan portfolios, and since the domestic banks had over-loaned on many speculative projects, the assets were overvalued.

Thus, the boom-and-bust cycle in the asset markets due to speculative lending by banks preceded the currency crises in all affected nations. In the aftermath of the Asian financial crisis, the IMF provided more than $120 billion to four countries in an effort to improve the performance of the once-strong economies. The majority of economists called for stricter regulation in the banking sector, and many banks in the region were closed. Large commercial banks have also recently agreed to an overall system of quantifying risk at major international banks, in a system called the **Basel Accords**. Under this system, the amount of capital held in the financial institutions must reflect the amount of risk in the loan portfolios. This calculation is done via a standardized bank credit-scoring system. Other suggestions for improvement include increased levels of financial reporting for companies (or "transparency guarantees," in the words of Amartya Sen).

EU Sovereign Debt Crisis

The European Union sovereign debt crisis (or Eurozone crisis), which began in 2008, involved the inability of various European nations (i.e., Greece, Ireland, Spain, and Portugal) to either repay or refinance their government debt without the assistance of other parties. A primary cause of this crisis was the inability of the European Central Bank to adequately manage the vagaries of the economic cycle for a multitude of nations who all shared a common currency but not a common fiscal policy. While convergence criteria were memorialized by the Maastricht Treaty, there were numerous examples over the last decade of countries (both big and small) that breached the budget deficit and debt limitations with little or no punishment. While the exchange rates of the members of the European Monetary System are no longer an issue, differences in national fiscal policy and inflation rates led to a crisis that threatened the very life of the European Union.

As one of the few large EU member states with a budget and trade surplus, Germany was sought as the primary underwriter for the profligacy of others, a role that began to erode support domestically for the continued bailouts of southern EU member nations. An early proposal to stem the tide of the Eurozone crisis was the creation of a pan-European bond, whereby the debts of all EU members would be underwritten by all other members. The goal of this proposal was to reduce the variability in interest rates among member states, as states with higher perceived risks were required to pay higher interest rates on their sovereign bonds. As bond interest rates approached 7 percent, many of the less solvent EU members could not pay back the debts. Another discarded solution was a planned "Eurozone banking union" whereby Germany would serve as the paymaster for other nations that required banking bailouts. This proposed solution was also vetoed by Germany. Finally, after much negotiation and debate, the (then) twenty-seven EU member nations agreed on a temporary solution via the European Financial Stability Facility (EFSF) in 2010. This legal instrument aimed at preserving financial stability in Europe by providing assistance to EU states in difficulty. The EFSF could issue bonds or other debt instruments with the support of the German Finance Agency to provide loans to EU nations in trouble, to recapitalize banks, or to buy sovereign debt. In September 2012, the European Stability Mechanism (ESM) was created to replace the EFSF as the permanent firewall for protection of the Eurozone with a maximum lending capacity of €500 billion. All new requests for bailouts will come through the ESM. All ESM applications require that the applicant nation sign a memorandum of understanding concerning the necessary reforms required to bring the nation back to financial stability. It remains to be seen if the maximum lending capacity will be breached and how the process will be handled in an emergency situation. Failure to return the EU to a sustainable financial path may have dire consequences for the EU monetary system.

ISSUES FOR REFORM

The violent fluctuations in exchange rates ever since the inception of the floating-rate era have raised serious questions about the efficiency and desirability of the present arrangements for settlement of international financial obligations. It is evident that the system has not proved to be perfect, and there have been several adverse effects, especially for the less-developed nations of the world. Some of the main issues that have to be addressed in this context are the following:

1. International exchange-rate stability
2. Enhancement of international liquidity
3. A more equitable international monetary system from the point of view of the LDCs
4. Bank reform in national markets (as discussed in the Asian financial crisis section)

INTERNATIONAL EXCHANGE-RATE STABILITY

While there is general agreement that the current state of violent fluctuations in exchange rates is not desirable, there is no definite agreement on how this should be resolved, if such resolution is at all possible.

Some proponents of the extreme view seek a return to the gold standard, citing the stabilizing role of gold and the near-complete exchange stability the world enjoyed during the days of the gold standard. Conditions have since changed drastically, however, and it is hardly likely that there would be enough gold to back the enormous volume of international obligations now in circulation. Another proposal to restore international exchange-rate stability is to return to fixed exchange rates. It is argued that a return to fixed rates would reduce international currency volatility, which would improve international trading efficiency and remove the costs involved in avoiding possible losses because of currency fluctuation. Fixed rates are also claimed to have a moderating influence on domestic monetary and fiscal policies and engender a conservative approach that fosters macroeconomic stability. Moreover, fixed rates would allow a consistent approach toward domestic resource allocation, and the patterns of domestic resource allocation would not have to change to take into account major movements in exchange rate and competitive positions of different industries. Fixed exchange rates also do not permit speculation, which has caused serious disruption in the international markets and substantial losses to persons involved in international trade transactions.

Fixed exchange rates, however, do have downside risks. First, they hold domestic policies ransom to external conditions, as external conditions force changes in domestic policies if exchange rates have to be maintained at a predetermined level. Defending a particular exchange rate requires the maintenance of substantial foreign exchange reserves and incurring considerable losses on the foreign exchange markets during intervention operations. Large reserves tend to be a wasteful use of resources because they do not yield the highest possible rate of return, and return considerations are overshadowed by safety and liquidity requirements. Moreover, some countries, especially the less-developed ones, simply may not have access to sufficient amounts of foreign currencies to maintain the needed levels of exchange reserves.

As of now, it is not likely that the IMS will revert to a system of fixed exchange rates, at least in the foreseeable future, but it does remain as an option at the back of the minds of a large number of international economists.

TARGET ZONES

The target zone arrangement was perhaps the most actively and seriously discussed arrangement of the late 1980s, as an alternative to the present market-based system.[12] The target zone system envisions the establishment of relative wide bands around certain parities, within which currencies of countries participating in the system can fluctuate with reference to one another. Once a currency approaches the limit at the edge of a band, the central banks would intervene in the exchange market to bring it back into line. The major mechanism, however, would be the long-term coordination of national economic policies that would keep the values of participating currencies within the target zones so that frequent intervention by central banks would not be required. The target zone proposal has definite merit, inasmuch as it seeks to provide exchange-rate stability while making necessary provisions for flexibility, which is essential in the current international economic environment. Implementation of target zones, however, faces a number of hurdles. First, there must be agreement on what the range of permitted fluctuations should actually be, and, even before that is determined the basic parity of exchange rates around this range should be established. Second, mechanisms have to be established to prevent speculation in the international foreign exchange markets taking advantage of the system. Third, if the system is to work, a serious commitment is needed from participating countries to coordinate their national economic policies. This commitment, even if made initially, is difficult to maintain, given the varied pressures that national governments face at home. Moreover, with changes in governments taking place periodically, there is no real guarantee that the policy commitments given by one government will be honored by the next.

INTERNATIONAL LIQUIDITY

International liquidity depends on the amounts of internationally acceptable monetary reserves available to different countries. The importance of international liquidity clearly stems from its role in financing the external transactions of all countries. Through the 1980s the liquidity position of the developing countries tended to worsen because of a number of factors: lower export earnings, higher export costs, reduced access to external commercial borrowings because of the debt crisis, large debt-service requirements, and reductions in official development assistance in real terms, all of which have limited the capacity of these countries to continue to finance crucial imports needed for sustaining their ongoing developmental efforts and to give them the elbow room to make necessary adjustments in their economies.

As a result, many developing countries have sought an enhancement of international liquidity through greater access to IMF resources. This access is sought through attempts to increase the quota sizes allocated to different countries. The argument of the developing countries is that the quota sizes should be determined not by the existing criteria, but by assessing the financing requirements of individual countries. A link of SDR allocations to the aid requirements of developing countries has been strongly advocated for several years. This view historically has been opposed by the developed countries, which saw no real need to increase the present level of liquidity in the international economy. Developed countries have historically felt that the resources of the IMF were meant for specific purposes and that the present procedures are designed to ensure their optimal utilization. According to this line of thinking, developmental assistance is best routed through the World Bank, because it is accompanied by serious appraisal and follow-up procedures. Discretionary use of the resources of the IMF could lead to excessive borrowing, which could prove counterproductive and promote a lax attitude toward the tough decisions needed to be taken by the developing countries to improve the efficiency and productivity of their economies. Moreover, according to the industrialized countries, enough resources are available to countries that can prove their creditworthiness to receive them.

Obviously, the historical position of the developed countries in this regard has proven problematic in the wake of the recent financial crisis and the sovereign debt crisis in Europe. The IMF was seen as a funding resource for developed countries such as Iceland, Spain, and Ireland over the last few years, which seems contrary to the traditional viewpoints about when IMF resources should be accessed and to the resultant moral hazard that may ensue when international liquidity is accessed for inappropriate reasons.

A More Equitable International Monetary System

Many developing countries have raised the issue that the international monetary system as it exists today is weighted heavily in favor of the industrialized countries. All key decisions of the IMF, for example, are subject to a veto by the United States, because an 85 percent majority is needed to make these decisions, and the United States holds 16.75 percent of the total votes. Moreover, although the developing countries comprise more than 70 percent of the world's population, their share of IMF votes is only 40 percent. One way for the LDCs to achieve a greater voice in the international monetary arena is an increase in their IMF votes to 50 percent. Little progress has been made in this direction. Another route that can be taken by developing countries is to reduce their reliance on the currencies and financial systems of industrial countries in settling transactions among themselves. As a result, several regional clearing arrangements have been established to promote the use of the currencies of developing countries. Most of them, however, have not been able to achieve any great success because of a number of different problems that have arisen since their introduction. Regional clearing arrangements have not been abandoned, however, and efforts are under way to find ways to make these systems more effective and beneficial to the developing countries. One example of such an arrangement is the Asian Clearing Union.

SUMMARY

The ability to properly value and exchange one currency for another is fundamental to conducting international business. Hard currencies, such as the US dollar, the euro, and the British pound, are easily acquired and disposed of in a free and open market. Soft currencies are not easily exchanged because of government controls. The IMS serves as the basis for currency exchange by establishing the internationally accepted framework and methodologies of valuation.

The early forms of the IMS used gold as the basis for exchanging one currency for another. International events, such as World War I, large balance of payments deficits in the United Kingdom and Europe, and World War II, along with the emergence of the United States as the world's largest creditor, ultimately led to the development of the gold exchange standard at Bretton Woods. The International Monetary Fund was designed to administer and enforce the Bretton Woods Agreement by providing financial assistance for member countries with balance of payments problems through its facilities operations. Gaining IMF assistance, however, required implementation of conditionalities that aimed at stabilizing the economies of borrowers.

Special drawing rights were created as reserve assets by the IMF when the United States began experiencing large balance of payments deficits and gold production could not keep pace with the increasing volume of international trade. Initially fixed in terms of gold, valuation of the SDR in 1974 was changed to a basket of sixteen currencies and, in 2000, a basket of the developed world currencies (the US dollar, the British pound, the euro, and the Japanese yen).

The US dollar was the key component of the Bretton Woods Agreement and provided the liquidity required by the IMS. As US deficits grew, however, confidence in the dollar as a reserve currency fell, requiring its devaluation. Two unsuccessful attempts in 1971 and 1974, along with the abandonment of rights to convert US dollars into gold, resulted in the development of the modern IMS, the floating-rate era. A variety of exchange-rate methods have developed, including managed or dirty floats, crawling pegs, and fixed rates.

The floating-rate era has been harmed by extreme volatility caused by a variety of factors. These include the oil crises of the 1970s, the chronic fiscal and balance of payments deficits of the United States, and the appreciation of the US dollar because of its relative political stability and position as a safe haven. In 1985 and 1987, the Plaza and Louvre agreements, respectively, implemented policies to bring down and then arrest the decline of the value of the US dollar. In the 1990s, the Asian financial crisis exposed the problem of moral hazard in the banking sector in multiple Southeast Asian nations. The aftermath of this crisis was a concentrated effort to improve the risk assessment of credit portfolios for internationally active banks via the Basel Accords. In the next decade, the EU sovereign debt crisis and global recession again exposed the flaws of an inappropriately regulated floating-rate regime.

The current monetary system has clear shortcomings, particularly for developing countries. The current system also is exposed to the recurring theme of government guarantees begetting poor bank lending, with the eventual necessity of a public bailout. Monetary system reformists suggest that new policies be implemented to increase international exchange-rate stability, enhance international liquidity, and lessen the impact of speculation.

DISCUSSION QUESTIONS

1. What is the difference between a hard currency and a soft currency?
2. What was the importance of gold in the early international monetary system? What problems arose under this system?
3. Describe the Bretton Woods Agreement. What position did gold hold in this system?
4. Outline the structure of the International Monetary Fund. What are its aims? What is conditionality?
5. What is a special drawing right?
6. Discuss the difficulties that occurred in the late 1960s and early 1970s that required the United States to abandon the gold exchange system.
7. What is the difference between a pure floating rate and a managed, or dirty, floating rate? Provide an example of currencies that are managed.
8. Why are international exchange-rate stability and liquidity important for conducting international business?

NOTES

1. If a currency is fixed against another currency, any formal upward adjustment of its value against the reference currency is termed a revaluation. Correspondingly, any formal downward adjustment is termed a devaluation.

2. Galbraith, *Money*.

3. This situation prefigures current complaints that China keeps its currency value low by fixing its currency to the US dollar. The primary difference is that the Chinese balance of payments is closer to equilibrium.

4. Another Bretton Woods institution, the World Bank, is discussed in detail in Chapter 6.

5. The largest quota holders as of 2012 are the United States, Japan, Germany, France, and the United Kingdom.

6. The World Bank, as discussed in Chapter 6, provides loans for productive purposes (i.e., projects that improve sectors or industries within the borrowing country).

7. The Communauté Financière Africaine (CFA) franc was formerly tied to the French franc.

8. The ten additional member states in 2004, and the two additional members in 2008, were not given the option of opting out of the currency union.

9. The Copenhagen Inter-Bank Offering Rate (CIBOR) typically has been twenty-five basis points higher than the ECB rate.

10. *Economist*, "Survey of Asian Finance."
11. Krugman, "What Happened in Asia?"
12. Some would call this a non-system.

BIBLIOGRAPHY

Aliber, Robert Z. *The International Money Game*. 2nd ed. New York: Basic Books, 1976.

Deane, Marjorie. "At Quiet Bank-Fund Meetings: Thoughts of Monetary Reform." *Financier* (November 1988): 13–16.

Galbraith, John Kenneth. *Money: Whence It Came and Where It Went*. Boston: Houghton Mifflin, 1995.

Glascock, John L., and Donald J. Meyer. "Assessing the Regulatory Process in an International Context: Mixed Currency SDRs and U.S. Bank Equity Returns." *Atlantic Economic Journal* (March 1988): 39–46.

Heinonen, Kerstin. "The Role and Future of the SDR." *Kansallis-Osake-Pankki Economic Review* (July 1990): 567–77.

Hosefield, J. Keith *The International Monetary Fund, 1945–1965*. Washington, DC: International Monetary Fund, 1969.

International Monetary Fund. "IMS Survey." Washington, DC: International Monetary Fund, October 2004.

International Monetary Fund. *Annual Report*. Washington, DC: International Monetary Fund, 2005.

Krugman, Paul. "What Happened in Asia?" 1998. www.hartford-hwp.com/archives/50/010.html.

Pozo, Susan. "The ECU as International Money." *Journal of International Money and Finance*, June 1987, 195–206.

Saxena, Ramesh B., and Heena R. Bakshi. "IMF Conditionality: A Third World Perspective." *Journal of World Trade*, October 1988, 67–79.

Scammell, William M. *The Stability of the International Monetary System*. Totowa, NJ: Rowman and Littlefield, 1987.

Suzuki, Yoshiro, Junichi Miyake, and Mitsuaki Okabe. *The Evolution of the International Monetary System: How Can Efficiency and Stability Be Attained?* Tokyo: University of Tokyo Press, 1990.

Tew, Brian. *The Evolution of the International Monetary System: 1945–1988*. London: Hutchinson Education, 1988.

Triffin, Robert. *Our International Monetary System: Yesterday, Today and Tomorrow*. New Haven, CT: Yale University Press, 1968.

Ziegler, Dominic. "Survey of Asian Finance," *Economist,* February 8, 2003.

APPENDIX 4.1: BALANCE OF PAYMENTS

The **balance of payments (BOP)** is an accounting system for the financial transactions of a country with the rest of the world. The BOP shows trade inflows and outflows for a country and draws a picture of how the nation has financed its international economic and commercial activities. It measures the value of all export and import goods and services, capital flows, and gold exchanges between a home country and its trading partners. This accounting of the flows of goods and capital between nations provides crucial information in determining a nation's economic health. Thus, it becomes critical information for policy-makers and officials on the domestic front and within supranational organizations, as well as for all international business people, especially potential investors of resources across national borders.

Identifying just how a nation finances its activities and what claims other countries hold on its assets provides one measure of its economic strength. Is the country in a good position to meet claims against its assets? How able is the country to purchase goods or services from other countries? The measures provided by the BOP system are not entirely instructive on an annual basis; what is more important are the displays it shows over time in trading patterns and aggregate annual flows of goods, capital, and reserves between nations.

PRELIMINARY DEFINITIONS

In order to understand the balance of payments, it is important to comprehend some of the terminology used in the process. First of all, the balance of payments is a system based on the double-entry accounting method. Thus, for each transaction, two entries are made: a debit and a credit. For example, if a country imports goods and services, the value of the payment made for such imports will be debited in one account that records transactions relating to trade and credited in other accounts that either record the increase of assets of the country held by foreigners or the decrease in short-term foreign assets held by residents. For example, if the United States imported $50,000 of wines from the United Kingdom, the payment would be recorded as a debit in the current account, which records the transactions in goods and services, and be recorded as a credit in the capital account, which records inflows and outflows of financial assets from the country. The entry in a particular subhead of the capital account will depend upon the manner in which payment is made for imports. If payment is made out of the foreign exchange reserves of the country, the account subhead for the decrease in short-term foreign assets is credited to the account. On the other hand, if the payment is made in the local currency and the local currency continues to be held by the UK firm, then the account subhead credited is the increase in short-term domestic assets held by foreigners.

Because each entry in the balance of payments is matched by an equal and opposite entry by definition, the account has to balance. The following chart illustrates the organization of information in a balance of payments. Table 4.1A is a complete balance of payments for the United States in ten-year intervals from 1960 through 2010. The trade flows are organized into four separate categories or accounts, as described below: the current account, the capital account, the official reserves account, and the net statistical discrepancy.

Information on the flow of goods in and out of a country is usually provided by customs information collected as merchandise crosses international borders. Information on service flows is generally estimated through the use of statistical sampling of actual expenditures. Information on payments made for exports and imports, as well as outflows and inflows because of credit and capital flows, is provided by commercial banks. Financial institutions also provide information on capital and credit flows across the borders of a country. Finally, the monetary authority or central bank of each country reports official borrowings, and each country maintains its own accounts. In the United States, the Department of Commerce maintains the records of national accounts. The figures for each country are then synthesized by two agencies, the United Nations and the International Monetary Fund, into an aggregate global snapshot of flows between nations.

Table 4.1A   Balance of Payments Trends for the United States
US International Transactions Account Data (ten-year intervals in millions of dollars)

	1960	1970	1980	1990	2000	2010
Current account						
1. Goods, balance of payment basis	$19,650	$42,469	$224,250	$387,401	$784,781	$1,288,882
2. Services	$6,290	$14,171	$47,584	$147,832	$288,002	$553,603
3. Income receipts	$4,616	$11,748	$72,606	$171,742	$352,478	$676,282
4. Exports of goods and services and income receipts	**$30,556**	**$68,387**	**$344,440**	**$706,975**	**$1,425,260**	**$2,518,767**
5. Goods, balance of payments basis	$(14,758)	$(39,866)	$(249,750)	$(498,438)	$(1,230,568)	$(1,934,006)
6. Services	$(7,674)	$(14,520)	$(41,491)	$(117,659)	$(218,964)	$(403,216)
7. Income payments	$(1,238)	$(5,515)	$(42,532)	$(143,192)	$(333,300)	$(492,423)
8. Imports of goods and services and income payments	**$(23,670)**	**$(59,901)**	**$(333,774)**	**$(759,290)**	**$(1,782,832)**	**$(2,829,645)**
9. Unilateral current transfers, net	**$(4,062)**	**$(6,156)**	**$(8,349)**	**$(26,654)**	**$(58,767)**	**$(131,074)**
10. Balance on current account (lines 4, 8, and 9)	**$2,824**	**$2,331**	**$2,317**	**$(78,968)**	**$(416,338)**	**$(441,951)**
11. Capital account						
12. Capital account transactions, net	**$0**	**$0**	**$0**	**$(7,220)**	**$(1)**	**$(157)**
13. Financial account						
14. US owned assets abroad, excluding financial derivatives (increase/financial outflow (−))	$(4,099)	$(9,337)	$(86,967)	$(81,234)	$(560,523)	$(939,484)
15. Foreign-owned assets in the United States, excluding financial derivatives (increase/financial outflow (+))	$2,294	$7,226	$63,037	$139,357	$1,038,224	$1,308,279
16. Financial derivatives, net	$	$	$	$	$	$14,076
17. Balance on capital account (lines 12, 14–16)	**$(1,805)**	**$(2,111)**	**$(24,930)**	**$50,903**	**$477,700**	**$382,714**
18. Statistical discrepancy (errors and omissions)						
19. Statistical discrepancy (sum of lines 10 and 17 with sign reversed)	**$(1,019)**	**$(219)**	**$(22,613)**	**$28,066**	**$(61,361)**	**$(59,237)**

Source: US Bureau of Economic Analysis, 2012, www.bea.gov/international/.

The position of a country in any of these accounts is in equilibrium when outflows equal inflows; it is in deficit when outflows of foreign exchange because of imports and other payments exceed inflows because of exports or other receipts. A country can be in surplus when total foreign exchange inflows exceed total outflows. The final balance is done in an attempt to capture a history of all flows between nations, whether they are because of reserves of gold, currencies, foodstuffs, manufactured goods, investments of home country funds abroad, the provision of insurance, travel facilities, and hotel accommodations or other services.

Current Account

The **current account** takes note of three separate types of flows between nations, similar to the concept of revenues (credits) and expenses (debits) in business operations. The first type of transfer is **visibles**: financial inflows and outflows arising out of actual exchanges of merchandise between countries through exporting and importing. Exports add to the account and imports subtract from the balance of the account. The net position of this section of the BOP is the **balance of trade** (BOT).

Flows of imports and exports are not only evaluated according to volumes, but also according to the **terms of trade** of a nation. Terms of trade refer to the ratio of the export prices of a country to its import prices. A rise in export prices in relation to import prices improves the balance of trade if the trade volumes remain constant. Generally, rising prices for exports will tend to eventually squeeze the volume of exports in relation to imports. Quantities of goods traded between nations tend to change slowly; thus initially a rise in the terms of trade will improve a country's trade balance in the short term, with deleterious effects on the balance becoming apparent only in the long term.

The second category of transfers within the current account are **invisibles**: services between nations, including such items as transportation of people or goods, tourist services provided by other countries, supplying insurance for foreign policy buyers, international consulting services, and such financial and banking services as loans or fees for establishing lines of credit or acting as brokers in foreign exchange transactions. This category also includes the transfer of investment income from international investments overseas back to home-country residents and the remittance of profits back to parent corporations. These transfers are considered to be income resulting from the employment of production factors abroad, such as investment capital. The actual movement of the factors of production, that is, capital in the form of dollars going into plant and equipment overseas, is differentiated as a capital movement because the factor itself is moved across borders.

The third category within the current account keeps track of unilateral (or unrequited) transfers by countries to other countries, which is the flow of funds or goods for which no quid pro quo is expected. These items include aid provided by a government or private interests to other countries, which can be in the form of grants issued by the government, money sent home to their families by immigrants, and private funding and aid by foundations and international aid agencies, such as the Red Cross. Unrequited transfers can be private funding and aid by foundations and international aid agencies that provide financial and physical assistance in the event of national disasters. Unrequited transfers are made to institutions and private individuals alike.

The current account is considered the most important of the four BOP accounts because it measures all income-producing activity generated through foreign trade and is considered the prime indicator of the trading health of a nation. A balance of trade deficit, however, is not in itself a negative condition in certain instances, and it could be considered normal for a country as long as other services, transfers, and capital accounts can finance the deficit within the merchandise sector. Some countries have chronic balance of trade deficits but are economically healthy, because of their strength in other sectors, such as Switzerland, whose forte is the financial services sector. Other countries exhibit continuing deficits in their balances of trade because they are in the process of development.

The balance of trade and the current account are not the only indicators of the position of a country. The history and level of development of a nation must also be considered in assessing its relative health. Another important indicator in weighing national economic strength in relation to other countries is the BOP capital account.

Capital Account

The **capital account** of a nation measures its net changes in financial assets and liabilities abroad. It also chronicles the flow of investment funds across national borders. The capital account notes an inflow when residents of a country receive funds from foreign investors. These funds may be invested in stocks (equity) or bonds (debt) or any other financial assets that foreign owners hold and for which resident borrowers are liable for payment. The resident is then required to remit to the foreign financiers returns on the investment in the form of dividends or profits. Naturally, an outflow of funds occurs when a resident of the home country acquires assets abroad; the overseas counterpart then incurs an international liability.

The capital account is made up of three separate segments. The first is long-term capital movements, which can be in the form of either direct or portfolio investments. Direct investments are those made by individuals or multinational corporations in facilities or assets abroad where the investor has control over the use and disposition of the assets. For balance of payment purposes, effective control is determined as that time when foreign owners from one country hold more than 50 percent of voting stock or when a single resident or an organized group from one country owns more than 25 percent of voting stock in a foreign company.

Long-term portfolio investments are those in which investors contribute capital to a foreign concern and invest their funds in stocks or bonds but do not control the facility or the assets of the enterprise. These investments are considered long-term if they are held for more than a year. Portfolio investments that mature in less than a year are considered short-term capital flows, the third segment of the capital account. Some short-term movements are considered as being compensatory, in that they finance other activities, such as those in the current account. Others represent autonomous international financial movements undertaken for their own sake in order to speculate on fluctuations in exchange and interest rates. Many of these actions consist of trading and hedging activity undertaken in international financial forward, futures, options, and swaps markets.

These capital outflows can have the effect of increasing aggregate demand overseas or of displacing exports from the home country. By the same token, however, investment outflows may also provide for returns from abroad in the form of dividends, profits, or increased equity.

Official Reserves Account

This balance of payments account exists for government use only, to account for the official reserves position of one government against other; that is, it reflects the actual holdings of a country and what might be the equivalent of cash or near-cash assets for a corporate entity. This account reflects holdings of gold and foreign exchange. It also takes into account loans between governments and decreases and increases in liabilities to foreign central banks and the country's balance in special drawing rights with the International Monetary Fund.

Net Statistical Discrepancy

In theory, the balance of payments should balance perfectly within the account of one single country and among all countries of the world as trade flows progress in an orderly fashion and as all nations of the world report those flows consistently and accurately. In actuality, this scenario is far from the truth, because of differences in accounting practices, functions, mistakes, and unsanctioned transfers of funds between countries through *smuggling*, underground economic activity, and the sale of illegal items. Thus, the balance of payments includes a separate account that adjusts for these discrepancies, which can be sizable amounts. In 2010, for example, the *net statistical discrepancy* (also known as the errors and omissions account) for the US balance of payments reached $59 billion.[11]

PROBLEMS IN BALANCE OF PAYMENTS

Balance of payments problems occur when a country's external assets or liabilities increase beyond proportion—that is, when the balance of payments shows either a surplus or deficit of external resources. Although surpluses and deficits in the balance of payments are a normal feature, they pose a problem when they are excessive and persistent to a point where they cannot be sustained. While surpluses also pose certain problems for a country, it is the deficits that present the real difficulties. Deficits generally occur when a country is not able to match the outflows of foreign exchange because of imports, debt service, or other payments with its export or other inflows. If the deficit remains persistent, a country is faced with several options:

- The country can borrow from other governments and multilateral institutions (e.g., the IMF) to fill the gap between the inflows and outflows.
- The country can draw down its level of foreign exchange reserves to meet the shortfall.
- The country can devalue its currency in order to make exports attractive and imports unattractive, so that the gap between inflows and outflows is corrected.
- The country can make fundamental adjustments in its economy to reduce the outflows and increase the inflows of foreign exchange, which could include reducing the level of nonessential imports, controlling local inflation, improving domestic productivity and efficiency, and improving the allocative efficiency of the economy.

The issue of BOP problems has attracted considerable attention, especially after 1973, when the less-developed countries of the world faced huge increases in their oil bills, which increased their expenditures of foreign exchange and, by creating a recession in Western countries, reduced their foreign exchange earnings. BOP difficulties lead to problems in the domestic sector. When external creditors find that a country is not able to service its borrowings, they are reluctant to lend it additional money or tend to charge higher rates of interest for a perceived higher risk. The country facing the crisis loses access to external credit with which to finance essential imports for meeting developmental and consumer needs. Moreover, it is not easy to make fundamental economic adjustments. Many developing countries have large sections of population at or below poverty levels, and any economic adjustment measures calling for reduction in government subsidies or assistance for these sections of the population are not likely to be politically acceptable. Moreover, entrenched vested interests in different sectors of the economy are eager to maintain the status quo and may even resort to disruptive activities to prevent their privileges from being disturbed.

The intention of the adjustment measures, however, has a reasonably sound theoretical basis. Devaluing the currency to bring it closer to its actual market value boosts exports and discourages imports by making them more expensive. Controlling inflation also increases export competitiveness, as does the increase in productivity and efficiency of the domestic industries. Reducing the demand for imports automatically reduces the outflows of foreign exchange.

Although the BOP problems can be resolved through these actions, there is considerable cost involved. Devaluation can lead to an increase in domestic inflation because import prices will be higher. Moreover, the advantage of devaluation is lost if the export sector of a country is using a large proportion of imported inputs. The terms of trade of a country also worsen with devaluation, as it is forced to part with a greater quantity of exports for the same quantity of imports. Reduction in import demand leads to economic slowdowns, which exacerbate existing problems of stagnant growth and high unemployment. Additionally, any government intervention in the financial markets is not performed in a vacuum. If a sovereign entity attempts to orchestrate BOP improvement, other nations may follow suit.

The policy-makers of a country, therefore, have to tread very carefully and balance these diverse and often conflicting considerations while attempting to correct imbalances in the position of their external payments. Creditors, trading partners, and multilateral institutions play a vital role in determining the success of the efforts of a country to resolve BOP problems. If they follow supportive policies, a country can overcome its fundamental constraints and recover its external balance. Its problems can be exacerbated, however, if the creditors and trading partners follow a "beggar thy neighbor" policy, for example, by indulging in competitive devaluation or manipulating interest rates to attract foreign capital that might be needed by other countries in difficulty.

US Trade Deficits

The historical position of the United States in world trade illustrates these problems. Some form of balance of payments statistics have been maintained by the US government since 1790, when America had a deficit of $1 million in goods and services.[2] In the twentieth century, the United States had a positive balance in goods and services for more than six decades. During that period, the largest surpluses were during the war years of 1943 and 1944, when surpluses were $11.038 billion and $12.452 billion, respectively, reflecting US exports directed toward the war effort. In 1947 the balance in goods and services also reflected US efforts toward war-torn countries, and the surplus was $11.617 billion.[3]

In the late 1960s the US balance of payments began to come under pressure, and in the 1970s the current account began to show substantial deficits. A number of factors contributed to the reversal of trends, including the huge increase in US imports, the emergence of strong competition in world export markets from Europe and Japan, and the quadrupling in the price of oil.

In the 1980s the situation continued to worsen. Imports rose from $333 billion in 1980 to nearly $500 billion in 1986. On the other hand, exports remained relatively stagnant, growing only marginally from $342 billion to $372 billion over this period. The large gap between inflows and outflows because of exports and imports was financed primarily by private capital transfers into the United States. The effect of the private capital flows into the United States nullified the effect of the huge trade deficit on the US currency, which continued to appreciate between 1980 and 1985.

The strength of the dollar, however, further weakened US competitiveness in international markets, enabling Europe, Japan, and some of the Pacific Rim countries to build substantial market shares not only in overseas markets, but also in the US domestic market. In fact, the years of an overvalued dollar had tended to make the deficit structural, or built-in, in character, which occurred because overseas manufactures, taking advantage of the high dollar, were able to underprice their products and capture US domestic market shares in such areas as consumer electronics and automobiles. Having achieved market penetration, the long period of dollar overvaluation gave overseas exporters opportunity to consolidate and secure their gains by building dealer networks, after-sales service arrangements, and consumer brand loyalty. Thus, even though the dollar depreciated substantially after 1985, there was no significant drop in either the market shares covered by the overseas exporters or the overall volume of imports.

The widening of the current account deficit has only worsened since the 1990s. The increased competition from China and Southeast Asia led to the movement of many manufacturing jobs from the United States to the Asian continent; and this led to the further decrease in the amount of manufacturing output in the United States from the 1990s to the present. The US has continued to maintain a surplus in the trade of invisibles (or services) with the rest of the world. The US dollar began to depreciate heavily against the euro and the yen over the last few years, which has tended to make US exports priced more favorably abroad, and imports to the US priced less favorably. It remains to be seen just how long the dollar will drop and what affect this will have on the balance of payments of the United States in the coming years.

Given the size of the economy, however, the trade deficits do not create a calamity. While there is cause for concern and reason for remedial action, there is no reason for panic, both because of the size of the deficit and its nature.

Some analysts, such as economist Robert B. Reich, believe that attention should be focused on the reasons behind these deficits. For example, the United States currently runs a deficit with China and much of the rest of Asia. Some Americans worry about this situation, but Reich asks exactly what are US interests in world trade and who are "we." He notes that while Americans are exporting less, they may not be selling fewer goods in world markets because "these days about half of the total exports of American multinational corporations come from their factories in other countries," compared to a one-third equivalent twenty years ago.[4] Thus, he maintains that nearly one-third of our imbalance with the Pacific Rim countries, for example, results from the multinationalization of industry and US subsidiaries making products there and selling them back to Americans on domestic soil. He also notes that some US companies are key export players in other market arenas. Many large US companies, for example, have moved overseas in the past few years to capitalize on the low wage rates in countries such as India and China.

APPENDIX 4.1 DISCUSSION QUESTIONS

1. What is the balance of payments?
2. What are the four basic accounts under the balance of payments?
3. Name a source for the US balance of payments. What source(s) exist for international balance of payments?
4. Examine the US balance of payments (Table 4.1A). What do you observe about the current account over time? Are US exports greater or less than US imports? Do services improve the merchandise import and export balance?

APPENDIX 4.1 NOTES

1. US Bureau of Economic Analysis.
2. US Department of Commerce, *Historical Statistics of the United States*.
3. Ibid.
4. Reich, "The Trade Gap."

APPENDIX 4.1 BIBLIOGRAPHY

Asheghian, Parvis. "The Impact of Devaluation on the Balance of Payments of Less Developed Countries: A Monetary Approach." *Journal of Economic Development* (July 1985): 143–151.

Business Council for International Understanding. Descriptive brochure. Washington, DC, 2003.

Crook, Olive. "One Armed Policy Maker." *Economist* (September 1988): 51–57.

Gladwell, Malcolm. "Scientist Warns of U.S. Reliance on Foreigners." *Washington Post*, September 9, 1988.

Gray, H. Peter, and Gail E. Makinen. "Balance of Payments Contributions of Multinational Corporations." *Journal of Business* (July 1967): 339–343.

International Monetary Fund. *Balance of Payments Yearbook*. Washington, DC: International Monetary Fund (annual).

McGraw, Thomas K. *America Versus Japan*. Boston: Harvard Business School Press, 1986.

Nakamal, Tadashi. "Growth Matters More Than Surpluses." *Euromoney* (February 1984): 101–103.

Obstfeld, Maurice. "Balance of Payments Crises and Devaluation." *Journal of Money, Banking and Credit* (May 1984): 208–217.

Reich, Robert B. "The Trade Gap: Myths and Crocodile Tears." *New York Times*, February 2, 1988.

Solop, Joanne, and Erich Spitaller. "Why Does the Current Account Matter?" *International Monetary Fund Staff Papers* (March 1980): 101–134.

Striner, Herbert E. *Regaining the Lead: Polities for Economic Growth*. New York: Praeger, 1984.

US Bureau of Economic Analysis. www.bea.gov/international/.

US Department of Commerce. *Historical Statistics of the United States: Colonial Times to 1970*. 1976.

World Bank. *The World Development Report, 2003*. Washington, DC: Oxford University Press, 2003.

Yoder, Stephen Kreider. "All Eyes Are on MITI Research Wish List." Washington, DC: *Wall Street Journal*, April 29, 1988.

CASE STUDY 4.1

GLOBAL BANK CORPORATION

Global Bank Corporation is a major international bank headquartered in New York City, with branches in eleven other countries: Australia, Brazil, Canada, Dubai, France, Germany, Great Britain, Hong Kong, Japan, Netherlands, and Singapore. Total assets in 2010 were $90 billion, and the bank was among the top 500 banks in the world. The bank is organized into three main divisions: retail banking, institutional banking, and investment banking. Global retail banking undertakes transactions with individual customers—for example, savings accounts, checking and money market accounts, issuance of certificates of deposit, operation of auto-mated teller machines, loans to individual customers for different purchases, funds transfer facilities, and so on. The institutional banking division carries out business with the bank's institutional and corporate customers: the trusts of major companies and other large clients. Much of the work of the institutional banking division is concerned with devising comprehensive financing arrangements for its clients. The investment banking division of Global has three main functional areas:

1. The capital markets group, which provides a wide range of services to companies seeking to raise funds in the international financial markets
2. The private banking group, which provides fund management and advisory services to large net worth clients
3. The foreign exchange division, which carries out exchange trading, handles foreign exchange transactions, and provides advisory services

The foreign exchange trading function of the bank is decentralized to levels of operation for each country and further to each individual trading operation. Each level of decentralization, however, has to operate within established trading and exposure limits that are laid down by the corporate risk management committee of the bank, which meets every month at the headquarters in New York City. A typical trading operation at Global Bank Corporation is divided into two main areas: interbank exchange market trading and customer-based trading. The former is primarily a speculative operation aimed at generating substantial profits for the bank from interbank trading, while the latter operation provides customers with a wide range of foreign exchange services, ranging from risk management to a simple sale or purchase of different foreign currencies. The interbank trading division has been fairly successful in the past four years and has consistently made profits, although the level of profits has varied over the years. The main focus of the trading activity is the Tokyo, New York, and London markets. At other centers, the trading operations of the bank are more oriented toward meeting the foreign exchange needs of customers.

In the past twenty years, the Singapore and Hong Kong markets have become extremely active and a large number of international banks have set up trading operations to generate profits from the booming interbank market. The investment banking division is planning to set up new operations in this area. Both markets have an environment relatively free of regulation and excellent communication and other infrastructural facilities for establishing trading operations. Hong Kong seems to be a less stable alternative because the pro-business climate there could eventually be hindered by decisions of the Chinese government. While the Chinese government has said that Hong Kong will operate as it has historically, some business leaders and political activists in Hong Kong fear that free speech will be eliminated by new regulations out of the mainland. While this has not occurred as of this time, business professionals in Hong Kong remain skeptical.

Singapore, therefore, seems a better choice for Global Bank Corporation's new operations. Singapore has all of the technological advantages of Hong Kong without the political uncertainty. Despite its advantages, however, the possibility of establishing a new interbank trading center in Singapore has given rise to some doubts. The bank has not opened a new trading center for the past seven years and will have to

(continued)

Case Study 4.1 *(continued)*

hire a new team. Some senior investment banking division executives feel that while interbank trading is a good source of profit that helps to strengthen the company's bottom line, it is also risky. Having a fourth interbank trading operation will increase the overall exposure of the bank and will make controls more difficult to enforce. Other executives feel that because the exchange market is an around-the-clock operation, a presence in the Singapore market will allow the bank to have an active presence in all time zones and increase the effectiveness of overall global trading operations. Further, the proponents of the Singapore trading location argue that once this trading location has stabilized, a fifth location can be opened somewhere in the Middle East, for example, in Bahrain. The profits from the Singapore trading center in the interbank market could be used for aggressive pricing of corporate foreign exchange products to later capture increased market share.

DISCUSSION QUESTIONS

1. Should Global Bank Corporation set up a new foreign exchange operation at Singapore? If so, what functions, such as interbank trading or customer Telex sources, should be given priority?
2. What additional information would you consider relevant in evaluating a proposal to set up a new foreign exchange trading operation?

CASE STUDY 4.2

SCRINTON TECHNOLOGIES

The party at the banquet hall of Grosvenor House Hotel in London is a glittering affair. Dozens of top bankers, CEOs of industrial companies, and important government officials are attending the formal celebration marking the commissioning of Scrinton Technologies' new plant in Southampton, England, which will be manufacturing a small range of state-of-the-art medical diagnostic equipment, including computer-enhanced imagery and high-tech scanning systems. Scrinton is a world leader in diagnostic equipment, and the new plant represents the most advanced manufacturing facility of its type in the world. Only Scrinton's own plant in Sacramento, California, approaches this facility in technical sophistication and advanced production equipment and processes.

The Southampton plant was a major commitment for Scrinton, involving an outlay of US$110 million. Scrinton's top management had viewed this project as a strategic move, to have a manufacturing facility in Europe. At the same time, it was considered essential that only the newest technology and processes be used in the plant to ensure products of futuristic sophistication and unquestioned quality and reliability. The European market is large and growing, but at the same time highly sophisticated and competitive. Competition is particularly strong from German and Swiss companies, many of which have been supplying hospital equipment to medical centers all over Europe for several decades. Although it lacked the long-standing relationships of its competitors, Scrinton was confident that, with its edge in technology, it would be able to catch up with the competition and successfully wrest market share. Some European hospitals and clinics already use Scrinton's equipment and appreciate the quality and reliability of the company's products. The need to keep a distinct technological edge over the competition, now and in the future, meant that the company had to find considerable resources to finance this ambitious and extremely expensive venture.

Scrinton had decided to go ahead with the Southampton plant. The financing was raised from five sources:

1. Syndicated Euromarket loan: US$40 million
2. Bond issue in the US market repayable in seven years: US$38 million
3. Long-term loan from a consortium of major main commercial banks: US$16 million
4. Equity issue on Wall Street: US$12 million
5. Internal resources: US$4 million

The project took three years to complete, and the debt service schedule of Scrinton UK, a wholly owned subsidiary that had taken the loans and made the equity and bond issues, was repayment of the bank loan in five years, repayment of the syndicated loan in seven years, and redemption of the bond issue in seven years.

Revenues of the company would be principally in three currencies: pounds sterling, euros, and Swiss francs. It was decided not to invoice products in other currencies, and as a matter of policy, all attempts would be made to invoice in only these currencies. Exceptions would be made only in rare cases, generally when a particular sale was of strategic or critical importance to the company.

The company expects to make substantial sales and generate adequate revenue to cover its entire amortization schedule (see below) without any need to draw on the resources of the parent company, but a major issue remains: the possible fluctuation of interest and exchange rates over the life of the repayment plan. The company is

(continued)

Case Study 4.2 *(continued)*

exposed because its syndicated loan in the Euromarket is at variable rates, and its liability could increase substantially if interest rates go up. Further, although its revenues are going to be denominated in three European currencies, it has substantial liabilities in US dollars, and any major appreciation of the dollar against the European currencies would place the entire debt servicing of the project in serious jeopardy.

Bill Smythe, finance director of Scrinton UK, is concerned about these issues as he makes small talk with a London investment banker at the party. "I'll deal with this in the morning," he thinks, forcing the problem away and beginning to pay more attention to his companion, who has moved away from the subject of a possible minicrash in the stock market in the next three months to the timelier subject of the latest rumors about the British royal family.

The next morning, Bill Smythe looks over the projection of estimated revenues for each year. The pound liability is apparently no problem from an exchange-risk point of view, because the pound revenues of the company are sufficient to cover the liability. The syndicated loan, however, is at a variable rate of 0.25 percent over the London interbank offered rate (LIBOR). If LIBOR moves up, the value of the pound liability could increase considerably, significantly increasing the company's debt service costs.

The dollar borrowings present a bigger problem. Both exchange-rate and interest-rate exposure are present because the repayment obligations are denominated in dollars. Further, the long-term loan from the consortium of banks is at a variable rate of 0.5 percent over the prime rate.

"There are so many options available to hedge these risks," thinks Smythe, "but should we? After all, there is going to be a substantial hedging cost and I wonder whether it will be worth the cost."

DISCUSSION QUESTIONS

1. What are the main options for dealing with the company's exposure?
2. Under what circumstances would the company suffer the greatest loss if its exposure were left completely uncovered?

Syndicated Euromarket Loan (in millions of US dollars)

Year	Principal	Interest	Total
1	5	0.6	5.6
2	5	0.6	5.6
3	5	0.5	5.5
4	5	0.5	5.5
5	5	0.4	5.4
6	5	0.3	5.3
7	10	0.3	10.2

Long-Term Consortium Loan (in millions of US dollars)

Year	Principal	Interest	Total
1	2	0.25	2.25
2	2	0.25	2.25
3	2	0.25	3.25
4	2	0.25	3.25
5	6	0.25	6.25

Bond Issue (in millions of US dollars)

Year	Principal	Interest	Total
1	0.4		0.4
2	0.4		0.4
3	0.4		0.4
4	0.4		0.4
5	0.4		0.4
6	0.4		0.4
7	0.4	38	38.4

Total Dollar Liability

Year	Amount (in millions)
1	2.65
2	2.65
3	3.65
4	3.65
5	6.65
6	0.40
7	38.40

Estimated Revenues (in millions)

Year	Euro	Swiss Franc	Pound
1	35.00	30.00	15.00
2	38.50	33.60	17.83
3	42.50	37.60	19.83
4	46.50	42.10	22.80
5	51.00	47.00	26.22
6	56.10	52.60	30.15
7	61.71	58.90	

CHAPTER 5

Foreign Exchange Markets

"Two and two are four, and five will get you ten if you know how to work it."
—Mae West

CHAPTER OBJECTIVES

This chapter will:

- Suggest the underlying need for foreign exchange markets
- Introduce the terms and definitions used in the foreign exchange markets
- Describe the structure and operations of the foreign exchange markets
- Present the mathematical formulas used to compare currency movements in the foreign exchange markets
- Discuss common techniques used to manage currency risk and exposure
- Explain the need for and problems associated with forecasting foreign exchange rates

---

BACKGROUND

Nearly all international business activity requires the transfer of money from one country to another. Trade transactions must be settled in monetary terms: Buyers in one country pay suppliers in another. Repatriation of dividends, profits, and royalties from overseas investments, contributions of equity and other kinds of financial dealings from such investments also involve the transfer of funds across national borders. The transfer of funds poses problems quite different from those associated with the transfer of goods and services across national borders. Buyers and sellers are willing to accept and use goods and services from other countries quite routinely. For example, US consumers are content to drive Japanese cars, such as Toyotas and Hondas, while the Japanese are quite willing to use US operating systems or other high-tech products.

This internationalization that applies to product usage is not found when it comes to accepting the currency of another country, however. While the US importer is happy to receive Japanese products and the Japanese importer is glad to accept US products, neither is normally in a position to accept the other's currency. A US importer usually has to pay a Japanese exporter in Japanese yen, while a US exporter will generally want to be paid in US dollars. This is quite logical, since each country has its own currency, which is legal tender within its borders, and exporters are likely to prefer the currency that they can use at home for meeting costs and taking profits.

A US importer who must pay a Japanese exporter has to acquire Japanese yen. To do so, he must exchange his own currency, dollars, into yen. Such an exchange of one currency for another is called a **foreign exchange** transaction.

For example, a German company invests in an electronics manufacturing facility in Australia. Therefore, it must convert its euros into Australian dollars to meet project costs in Australia. In another example, a US multinational has a plant located in Great Britain. At the end of the financial year, it wants to repatriate its profits to corporate headquarters in the United States. Therefore, it will convert British pounds sterling—profits earned by the plant in Great Britain—into US dollars. As another example, suppose a Japanese investor has a large stock holding on Wall Street. After a rally in which her holdings appreciate substantially, she wants to repatriate her profits to Japan. To do so, she would convert her US dollar profits into Japanese yen.

How do the German company, the US multinational, and the Japanese investor convert the currency in their possession into the currency they desire? The answer is provided by the foreign exchange markets.

THE STRUCTURE OF THE FOREIGN EXCHANGE MARKETS

The need to convert one currency into another currency gives rise to the demand for foreign exchange transactions. The foreign exchange markets of the world serve as the mechanism through which these numerous and complex transactions are completed efficiently and almost instantaneously.

The main intermediaries in the foreign exchange markets are major banks worldwide that deal in foreign exchange. These banks are linked together by a very advanced and sophisticated telecommunications network that connects them with major clients and other banks around the world. There is no physical contact between the dealers of various banks in the foreign exchange markets, unlike in the stock exchanges or the futures markets, which have specific trading floors or pits.

Banks that are active in foreign exchange operations set up extremely sophisticated facilities for their foreign exchange traders in trading (or dealing) rooms, which are equipped with instantaneous telecommunication facilities. A very important feature of modern trading rooms is their access to information about political, economic, and other current events as they unfold. A major source of this information is the British news agency Reuters, which furnishes subscribing banks with a dedicated communication system that provides on-screen information beamed from the central newsroom of the agency. There are also many services, including Reuters and Telerate, which provide up-to-the-second information on the prevailing exchange rates quoted by banks worldwide. Any changes in exchange rates anywhere in the world can be immediately brought to the notice of traders.

Exchange trading is an extremely specialized operation that puts enormous pressure on traders because rates change rapidly, providing chances to make huge profits or incur massive losses. Bank management continually monitors the activity and progress of its dealing rooms, while setting very clear guidelines in order to limit the level of risk the traders can take while trading currencies on behalf of the bank.

To relieve traders from the task of booking orders, trading rooms are supported by backup accounting departments that record the transactions made by the traders and do the necessary computations to track the trading activity. They also supply the traders with background data and analytical reports to optimize the traders' strategy and performance. Such information is fed into electronic trading boards that are clearly visible to traders. Generally, this information includes the risk exposure of the bank in each currency and the current rates for different currencies, as well as a host of other information.

Exchange trading at a bank usually begins every day in the early morning with an in-house conference of traders and senior managers to discuss the currency expectations and the strategy for the day. Most trading is conducted during local business hours, but the ease of communication made possible by the latest technology enables banks to continue to trade with banks in other time zones after the local business day is over. Therefore, some major banks have a system of shifts, allowing traders to come in at night to trade in markets in different time zones. By using night trading desks, many major banks have been able to establish twenty-four-hour trading operations.

There are two levels in the foreign exchange markets. One is the customer, or retail, market, in which individuals or institutions buy and sell foreign currencies to banks dealing in foreign exchange. For example, if IBM wishes to repatriate profits from its German subsidiary to the United States, it can approach a bank in Frankfurt with an offer to sell its euros in exchange for US dollars. This type of transaction occurs in what is called the customer market.

Suppose the bank does not have a sufficient amount of US dollars to exchange for the subsidiary's euros. In this situation the bank can approach other banks to acquire dollars in exchange for euros or some other currency. Such sales and purchases, termed interbank transactions, collectively constitute the interbank market. Interbank transactions are both local and international.

The interbank market is extremely active. Banks purchase currencies from and sell currencies to one another to meet shortages and reduce surpluses that result from transactions with their customers. Transactions in the interbank markets are almost always in large sums. Amounts less than US$250,000 are not traded in interbank markets. Values of interbank transactions usually range from US$1 million to US$10 million per transaction, although deals involving amounts above this range are also known to take place. A large proportion of the transactions in interbank markets arise from banks trading currencies to make profits from movements in exchange rates around the world.

It is important to note that in all this trading activity in foreign exchange markets, billions of dollars of international currency are exchanged without any physical transfer of money. How are the transactions settled? The answer lies in a system of mutual account maintenance. Banks in one country maintain accounts at banks in other countries. These accounts are generally denominated in the home currency of the bank with the account. In banking parlance these are called *vostro* accounts, which essentially means "your account with us," or *nostro* accounts, which means "our account with you." Thus, if Citigroup New York has a euro account with Deutsche Bank in Frankfurt, it will term the Deutsche account its nostro account. For Deutsche, this will be a vostro account. Similarly, Deutsche Bank would have a US dollar account with Citibank or another bank in the United States. For Deutsche this will be a nostro account, while for the US bank it will be a vostro account. Foreign exchange transactions are settled by debits or credits to nostro and vostro accounts.

MARKET PARTICIPANTS

The foreign exchange markets have many different types of participants. These participants differ not only in the scale of their operations but also in their objectives and methods of functioning.

INDIVIDUALS

Individuals may participate in foreign exchange markets for personal as well as business needs. An example of a personal need would be sending a monetary gift to an overseas relative. To send the gift, the individual would utilize the market to obtain the currency of the relative's country. Individual business needs arise when a person is involved in international business. For example, individual importers use the foreign exchange markets to obtain the currencies needed to pay their overseas suppliers. Exporters, on the other hand, use the markets to convert the currencies received from their foreign buyers into domestic or other currencies. Business or leisure travelers also participate in the foreign exchange markets by buying and selling foreign and local currencies to meet expenses on their overseas trips.

INSTITUTIONS

Institutions are very important participants in the foreign exchange markets because of their large and varied currency requirements. Multinational corporations typically are major participants in the foreign markets, continually transferring large sums of currencies across national borders, a process that usually requires the exchange of one currency for another. Multinational corporations utilize foreign exchange markets to hedge transactions conducted in more than one currency whereby the initial exchange rate at the time a transaction is agreed will remain constant once the deal is settled at a future date. Corporations that utilize foreign exchange as a hedging tool have decided that they are not in the currency speculation business and are seeking to minimize the effects of currency movements on their business transactions, operating performance, and financial statements. Financial institutions that have international investments are also important foreign exchange market participants. These institutions include pension funds, insurance companies, mutual funds, and investment banks. They need to switch their multicurrency investments quite often, generating substantial transaction volumes in the foreign exchange markets.

Apart from meeting their basic transaction needs, both the individual and institutional participants use the foreign exchange markets to reduce the risks they incur because of adverse fluctuations in exchange rates.

BANKS

Banks are the largest and most active participants in the foreign exchange markets. Banks operate in the foreign exchange markets through their traders. (British banks and many others use the term "exchange dealer" rather than "exchange trader." These terms can be used interchangeably.) Exchange traders at banks buy and sell currencies, acting on the requests of their customers and on behalf of the bank itself.

Customer-requested transactions form a very small proportion of trading operations by banks in the foreign exchange markets. To a very large extent, banks treat foreign exchange market operations as an independent profit center. In fact, some major banks make substantial profits on the strength of their market expertise, information, trading skills, and ability to hold on to risky investments that would not be feasible for smaller participants. On occasion, banks can also incur substantial losses. As a result, foreign exchange operations are closely monitored by bank management teams.

CENTRAL BANKS AND OTHER OFFICIAL PARTICIPANTS

Central banks enter the foreign exchange markets for a variety of reasons. They can buy substantial amounts of foreign currencies to either build up their foreign exchange reserves or bring down the value of their own currency, which in their opinion may be overvalued by the markets. They can enter the markets to sell large amounts of foreign currencies to support their own currencies. In the latter part of the 1980s, central banks and treasurers of the United States, Japan, and West Germany intervened quite often to correct the imbalances between the values of the yen and deutsche mark (then the currency of West Germany; the unified Germany now uses the euro) versus the US dollar.

The main objective of central banks is not to profit from their foreign exchange operations or to avoid risks. It is to move their own and other important currencies in line with the values they consider appropriate for the best economic interest of their country.

Central banks of countries that have an official exchange rate for their currency must continually participate in the foreign exchange markets to ensure that their currency is available at the announced rate.

SPECULATORS AND ARBITRAGERS

Participation by speculators and arbitragers in the foreign exchange markets is driven by pure profit motive. These traders seek to profit from the wide fluctuations that occur in foreign exchange markets.

In other words, they do not have any underlying commercial or business transactions that they seek to cover in the foreign exchange market. Typically, speculators buy large amounts of a currency when they believe it is undervalued and sell it when the price rises. **Arbitrage** opportunities occur when investors try to exploit the differences in exchange rates between different markets. If the exchange rate for the pound is cheaper in London than in New York, they would buy pounds in London and sell them in New York, making a profit. Arbitrage opportunities are now increasingly rare, however, because instantaneous communications tend to equalize worldwide rates simultaneously.

A substantial part of the speculative and arbitrage transactions comes from exchange traders of commercial banks. Often these transactions represent a conscious effort to maximize profits with clearly defined profit objectives, loss limits, and risk-taking boundaries. In fact, the majority of foreign exchange market transactions today are driven by speculation. Unlike corporations that seek to hedge their transactions via foreign exchange, speculators seek to profit by the future movements in exchange rates.

FOREIGN EXCHANGE BROKERS

Foreign exchange brokers are intermediaries who bring together parties with opposite and matching requirements in the foreign exchange markets. They are in simultaneous contact through hotlines with scores of banks, and they attempt to match the buying requirements of some banks with the selling needs of others. They do not deal on their own account and are not a party to the actual transactions. For their services they charge an agreed-on fee, which is often called brokerage.

By bringing together various market participants with complementary needs, foreign exchange brokers contribute significantly to the "perfection of information" that makes the foreign exchange markets as efficient as they are. Apart from this, brokers also perform another important function: they preserve the confidentiality and anonymity of the participants. In a typical deal, the broker will not reveal the identity of the other party until the deal is sealed. This achieves a more uniform conduct of business as deals are decided purely on market considerations and are not influenced by other considerations that might be introduced if the parties' identities became known.

LOCATION OF FOREIGN EXCHANGE MARKETS

The foreign exchange markets are truly global, working around the clock and throughout the world. The very nature of foreign exchange trading, as well as the revolution in tele-communications, has resulted in a unified market in which distances and even time zones have been compressed. Traditionally, London and, later, New York were the main centers of foreign trading. Other centers, however, such as Tokyo, Hong Kong, Singapore, and Frankfurt, have become extremely active. Smaller but significant markets exist in many European and some Asian countries.

The individual foreign exchange trading centers are closely linked to form one global market. Trading spills over from one market to another and from one time zone to another. Price levels in one trading center immediately affect those in other centers. As the market closes in one time zone, others open in different time zones, taking cues from the activities of the earlier market in setting up trading and price trends. A continuous pattern is thus established, giving the impression of one unified market across the world.

JAPAN

Because of its geographical position, Japan can be considered the market where the world's trading day begins. The Japanese markets, led by Tokyo, are extremely active, with a very high daily turnover. Most of the deals are backed by customer-related requests to finance or settle international commercial transactions. Dollar-yen deals predominate in the market because of the large share of US-related business in the international transactions of Japan.

Since the deregulation of Japanese foreign exchanges, the element of speculative activity has increased considerably, especially in the Tokyo market. The volume of trading in the market has also increased as the securities and equity markets of Japan have opened up to foreign investment and some foreign investment banks have been allowed to operate in Japan. Brokers are used extensively in the Japanese markets, especially in transactions between banks located within the country. The market, however, closes at a set time in the afternoon, thus putting a limit on the volume of transactions that can take place. This system has somewhat inhibited the development of the Tokyo market, which would otherwise be significantly larger.

SINGAPORE AND HONG KONG

Singapore and Hong Kong are the next markets to open, about one hour after Tokyo. These markets are much less regulated, and in pursuit of their aim to become major international financial centers, both markets offer liberal access to overseas banks and commercial establishments. At the same time, the governmental authorities have attempted to create a friendly market environment to promote maximum trading activity. Market activity has increased considerably because several overseas banks, attracted by the incentives offered, have opened branches in both centers. Brokers are heavily involved in local transactions in Singapore, while international transactions are handled primarily through direct deals between banks. The trading activity of Hong Kong is a mix of direct deals and broker-intermediated transactions. Both of these markets have grown tremendously in the past few decades.

BAHRAIN

The Bahrain market in the Middle East emerged as an important center of foreign exchange trading in the 1970s, when oil-linked commercial transactions grew considerably. Located in the middle of overlapping time zones, Bahrain is often used by traders in other markets to serve as a link in their global cycle. Bahrain provides a bridge between the closing of the Far Eastern and opening of the European markets because it is open during the time when the markets in those locations are closed.

EUROPEAN MARKETS

Europe, taken as a whole, is the largest foreign exchange market. Its main centers are London, Frankfurt, and Zurich. European banks have no set closing time for foreign exchange trading and are free to trade twenty-four hours a day, but they generally cease trading in the afternoon. Both direct and brokered deals are common in European trading. In the past, some of Europe's markets, such as that in Paris, have exhibited a unique feature: rate fixing. Once a day, representatives of the larger banks and the central banks met to fix the exchange rate of the US dollar against local currencies and hence against one another. The fixed rate represented the balance of offers and bids and was close to what the rate would be internationally. There was sometimes a small discrepancy, however, which offered an opportunity for arbitrage. This opportunity, of course, existed for only a very short time, as market pressures quickly equalized the prices. The fixed rate was important primarily because it was considered the legal official rate and was often specified in contracts. This practice is less important in the European markets now, given that many of the countries are using the same currency (the euro).

US MARKETS

The New York market opens next. It is one of the world's largest markets, and the top foreign exchange trading firms are headquartered there. The volume of business in New York has increased tremendously since deregulation of the banking system and the increasing presence of overseas banks. Both brokered as well as direct dealing are common in the New York exchange market. The West Coast markets are essentially tied to New York and closely follow the trading patterns that are established there.

Market Volumes

Foreign exchange markets are clearly located in the largest financial markets in the world. Their turnover exceeds several times that of securities, futures, options, and commodities markets. The actual turnover figures, however, are difficult to ascertain, because banks do not publish data on the volume of their transactions.

In 1979 one study estimated the daily turnover of the world foreign exchange market to be about US$200 billion.[1] The 2010 triennial central bank survey compiled by the Bank for International Settlements places worldwide daily trading of spot and forward foreign exchange markets at US$3.73 trillion. This is the equivalent to $540 in daily transactions for every person on earth.[2] The currencies that predominate in foreign exchange trading activity on a worldwide basis are the US dollar, the euro, the yen, the Swiss franc, the pound, the Canadian dollar, and the Australian dollar. Some other currencies of increasing importance in foreign exchange markets are the Swedish krona, the Indian rupee, and the Chinese yuan.

A daily turnover of US$3.73 trillion would amount to an annual figure of US$1,361 trillion. This enormous figure, which estimates the annual volume of global foreign exchange trading, can be appreciated by comparing it with the global GDP, which was US$63.25 trillion in 2010.

Uses of the Foreign Exchange Market

Besides providing the means by which different categories of individuals and institutions acquire foreign exchange to meet different needs, foreign exchange markets perform several basic functions. It is important to understand the economic functions performed by the foreign exchange markets and their role in international trade in goods and services. Two basic functions are the avoidance of risk and the financing of international trade.

International trade transactions, which must be settled monetarily, carry significant risks both to the buyer and to the seller. If the transaction is invoiced in the currency of the seller, the seller stands to lose if the currency depreciates in the time lag between agreement on the price and the actual date of payment. Consider, for example, a British importer of US computers. The importer agrees to buy the shipment of computers for US$150,000, and the current exchange rate is US$1.5 to £1. At this rate, the cost to the British importer is £100,000. Usually, in such instances payments are made after goods are shipped or received. In this example, assume a lag of three months between the signing of the contract and the actual payment by the British importer. Suppose that in this period the value of the US dollar appreciates and US$1 becomes equal to £1. In this event, the British importer will have to part with £150,000 to purchase the US$150,000 needed to meet the contractual obligation. As a result, the importer stands to incur a substantial loss: £50,000. Although this is an exaggerated example, the risks are indeed real and can often wipe out the entire profit from a transaction.

Foreign exchange markets provide mechanisms to reduce this risk and ensure a certain minimum return. Foreign exchange markets also provide the financing mechanism for international trade transactions. Financing is required to cover the costs of goods that are in transit. These costs are considerable if goods are sent by sea. At the same time, the risks are also high because the parties are in different countries, and, in the event of default, the recourse for the party defaulted against is limited. These problems are solved efficiently through the foreign exchange markets, specifically through the use of internationally accepted documentation procedures, the most important being letters of credit, which will be discussed in Chapter 12.

TYPES OF FOREIGN EXCHANGE MARKETS

There are two main types of foreign exchange transactions that are often characterized as different markets—spot transactions and forward transactions. Often dealers specialize in one of three transaction categories: cash, tom, or spot.

THE SPOT MARKET

The spot market consists of transactions in foreign exchange ordinarily completed on the second working day of the deal being made. Within the spot market, there can be three types of transactions:

1. *Cash*, in which the payment of one currency and delivery of the other currency are completed on the same business day
2. *Tom* (short for "tomorrow"), in which the transaction deliveries are completed on the next working day
3. Spot exchange, in which the transaction deliveries are completed within the same day of the deal being struck

Price Quotation in Exchange Markets

The prices of currencies in the spot market can be expressed as direct quotes or indirect quotes. When the price of one currency is expressed as a direct quote, it reflects the number of units of home currency that are required to buy the foreign currency. A **direct quote** on the New York market would be US$1.30 = €1. An **indirect quote** is the reverse; the home currency is expressed as a unit, and the price is shown by the number of units of foreign currency that are required to purchase one unit of the home currency. For example, in the New York market an indirect quote would be US$1= €0.77 (to purchase one unit of the home currency, the US dollar, €0.77 are needed).

An important feature of foreign exchange price quotation is the number of decimals used. Since large amounts are traded, quotes are usually given at least up to the fourth decimal, especially for such major currencies as the pound and the US dollar. Thus, a quote for the pound would be £1 = US$1.7643.

Long and Short Positions

A bank can be in the spot market in three positions:

1. *Long*, when it buys more than it sells of a currency
2. *Short*, when it buys less than it sells of a currency
3. *Square*, when it buys and sells the same amount of currency

Whenever a bank is long or short in a currency, it is exposed to a certain amount of risk. The risk arises in a **long position** because the value of the bank's excess currency could depreciate if that currency falls in price. Thus, the market value of the assets of a bank would be lower than the cost price. In a **short position**, the bank agrees to sell more currency than it has in its possession. If the price of the currency in which the bank is short rises, the bank will experience a loss. The bank will have to acquire and deliver the currency at a higher price than the agreed-upon selling price. Both long and short positions can also result in profits, if the currency in question appreciates or depreciates. Since large losses are possible, banks must carefully evaluate the amount of exposure they can withstand. Specific limits are laid down for long and short positions in each currency, as well as aggregate limits for all major currencies.

There are usually two types of trading strategy followed by banks in the spot market. One strategy is to determine whether the currency is going to appreciate or depreciate and then assume a long or short position, allowing the trader to profit from the currency movement. This strategy is often called running a position, or positions trading. The other strategy is to assume and liquidate long and short positions very quickly (often within minutes) as exchange rates fluctuate during the business day. This strategy is known as in-and-out trading.

THE FORWARD MARKET

The forward market consists of transactions that require delivery of currency at an agreed-upon future date. The rate at which this forward transaction will be completed is determined at the time the parties agree on a contract to buy and sell. The time between the establishment of contracts and the actual exchange of currencies can range from two weeks to more than a year. The most common maturities for forward contracts are one, two, three, and six months. Some forward transactions are termed outright forwards, to distinguish them from swap transactions.

Forward transactions typically occur when exporters, importers, or others involved in the foreign exchange market must either pay or receive foreign currency amounts at a future date. In such situations there is an element of risk for the receiving party if the currency it is going to receive depreciates during the intervening period.

For the purposes of a quick example of this concept, assume that the owner of a small business wished to purchase an amount of softwood lumber from a Canadian company in June 2004. At that time, the Canadian dollar was worth US$0.74. If the purchase was made in June, the total purchase of Can$3,000 would cost the business owner US$2,220 (3,000 × 0.74). If for some reason the business owner waited until November 2004 to purchase the lumber, the Canadian dollar would have risen to US$0.84 by that time. Thus, the same Can$3,000 purchase would now cost the business owner US$2,520—or US$300 more than the same product would have cost in June! The owner of the small business could have eliminated all or part of this risk by purchasing a forward currency contract over this period of time.

To fix a minimum value on the foreign exchange proceeds, these recipients can lock into a rate in advance by entering into a forward contract with a bank. Under such a contract, the bank is obligated to purchase the currency from the exporter at the agreed-on rate, regardless of the rate that prevails on the day when the foreign currency is actually delivered by the exporter. Banks in turn enter into contracts with other banks to offset these customer contracts, giving rise to interbank transactions in the forward market.

The date on which the currencies are to be delivered under a forward contract is fixed in advance and is usually specific. In some customer contracts, however, the banks provide an option to the customers to deliver currencies within a certain time that can range up to ten, twenty, or thirty days. The costs of such contracts are, naturally, higher than the cost of contracts with specific maturity dates, because banks have to incur additional costs and efforts to create offsetting contracts in the interbank market. Forward contracts are popular with customers who are not certain of the dates on which they will have to pay or receive foreign currency amounts and would therefore like some leeway in executing their contractual obligations.

FOREIGN EXCHANGE RATES

A foreign exchange rate can be defined as the price of one currency expressed in units of another currency. The price of pounds expressed in terms of US dollars could be 1.8391. Therefore, 1.8391 would be the foreign exchange rate of the pound. Many journals and newspapers report foreign exchange rates either daily or periodically. Table 5.1 shows the major currency *cross rates* on October 15, 2012, as shown on Yahoo Finance. Notice that you can determine both the direct and the indirect exchange rates for each of the currencies listed in the table.

Since it is often confusing to decide whether a rate is an indirect or direct quote, a uniform standard of exchange-rate quotation was adopted in 1978. Under this standard, the US dollar was to be the unit currency and other currencies were expressed as variable amounts relative to the US dollar. This method, where foreign currency prices are quoted as US$1, is known as stating the price in **European terms**. The prices of some currencies, such as the British pound and Australian dollar, however, are quoted in terms of variable units of US dollars per unit of their currency. Such quotations are known as **American terms**.

Table 5.1 **Major Currency Cross Rates as of October 15, 2012**

	US dollar	Yen	Euro	Canadian dollar	British pound	Australian dollar	Swiss franc
1 US dollar	1	78.644	0.7722	0.9805	0.6222	0.9749	0.9330
1 yen	0.0127	1	0.00098	0.0125	0.0079	0.0124	0.0119
1 euro	1.2951	101.8503	1	1.2698	0.8059	1.2626	1.2083
1 Canadian dollar	1.0199	80.2105	0.7875	1	0.6346	0.9944	0.9516
1 British pound	1.6071	126.3879	1.2409	1.5757	1	1.5668	1.4994
1 Australian dollar	1.0257	80.6651	0.7920	1.0057	0.6382	1	0.9570
1 Swiss franc	1.0718	84.2911	0.8276	1.0509	0.6669	1.0450	1

BID AND OFFER RATES

Rates in the foreign exchange market are quoted as bid and offer rates. A bid is the rate at which the bank is willing to buy a particular currency, and an offer is the rate at which it is willing to sell that currency. Banks in the market are generally required by convention and practice to quote their bid and offer prices for particular currencies simultaneously.

When quoting their bid and offer rates for a particularly currency, banks quote a price for buying the currency that is lower than the price they charge for selling it. The difference between the buying and selling price is called the **bid-offer spread**. In a typical spot market transaction, a US dollar–pound sterling quote might be 1.8410–1.8420. The quote on the left side is the bid rate, at which the bank would be willing to sell US$1.8410 in exchange for a pound. The quote on the right side is the offer rate, at which the bank would be willing to buy US$1.8420 for a pound. Notice that the selling rate is higher because the bank is prepared to sell fewer dollars for a pound (US$1.8410) than it is prepared to buy. The use of both American and European terms reverses the bid-offer order. Moreover, a bid quote for one currency is an offer quote for the other currency in the transaction. To avoid confusion, a useful rule of thumb is to remember that in its quote the bank will always part with smaller amounts of the currency it is selling than it will receive when it is buying. In the example, the bank is willing to part with US$1.8410 per unit of pound sterling when selling them, but it wants to receive US$1.8420 per unit of pound sterling when it is buying.

In practice, exchange traders quote only the last two decimals of the exchange rate, especially in the interbank market. The interbank quotations of bid-offer rates feature extremely fine spreads because transactions are in huge volumes and the competition is intense.

CROSS RATES

Exchange rates are quoted prices of one currency in terms of another currency. In practice, however, prices of all currencies are not always quoted in terms of all other currencies, which is particularly true of currencies for which there is no active market. For example, rate quotations for Malaysian ringgits in terms of Swedish krona are not easily available, but both currencies are quoted against the US dollar. Their rates with reference to the dollar can be compared, and a rate can be determined between these two currencies (see Table 5.1). For example, if one US dollar buys 10 Malaysian ringgits, and if one US dollar buys 2.5 Swedish krona, the cross rate (not including transaction costs) can be calculated as follows:

MYR10/US$1 divided by SEK2.5/US$1 equals 4 ringgits to 1 krona

PREMIUMS AND DISCOUNTS

The spot price and forward price of a currency are invariably different. When the forward price of the currency is higher than the spot price, the currency is said to be at a premium. The difference between the spot price and forward price in this case is called the forward premium. When the forward rate of a currency is lower than the spot rate, the currency is said to be at a discount. The difference between the spot and forward rate in this case is called the forward discount. Here are some illustrations of forward premiums and discounts:

Spot rate for U.S. dollar/Can. dollar = Can$1.19
Forward rate for U.S. dollar/Can. dollar = Can$1.29

Notice that in the forward rate, it will require Can$1.29 to buy US$1, while in the spot rate only Can$1.19 is required. The US dollar is costlier in the forward quote than in the spot quote and is therefore at a premium against the Canadian dollar. The premium on forward quotes of the US dollar is Can$0.10.

Now, assume the following exchange rates between the US dollar and Canadian dollar:

Spot rate: Can$1.29 = US$1
Forward rate: Can$1.09 = US$1

In this case the spot rate for the US dollar is more expensive, in terms of Canadian dollars, than the forward rate. In other words, the US dollar is cheaper in the forward market because only Can$1.09 is needed to buy US$1 forward, whereas Can$1.29 is needed to buy US$1 in the spot market. Thus, the US dollar is at a discount of Can$0.20 in the forward market.

It is very important to recognize the type of quotation when considering forward premiums and discounts. When the quotes are indirect, that is, when the home currency is expressed as a unit and the foreign currency as variable, forward premiums are subtracted from the spot rate to arrive at the forward rate. Similarly, forward discounts are added to the spot rate to get the forward rate. Following are examples showing premiums and discounts.

Premium:

Spot rate: US$1 = Can$1.29
Forward premium on Can$ = Can$0.010
Forward rate for US$/Can$ = Can$1.28

Discount:

Spot rate: US$1 = Can$1.29
Forward discount on Can$ = Can$ 0.020
Forward rate for US$/Can$ = Can$1.31

When the exchange rates are quoted as direct rates, that is, when the foreign currency is the unit, premiums are added to the spot rate to arrive at the forward rate; discounts are subtracted.

Consider a situation in which the pound sterling is at a premium:

Spot rate: £1 = US$1.78
Forward premium on £ = 0.10
Forward rate for £1/US$ = US$1.88

Consider a situation in which pound sterling is at a discount and direct quotations are used. The forward rates will be calculated as follows:

Spot: £1 = US$1.864
Forward discount: US$ 0.020
Forward rate: £1 = US$1.844

Notice that the method of arriving at the forward rate is reversed when moving from direct to indirect rates. However, the basic rule applicable to all types of quotations is that a currency at a premium will buy more units of the other currency in the forward market than in the spot market, while the reverse will be the case when the currency is at a discount. Also, the premium and discount calculations will be applied at the variable currency, either in a direct or indirect quote. Thus, in the examples above, currencies that are at a premium or discount are the ones that are variable—that is, the ones whose rates are not expressed as a unit.

Forward premiums and discounts arise when the exchange markets expect the future value of currencies to be either higher or lower. The amount of premium can and does vary quite often with the length of the forward quote, and banks often quote a series of exchange rates indicating the forward premium or discount over a range of forward deliveries. Table 5.2 illustrates a typical foreign exchange forward quotation.

Table 5.2   **Foreign Exchange Forward Quotation**

Transaction	US$
Spot	1.6560
30-day forward	1.6550
60-day forward	1.6540
90-day forward	1.6530

In this quotation, the thirty-day forward quote shows Canadian dollars at a premium of ten points, while sixty-day and ninety-day premiums are at twenty and thirty points, respectively. Points here represent values in terms of the fourth decimal place of the exchange-rate quotation.

Another important consideration is that forward premiums and discounts are relative. When one currency is at a premium against another, the other currency is simultaneously at a discount against it. This is only natural, because the exchange rate is the value of one currency in terms of another currency. As an example, the Canadian dollar could be at a ten-point premium against the US dollar for thirty-day forward rates. Therefore, the US dollar would be at a ten-point discount against the Canadian dollar for thirty-day forward rates.

Forward Rates in Percentage Terms

Another way of expressing forward premiums and discounts is by quoting them as annualized percentages. There are two ways these can be calculated, one for indirect rates and the other for direct rates. The formula for computing forward rates when direct rates are used is as follows:

$$\text{Forward premium or discount} = \frac{\text{Forward rate} - \text{Spot rate}}{\text{Spot rate}} \times \frac{12}{n} \times 100$$

where n = number of months.

Consider a situation in which the US dollar and pound sterling rates are quoted as follows:

A.

$$\text{Spot US\$/£} = \text{US\$1.6420}$$
$$\text{30-day forward US\$/£} = \text{US\$1.6400}$$

B.

$$\text{Spot US\$/£} = \text{US\$1.7435}$$
$$\text{30-day forward US\$/£} = \text{US\$1.7455}$$

Quotation A shows that the US dollar is at a premium of twenty points for the thirty-day forward rate against the pound sterling. This premium can be expressed in percentage terms using the following formula:

$$\frac{1.6400 - 1.6240}{1.6420} \times \frac{12}{1} \times 100 = 1.4616\%$$

Thus, the US dollar is at a premium of 1.46 percent against the pound sterling.

Quotation B shows that the US dollar is at a twenty-point discount against the pound in a thirty-day forward contract. This discount can be calculated as follows:

$$\frac{1.7455 - 1.7435}{1.7435} \times \frac{12}{1} \times 100 = 1.37\%$$

Thus, the US dollar here is at a 1.37 percent discount against the pound.

Forward Premiums and Discounts Using Indirect Quotes

The formula for calculating forward rates as annual percentages using indirect quotes

Forward discount or premium as a forward rate percent per annum:

$$= \frac{\text{Spot rate} - \text{Forward rate}}{\text{Forward rate}} \times \frac{12}{n} \times 100$$

Suppose the following quotes are available in the New York interbank market:

A.

Spot US\$/Can\$ = Can\$1.5670
3-month forward US\$/Can\$ = Can\$1.5570

B.

Spot US\$/Can\$ = Can\$1.5670
6-month forward US\$/Can\$ = Can\$1.5520

These rates can be expressed in percentage-per-annum terms, using the formula for indirect quotes.

Quotation A shows that the US dollar is at a 100-point discount against the Canadian dollar for a three-month forward contract. Expressing this as a percentage on an annual basis would work out as follows:

$$\frac{1.5670 - 1.5570}{1.5570} \times \frac{12}{3} \times 100 = 2.57\%$$

Thus, the US dollar is at a 2.57 percent per annum discount against the Canadian dollar.

Quotation B shows that the US dollar is at a discount of 150 points over the Canadian dollar for a six-month forward contract. In percentage terms on an annual basis, this is expressed as follows:

$$\frac{1.5670 - 1.5520}{1.5520} \times \frac{12}{6} \times 100 = 1.93\%$$

Thus, the US dollar is at a discount of 1.93 percent per annum against the Canadian dollar for a six-month forward contract.

DEVALUATION AND REVALUATION OF EXCHANGE RATES

Exchange rates move up and down almost continuously in the exchange market. A downward movement is termed devaluation, while an upward movement is termed revaluation. Devaluation has a specific meaning in the context of exchange-rate policy: it means a country lowers the officially fixed value of its currency. We are using the term to mean a downward movement in the currency. Similarly, revaluation has a specific meaning, which is the reverse of devaluation, but in this section it is used to mean upward movements in currency prices. Both devaluation and revaluation are considered on a spot basis. It is important to measure these changes in exchange rates to compute the actual implications they have for foreign exchange transactions. The formulas for calculating the changes are different for direct and indirect quotes. The formula for calculating direct quotes is as follows:

$$\text{Percent devaluation or revaluation} = \frac{\text{Ending rate} - \text{Beginning rate}}{\text{Beginning rate}} \times 100$$

For example, suppose the following quotes for pound sterling are available today, for spot transactions in the New York interbank market:

A.

10:00 A.M. US$/US$1.6800
12:00 A.M. US$/US$1.6400

B.

$$12:30 \text{ P.M. } £/US\$/ \; US\$1.6700$$
$$2:30 \text{ P.M. } £/US\$/US\$1.6900$$

In example A, the US dollar has seen a revaluation of 400 points against the pound. This revaluation expressed in percentage terms is calculated as follows:

$$\frac{1.6400 - 1.6800}{1.6800} \times 100 = -2.38\%$$

Thus, the dollar rose 2.38 percent against the pound.

In example B, the pound has been revalued against the US dollar by 200 points. Expressed in percentage terms, this revaluation is calculated as follows:

$$\frac{1.6900 - 1.6700}{1.6700} \times 100 = 1.19\%$$

Thus, the pound sterling appreciated or was revalued by 1.19 percent against the US dollar.

The formula for measuring changes in spot rates when indirect quotes are used is as follows:

$$\text{Percent change in spot rate} = \frac{\text{Beginning rate} - \text{Ending rate}}{\text{Ending rate}} \times 100$$

For example, suppose the following quotations are available in the New York interbank market for spot rates today, and two days for now:

A.

$$10:00 \text{ A.M. } US\$/ \text{€} = \text{€}1.2530$$
$$12:00 \text{ A.M. } US\$/ \text{€} = \text{€}1.2030$$

B.

$$10:00 \text{ A.M. } US\$/ \text{€} = \text{€}1.2700$$
$$12:00 \text{ A.M. } US\$/ \text{€} = \text{€}1.2150$$

In example A, the US dollar has suffered a depreciation of 500 points against the euro. This depreciation (devaluation) expressed in percentage terms is calculated as follows:

$$\frac{1.2530 - 1.2030}{1.2030} \times 100 = 4.16\%$$

Thus, the US dollar has fallen 4.16 percent against the euro.

In example B, the US dollar has seen devaluation (depreciation) of 550 points against the euro. This depreciation is expressed in percentage per annum terms as follows:

$$\frac{1.2700 - 1.2150}{1.2150} \times 100 = 4.53\%$$

Thus, the US dollar has been devalued (depreciated) 4.53 percent against the euro.

Triangular Arbitrage

Occasionally, prices of one currency can vary from one market to another. A currency may be cheaper in New York than it is in London. If such a situation arises, it provides an opportunity for market participants to buy the currency in New York and sell it in London. This activity is known as **triangular arbitrage**, or inter-market arbitrage (see Figure 5.1). Whether such arbitrage is possible is indicated by comparing a currency's actual price in one market and its price in another market, using cross-rate quotations. There are several steps an arbitrager must take to profit from such an opportunity. For example, assume that the following exchange rates are quoted in the interbank market:
New York:

$$£/US\$ = £1.8300$$
$$€/US\$ = €1.2700$$

Paris:

$$£/€ = £1.42$$

The euro and the pound sterling are quoted against the US dollar in New York and against each other in Paris, but also we can compute the exchange rate of the euro against the pound in the New York market through the mechanism of cross rates:

$$\frac{£1.83}{€1.27} = £1.44$$

It is evident that the two rates for pounds in terms of euros in New York and Paris are not the same. It would be profitable, therefore, to buy pounds in New York and sell them in Paris. Thus, a US arbitrager can get £183,000 in the New York market for US$100,000 and then sell these in Paris for €128,873. The euros can be sold in the New York mar-

Figure 5.1 **Triangular Arbitrage**

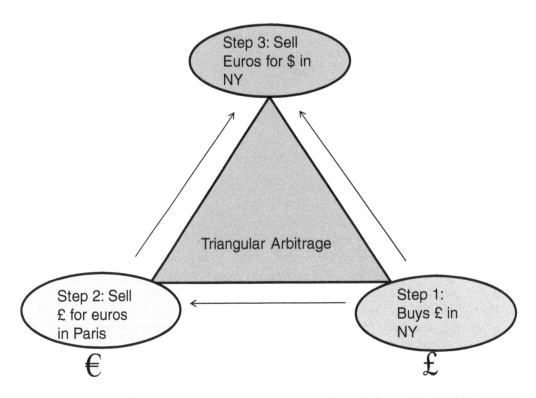

ket, bringing in US$101,474.99. The arbitrager can make a clean profit of US$1,474.99 without incurring any risk.

Arbitrage opportunities exist for a very short time in the interbank markets, because market movements quickly bring the rates back into line (refer to the steps in Figure 5.1). If such an opportunity were indeed present in the interbank market, there would be an enormous number of arbitragers acting on the same strategy. Thus, the first step, selling US dollars and acquiring British pounds, would push up the demand for British pounds and decrease the demand for US dollars. As a result, there would be upward pressure on the price of British pounds in the New York market. The second step, the sale of British pounds acquired in New York for euros in Paris, would lead to enormous selling pressure on British pounds and buying pressure on euros. This would push down the price of British pounds and push up the price of euros in this market. Large quantities of euros would be unloaded in the New York market for US dollars, again pushing down the price of euros and increasing the price of US dollars. The net effect of these pressures would be an increase in the price of British pounds in New York, while the price of British pounds in Paris would go down.

The converse movement would soon be enough to equalize prices in the two markets and eliminate the arbitrage opportunity. In fact, with modern information and computing technology, arbitrage opportunities hardly ever exist. If they arise momentarily, they are almost instantaneously eliminated as exchange traders are able to spot them simultaneously and execute transactions that move the rates back into proper alignment; in other words, the cross rates and quoted rates for currencies in different markets quickly become the same.

COVERED INTEREST ARBITRAGE

Covered interest arbitrage is a technique used to exploit the misalignment between the forward exchange rates of two currencies and their interest rates for the corresponding period. Usually, the differences in the interest rates of two countries for securities of similar risk and maturity should be equal but opposite in sign to the forward exchange premiums or discounts of their respective currencies, if transaction costs are ignored. This proposition is known as the theory of interest-rate parity. For example, assume that the following are US dollar and Canadian dollar exchange and interest rates:

US$/Can$ spot = US$1/Can$1.2750
US$ 3-month forward rate = US$1/Can$1.2758

3-month U.S. Treasury bill rate = 1.75%
3-month Bank of Canada Treasury bill rate = 2.00%

A US investor could invest US$100,000 in three-month treasury bills (T-bills) and earn 1.75 percent interest. At the end of three months, he would earn US$438 and end up with a total cash balance of US$100,438. If he chose to invest in three-month Bank of Canada treasury bills, he would first convert his US$100,000 into Canadian dollars at the prevailing rate of US$1 to Can$1.2750. He would receive Can$127,500, which he would invest in Bank of Canada treasury bills with a three-month interest rate of 2 percent. He would receive Can$128,138 at the end of three months as principal and interest. This sum would be convertible to US dollars at a forward rate of 1.2758, which would yield US$100,438. Thus, the investor would receive the same return regardless of the country in which he invests. The higher interest rate of the United States is compensated by the higher premium of the Canadian dollars. Thus, there is no transnational flow of investment funds between the two countries.

When these conditions are not present, that is, if the interest rate parity does not hold, an opportunity arises for arbitrage. This type of arbitrage takes advantage of the disequilibrium between the interest rates and forward exchange premiums and discounts between two currencies. The basic strategy is to invest in another country and cover the exchange risk at favorable terms, so that the profits being made are completely riskless. Moreover, arbitragers need not even invest their own funds. They can borrow funds and return them after taking their profits at the maturity of the transactions.

For example, assume that the following are the interest rates and spot and forward exchange rates for US dollars and pounds sterling:

$$US\$/\pounds \text{ spot} = US\$1.7840 = \pounds1$$
$$US\$/\pounds \text{ forward} = US\$1.7850 = \pounds1$$
$$US \text{ 3-month prime rate} = 3\% \text{ per annum}$$
$$UK \text{ 3-month prime rate} = 6\% \text{ per annum}$$

The arbitrager makes six steps:

1. The arbitrager borrows US$100,000 in the United States at a prime rate of 0.75 percent (3 percent/4).
2. She exchanges the dollars for pounds at the spot rate of £1 = US$1.7840, which yields £56,053.81.
3. The pounds are invested in three-month deposits in the United Kingdom at a rate of 1.50 (6 percent/4) percent, which yields £56,264.28 at the end of the three months.
4. The maturity proceeds of the UK deposit (interest and principal) are covered by a forward contract for reconversion into US dollars at the prevailing fund rate of £1 = $1.7720. The investor locks in 1.7850 × £56,264.28, or US$100,431.74.
5. The arbitrager repays the US loan taken at 0.75 percent, US$100,187.62.
6. The arbitrager takes a profit of US$244.12.

Thus, the arbitrager has made a completely riskless profit of US$244.12, without even investing any of her own funds. Obviously, as the size of the transactions increase, so would any riskless profit opportunity. Again, such opportunities arise only rarely, and when they do, they are quickly eliminated by market movements. If the situation described arises, there will be huge borrowings in the US dollar, conversions into pound sterling, investments in sterling deposits, and reconversion into US dollars. This situation will tend to raise US interest rates, appreciate the spot rate of pounds sterling, depress UK interest rates, and reduce the forward premium that the US dollar enjoys over the British pound. All these changes will make it less profitable to borrow funds in the US and convert them to pounds sterling for deposit in the United Kingdom and then reconvert back into US dollars. The arbitrage opportunity, therefore, is eliminated, and the interest rate and forward premiums and discounts move back into line.

CURRENCY FUTURES MARKETS

Currency futures are standard value-forward contracts that obligate the parties to exchange a particular currency on a specific date at a predetermined exchange rate. Currency futures are traded at the International Money Market Division (IMM) of the Chicago Mercantile Exchange (CME). These futures were introduced in 1972 because in the new environment of floating exchange rates, it was believed that the interbank market would not be able to provide foreign exchange services to small investors or corporations that wanted to speculate in currency fluctuations through a daily trading strategy. Speculators are the main participants in the currency futures market, which has a daily turnover in excess of US$40 billion. More recently, commercial banks have begun to deal in currency futures through arbitrage companies, which grew out of the IMM operations. The activity of the IMM adds liquidity to the interbank market.

DIFFERENCES BETWEEN FUTURES AND FORWARD MARKETS

Although futures are similar to forward contracts, in that they allow market participants to fix their forward liability by locking into a future exchange rate, there are important differences between the two.

One of the most important differences is that while forward contracts can be of any size, futures contracts are of specific sizes (e.g., Can$50,000 or CHF125,000). Thus, if a company wishes to buy a Swiss franc currency future, it will have to enter into a contract for at least CHF125,000. Larger contracts will be in multiples of this amount. Forward contracts are available in a variety of currencies, including some that are not actively traded. Currency futures contracts are available only in specific currencies, usually the currencies of the industrialized countries.

Futures contracts have standardized maturity dates that are regulated by the exchange authorities, while forward contracts have a relatively wide range of maturities. The element of standardization also affects the future margin requirements. (Margins are deposits paid by persons entering into contracts as security for ensuring compliance with contractual obligations.) Futures contracts stipulate specific initial and maintenance margins, but forward contract margins are negotiable between banks and their clients. The futures markets are highly regulated and brokers can charge only fixed commissions. Regulation in forward markets is almost nonexistent, and commissions can vary.

Futures markets are highly speculative in nature, and rate movements are more volatile than in the forward market. In fact, this extreme volatility has resulted in the fixing of maximum price changes that are permissible on a particular trading day. Similarly, standards of minimum movements in rates have been fixed to affect a change in futures quotes. Operationally, perhaps the greatest difference between the two markets is the facility to exit or liquidate a position in the futures market, which is not available in the forward market. In the futures market, corporations or individuals can liquidate their existing position before the settlement date by selling an equivalent futures contract. This facility makes it easier for the speculators and hedgers in the futures markets to cut their losses or take their profits without having to wait for the contract period to expire.

FOREIGN CURRENCY OPTIONS

Foreign currency **options** are contracts that give the buyer the right, but not the obligation, to buy or sell a specified amount of foreign exchange at a set price for an agreed-upon period.

For example, a US corporation enters into an option contract to buy CHF100,000 within a two-month period at a rate of CHF3.6 per US$1. If the rate of the Swiss francs appreciates against the US dollar to a point at which each Swiss franc is equal to one US dollar, the corporation can exercise the option and acquire the foreign currency at the previous rate and not the prevailing rate. On the other hand, if the Swiss franc depreciates to, say four Swiss francs to the dollar, then it would not be economical for the corporation to utilize the contract at the fixed rate of 3.6 Swiss francs to the dollar. Thus, the corporation would choose to buy its Swiss francs off the market and let the option go unexercised.

There are two types of options. A **call option** allows the option purchaser to buy the underlying foreign currency. A **put option** allows the option buyer to sell the underlying currency.

OPTION TERMINOLOGY

Options markets are characterized by their unique terminology, which describes essential features of the contracts. Here are eight of the important terms:

1. *Writer:* A person who confers the right but not the obligation to another person to buy or sell the foreign currency
2. *Strike price* or *exercise price:* The rate at which the option can be exercised, that is, the rate at which the writer of the option will buy or sell the underlying foreign currency to the purchaser in the event the latter exercises his or her option
3. *At-the-money option:* An option whose exercise, or strike, price is the same as the prevailing spot exchange rate
4. *In-the-money option:* An option whose exercise price is better, at the time of contract writing, than the spot price for the relative currency
5. *Out-of-the-money option:* A currency option whose exercise price is worse for the purchaser than the prevailing spot price
6. *American option:* An option that can be exercised at any date between the initiation of the contract and the maturity date
7. *European option:* An option that can be exercised only on the maturity date
8. *Option premium:* The price paid by the purchaser of the option to its writer. The option premium is higher for in-the-money options and lower for out-of-the-money options. Option premiums are higher than the prevailing forward premiums in the interbank markets for contracts of similar maturities.

FORECASTING FOREIGN EXCHANGE RATES

Forecasting exchange rates is often vital to the success of international business. Inaccurate foreign exchange forecasts or projections can eliminate entire profits from international transactions or result in enormous cost overruns that could threaten the viability of overseas operations. Exchange rates must be forecast for any decision that involves the transfer of funds from one currency to another over a period of time. For example, when companies approach foreign markets to borrow or invest foreign currencies, they must project future exchange rates to compute even roughly their possible costs and returns. If a British company is borrowing Japanese yen, it will have to forecast the long-term pound-yen rate to compute what its repayment liabilities are going to be over the life of the loan and amortization period. Similarly, decisions involving both financial and nonfinancial investments overseas require foreign exchange forecasts to calculate the returns profile, because it depends considerably on the rate at which the foreign currency is going to be acquired for investment and the rate at which earnings will eventually be repatriated. Even when it is simply a question of **hedging** foreign exchange risks, currency forecasts are important. Only when a corporation has a clear view of what it believes the future direction of exchange-rate movements will be can it make a proper hedging decision and decide which hedging strategy or instrument is best for its purposes.

PROBLEMS IN FORECASTING FOREIGN EXCHANGE RATES

It is generally recognized that there is no perfect foreign exchange forecast or even a perfect methodology to forecast foreign exchange rates. There is no accurate and precise explanation for the manner in which exchange rates move. Movements of exchange rates depend on the simultaneous interaction of a variety of factors. How these factors influence one another and how they influence exchange-rate movements is impossible to quantify or predict. Exchange rates have been known to react violently to single, unexpected events, which have thrown many forecasts and theories completely off balance for that period.

Participants in foreign exchange markets, especially corporate treasurers, grapple with uncertainty and use a variety of techniques to develop some sense of what exchange rates are going to do in the future.

FUNDAMENTAL FORECASTING

Fundamental forecasting is a technique that attempts to predict future exchange rates by examining the influence of major macroeconomic variables on the foreign exchange markets. The main macroeconomic variables that are used in this analysis are inflation rates, interest rates, the balance of payments situation, economic growth trends, unemployment trends, and industrial and other major economic activities. These variables are quantified through comprehensive models that build relationships between the different factors with various statistical techniques, especially regression analysis.

A major problem with fundamental forecasting is that the timing of the events that influence exchange rates, and the gap between the occurrence of these events and their impact on exchange rates, are very difficult to measure. The latest data to make precise quantitative estimates of the relevant macroeconomic variables are seldom readily available. Perhaps the greatest weakness of fundamental analysis in forecasting exchange rates is that it takes into account only some of the factors that influence the movement of rates in the foreign exchange markets. There are several other noneconomic, nontangible factors, such as market sentiment, investor fears, speculative intentions, and political events that have an enormous influence on exchange rates and can override, at least in the short run, other fundamental considerations and factors.

TECHNICAL FORECASTING

Technical forecasting relies on past exchange-rate data to develop quantitative models and charts that can be used to predict future exchange rates. Technical analysts try to see historical patterns in the previous exchange-rate movements and attempt to build future patterns on that basis. This approach relies more on personal views and perceptions than on strong economic analysis. There are other technical models that use economic techniques to forecast exchange rates. These complex models try to capture and incorporate as many variables as possible, ascribing to each variable a certain level of influence in the overall computation of the future exchange-rate movements.

Technical models have been found to be of questionable use in practice. Studies conducted over the past few years have shown that technical models have not proved to be accurate predictors of future exchange-rate movements, but their widespread adoption by many market participants has given them a unique influence as factors in forecasting exchange-rate movements. Because a large number of market participants using similar models will tend to behave in a similar manner, moving the exchange rate in the direction indicated by their model is a sort of self-fulfilling prophecy. Usually, technical models concentrate on the near term and are favored by participants who have an interest in short-term trading and speculation in the exchange markets. Many companies, however, use technical models to provide a way of looking at foreign exchange possibilities, and if they are in agreement with the corporate projections, they could serve to reinforce that view.

ASSESSING MARKET SENTIMENTS

Another forecasting technique is the assessment of market sentiment, as reflected in the spot and forward rates of currencies. If the spot and forward rates of currencies are expected to appreciate, there would be buying pressure from speculators, which would push the exchange rate up to the expected level. Thus, the spot and forward rates that prevail can be seen as the realized expectations of future movements of currency. Some market participants base their forecasts on this logic, especially for future rates, and treat the forward rate as an unbiased estimator of the future spot rate.

FORECASTING STRATEGY

As is evident, no one technique is truly adequate for forecasting future movements in the exchange rate. Usually, corporate participants base their expectations on a combination of techniques and their individual experience and expertise in the area. The importance given to each type of forecasting technique will depend on the views of the individual firm. It is important that a comprehensive and broad-based view be taken when making foreign exchange-rate projections. These projections should be constantly reviewed and updated.

TYPES OF EXPOSURE IN FOREIGN EXCHANGE MARKETS

There are four major types of risks or exposure that a corporation faces in the course of its international business activity: transaction exposure, economic exposure, translation exposure, and tax exposure.

TRANSACTION EXPOSURE

Transaction exposure is the risk that a company's future cash flows will be disturbed by fluctuations in exchange rates. A company that is expecting inflows of foreign currency will be faced with transaction exposure to the extent that the value of these inflows can be affected by a change in the rate of the company's currency against the preferred currency for conversion. Exchange rates are extremely volatile, and a sharp movement can adversely affect the real value of cash flows in the desired currency. A corporation can have both inflows and outflows in a currency. Moreover, it can have different amounts of inflows and outflows in different currencies. In this situation, the company nets out its exposure in each currency by matching a portion of its currency inflows and outflows. The net exposure in each currency is aggregated for all currencies to arrive at a measurement of the total transaction exposure for the company. The period over which the cash flows are considered for arriving at the figure for transaction exposure depends on the individual methods and views of the company. Organizations use a variety of methods to assess the degree to which their net exposed cash flows are at risk. These methods can center on the time lag between the initiation and completion of the transaction, the use of currency correlations, or statistical projections of exchange-rate volatility. Sophisticated strategies for assessing transaction exposure often include some element of all of these considerations.

Differences in Currency Exchange Rates

One of the most crucial problems that international firms face is accounting for a transaction that is conducted in a foreign currency. How is such a transaction to be recorded on the books or reported to management in a consistent manner?

Differences in exchange rates between currencies lead to two separate problems for the international business firm. The first is that of accounting for business transactions and gains and losses from currency-rate differentials that arise during such business activity. The second problem is interpreting financial results of transactions conducted in different currencies or devising translations of currencies to yield comparable and measurable results.

Accounting procedures designed to treat these transactions follow either the one-step transaction or the two-step transaction approach, both of which provide methods for recording business transactions in a home currency.

The **one-step method** records the transaction using the spot rate in effect on that day for the foreign currency. Assume, for example, that Bob of Bob's Lawn and Garden Store wants to acquire lawn ornaments from a German supplier to round out his inventory in anticipation of heavy summer sales. Thus, on January 1, Bob buys 10,000 gross of pink flamingos for €60,000 payable by February 1. On the first of January the euro is trading for $0.50 (i.e., each dollar is worth €2). Consequently, under the one-step method Bob's ledger entries would be as follows:

Purchases	
Pink Flamingos	$30,000
Accounts Payable	$30,000 (€ @ $0.50)

If, however, exchange rates change between the time Bob places his order, records it in his books, and pays his account with the German flamingo maker, he will need to change his records to record the facts and the rate of exchange when the transaction is completed or actually settled. For example, if the value of the dollar falls and it takes $0.75 to buy €1, Bob's costs for his pink flamingos will rise and must be accounted for as an adjustment to the original cost of the flamingos. Thus he would make the following entries:

Purchases	
Pink Flamingos	$30,000
Accounts Payable	$15,000
Cash	$45,000 (€ @ $0.75)

The **two-step method** of accounting for gains or losses in transactions separates business activity and currency exchanges. The key difference from the one-step method is that gains or losses from the transaction do not affect the value of the asset acquired but are treated separately, as a result of assuming risk in engaging in the activity and opening the firm to fluctuations in exchange rates. Consequently, under this method Bob's flamingo transaction would be noted as follows:

Accounts Payable	$30,000
Exchange Adjustment: Loss	$15,000
Cash	$45,000 (€ @ $0.75)

In this method, the pink flamingos retain their value of $30,000 on Bob's books, and the difference between the agreed-on price or costs and the actual amount paid is noted in an exchange adjustment account that is eventually netted and applied as an adjustment to shareholder equity.

Some countries require the use of the one-step method, while others employ the two-step method. The United States has historically employed the two-step method and has required the immediate recognition of gains or losses from foreign currency transactions. In other countries, it is common accounting practice to defer gains and losses from accounts payable and receivable until the transactions are completed, and these results are not included in the income statement.

These accounting steps become far more involved when firms engage in hedging to protect themselves from fluctuations in rates of exchange between countries. It must be remembered, however, that such complications arise only when the transaction is denominated in a foreign currency. Bob could have asked to pay his bill in dollars, in which case, he would have no risk because of changes in the rate of exchange between euros and dollars. Instead, the German manufacturer would take the currency risk and account for any changes in the dollar's value.

ECONOMIC EXPOSURE

Economic exposure is a relatively broader conception of foreign exchange exposure. The prime feature of economic exposure is that it is essentially a long-term, multi-transaction-oriented way of looking at the foreign exchange exposure of a firm involved in international business. The standard definition of economic exposure is the degree to which fluctuations in exchange rates will affect the net present value of the future cash flows of a company.

Economic exposure is a particularly serious problem for multinational corporations with operations in several different countries. Since currency fluctuations do not follow any set pattern, each operation is subject to a different degree and nature of economic exposure. Measuring the degree of economic exposure is even more difficult than measuring transaction exposure. Economic exposure involves operational variables, such as costs, prices, sales, and profits, and each of these is also subject to fluctuation in value, independent of the exchange-rate movements. Many techniques are used to measure economic exposure. Most of these techniques rely on complex mathematical and statistical models that attempt to capture all the variables. Use of regression analysis and simulation of cash-flow positions under different exchange-rate scenarios are two such techniques.

Managing economic exposure can involve extremely complex strategies and instruments, some of which are outside the foreign exchange market.

TRANSLATION EXPOSURE

Translation exposure is the degree to which the consolidated financial statements and balance sheets of a company can be affected by exchange-rate fluctuations. It is also known as **accounting exposure**. Translation exposure arises when the accounts of a subsidiary are consolidated at the head office at an exchange rate that differs from the rate in effect at the time of the transaction.

Differences in translation exposure also emerge in the way firms measure the value of assets and the way they determine income. These differences become apparent in a number of procedural areas, such as accounting for leases, carrying long-term debt, assigning value to shares of a company's own stock, R&D expenses, depreciation, and inventory valuing techniques. For example, in the United States, depreciation is calculated according to the normal life of an asset. The value of the asset, however, is adjusted for the amount of money expected to be gained when that asset is ultimately sold. This eventual sales price is referred to as the salvage value. While US firms are allowed to depreciate only assets minus salvage value, in other countries the final asset is depreciated according to its full purchase price.

Other valuation and income differences emerge when countries do not agree on the use of the matching concept of accounting, a term that refers to the cash method of accounting, in which a business attempts to match expenses to the revenues associated with the incurring of those expenses, despite any differences in timing. Still more differences occur when it is accepted practice to keep certain business items off the balance sheet and out of the public or regulatory eye. In recent years, for example, there has been some debate in accounting circles about how to account for stock options on a company's financial statements.

Occasionally, off-the-balance-sheet items derive from the pursuit of illegal activities (for example, illegal payments or bribery) by businesses in countries with little regulatory supervision. The United States, for example, imposes strict requirements on accounting for legal facilitative payments made to low-level foreign officials to smooth the progress of business in foreign countries. Payments or gifts made to high-level government officials are illegal. In other countries, these practices are considered to be ordinary expenses of doing business abroad and are deductible for tax purposes.

Problems arise for multinational firms with business operations that are carried out in different locales and reported in different currencies. When an MNC is required to translate local currency accounts into home currency at the close of the financial year, what criteria does it use to report and compare its operations in different environments? These are not problems of valuation (determining appropriate values for assets in terms of other currencies) or of converting currencies from foreign currencies to a uniform home currency, but rather are involved in restating operational results. The objective is for results to be integrated so that they can be analyzed by management and reported to regulatory authorities. The process of restating financial statements into a uniform currency is called **translation**. When the financial statements from all operating units of an MNC are combined, they are said to be consolidated.

Foreign statement translation is a two-step process for the controller of an MNC. First, the accounts must be made consistent by being restated according to the same accounting principles, such as those for valuing inventories and assets and determining depreciation.

Table 5.3   **Exchange Rates Employed in Different Translation Methods for Specific Balance Sheet Items**

	Current	Current-Noncurrent	Monetary-Nonmonetary	Temporal
Cash	C	C	C	C
Accounts receivable	C	C	C	C
Inventories				
Cost	C	C	H	H
Market	C	C	H	C
Investments				
Cost	C	H	H	H
Market	C	H	H	C
Fixed assets	C	H	H	H
Other assets	C	H	H	H
Accounts payable	C	C	C	C
Long-term debt	C	H	C	C
Common stock	H	H	H	H
Retaining earnings	*	*	*	*

Note: C = current rate; H = historical rate, and * = residual, balancing figure representing a composite of successive current rates.

After the basis of the accounts has been adjusted to provide for consistency, the foreign currency amounts represented in the results can be translated into the reporting or home currency. Translation must not be confused with conversion. Translating is merely the restating of currencies, while conversion refers to the actual physical trade or exchange of units of one currency for another.

Accountants use four different methods of translating statements from local currencies to the reporting or home currency: the current-rate method, the current-noncurrent method, the monetary-nonmonetary method, and the **temporal method** (see Table 5.3).

Statement 52 of the Financial Accounting Standards Board FASB introduced some new definitional concepts to the translation of foreign exchange accounts. The first is the use of a **functional currency**, which is defined as the "currency of the primary economic environment in which the entity operates." It is differentiated from the reporting currency, which is the currency that the parent company uses in its consolidated financial statements. The determination of a functional currency is tricky for some subsidiaries. It could be the local currency if most of the subsidiary's business of buying, selling, or manufacturing is conducted using the local currency. The parent company's reporting currency could also be the functional currency, if the subsidiary's operations consist mostly of selling goods to the parent, or it could even be the currency of a third country, if the bulk of the entity's business is conducted in a third country.

The responsibility for choosing the functional currency rests with each firm, based on operational criteria regarding currencies involved in cash flows, prices, sales market, expenses, financing, and intercompany indicators. Functional currencies can change, but only if there is a change in the initial underlying operational criteria, a stipulation imposed by the FASB to prevent arbitrary changes in functional currencies that aggressive accountants might make to put financial statements in the best possible light.

Once the functional currency is determined, a firm can begin its process of translating statements under FASB 52 and consolidating, or combining, the results of disparate operations. The use of either the current or the temporal rate is determined by the location of operations and resulting functional currency. If the books and records are kept in the currency of the parent, no restatement is necessary. If, however, the books and records are kept in a local currency, the subsidiary has three different translation routes, depending on the functional currency.

If the functional currency is the local currency of the subsidiary, the parent merely translates the statements into US dollars using the current-rate method. This situation holds unless the functional currency is a local currency in a high-inflation country, in which case the firm must use the temporal method of translation. High-inflation countries are defined as those with inflation rates greater than 100 percent for three consecutive years.

If the functional currency is the parents' home currency, even if the books are kept in the local currency, the firm uses the temporal method to re-measure results. If the functional currency is a third currency, the firm re-measures from the local to the functional currency using the temporal method and then translates the result into the home currency using the current-rate method. Figure 5.2 provides a graphic description of this process.

CONSOLIDATION PROBLEMS

The results of these financial machinations are then integrated into a firm's comprehensive reckoning of operations and results. This consolidation process raises some special considerations for an MNC and questions about a firm's organizational and investment decisions. For example, what operations should be consolidated into the firm's overall operations? Some countries require only that the parent report the results of its operations and do not require the integration of the results of subsidiary or affiliated arms. In the United States, for example, tax laws require that firms consolidate their operations globally, because firms are taxed on worldwide income (although they are given credit for taxes paid to other governments). Some other issues raised are the following: What if a parent corporation owns only part interest in a subsidiary? What level of investment determines ownership or control? What distinction is made between having an investment in another concern and that concern's being an integral part of the parent corporation's network?

CONSOLIDATION RULES IN THE UNITED STATES

In the United States the questions about whether a parent consolidates the results of subsidiary operations into its own depends on the level and type of involvement of the parent

Figure 5.2   **Translating a Firm's Functional Currency into a Reporting Currency**

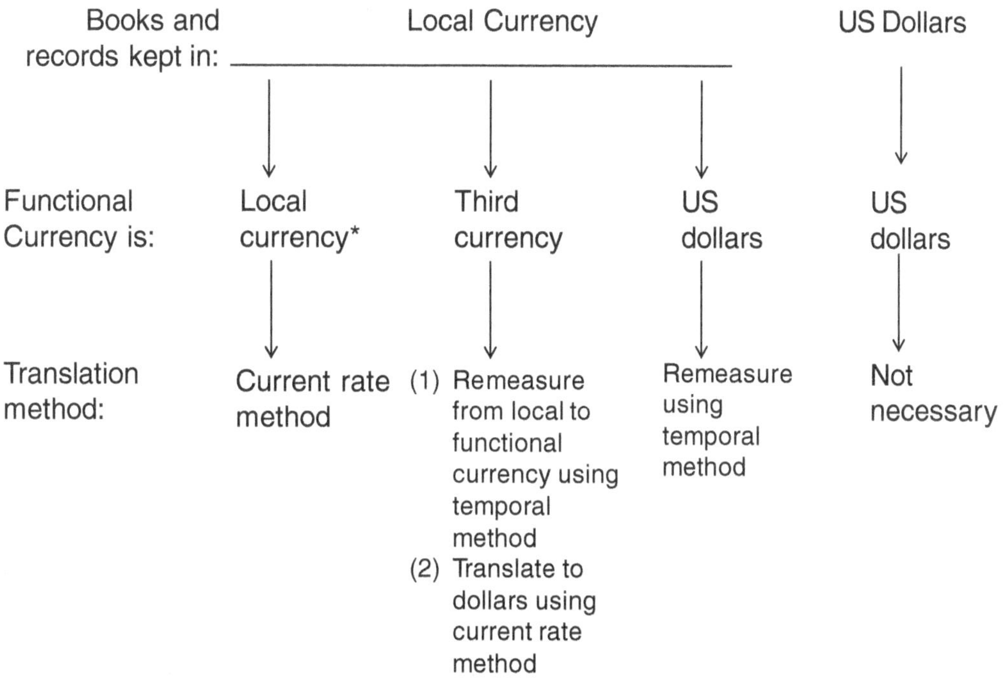

Books and records kept in:	Local Currency			US Dollars
↓	↓	↓	↓	↓
Functional Currency is:	Local currency*	Third currency	US dollars	US dollars
	↓	↓	↓	↓
Translation method:	Current rate method	(1) Remeasure from local to functional currency using temporal method (2) Translate to dollars using current rate method	Remeasure using temporal method	Not necessary

*In the case of a highly inflationary economy, the local currency may be the functional currency from an operating standpoint, but the dollar is considered the functional currency from a translation standpoint.

in the activities of the subsidiary. There are three different ways an investment in another enterprise can be handled under accounting rules: the cost method, the equity method, and consolidation. The cost method is employed when the parent firm holds an unsubstantial investment in the subsidiary. Under this method, the parent carries the investment as such and reports income from the subsidiary only when the subsidiary declares a dividend to the parent. Typically, the cost method is used in the United States when the parent owns less than 20 percent of the voting stock of the affiliate and that stock was acquired initially through purchasing. Monies flowing back to the parent are treated as dividends and do not change the level of the investment account of the parent.

If the parent owns a substantial portion of the stock of the subsidiary, from 20 percent to 50 percent, it uses the **equity method**, reporting income from the subsidiary as it is earned, not as it is received. The investment is carried on the parent's books at original cost and is adjusted according to earnings or dividends received from the subsidiary. Income from the foreign subsidiary increases the value of the parent's investment (whether it is received or not), and thus the value of the holding is adjusted upward to reflect an increase in the share of profits. Any dividends received by the parent from its holdings in the subsidiary have the effect of reducing the investment's book value, because they are considered to have the effect of lowering the profits of the subsidiary.

If the parent owns more than 50 percent of the subsidiary, it has a controlling interest in the foreign affiliate and must consolidate the results of the affiliate into its own reports. The consolidation process is carried out line by line to agree with the financial statements of the parent. Thus, before the two sets of figures are aggregated, they must be adjusted to agree according to the accounting principles used, and foreign currencies must be translated into the reporting currency. The parent and the affiliate must also adjust their books to correct for their inter-corporate transactions and profits that have resulted from business dealings between the two entities.

INFLATION

Companies doing business in high-inflation countries must develop special procedures for dealing with the effects of inflation on the valuation of assets. Inflation also raises problems for MNCs in their attempts to evaluate and predict purchasing power for foreign operations and in evaluating their financial reports. As long as there are few changes in prices in a country, MNCs attempting to value their assets can use historical costs for those assets as appropriate measures. When inflation is significant, however, the value of those assets stated in historical terms inaccurately represents the wealth of the firm.

There are basically two responses when dealing with inflation. One can either reestablish a new basis for historical values that reflects the effects of inflation, or one can put into place a system that constantly corrects for changes in prices. In practice, under the first model, all financial statements are adjusted at a single point in time, and these adjusted costs become the new historical basis; under the second model, values are indexed on a continual basis according to changes in prices.

In accounting practice the use of models depends on the objectives of the financial reports. The two accounting methods for handling inflation are constant-dollar (or general-purchasing-power) accounting and current-cost accounting.

The goal of **constant-dollar accounting** is to report assets, liabilities, expenses, and revenues in terms of the same purchasing power. The original basis of the valuations, the historical costs, does not change under this accounting method. Instead, nonfinancial items are restated to reflect the purchasing power in effect on the date of the balance sheet. Financial items on the statements, such as cash, receivables, and payables, would not be restated, because their monetary valuation would already reflect the purchasing power of the currency on the date of the report.

In **current-cost accounting**, the emphasis is not on the loss of purchasing power associated with a specific currency but on the amount of money it would take to replace assets because of price increases. Thus, under current-cost accounting, historical costs are supplanted by new, adjusted costs, such as replacement costs. This method's objective is to account for the effects of inflation as it relates to the increases in the costs of specific assets and not overall prices.

The treatment of inflation in the presentation of accounting records differs around the world. In the United States, firms are required to continue to use the historical cost standard as their basis for reporting financial results, but also they are required to disclose supplementary information regarding both price level and current-cost accounting. Other countries have different requirements. In Great Britain, current-cost balance sheets and income statements must be presented, and such financial statements may be presented as supplements to or in place of historical costs financial statements. Some high-inflation countries require that firms adjust their statements to reflect the enormous rates of inflation and require the use of an inflation index and a monetary correction system.

The result of these different methods of accounting for inflation is that the MNC operating in a multitude of foreign environments must often keep multiple sets of books to adhere to the reporting requirements of each jurisdiction and the parent firm's home authorities.

TAX EXPOSURE

Tax exposure is the effect that changes in the gains or losses of a company because of exchange-rate fluctuations can have on its tax liability. An unexpected or large gain based solely on exchange-rate fluctuations could upset the tax planning of a multinational by causing an increased tax liability. Gains and losses from translation exposure generally have an effect on the tax liability of a company at the time they are actually realized.

TAX HAVENS

Despite extensive nets cast by US tax authorities to capture taxes owed, many individuals and corporations attempt to avoid being taxed on their income earned abroad. Although this activity has been limited by the imposition of regulations and taxes on unremitted earnings, crafty financiers continue to attempt to shelter income. One method of accomplishing that objective is to keep income overseas (and, thus, off domestic books) in countries without tax treaties with the MNC's home government. These countries, which provide sanctuary for foreign-earned income and impose few taxes or no taxes at all, are termed "**tax havens**." Monies deposited in these nations are safe from taxation until the subsidiary declares a dividend to the parent, at which time the remittance becomes taxable by the home tax authority.

To be efficient sanctuaries for a corporation's worldwide income, tax havens must satisfy several criteria:

- They must not have a tax treaty with the corporation's domestic government that allows for the reciprocal tax treatment of income. Such a treaty would entail the sharing of earnings information and data.
- These nations must have low or no taxes on foreign-source funds. (Some tax haven countries do not provide equivalent tax amnesty for earnings within their own countries.)

- The countries must provide stable political and economic environments, so that funds deposited there will remain safe.
- The nations must allow for the free convertibility of currencies and have few if any restrictions on the inflow and outflow of currencies.
- The policies of the nations must be centered on a positive attitude toward businesses and their activities and, thus, have liberal incorporation laws.
- To accommodate financial flows, the countries must have well-developed banking systems with some degree of banking secrecy.
- The countries must also have infrastructures that support and facilitate general business operations, including such amenities as dependable telecommunications and transportation systems. A tax haven's close physical proximity to the home country makes it easier for depositors, who may then use the same lines or systems of communication and be in the same time zones.

Tax havens vary in their structure. Some countries, such as Caribbean tax havens, have very low or zero taxes on foreign or domestic income. These tax haven countries, including the Bahamas, the Cayman Islands, Bermuda, the British Virgin Islands, and the Netherlands Antilles, are often used by US nationals and corporations.

Other nations, such as Panama and Liechtenstein, provide sanctuary for foreign sources of funds but tax domestically produced income. Still other countries provide havens from taxation only for specific purposes or industries. These countries encourage investment within their boundaries by providing for tax exemptions for certain periods of time to promote industrial development. Two such countries that provide tax holidays are Ireland and Singapore, which provide tax incentives or lowered tax rates for the establishment of facilities in specific regions or zones.

TRANSFER PRICING

Multinational firms use the pricing of goods and services between their different operating arms to achieve a number of objectives, such as increasing rates of return in specific operating locations, lowering product prices in specific markets, circumventing restrictions regarding repatriation of parent-company profits, and getting around inconvertibility of host-country currencies. In addition, the uses of transfer pricing in intra-company transactions can also provide a method for MNCs to manage their international tax liability.

By shifting costs to countries with high tax rates, an MNC can enjoy savings on its tax bills, because by raising the costs of goods sold, a company can lower its taxable income, shifting profits to countries where tax rates on corporate profits are lower. US companies usually attempt to shift deductible costs to themselves or to a parent corporation's accounts from the books of the affiliates. Thus, the costs of such items as intra-company loans, the sale of inventory and machinery, and the transfer of intangible property and their associated deductibility are transferred to high-tax-rate environments.

Such practices have come under intense scrutiny both by host governments and by the US Internal Revenue Service, which can now challenge prices set by MNCs. Under certain circumstances, the IRS has the authority to recalculate those prices and assess tax liabilities according to prices set at arm's length—those prices that would have been reached if two independent parties engaged in the same transaction.

TRANSFER PRICING AND COSTING

The international nature of the business of MNCs introduces a number of factors that have to be accounted for in determining the costs of their products around the world. Although multinational firms use the same methods as domestic enterprises for determining costs, their efforts are greatly complicated by the nature of operations in a global environment. For example, products and raw materials are affected not only by domestic forces, such as inflation and availability, but also by such international forces as changes in exchange rates, transportation fees, insurance costs, customs duties, and facilitating payments. Similarly, costs involved in conducting international trade are often influenced by government subsidies that are intended to promote exports sales.

Such costing and pricing problems are significant for exported products manufactured domestically; they are even worse for firms that have raw material and parts sources in several parts of the world. The complications become enormous as accountants attempt to allocate costs to different products and operating units within different countries.

Transfers within an MNC's various affiliated arms, especially transfer pricing for goods and services between different parts of the company, create complex accounting issues. MNCs can use transfer pricing to achieve a variety of corporate objectives, such as reducing overall tax burden, avoiding restrictions on repatriation of earnings, or exchanging local for home-country currencies. Thus, transfer prices set by MNCs not only concern the strategic decision-makers in the company, but also often come under the scrutiny of external government officials. An MNC can deal with this problem to some extent by adjusting its performance measures for the subsidiary to focus on different criteria, such as achieving production efficiencies and maintaining low costs.

Companies have three ways of valuing goods and services that pass between arms or branches of the same corporation. They can use a cost-plus method, whereby they take actual costs of production and add a fixed monetary amount or percentage. Alternately, they can use the market price, less a certain percentage discount. Under arm's-length pricing they can charge the same price to affiliates or parents as they do to third-party buyers. While cost-based transfer pricing has the advantage of providing the firm with flexibility, most governments prefer that MNCs use the easily determined and monitored market-based pricing systems. The United States requires that firms use arm's-length prices unless they can justify why different prices based on costs are more reasonable than those based on market prices.

SUMMARY

The foreign exchange markets act as the intermediary through which complex transactions between different currencies are completed. Individuals and institutions, such as multinational corporations, pension funds, commercial banks, central banks, arbitragers, speculators, and foreign exchange brokers, all participate in the markets to varying degrees, with the large international banks being the most active. Located in major business centers around the world (London, New York, and Tokyo are the largest), the foreign exchange markets have three basic functions: settlement of trade transactions, avoidance of risk because of currency fluctuations, and the financing of international trade.

The three major transactions in the foreign exchange markets are the spot, forward, and swap transactions. Based on the prices of currencies and using various formulas, traders attempt to take advantage of momentary disequilibrium in the prices of currencies, or currency and interest disparities, by trading in different locations or markets. They also try to minimize losses associated with unanticipated changes in currency values. Some of the techniques used are triangular arbitrage, covered interest arbitrage, and hedges.

Forward contracts, which are generally used by large international banks and MNCs, can be tailor-made for any contract size or currency, but they require execution of the transaction on the date of contract maturity. Futures contracts differ from forward contracts by offering standardized, regulated contracts of smaller sizes, which can be easily liquidated. Options are yet another form of currency contract, which, like futures contracts, are standardized and can be easily liquidated. Options offer the right, not the obligation, to buy or sell a foreign currency at a set price up to an agreed date.

Corporations face four major types of risk or exposure in their international activities: transaction exposure, economic exposure, translation exposure, and tax exposure. Forecasting foreign exchange rates is often vital to conducting international business, but generating accurate forecasts is extremely difficult. Fundamental forecasting examines macroeconomic variables, such as balance of payments, inflation rates, and unemployment trends, to predict future exchange rates, while technical forecasting relies on historical exchange-rate data to predict future currency exchange rates.

DISCUSSION QUESTIONS

1. Why does international business need a foreign exchange market?
2. Who are the participants in foreign exchange transactions?
3. Where are foreign exchange markets located? Where are the main centers of foreign trading?
4. Discuss the four types of risk facing multinational corporations.
5. What is the difference between the spot and the forward markets?
6. You currently hold US$1 million and are interested in exchanging US dollars for Swiss francs. The current spot rate of US$1 = CHF1.475 is a direct quote. Is this true or false?

7. What is a long position? What is a short position? What is a square position?

8. What is the bid-offer spread for a US$/£ quote of US$1.8410–$1.8420?

9. What is covered interest arbitrage?

10. What is the difference between the futures and forward markets?

11. What is an option?

12. What is the difference between fundamental forecasting and technical forecasting?

NOTES

1. Federal Reserve Bank of New York, *Summary Results of U.S. Foreign Exchange Markets Survey Conducted in March 1986.*

2. Eun and Resnick, *International Financial Management.*

BIBLIOGRAPHY

Aliber, Robert Z. *The International Money Game.* 2nd ed. New York: Basic Books, 1976.

Black, Fisher, and Martin Scholes. "The Pricing of Options and Corporate Liabilities." *Journal of Political Economy* (May–June 1973): 637–659.

Buckley, Adrian. "Multinational Finance: The Risks of FX." *Accountancy* (February 1987): 80–82.

Choi, Jau J. "Diversification, Exchange Risk and Corporate Risk." *International Business Studies* (Spring 1989): 145–155.

Dornbusch, Rudiger "Equilibrium and Disequilibrium Exchange Rates." *Zeitschrift fir Wirtschafts und Sozialwissenshaften* 102 (1983): 573–599.

Dufey, Gunter, and Ian. Giddy. "Forecasting Exchange Rates in a Floating World." *Euromoney,* November 1975, 28–35.

Ensig, Paul. *The Theory of Forward Exchange.* London: Macmillan, 1937.

Eun, Cheol S., and Bruce G. Resnick. *International Financial Management.* 6th ed. New York: McGraw-Hill/Irwin, 2012.

Federal Reserve Bank of New York. *Summary Results of U.S. Foreign Exchange Markets Survey Conducted in March 1986.* New York: Federal Reserve Bank of New York, 1986.

Griffiths, Susan H., and Paul S. Greenfield. "Foreign Currency Management: Part I—Currency Hedging Strategies." *Journal of Cash Management* (July–August 1989): 141.

Kwok, Chuck. "Hedging Foreign Exchange Exposures: Independent Versus Integrative Approaches." *Journal of International Business Studies* (Summer 1987): 33–52.

Ma, Christopher K., and G. Wenchi Kao. "On Exchange Rate Changes and Stock Price Reactions." *Journal of Business Finance and Accounting* (Summer 1990): 441–449.

Madura, Jeff. *International Financial Management.* 2nd ed. St. Paul, MN: West, 1989.

Mckinnon, Ronald I. "Interest Rate Volatility and Exchange Risk: New Rates for a Common Monetary Standard." *Contemporary Policy Issues* (April 1990): 1–17.

Soenen, Luc A., and Raj Aggarwal. "Corporate Foreign Exchange and Cash Management Practices." *Journal of Cash Management* (March–April 1987): 62–64.

Sweeney, Richard J. "Beating the Foreign Exchange Market." *Journal of Finance* (March 1986): 163–182.

Taylor, Mark P. "Covered Interest Arbitrage and Market Turbulence." *Economic Journal* (June 1989): 376–391.

Walsh, Carl E. "Interest Rates and Exchange Rates." *FRBSF Weekly Letter,* June 5, 1987, 41.

Woo, Wing Thye. "Some Evidence of Speculative Bubbles in the Foreign Exchange Market." *Journal of Money, Credit, and Banking* (November 1987): 499–514.

Yahoo Finance. "International Currency Tables." October 15, 2012. http://finance.yahoo.com/currency-investing.

CASE STUDY 5.1

SKYTRACK INSTRUMENTATION

Jerry Turner and William McKensie are in good spirits. Having finished a round of golf at the Green Holes Country Club in Quintacera, a resort town north of Divotia, the main business center in the Latin American nation of Celida, they head for the clubhouse for a couple of drinks before lunch and an afternoon meeting with José Cervantes, their main consultant on government regulations. Turner and McKensie are president and chief financial officer of Skytrack Instrumentation, a British-based multinational specializing in air traffic control instruments for civilian aircraft. Their annual sales are about US$6 billion, spread over forty-five countries on four continents. Skytrack Instrumentation Celida was established as a wholly owned subsidiary in 2010. The company had set up a highly automated manufacturing facility in a small industrial park just outside Divotia that had been created by the government of Celida to attract investment from overseas. With considerable cooperation from the government and the availability of many infrastructural facilities in Celida, Skytrack was able to set up the plant within two years, and production is now expected to begin within the next three weeks. Turner and McKensie are taking a well-deserved vacation before the commencement of operations. Meanwhile, McKensie also has to start charting the tax strategy of the company, something he has not yet done. A preliminary meeting with Cervantes, a leading expert on government regulations for multinational enterprises in Celida, seems to be a good first step.

Cervantes comes to their meeting well prepared for the discussion. He pulls out two separate briefs, detailing comprehensive outlines for two approaches that Skytrack could take to minimize its tax liability in Celida.

One of the approaches is based on the technique of transfer pricing, which the brief euphemistically calls the "price adjustment approach." There is considerable scope with this technique because the subsidiary is importing nearly every component of its products from Great Britain and assembling them in Celida. In fact, the cost of components is almost 50 percent of the total costs of goods to be sold in Celida, according to early projections made by the company's accountants. If the import price is raised, the profit margins would be lowered and so would the tax liability. The tax rates on overseas corporations in Celida are as follows:

35 percent corporate income tax	Computed on earnings, including interest earnings, for the financial year
15 percent withholding tax	Computed on the amount of profits sought to be repatriated by the company

Projected sales of Skytrack Celida for the first year are about £160 million (calculated at the day's exchange rate of £1 for 34 Celidan pesos). The estimated costs of goods sold, selling expenses, interest expenses, and other costs are in aggregate £130 million. Net profit before taxes is thus estimated to be £30 million; of this, 35 percent, that is, £10.5 million, is to be paid as corporate income tax, which would leave the company with £19.5 million in profits. According to the local regulations, overseas companies are allowed to repatriate 75 percent of their posttax profits each year. Under this provision, Skytrack could repatriate £14 million to Great Britain. There would be, however, a withholding tax of 15 percent on this amount, or £2.2 million. The total tax liability of Skytrack Celida would thus be £12.69 million on a profit of £30 million, or about 42.3 percent.

If, however, Skytrack UK could increase the price of components sold to Skytrack Celida by 15 percent (on total annual sales of approximately £85), the tax liability could be reduced substantially. Cervantes shows Turner and McKensie the computation (in millions of pounds):

Original cost of sales	130
Increase in equipment prices	12.75 (15 percent of £85)
New cost of sales	142.75
Profit	17.25
Corporate income tax	6.0375
Net profit	11.21
Repatriated amount (75 percent)	8.40
Tax on repatriated amount	1.26
Total tax	7.296
Tax savings	5.40
Increase in headquarters tax liability on account of increase in income	3.2
Net tax savings	**2.2**

The other approach suggested by Cervantes is to use a tax haven, which would make the tax savings even greater. Skytrack could ship components, on paper, to Skytrack Cayman Islands, at the same price it would be shipping to Skytrack Celida. Thus, there would be no increase in Skytrack UK income because of higher prices, but Skytrack Cayman Islands would notionally resell these components to Skytrack Celida at a markup of 15 percent and in the process make a "profit" of £12.75 million, on which there would be no tax liability because the Cayman Islands is a tax haven. At the same time, Skytrack Celida would have a reduced tax liability of £5.4 million. The net savings would be £3.2 million over the direct approach.

(continued)

Case Study 5.1 *(continued)*

The tax haven approach, however, is more complex. It requires documentation to be routed through the Cayman Islands and increases the risk of making Celidan authorities suspicious. On the other hand, £3.2 million a year is a large sum, even for a company of Skytrack's size, and the use of tax havens is quite common.

DISCUSSION QUESTION

Which of the following options should Turner and McKensie choose? Explain your reasons for accepting or rejecting each option.
  A. No transfer pricing
  B. Transfer pricing
  C. Transfer pricing and using a tax haven
  D. Are there other alternatives? If so, what are their advantages and disadvantages?

CASE STUDY 5.2

CHEMTECH INC.

As he walks into his office in downtown Frankfurt one Tuesday morning, Jorge Muller, corporate treasurer of Chemtech, smiles at his secretary. "Good morning, Marita," he says. "Anything important happen while I was away?" he continues, referring to his short trip to Paris that had spilled over from the weekend to Monday. "Nothing much," replies Marita, "except there was a call from Mr. Karl Volten of Hamburg Bank. He wants you to call him as soon as possible." "Thanks," Muller replies as he sits down to begin work on what he knows will be a critical week.

Chemtech Inc. is a leading pharmaceutical manufacturer in Germany with total sales of more than $26 billion in 2010. Founded just after World War II, the company has established a strong market presence in both the German domestic market and several international markets. The emphasis of the company has always been to push ahead in the export markets of the industrialized countries, because opportunities to sell its sophisticated and fairly high-priced products in markets of less-developed countries are limited. Total export sales come from the following countries:

United States	$6.00 billion
United Kingdom	2.00 billion
France	2.00 billion
Italy	1.50 billion
Canada	0.75 billion
Sweden	0.70 billion
Japan	1.20 billion
Total	**$14.15 billion**

While Chemtech has enjoyed great success in its export markets, with sales growing at an average of 11 percent over the past seven years, profits from exports have not grown at the same pace. International competition has intensified in most markets due to US and Swiss pharmaceutical manufacturers, and the firm has been forced to give greater discounts to retain market share. Although productivity has risen, it has not risen enough to offset increasing production costs, especially the higher labor costs that Chemtech encountered over the past three years following a settlement with the labor unions. One of the most important problems, however, is the continued appreciation of the euro against the US dollar and pound sterling, which has reduced export profits considerably. The problem has been particularly acute in the past eight months, because a continuously weakening dollar has hurt export revenues and therefore profitability by as much as 9 percent.

Muller was asked by Chemtech's director of finance to come up with a strategy to guard against foreign exchange fluctuation losses. Muller called his friend and longtime adviser Karl Volten, vice president of corporate foreign exchange services at Hamburg Bank, for suggestions. Volten is a foreign exchange expert with many years of top-level experience in advising large corporations on managing their foreign exchange exposures. He has an MBA in finance from a major US university and worked as an exchange trader in the New York branch of the Hamburg Bank for six years. He had been assistant vice president of corporate foreign exchange advisory services for three years and has held his current position for the past two and a half years.

When the two friends meet, Volten suggests that Chemtech should buy US$ call options on the IMM exchange through the New York branch office of the Hamburg Bank. By purchasing an option, the company could lock in a minimum euro price for the dollar revenues it earns from US operations, and if the euro weakens before maturity of the contract, the company could choose not to exercise the option. As a matter of policy, Chemtech repatriates US dollar profits every six months, and options could be bought for six-month maturities. Options could also be sold off before the due date.

(continued)

Case Study 5.2 *(continued)*

For example, the prevailing US$/€ rate today is US$1 = €1.5. It is expected that the euro will be strengthened further, although no one can predict by how much. Chemtech can lock in a particular level of exchange rate by buying a euro call option for the strike price of €1.3 per dollar. There would be an up-front cost for the option of €0.3 for every dollar of the contract amount. The company would therefore be locking into an effective rate of €1 = $1.

The strategy has several advantages. For one, the company is covered against excess depreciation of the dollar. If the dollar appreciates beyond €1.3, the company could simply forgo the option and buy euros in the open market. In fact, if the dollar goes beyond €1.6, the company can recover its entire hedging cost of €0.3 per dollar and actually profit from the option transaction. If, on the other hand, the dollar weakens beyond €1.3, the company can exercise the option and buy the euros at this price. Hedging costs will be fully recovered if the dollar weakens to €1 = $1, and any further weakening of the dollar will mean additional profits for Chemtech.

The strategy appears extremely attractive to Muller. "We win on both sides," he figures, "since we are saved from any excess strengthening of the euro and still have the opportunity of making substantial gains on any large weakening of the currency. It's a lot better than going for the plain old forward contract for €1.2 per dollar. True, we lock in our price at €1.2 and we are saved against any depreciation of the dollar beyond that, but if the dollar strengthens against the euro, we would be locked out of the opportunity to profit from it. I think I will prepare a report for the treasurer," he decides.

DISCUSSION QUESTIONS

1. Is the suggested options strategy completely risk-free?
2. If you were the treasurer, what would you think of this proposal? Are there any reasons for rejecting this strategy in favor of forward contracts?
3. Under what circumstances would a forward contract be a better alternative to achieve the objectives of the company?

CHAPTER 6

Supranational Organizations and International Institutions

"Mankind always takes up only such problems as it thinks it can solve."
—Albert O. Hirschman

CHAPTER OBJECTIVES

This chapter will:

- Identify major international trade organizations, such as the World Trade Organization and the United Nations Conference on Trade and Development, and the roles they play in shaping the international business environment
- Describe the major financial institutions, such as the World Bank and the International Finance Corporation, and the assistance they provide in channeling financial resources to developing countries
- Review the growth of regional financial institutions and their important positions as providers of financial resources

---

BACKGROUND

Increasing economic, financial, and commercial interdependence among nations of the world after World War II created a need to coordinate international action and policies to secure the smooth flow of trade. Apart from regular, periodic meetings of officials and business leaders from different countries, these nations recognized a need for the establishment of permanent organizations to provide stability and continuity to the process of international economic interchange. Some supranational bodies were set up in the period immediately following World War II, while more were established in the following decades. Two major categories of international organizations can be identified as those having a global focus and those set up to meet the needs of particular regions.

GENERAL AGREEMENT ON TARIFFS AND TRADE

The **General Agreement on Tariffs and Trade (GATT)** was established initially as a temporary measure to reduce trade barriers among its founding members. Since its inception in 1947, GATT evolved into a permanent body to include most industrial and developing countries, excluding those of the socialist bloc.

GATT was originally established to avoid the kind of competitive protectionism that had plagued international trade in the period between the two world wars, which was reflected in high tariff barriers and a major slump in trade volumes. The objectives of GATT—liberalization of international trade restrictions and the lowering of tariff barriers—were to be achieved by multilateral negotiations and voluntarily agreed-upon rules of conduct. As a permanent international body, GATT was to provide the forum for the conduct of these negotiations and the development of necessary ground rules for liberalizing the international trade environment. GATT was also intended to serve as an agency for mediation and settlement of trade disputes.

One of the main tenets of GATT regulations is the requirement for its members to comply with the most-favored-nation clause, which obligates all member countries to give the same tariff concessions to all GATT countries that they give to any one member country. For example, if Germany reduces the import duty on Japanese television sets from 40 percent to 10 percent, then it must level the same rate of duty on television sets from other countries.

There have historically been important exceptions to the most-favored-nation clause, which recognized the need for preferential treatment to be given to the less-developed countries (LDCs), which without special treatment have not historically been able to compete on a one-to-one basis with the industrialized countries. The developing countries thus have had preferential access to the markets of developed countries for some of their products under the generalized system of preferences, an advantage that has begun to erode in recent years.

Another major exception relates to the establishment of regional trading alliances: members of regional trade agreements can extend trade concessions to one another without extending these concessions to countries that are not members of the alliance. The European Union (EU), the North American Free Trade Agreement (NAFTA), and the Association of South East Asian Nations (ASEAN) are three examples of regional trade agreements. To ease the problem of dealing with tariffs and duties on individual products, most negotiations concern making generalized reductions in tariff rates for a large number of products in certain categories.

In the eight rounds, or negotiating sessions, under GATT,[1] significant changes were made. The average tariffs on industrial products, levied by the developed countries,

Figure 6.1   **Proliferation of (In-Force) Regional Trade Agreements (RTAs) Since 1958**

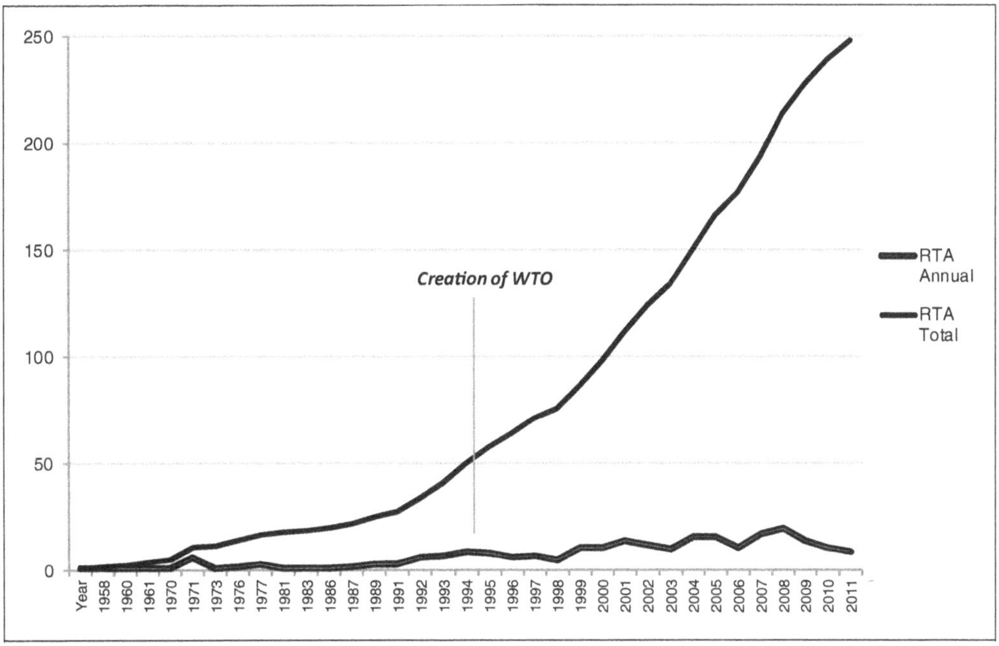

Source: World Trade Organization, "Welcome to the Regional Trade Agreements Information System (RTA-IS)," http://rtais.wto.org/UI/PublicPreDefRepByEIF.aspx.

came down significantly. GATT countries have accounted for 85 percent of world trade since its inception. This trend has only improved since the creation of the World Trade Organization in 1995, as is shown in Figure 6.1.

There were still several problems with GATT, however, such as an increasing emphasis on protectionism, not only in the developing countries, but also in the industrialized world. The use of nontariff barriers to discriminate against imports from other countries has enabled many member countries to negate the intended effects of the tariff reductions agreed to under the GATT rules of conduct. Further, since GATT regulations were imprecise, many signatory states found loopholes to evade the requirements, almost on a routine basis. Many trade issues arose in the 1970s and 1980s that had not been foreseen by earlier negotiations, and provisions for regulating them were not included in the agreements. There are also substantial difficulties between major trading partners, as relative economic and competitive strengths change and new arrangements and terms are sought by old trading partners. In the mid-1990s, the increasing importance of both the service sector and intellectual property rights led to the need for a fundamental change in GATT. In 1994, at the end of the Uruguay Round of trade talks, the decision was made to expand GATT into a new organization known as the World Trade Organization (WTO).[2]

World Trade Organization

Since GATT had been successful in reducing tariffs worldwide since 1948, and given the increasing importance of the service sector and intellectual property rights in the modern economy, the members of GATT formed the **World Trade Organization** in January 1995 to increase the scope of the trade agreements beyond manufactured products. The WTO currently has more than 150 member nations that participate in trade discussions. The WTO is both a forum for resolving trade disputes and an arena for agreeing on the rules of operation for international trade. Since we have already outlined GATT, we will next focus on providing a brief description of the other two primary areas of the WTO, the General Agreement on Trade in Services and the Agreement on Trade-Related Aspects of Intellectual Property Rights.

General Agreement on Trade in Services

The **General Agreement on Trade in Services (GATS)** is the first and only set of multi-lateral rules governing international trade in services. The inclusion of services, negotiated in the Uruguay Round, was developed primarily due to the increase in importance of the service sector in the developed world and also due to the greater potential for trading services brought about by the advancement in communications technology over the past few decades. All services are covered under GATS, and the most-favored-nation treatment applies to all services as well.[3] GATS identifies four modes of trading services:

1. *Cross-border supply*: services supplied from one country to another
2. *Consumption abroad*: consumers or firms making use of a service in another country (i.e., tourism)
3. *Commercial presence*: foreign company setting up a branch or subsidiary in another country
4. *Presence of natural persons*: individuals traveling to another country to supply services

The reason that these definitions are necessary is that the trade in services is a much more diverse area than the trade in manufactured goods. The business models of service sector industries such as financial services, telecommunications, tourism, and even restaurants are very different. These varied industries under the service sector umbrella perform their operations in very different ways.

GATS requires member governments to regulate their services reasonably, objectively, and impartially, and the agreement does not require that any service be deregulated. As you will recall from the discussion concerning the Asian financial crisis, the lack of effective regulation in the banking sector was at the heart of the problem. Thus, if GATS had required deregulation of the service sector by its member nations, the problem of moral hazard could not have been improved.

Another important tenet of GATS is **transparency**. GATS specifies that all governments should adequately publish all laws and regulations that deal with the service sector. This will provide for easy access to the domestic service regulations for foreign companies and governments wishing to conduct business in another country. The guiding principle of these transparency rules is **nondiscrimination**, or the treatment of foreign enterprises on the same basis as domestic enterprises. The industrialized countries are likely to press for progressive liberalization of trade in services, while the developing countries may demand greater shares in the international services market and greater mobility of their workforces to move to the developed countries as a part of the liberalization of rules regarding manpower services.

AGREEMENT ON TRADE-RELATED ASPECTS OF INTELLECTUAL PROPERTY RIGHTS (TRIPS)

Another creation of the Uruguay Round was the **Agreement on Trade-Related Aspects of Intellectual Property Rights (TRIPS)**. The purpose of TRIPS is to allow for the creation of domestic laws that concern the protection of intellectual property rights, as well as the enforcement of such laws in violating countries. TRIPS established minimum levels of protection that each WTO member government must provide to the intellectual property of fellow WTO member states. TRIPS covers the following types of intellectual property.[4]

- Copyrights
- Trademarks (including service marks)
- Geographical indications, such as "Champagne," "Scotch," and "Tequila"
- Industrial designs
- Patents
- Layout designs of integrated circuits
- Undisclosed information, including trade secrets

TRIPS provides guidelines for how basic principles of the trading system and other international intellectual property rights agreements should be applied. It also spells out how various WTO member governments must provide adequate protection of intellectual property rights in their domestic laws, and it sets rules for how countries should enforce intellectual property rights within their own borders. TRIPS also provides a means of settling disputes regarding intellectual property between members of the WTO.

When the WTO came into being in January 1995, the developed countries of the world were given one year to harmonize (or equalize) their intellectual property laws so that they were in compliance with the specifications required by TRIPS. Some developing countries were given until the year 2000 to ensure that their laws and practices conform to the TRIPS agreement. LDCs were initially provided eleven years (until 2006) to meet these requirements.[5] Currently, there is a phase-in period for LDCs regarding the implementation of pharmaceutical patent protection until 2016.

The TRIPS agreement has been a point of contention for many years between the developed world and the developing nations. The countries of the developed world see the need for strict intellectual property rights enforcement as a way of recouping their research and development costs for products such as pharmaceutical drugs. The LDCs see these same protections as trade restrictions. In the case of pharmaceutical drugs, the LDCs argue that in lieu of intellectual property restrictions, much cheaper versions of the drugs could be provided for a greater number of people. This is similar to the utilitarian viewpoint made famous by such philosophers as Jeremy Bentham, who, in the eighteenth century, argued that moral values are reflected in policies that provide the greatest happiness to the greatest number of people. These same arguments have been made by students around the globe recently concerning online music sharing; high school and college students have found it reasonable to argue that music provided online or via Apple iPods should be provided either without cost or at a much-reduced cost. While the arguments are essentially the same, the impact of not being able to enjoy online music is of no comparison to the inability to access pharmaceutical drugs for the affected citizens. Discussions like these will only continue with the increased integration of world markets and with the continued importance of the TRIPS for all WTO member nations.

DOHA AGENDA

In November 2001, at a WTO conference in Doha, Qatar, the member nations of the WTO agreed to launch a new round of trade negotiations. One of the primary thrusts of the new trade round concerns the problems faced by the developing countries in implementing some of the changes decided upon in the Uruguay Round (e.g., TRIPS). Another important area for reform is agricultural trade barriers. The countries of the developing world claim that agricultural protectionism by the countries of the developed world (i.e., United States, Canada, and the members of the European Union) leaves them without the ability to sell their agricultural products to the most developed nations. Thus, their primary avenue for income growth has been closed. At the start of the Doha trade round, both developed and developing nations made promises to improve market access for agricultural and other products via reductions in export subsidies, quotas, and tariffs. To date, final agreements have not been possible owing to the inability to agree on the appropriate level of reduction of trade barriers for both the developed and the developing world.

UNITED NATIONS CONFERENCE ON TRADE AND DEVELOPMENT

The **United Nations Conference on Trade and Development (UNCTAD)** was established in 1964 to address concerns of developing nations regarding issues of international trade that affected their economic development. The main concern of most developing countries was that, under the old system, unequal players were asked to play on a level playing field. The LDCs, which were extremely weak economically and industrially backward, had no way of competing with the industrialized nations in the world market on the same terms. Moreover, they argued, given the structure of the international economy, they were parting with more of their goods as exports than they were receiving as imports. In effect, the prices of their exports were not rising as did the prices of their imports. This feature is conceptualized in economics as the terms-of-trade argument. Further, LDCs' exports suffered from low demand and low price elasticity, which meant that they could not raise export prices by reducing supplies. On the other hand, their imports were critical for them and their supplies were controlled by large monopolistic entities that could charge exorbitant prices.

UNCTAD was established to provide a forum for the developing countries to communicate their views on international trade issues to the industrialized countries and to seek trade concessions from them. After considerable and sustained pressure from the developing countries, the developed countries agreed to an across-the-board reduction of tariffs for developing countries under an arrangement known as the generalized system of preferences (GSP). The GSP tariff reductions, however, were for only limited amounts of imports from developing countries and did not create any significant niches for developing-country exporters in the markets of industrialized countries. Moreover, since the liberalization in tariffs was only for manufactured goods, many developing countries with little industrial activity cannot benefit from the reduced tariffs.

Membership of UNCTAD increased from 119 countries in 1964 to 194 countries in 2012. Although the deliberations and resolutions of UNCTAD have not solved the problems faced by developing countries in the international trade area, they have had important positive effects on the international trade environment in general. UNCTAD conferences have resulted in a better and more informed understanding of the respective positions on various issues of the developed and developing countries. In recent meetings of the Trade and Development Board in Geneva, issues concerning trade between the **developed countries** (the North) and the **developing countries** (the South) have been the topic of discussion. Under the current heading of "Prosperity for All," UNCTAD is committed to studying the factors that have left many African nations behind in their ability to participate in the benefits of globalization. The UNCTAD participants agree that it is the moral responsibility of the organization as well as other supranational organizations previously discussed to find ways of improving the performance of LDCs in the world economy.

A number of permanent working committees, such as the Commission on Trade in Goods, Services, and Commodities; the Commission on Investment, Technology, and Related Financial Issues; and the Commission on Enterprise, Business Facilitation, and Development, have been created to deal with major issues and analyze complex problems in depth, thereby contributing to an increase in the level of understanding of the problems by representatives and officials of different countries. Thus, UNCTAD has become a permanent international organization that focuses global attention on the trade development problems of LDCs. At the time of its inception, the creation of UNCTAD was hailed as one of the most important events since the establishment of the United Nations. Although the concrete impact of the organization has been limited, it has kept alive the dialogue between the industrial and developing world. Given the current impasse of the Doha Development Agenda in the WTO, organizations such as UNCTAD will continue the quest to allow all parts of the world to share in the benefits of globalization.

REGIONAL TRADE GROUPINGS

Regional trade groupings have emerged in the past two decades as major forces shaping the pattern of international trade. These arrangements have enabled countries located in different geographic locations to pool their resources and lower restrictions on trade among themselves in order to achieve greater economic growth.

Regional groupings offer several advantages over global trade arrangements to their members. Because there are fewer countries involved, and their state of economic development is relatively homogeneous, it is easier to find commonality of interest and arrive at a workable agreement on the basis of voluntary adherence by member countries. As was illustrated in Figure 6.1, the proliferation of regional trade agreements since 1995 has been unprecedented. Although some experts hail the accelerated pace of regional trade agreements as a success, others, such as economist Jagdish Bhagwati, refer to the various agreements as a "spaghetti bowl" with each successive arrangement moving the world further from true free trade. True free trade can be seen as an environment where no trade barriers, customs duties, or government interventionist policy limits international trade, whereby the cost of said trade is not increased by the barriers put into the marketplace.

The controversy surrounding the unprecedented increase in such arrangements aside, regional groupings do offer advantages of cultural, geographical, and historical homogeneity, which provides an environment conducive to the spirit of mutual cooperation. Even with all the positive factors, however, regional groupings can still face severe internal dissension among member states, especially if the general economic situation is poor and countries follow restrictive, inward-looking policies. The experience of regional groupings in international trade has therefore varied considerably. While the European Union and the Association of South East Asian Nations are notable successes, trade arrangements in Africa and Latin America have not achieved many significant benefits for their member countries.

FORMS OF REGIONAL INTEGRATION

Many nations have entered into **bilateral agreements** (involving two countries) or **multilateral agreements** (involving more than two countries) in the attempt to increase trade between member states. There are five different forms of regional economic integration. Some of these forms of economic integration also include some degree of political integration. Some have existed for many years, while others are relatively new. These forms of regional economic integration are listed in increasing order of integration as follows:

- Free trade area
- Customs union
- Common market
- Economic union
- Political union

FREE TRADE AREA

The first form of regional economic integration is the **free trade area**. The United States has entered into many of these bilateral agreements recently. Over the last few years, the United States has signed bilateral free trade agreements with countries as diverse as Singapore, Chile, Vietnam, and Jordan. These agreements are between just the United States and the designated bilateral partner (e.g., Chile); the agreements reached between these two countries pertain only to them. Free trade areas eliminate trade barriers among their members (at least the barriers agreed to in the free trade agreement), but members can set their own trade policies with nonmembers. Thus, while the United States has bilateral agreements with Chile and Vietnam, Canada does not have to honor these agreements. In fact, Canada has signed its own separate free trade agreement with Chile. Some observers argue that these agreements are really not free trade agreements at all, just reduced trade barriers for specific goods and services, with those items not addressed still being protected.

The most commonly known multilateral free trade agreement is the North American Free Trade Agreement (NAFTA). NAFTA, which came into effect in 1994, is a free trade agreement of the United States, Canada, and Mexico. The origins of NAFTA were in the United States-Canadian Automotive Agreement from 1965. NAFTA has been successful in increasing the volume of trade between its member nations, but critics cite the movement of jobs from the United States to Mexico as an example of a flawed system. Mexican companies have formed **maquiladoras**, or manufacturing facilities located in the northern part of Mexico, in an attempt to capitalize on the southern movement of manufacturing plants from the United States.

A weakness of free trade agreements is that they are vulnerable to **trade deflection**, a process in which nonmember nations reroute their exports to member nations with the lowest external trade barriers. Thus, free trade areas require **rules of origin** specifications to clarify what actually constitutes member goods and services within the free trade agreement. As an example, if Mexico had the lowest external trade barriers when compared with Canada and the United States, a country that is not a member of NAFTA (such as Brazil) could attempt to access the US and Canadian markets more cheaply by sending goods to Mexico for re-export into the United States or Canada. Another weakness of free trade areas is that they are vulnerable to **trade diversion**. This occurs when member nations stop importing from lower-cost nonmember nations in favor of member states. Since the goal of a free trade area is the reduction in the prices that consumers pay for products via the reduction of protective trade barriers, such trade diversion would seem to be counterproductive.

CUSTOMS UNION

The second form of regional economic integration, **customs union** agreements, combine the elimination of internal trade barriers among member nations with the adoption of common external trade policies toward nonmembers. Thus, a customs union is a free trade area with a common external trade policy. This eliminates the trade deflection problem that is associated with free trade areas. The most well-known customs union is the **Mercosur Accord**, an agreement signed by Argentina, Brazil, Paraguay, and Uruguay in 1995; Venezuela joined in 2012. The Mercosur Accord covers 260 million people, with a combined annual GDP of $2.9 trillion. Within three years of the formation of the customs union, the trade between the member nations doubled. The Mercosur Accord nations have recently been talking with European Union officials about forming the world's largest free trade area.[6] Thus far talks have not produced a new agreement. This idea was inspired by the existing example of a customs union between the European Union and Turkey.

Another example of a customs union is the **Andean Community**, an agreement signed by five Latin American countries—Bolivia, Chile, Colombia, Ecuador, and Peru—in 1969, in effect creating a sub-regional trading arrangement. An important motivation for the creation of the Andean Community was a growing dissatisfaction among several Latin American countries about restrictions on trade in goods and services. The Andean Community works through a secretariat that handles all administrative and executive matters. The decisions of the community are made through a commission made up of a representative from each member country. Disputes between members on the interpretation of the pact's statutes are heard and settled by the Court of Justice of the Andean Community. Although progress has been relatively slow, some important steps toward regional integration have been taken by the Andean Community countries. The community covers 1.8 million square miles and 98 million people.

Under the industry sectoral programs, a number of industry sectors are selected for the implementation of coordinated or rationalized development plans that aim to achieve the best utilization of competitive advantages available in different countries in the region. Thus, the country having a competitive advantage in a particular industrial product will concentrate on the production of that product, while other products related to that industry will be manufactured by other member countries. Countries exchange their allocated products with other member states on a tariff-free basis. At present, sectoral cooperation in industrial activity encompasses petrochemicals, automotive products, and metals.

The members of the Andean Community have been able to establish coordinated policies to promote and control foreign direct investments, with the goal of achieving a certain similarity of restrictions in all member countries in order to develop leverage in negotiating investment permissions with overseas investors. At the same time, by creating intraregional competition to attract foreign investment flows, the community aims to prevent the possibility of the investors gaining unfair advantages by playing one country of the region against another. Chile, however, wanted to attract greater levels of foreign direct investments but could not hope to do so under the community's restrictive provisions, so it left the Andean Community (at the time called the Andean Pact) in 1976.

The Andean Community has made little progress in tariff reduction among its member countries. Further regional cooperation in Latin America has been limited because most countries have been repeatedly beset by serious internal economic problems.

COMMON MARKET

The third form of economic integration, the **common market**, increases the agreements in place for a customs union to include the elimination of barriers that inhibit the movement of the factors of production. The member nations involved in a common market agree that labor, capital, and technology are able to move across borders without any barriers. Many of the countries engaged in customs unions have the eventual goal of becoming common markets.

The Central American Common Market was formed by a 1960 treaty signed by El Salvador, Guatemala, Honduras, and Nicaragua; Costa Rica joined later. The Caribbean Community and Common Market was formed in 1973. This group includes many island nations in the Caribbean, including the Bahamas, Belize, Haiti, Jamaica, Saint Lucia, and Trinidad and Tobago.

The most famous example of a common market is the **European Economic Area (EEA)**. This group includes the European Union plus Iceland, Liechtenstein, and Norway. The three countries outside of the European Union decided to keep the common market status that they had prior to increased integration in the European Union in 1992. The common market status of the EEA allows these three countries to participate in the internal market of the European Union, but not in the full integration of the twenty-eight nations that currently make up the European Union. One weakness of this approach for EEA members is that they must accept the regulations and laws of the European Union without influencing the vote in the European Parliament.

Each of the non-EU members of the EEA has its own economic reasons for not joining the European Union in its entirety. Norway and Iceland have historically depended on the fisheries industry and have objected to some of the provisions of the European Union's **common agricultural policy (CAP)**. While the fisheries industry represents less than 1 percent of Norway's GDP, it remains its most protected industry.[7] Additionally, Norway has a large current account surplus due in large part to the export of oil and gas. Norway's current account surplus has trended upward since 1998, as shown in Figure 6.2.

Since 1990, Norway has saved the surplus in its annual government accounts into the State Petroleum Fund. The existence of this fund may shed additional light on why Norway has not thus far been interested in pursuing further European Union integration: many citizens in Norway fear that this fund could be used to fund problem areas of other nations in an integrated Europe.[8] In the wake of the recent financial crisis, this fear may have been proved correct.

Liechtenstein has not integrated further than the EEA with the European Union given

Figure 6.2 **Norway's Current Account Surplus, 1998–2011** (US$ millions)

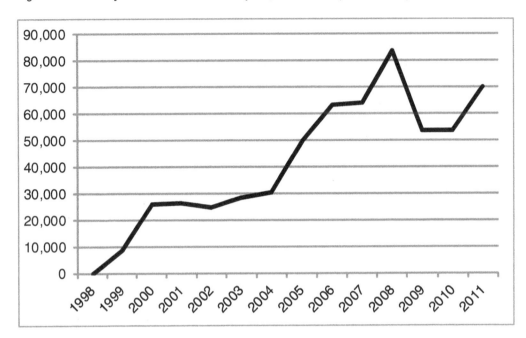

Sources: World Trade Organization, "Trade Policy Review Norway," September 2004, www.wto.org. and indexmundi.com, October 2012.

the country's high level of integration with Switzerland. Liechtenstein has had a customs union with Switzerland since 1924, has the same currency as the Swiss, and relies on the Swiss for defense. Since the Swiss failed to ratify the EEA amendment in 1992, any further integration by Liechtenstein with the European Union has been stalled. Both countries are known to maintain higher bank secrecy than other European nations, which also has slowed momentum for joining the EU.

ECONOMIC UNION

The fourth level of economic integration, economic union, involves eliminating internal trade barriers, adopting common external trade policies, abolishing restrictions on the mobility of the factors of production, and coordinating economic activities. As discussed in Chapter 4, the European Union (EU) is the primary example of this form of integration. The original fifteen EU member states agreed to coordinate their monetary, fiscal, taxation, and social welfare programs in an attempt to blend these formerly sovereign nations into a single economic entity. As evidenced by the EU sovereign debt crisis, some EU member nations—such as Greece, Ireland, and Spain—did not maintain the level of fiscal responsibility relative to other EU member states. Chapter 4 itemizes the various methods used to converge various member states into one economic entity. The

European Central Bank (ECB), based in Brussels, Belgium, was created to serve as the central bank for all members of the European Monetary Union. While the ECB formulates monetary policy for the European Union, the European Commission and the European Parliament are in charge of the European Union's fiscal policy. Managing the fiscal and monetary integration of the EU member states has proved challenging. In the wake of the EU sovereign debt crisis, a concerted effort has been made to ensure that the future fiscal irresponsibility of a few member states does not cause contagion for the EU at large. If the EU is to continue successfully, more fiscal oversight by the EU on member states is to be expected, as has been seen in the past.

Political Union

The fifth and final level of economic integration is political union. This represents the complete political and economic integration of all member states, in essence making them one unified country. Many Euro-skeptics believe that this will be the eventual result of the integration process of the European Union, although it remains to be seen how successful the current level of economic integration will be over the long term. The primary example of a successful political union was the Articles of Confederation, which made the thirteen separate colonies into the United States of America. The founders of the United States who assembled for the Second Continental Congress agreed to the formation of the union in 1776, but it was not without compromise. The member states retained freedom in all matters that were not expressly delegated to the Congress, and the politically divisive issue of how to handle slavery was eliminated from the discussions so that the union could be formed expeditiously.[9]

ASSOCIATION OF SOUTH EAST ASIAN NATIONS

The Association of South East Asian Nations (ASEAN) was founded in 1967 by Indonesia, Malaysia, the Philippines, Singapore, and Thailand. Brunei joined when it attained its independence in 1984. The association has been expanded over the years to include Cambodia, Laos, Myanmar, and Vietnam.

Over the past twenty years, ASEAN has made significant progress. Preferential trading arrangements have been established under which special, lower tariffs are levied on the import of goods from member states. Members cooperate on the coordinated development of industry in the region through the industrial project scheme, whereby member states select a particular project for establishment in a country and in which every other member state holds equity. To counter the problem of food shortages in some parts of the region, member states created the food security reserve scheme, under which a common stockpile of rice is maintained for supplementing the needs of any member country experiencing a shortfall.

Several other coordinated projects have proved that this regional arrangement has worked. An ASEAN finance corporation was established to finance joint ventures, and agreements between central banks of member countries reduce exchange-rate fluctuations and exchange imbalances by using currency exchange arrangements among themselves. ASEAN has fostered regional cooperation in other categories, such as projects for education, population control, and cultural exchanges among member states.

ASEAN has enabled the member states to represent their region as a collective body and improve their bargaining position with nonmember states, especially the industrialized countries. The aura of political stability and regional amity engendered by the body has also been a major factor in attracting overseas investment in several member countries. In recent years, the region has been one of the leading recipients of foreign direct investment, trailing only China and India.

Active cooperation between members is supported by a small secretariat located in Jakarta, Indonesia. Among the other notable achievements of ASEAN in the more than four decades of its existence are the following:

- An emergency sharing scheme on crude oil and oil products
- Joint approaches to problems in international commodity trade
- A program for cooperation on the development and utilization of mineral resources
- A planning center for agricultural development
- A program for tourism cooperation
- An agreement to align national standards with international standards (such as the International Organization for Standardization)

ASEAN has not been an unqualified success, however; progress has been slow, particularly in coordinated industrial development, because of several constraints. The level of complementarity between the member states is low, and many of them have competitive economic structures, especially because industrial output in most countries tends to be quite similar. Additionally, some ASEAN members are under significant financial stress, making it difficult to mobilize the resources needed to fund their ambitious development programs and government expenditures. Because import duties constitute a major source of revenue for the ASEAN countries, tariffs can be reduced only to the extent that members are able to absorb the resulting revenue loss. The lack of financial resources also constrains the development of joint industrial projects. The issues of equitable distribution of benefits from jointly owned or jointly run projects and of tariff preferences are difficult to resolve, given their complex implications.

In 1992, the **ASEAN Free Trade Area (AFTA)** was established. The goal was to integrate the ASEAN economies into a single production base in order to create a regional market of 500 million people. This agreement required that tariff rates levied on a wide range of products traded within the region be reduced to no more than 5 percent by 2008.[10] The free trade area covers all manufactured and agricultural products, but approximately 1 percent of products are not included in the agreement. These products, listed in the

General Exception List, are typically excluded in order to maintain national security, to protect human, animal, or plant life and health, and to preserve things of artistic, historic, or archeological value. The eventual goal of AFTA is the elimination of all import duties and the creation of the ASEAN economic community by 2015.

On balance, ASEAN has been a significant success. Trade among ASEAN countries grew from US$44.2 billion in 1993 to US$376.2 billion in 2009. This represents an annual increase of 13.42 percent.[11] If the member countries have the political will to sustain the progress of cooperation, there is no doubt that the arrangement will bring greater economic and political coordination to the region, which has already emerged as an important economic zone, even by global standards. The leaders of ASEAN established the ASEAN-China free trade area in 2010. This has the potential to significantly increase ASEAN's exports to China and China's exports to ASEAN nations. Similar discussions have also taken place with Japan, Korea, India, and Australia. The group is also interested in forging trade alliances outside of the Asia-Pacific region and has been discussing possible agreements with the European Union, the United States, and Canada as well.

ASIA-PACIFIC ECONOMIC COOPERATION FORUM

In response to the growing interdependence among the economies of the Asia-Pacific region, the Asia-Pacific Economic Cooperation Forum (APEC) was established in 1989. It has become the primary regional vehicle for promoting open trade and economic cooperation. The goal of APEC is to advance Asia-Pacific economic dynamism and the sense of community among the member economies. APEC now has twenty-one members, including the People's Republic of China, the Republic of Korea, New Zealand, Peru, Russia, and the nations composing such smaller groups as ASEAN and NAFTA. The membership totals more than 2.5 billion people with a combined GDP of approximately $20 trillion. The nations of APEC comprise almost half of world trade, which while impressive, illustrates the high importance of agreements made by the members.

In 1994, the leaders of APEC agreed on the future vision of the organization at their annual meeting in Bogor, Indonesia. The "Bogor Goals" include three areas of cooperation, which are known as the "three pillars" of APEC: trade and investment liberalization; business facilitation; and economic and technical cooperation. These goals would seem to be complementary to those of the WTO. Unlike the WTO, APEC does not require any treaty obligations of its participants. APEC is the only intergovernmental group in the world that operates on the basis of nonbinding commitments, open dialogue, and equal respect for the views of all participants.[12, 13] The decisions made in APEC are reached via consensus, and the commitments are undertaken voluntarily by the member economies.

FINANCIAL ORGANIZATIONS

WORLD BANK

The **World Bank** was created (along with the IMF) at the Bretton Woods Conference in New Hampshire in July 1944, and it officially came into existence on December 27, 1945. The objective of the World Bank was initially to make financial resources available to European countries to rebuild their war-shattered economies and later to provide critically needed external financing to developing countries at affordable rates of interest. The creation of the World Bank, together with the IMF, was also intended to strengthen the structure and encourage the development and efficiency of international financial markets. The World Bank consists of four main agencies: the International Bank for Reconstruction and Development (IBRD, generally known as the World Bank); the International Development Association (IDA); the International Finance Corporation (IFC); and the Multilateral Investment Guarantee Agency (MIGA).

International Bank for Reconstruction and Development

The main objective of the World Bank today is to support social and economic progress in developing countries by promoting better productivity and utilization of resources so that their citizens can live better and fuller lives. The World Bank seeks to achieve its objectives by making financial assistance available to developing countries, especially for specific, economically sound infrastructural projects, for example, in the areas of power and transport. The basic rationale for the emphasis on such projects is that a good infrastructure is necessary for the developing countries to carry out programs of social and economic development. In the 1970s World Bank loans were also given to promote the development of the social services sectors of borrowing countries: education, water supply and sanitation, urban housing, and so on. Loans were also provided for the development of indigenous energy resources, such as oil and natural gas. Since the early 1980s much World Bank lending has been policy-based; that is, it has aimed to support economic adjustment measures by borrowing countries, particularly those faced with heavy external debt-service requirements. Policy-based lending, sector-policy lending, and structural-adjustment lending programs of the World Bank provide critically needed financial assistance to countries attempting to alter the current orientation of their economies by enhancing productivity and efficiency in the allocation of resources, improving external competitiveness, reducing overburdening subsidies, and repairing other economic distortions that prevent a higher rate of growth and create macroeconomic instability.

Another important aspect of financial assistance provided by the World Bank is loan guarantees. The World Bank helps member developing countries to obtain increased access at better terms to international financial markets by guaranteeing repayment of loans. This form of assistance has been increasingly used to improve resource flows from private creditors to the highly indebted developing countries. The use of guarantees is also being considered by the World Bank in order to help member-country borrowers issue securities in the international financial markets.

World Bank Lending

There are five major categories of World Bank loans:

1. *Specific investment loans* are loans made for specific projects in the areas of agricultural and rural development, urban development, energy, and so on. They have a maturity ranging from five to ten years.
2. *Sector operations loans*, which constitute about a third of the World Bank's lending, are aimed at financing development of particular sectors of a country's economy such as oil, energy, or agriculture. Loans under this category are also provided to the borrower's financial institutions, which then lend the funds to actual users in a particular sector of the economy.
3. *Structural adjustment and program loans* are targeted at providing the financial support needed by member countries that are undertaking comprehensive institutional and policy reforms to remove imbalances in the external sector. These loans, therefore, support entire programs of structural adjustment and are not specific to any particular project or sector of the economy.
4. *Technical assistance loans* are provided to member countries that need to strengthen their technical capacity to plan their development strategies and design and implement specific projects.
5. *Emergency reconstruction loans* are provided to member countries whose economies, especially the infrastructure, have experienced sudden and severe damage because of natural disasters, such as earthquakes or floods. The emphasis of these loans, apart from restoring the disrupted infrastructural facilities, is also on strengthening the capacity of borrower countries to handle future events of this type.

Since 1982 World Bank loans have been made at variable rates of interest that are adjusted twice a year and are based on a spread of 0.75 percent on the average cost of the outstanding borrowings of the bank.[14] Apart from interest, World Bank borrowers have to pay a front-end fee and a commitment fee on their borrowings. Repayment terms, including grace periods and final maturity, are determined on the basis of the per capita income of the borrowing country. Final maturity can range up to twenty years for countries with the lowest per capita income. In 2012, the World Bank loaned a total of US$20.6 billion in support of ninety-three projects throughout the world. The total outstanding loan commitments by the bank surpassed US$136 billion in 2012.[15]

Fund-Raising by the World Bank

The primary capital resources of the World Bank come from contributions made by its 188 member countries, but nearly all loan funds are raised by borrowings in international financial markets. The bank enjoys a credit rating of AAA in the world's financial markets, which enables it to obtain easy access to funds and excellent borrowing terms in its chosen markets. Funds borrowed by the bank had surpassed US$100 billion by the end of 2003. Borrowings are made in a variety of major international currencies that reflect the nature of the bank's loan portfolio. Approximately twenty different currencies have been used by the bank to raise funds in the international markets. The World Bank typically borrows at variable interest rates, which are adjusted twice a year. Fixed-spread loans were introduced by the bank in 2000; these loans have a fixed spread over the **London Inter-Bank Offered Rate (LIBOR)** for the life of the loan.

The World Bank has played a pioneering role in the development of the currency swap market, whereby it improves its access and terms to preferred markets or adjusts its borrowing currency mix with the lending currency mix. The bank also uses **interest-rate swaps** to adjust mismatches in its borrowing and lending portfolios and improve the management of interest-rate risk.

The bank has made significant profits on its operations over the years, even though it charges a relatively low spread to its borrowers. As a matter of policy, all profits are transferred to the general reserve, which is maintained as a safeguard against the contingencies of loan or other financial losses.

Organizational Structure

Each World Bank member country subscribes to a certain proportion of the total paid-in capital of the bank. The subscription of each country differs and depends generally on its international economic importance. The member countries are, in effect, the shareholders of the bank and the ultimate guarantors of its financial obligations. The United States has the largest share of paid-in capital (28.9 percent) and is, therefore, the largest shareholder of the bank. Major industrialized countries, such as Japan, Germany, United Kingdom, and France, are among the other important shareholders.

The board of governors of the bank is the highest policy-making body, and each member state appoints one representative to the board, usually either its finance minister or the governor of its central bank. Each country also appoints an alternate member to the board of governors. The board of governors makes only major policy decisions about the functioning of the bank, such as capital increases, major changes in lending emphasis, and the creation of new affiliates, which are approved at its annual meetings.

Day-to-day administration of the bank's work is entrusted to the president of the bank, who has traditionally been from the United States. The president is supported by a twenty-five-member board of executive directors, who are appointed by member governments. The major industrial countries, Saudi Arabia, and China have their own executive directors, while other member states, with lesser shares, form regional groupings to appoint executive directors. The bank has four major administrative divisions:

- The *operations division*, which is essentially responsible for World Bank lending
- The *financial operations division*, which is responsible for raising and managing the financial resources of the bank
- The *policy, planning, and research division*, which is concerned with in-depth economic studies, analysis, and planning to support the objectives of the bank
- The *administration and personnel division*

World Bank headquarters are in Washington, DC, and there are regional representative offices in many developing countries. The World Bank's staff, which at the end of 2012 numbered more than 9,000, consists of personnel drawn from more than 150 nationalities and represents a wide variety of professional skills.

International Development Association

The **International Development Association (IDA)** was established in 1960 to provide long-term funds at concessionary rates to the poorest member countries of the bank. This affiliate does not have a separate organizational structure, and its operations are conducted by the staff of the World Bank. The president of the World Bank is also the president of the IDA. The basic objective of the association is to provide long-term financing to those members who cannot afford to borrow on normal World Bank terms. IDA funds are used to promote long-term, long-gestation development projects.

As member countries grow economically and their per capita income increases beyond a particular level,[16] they graduate from IDA assistance and become eligible for World Bank loans under its various lending programs.

IDA loans have long maturities, sometimes as long as forty years, with a ten-year grace period for the repayment of principal. Historically, a nominal service charge of 0.75 percent per annum has been levied, and a commitment fee of 0.5 percent has been charged on approved but non-dispersed credits. IDA funds are raised from member-country subscriptions, repayments of outstanding credits, and allocations from the income of the bank. IDA funds are periodically replenished by member countries.

In fiscal 2012, IDA provided US$14.7 billion in financing for various projects in low-income countries (most of them in Africa and South Asia). The five largest recipients of IDA credits are India, Vietnam, Bangladesh, Pakistan, and Ethiopia. Although in recent years IDA replenishments have led to a certain amount of debate about the amount of contributions to be made by the industrialized countries, there is no doubt that the role of the IDA is critical in providing sorely needed external assistance to many countries with large populations that are at the lowest rung of the global economic ladder.

International Finance Corporation

The **International Finance Corporation (IFC)** was established in 1956 with the objective of promoting the development of private enterprises in member countries. The IFC operates primarily through its own staff, but it is overseen by the World Bank's board of executive directors. The president of the World Bank is also the president of the IFC.

The IFC makes equity investments and extends loans to private enterprises in developing countries. In accordance with its mandate, the IFC cannot accept government guarantees of its loans. The primary role of the IFC, however, is not providing financial assistance alone. It serves as a catalyst to promote private capital flows to the private sector in developing countries. The IFC is never the sole financier in any particular transaction, and its contribution is usually a minor proportion of the total mobilized amount. The corporation also does not accept management positions or seats on the boards of directors of the organizations to which it lends funds. In addition, the IFC provides financial, technical, and legal advice to the companies in which it invests. Advisory services are also provided to companies who do not borrow directly from the IFC.

As a matter of policy, the IFC typically exits from companies in which it has invested as they develop and mature, usually selling its interests to local parties. The importance of the activities of the IFC has grown in recent years, with increasing emphasis on the development of the private sector by the industrialized countries and its growing acceptance by many developing countries, which are increasingly disillusioned by the lackluster performance of parastatal enterprises in their countries.

Apart from its traditional investment activities, the IFC also plays an important role in strengthening the financial infrastructure of developing countries through its capital markets department. The department provides needed technical and legal assistance to many developing countries to strengthen their financial markets. The IFC provides assistance in this area for such issues as framing legal statutes to regulate securities markets and the development of financial institutions, such as leasing companies, venture capital companies, commercial banks, credit-rating agencies, and export-import financing institutions.

The IFC also plays an important catalyzing role in setting up depository institutions; establishing trading, disclosure, and market practice standards; and directing external flows toward developing countries by helping to establish and develop capital markets and financial institutions and by participating in and promoting international investment efforts through pooled investment vehicles, such as country funds.

Although in the past the IFC had funded its investments from its own capital and borrowings from the World Bank, it has also raised substantial amounts on its own by directly borrowing in the international capital markets. The IFC is rated an AAA borrower by major US credit-rating agencies.

Multilateral Investment Guarantee Agency

The **Multilateral Investment Guarantee Agency (MIGA)** was established in 1988. Its main objective is to promote overseas direct investment flows into developing countries by providing guarantees against noncommercial risks that investors face in most economies. Noncommercial risks are generally risks arising out of political actions by most governments, such as confiscation, expropriation, and nationalization of the assets of the overseas enterprise. Other noncommercial risks covered by MIGA include risks arising out of such unforeseen circumstances as wars and civil disturbances.

The Future Role of the World Bank Group

The role of the World Bank group has constantly evolved ever since its inception. The next few decades pose several major challenges to the organization as it pursues its fundamental objectives of improving the living standards of people in poor countries by catalyzing greater economic growth and sustainable development. In the past decade, the World Bank has had to deal with a whole new set of issues created by the Asian financial crisis and the flow of much-needed external capital to industrial countries instead of the developing world. Given the significant gaps in the demand and supply of external resources for the developing countries as a whole, the bank will have to make additional efforts to meet the enhanced requirements of its member countries. Further, it will be required to increasingly collaborate with other multilateral institutions, such as the IMF, on the important issue of providing economic and institutional resources to many developing countries with a view to improving their levels of productivity and efficiency. The bank may also increasingly adopt a regional approach to solving difficult problems that need a broader geographical approach than do specific country operations.

Along with the main objective of fighting poverty in many countries across the world, the World Bank is likely to pay increasing attention to fragile global ecosystems and their interrelationships with the consequences of development, particularly in the context of the environmental impact of bank-financed projects. Another new direction for the World Bank is its increasing association with the work of nongovernmental organizations (NGOs) in developing countries. The World Bank has become increasingly involved in the support of organizations such as the **International Centre for Settlement of Investment Disputes (ICSID),** which has assisted in mediation or conciliation of over 375 investment disputes between governments and private foreign investors since its inception in 1966. The number of cases submitted to this organization has increased in recent years; the group saw thirty-eight cases in 2011 alone.

Internally, there is likely to be an ever-greater need of political and financial support for the bank from member governments, especially those of the industrialized countries.

INTER-AMERICAN DEVELOPMENT BANK

The **Inter-American Development Bank (IADB)** was established in 1959 with the primary objective of promoting social and economic development in Latin America.

The bank, headquartered in Washington, DC, has forty-eight member countries, including twenty-two non-borrowing members that only provide capital and have voting representation.

The main operations of the IADB are focused on providing long-term public financing to member countries. The main areas for which loans are extended include agriculture and rural development, transport, communications, and mining. Since the onset of the debt crisis in the 1980s in Latin America, the IADB has adopted special lending programs that direct financing where it is most urgently needed. Loans are made on a project basis, with proposals initiated by borrowing countries and examined and approved by the bank. The bank also provides technical assistance to the member countries for the preparation of project proposals and their implementation.

Unlike the World Bank, the IADB obtains a significant portion of its funding from member contributions to the paid-in capital of the bank. The United States has the largest contribution of paid-in capital (30 percent), followed by Brazil and Argentina. Loans are made only to Latin American and Caribbean countries, however, and only to governments. Since inception, the bank has loaned more than US$169 billion for over 13,000 projects in twenty-six countries throughout Latin America and the Caribbean. The announced policy of the IADB is to stop lending to a country whose account falls in arrears. In recent years the IADB has borrowed substantial funds in the international financial markets to supplement its resources for financing development in member countries. It continues to be well regarded in the international capital markets, despite the debt crisis faced by many of its member nations in the 1980s.

The role of the bank has been expanded to undertake financing of social projects, such as health, education, and rural development. Moreover, the smaller and economically weaker countries of Latin America have been given the highest priority in the extension of loans. Loans typically have a maturity period of between thirty and forty years. In addition, the IADB assists member states in mobilizing resources in their internal markets, especially through co-financing arrangements.

ASIAN DEVELOPMENT BANK

The **Asian Development Bank (ADB)** was founded in 1966 with the objective of promoting economic growth and cooperation in Asia and the Far East, including the South Pacific region. Although membership is primarily concentrated among countries of the region, major industrialized countries, such as Japan, the United States, Canada, and Germany, are also members in the capacity of donors. The bank currently has sixty-seven member nations. Traditionally, the president of the bank has been Japanese. Indonesia has been the largest borrower from the bank historically, but Vietnam, India, Pakistan, and Bangladesh were granted the most loans in 2011, taking up 55 percent of the total for the year. The ADB approved 114 loans totaling US$21.7 billion in 2011, for the purposes of 104 projects.[17]

The ADB provides different types of financial and technical assistance to member countries in the region, including guarantees, investment loans, and direct technical assistance. The important areas that receive ADB assistance are agriculture, industry, energy development, transport and communications, development of finance institutions, water supply, sanitation, and urban development. In recent years, the ADB has promoted inclusive growth in Southeast Asia as evidenced by a focus on microfinance programs throughout the region. Additionally, the ADB has partnered with ASEAN in creating an infrastructure fund for improvement in Southeast Asia.

Most ADB loans are long-term, and maturities range from ten to thirty years. Loans carry a fixed rate of interest that varies according to the prevailing rates in the international financial markets at the time of the extension of the loan, although in recent years the ADB has also started to lend at variable rates, like the World Bank. Repayment and grace periods vary, depending on the per capita income of the borrowing country. Grace periods range from two to seven years.

The ADB has a **soft-loans** facility known as the Asian Development Fund, in which concessional terms are granted to borrowing countries. This facility is funded by member-country contributions. Loans from this facility are provided free of commitment fees and require a nominal service charge of 1 percent per annum.[18] Repayments have traditionally been spread over a thirty-two year period, including a grace period of eight years.

AFRICAN DEVELOPMENT BANK

The **African Development Bank (AfDB)** was established in 1963 with the primary objective of accelerating the development process and improving socioeconomic conditions in the newly independent countries of Africa. The bank is headquartered in Abidjan, Ivory Coast. An important characteristic of the AfDB is its strong emphasis on maintaining its fundamentally African character and orientation. In fact, until 1982 non-African countries were not permitted to become members of the bank. Non-African countries are now allowed to become members only with certain specific safeguards aimed at preserving the unique African orientation and identity of the bank. Currently, the bank has fifty-three members from Africa and twenty-five non-African members, including the United States, Canada, France, China, and the United Kingdom. Since inception, the bank has funded more than 3,600 loans and grants for a total of UA 60 billion.

The bank is organized into three different affiliates, the largest entity being the bank itself, which lends to the more economically advanced member states and charges rates of interest at a spread over the cost of its own borrowed funds. The second affiliate is a soft-loan window, known as the African Development Fund (ADF), which channels concessional assistance to poorer member countries. There is no interest on this assistance, and historically there has been only a nominal service charge of 0.75 percent per year. The ADF receives its resources from the non-African countries, including several industrialized countries. The third affiliate is the Nigeria Trust Fund (NTF), which lends funds at rates and maturities that are between those charged by the AfDB and those charged by the ADF. The NTF, set up in 1976, is funded entirely by the Nigerian government. The bank raises its resources from paid-in capital by member countries, concessional loans from governments of industrialized countries, and, more recently, significant borrowings in the international financial markets that have been supported by the excellent credit ratings earned by the bank from major US credit-rating agencies.

The AfDB's strategic plan for the years 2003–2007 included some new methods for reducing the level of poverty on the continent, and ways of improving the governance, environmental protection, and treatment of women in Africa. This included the creation of the Central Microfinance Unit. Microfinance, or lending small amounts to the poorest individuals on an unsecured basis for the creation of small businesses, has been successful in other areas of the world and is seen as an avenue of great opportunity for improvement in Africa. In recent years, the AfDB has focused on the additional goals of creating more solid financial markets in Africa and other strategies to reduce poverty and improve living conditions on the continent.

EUROPEAN INVESTMENT BANK

The **European Investment Bank (EIB)** was established in 1957 by the Treaty of Rome, in conjunction with the creation of the European Economic Community. Although the bank is a separate legal entity, it is intimately connected with current EU activities and pursues four objectives:[19]

- Regional development and economic and social cohesion within the European Union
- Protecting the environment and improving the quality of life in the region
- Preparing the accession countries for future EU membership
- Community development aid and cooperation policy among member countries

The EIB attempts to implement these objectives by promoting funds for investment in projects that serve these ends. The EIB raises its resources both from paid-in subscriptions by member states and from borrowings in the international markets. Loans are made to finance projects in individual member countries and projects that serve the interest of the community as a whole, for example, projects to develop energy resources or infrastructural facilities that benefit all member states.

Germany, France, Italy, and the United Kingdom are the four largest shareholders of the EIB, and all EU member nations are also members of the EIB. Many of the EIB lending operations are for long-term loans at fixed rates of interest, with maturities varying from seven to twenty years. The bank is operated on a purely nonprofit basis, although it does generate income internally to meet its operating expenses and to build up a general reserve, which is prescribed as equal to 10 percent of its subscribed capital. In 2011 the EIB approved 60 billion in new loans, primarily for projects in the European Union. EIB projects included funds for port expansion in Rotterdam, sustainable transport in Warsaw, and small business lending in Croatia.

Support to developing countries is complemented by the operations of the European Development Fund (EDF), which is funded out of allocations made from the budgetary resources of the European Union.

EUROPEAN BANK FOR RECONSTRUCTION AND DEVELOPMENT

The **European Bank for Reconstruction and Development (EBRD)** was established in 1991 to promote development in eastern and central Europe following the collapse of communism. The bank uses investment and influence to transition formerly centrally planned economies to market-based democratic systems. In 2011, the EBRD invested 9.1 billion in 380 projects in thirty countries. The bank is headquartered in London and is owned by sixty countries worldwide, the European Investment Bank, and the European Union. The EBRD has made loans to improve the national railway system in Poland, the municipal water and wastewater systems in Latvia,[20] the operations of the oil and gas industry in Hungary, and the efficiency of the pharmaceutical industry in producing non-brand-name drugs in Serbia and Montenegro.

SUMMARY

The increasing interdependence of the nations of the world has increased the need to co-ordinate international actions and policies. Since World War II, permanent international institutions, or supranational organizations, have been formed to serve the vital role of providing economic stability and continuity in the world economy. Some institutions have a global focus, while others are designed to meet more specific regional needs. All of these institutions have the same goals: making the conduct of international business easier and more transparent for business people and the general citizenry.

The General Agreement on Tariffs and Trade, charged with liberalizing international trade restrictions, offers the most-favored-nation clause to member organizations. Eight rounds of GATT meetings were held, resulting in significant reductions in tariffs on industrial products. After the creation of the World Trade Organization in 1995, the Doha Round focused on the improvement of the economic performance of the developing countries. The GATT and WTO rounds highlight the differences in perspective that exist between developed and developing countries as negotiators attempt to establish a coordinated, non-protectionist global trade policy that serves the common interests of all parties.

In contrast to the WTO, the United Nations Conference on Trade and Development is a forum for developing countries to communicate their international trade perspectives as a group to the industrialized countries. Although limited in impact, UNCTAD has improved the dialogue between the developing and developed countries.

There are five different levels of economic integration: free trade area, customs union, common market, economic union, and political union. Groups such as the European Union, ASEAN, and the Andean Community have been established to coordinate regional trade policy, with the European Union and ASEAN being the most successful. The IMF and the

World Bank are international lending institutions, each performing specialized roles in the international monetary system. As discussed in Chapter 4, the IMF focuses primarily on lending for structural adjustments because of balance of payments problems, while as discussed in this chapter, the World Bank, which is comprised of four main agencies (IBRD, IDA, IFC, and MIGA), provides external financing to developing countries at affordable rates of interest. The IBRD, whose main objective is to support social and economic progress in developing countries, offers five major types of loans: specific investment loans, sector operations loans, structural adjustment and program loans, technical assistance loans, and emergency reconstruction loans. The IDA provides long-term funds to the poorest member countries in order to promote long-term development projects. The IFC promotes the development of private enterprises by making equity investments and providing loans. Operating as a catalyst, the IFC exits from an enterprise as it develops and matures. MIGA promotes overseas direct investment in developing countries by providing guarantees against noncommercial risks.

Other development banks, such as the IADB, the ADB, and the AfDB, have been formed to provide regional assistance in the Western Hemisphere, Asia, and Africa, respectively. The European Investment Bank and the European Bank for Reconstruction and Development promote investments in the European Union and in eastern Europe.

DISCUSSION QUESTIONS

1. Discuss the WTO and its role in international trade.
2. What is the most-favored-nation clause?
3. What trading organization represents the international trade objectives of developing countries? How do the concerns of developing countries differ from those of the industrialized, developed countries?
4. What is a regional trade group? What are the advantages provided by these groups?
5. Describe the structure at the World Bank and the services of its four main agencies.
6. What types of loans does the World Bank provide? How are these different from loans provided by the IMF?
7. What will the role of the World Bank be in the future?
8. Identify three regional financial institutions and outline their financial services.

NOTES

1. The ninth round, the Doha Development Agenda, was undertaken under the auspices of the World Trade Organization.

2. World Trade Organization, "Understanding the WTO."

3. There have been some temporary exemptions in cases in which preferential agreements had been signed prior to GATS. These exemptions cannot last longer than ten years, and new exemptions cannot be added or extended.

4. Specific forms of intellectual property are discussed further in Chapter 8.

5. The least-developed countries were provided an extension until 2016 for conforming with TRIPS (primarily for pharmaceutical patents).

6. In fact, the name "Mercosur" implies the eventual goal. It stands for Mercado Común del Sur, or "Common Market of the South."

7. World Trade Organization, "Trade Policy Review: Norway."

8. Ibid.

9. Ellis, *Founding Brothers*.

10. Association of South East Asian Nations, "Southeast Asia: A Free Trade Area."

11. Ibid. Prior to the Asian financial crisis, growth in the region was increasing by 29.6 percent annually.

12. Association of South East Asian Nations, *ASEAN Annual Report*, 2003–2004, Chapter 2, "Economic Integration and Cooperation."

13. Asia-Pacific Economic Cooperation.

14. Prior to July 31, 1998, the spread was 0.50 percent.

15. World Bank, *Annual Report*, 2004 and 2011.

16. In fiscal 2004, countries with annual per capita GNI of up to $865 were eligible for IDA assistance.

17. Asian Development Bank.

18. This charge is effective during the grace period; the interest moved to 1.5 percent during the amortization period as of December 1998.

19. European Investment Bank.

20. European Bank for Reconstruction and Development.

BIBLIOGRAPHY

African Development Bank. "Strategic Plan 2003–2007." www.afdb.org/en/publications/new_titles/adb_strategic_plan.

Asian Development Bank. www.adb.org.

Asia-Pacific Economic Cooperation. www.apec.org.

Association of South East Asian Nations (ASEAN). Secretariat. www.aseansec.org.

———. *Annual Report*, 2003–2004.

———. "Southeast Asia: A Free Trade Area." www.aseansec.org.

Bhagwati, Jagdish. *Termites in the Trading System*. London: Oxford University Press, 2008.

Ellis, Joseph J. *Founding Brothers: The Revolutionary Generation*. New York: Vintage, 2002.

European Bank for Reconstruction and Development. www.ebrd.com/pubs/general/6388a.pdf.

European Investment Bank. www.eig.org.

Inter-American Development Bank, *Annual Report*, 2005. www.iadb.org/exr/ar2005.

World Bank. *Annual Report*, 2004, 2011.

World Trade Organization. "Trade Policy Review: Norway." September 2004. www.wto.org.Indexmundi.com.

———. "Understanding the WTO." www.wto.org.

GLOBALIZATION AT THE CROSSROADS: WHITHER THE WTO?

As was shown in Figure 6.1, there has been a rapid acceleration of regional trade agreements since the formation of the WTO in 1995. When this is coupled with the lack of progress in the Doha Development Agenda, the question must be asked about the continued relevancy of the WTO in the future. A world without the WTO might not imply a lack of multilateral agreements, but as more and more regional alliances take place outside of the auspices of the WTO, there may be a tacit acknowledgment that the WTO's place as a supranational governing body may have peaked in importance. The recent formation of the Pacific Alliance among Chile, Colombia, Mexico, and Peru has the potential of returning Latin America to the "open regionalism" which led to the founding of the Mercosur Accord in 1991. This time, the founding members of the Pacific Alliance are free-market oriented, relatively fast growing economies which have embraced globalization. The Pacific Alliance is trying to resolve the difficulties of the spaghetti bowl of regional trade agreements by agreeing on rules of origin, border procedures, and harmonization of trading rules without WTO involvement.

Questions for Discussion

1. *How might the creation of yet another regional alliance threaten the WTO?*
2. *What does the "spaghetti bowl" of regional trade agreements mean for the notion of free trade?*
3. *Should free trade be the goal of international business?*
4. *What are the potential benefits and pitfalls of a free trade regime with or without the WTO?*

Case Study 6.1

Structural Adjustments in Masawa

Masawa is a small country located in southwestern Africa, with an area of 240,000 square miles and a population of about 60 million. The northern and western parts of the country are hilly terrain, while the southern and eastern areas are plains. Masawa has substantial natural resources: mineral deposits of manganese, copper, and tin in the northern hill areas and large tropical forests in the southeastern parts of the country. The eastern part has most of the cultivated land, and agricultural production, especially cereal crops, is concentrated there. There are some cocoa plantations in the western part of the country; cocoa is an important commercial crop. The main exports of Masawa are copper, tin, and cocoa. Manganese deposits are too small to be commercially viable for export.

   The country attained its independence from colonial rule in 1961 and since then has seen a few political upheavals. Emorgue Watiza, a leader of the country's freedom movement, was the first president. He ruled Masawa for six years before being ousted by the military, which installed General Ramaza, who was assassinated in 1974 and replaced by another military ruler, Colonel Waniki. Colonel Waniki instituted a series of political reforms, and after twenty-one years of power, handed over the reins of government to Dr. Sabankwa, the winner of the country's first democratic election. Dr. Sabankwa brought excellent credentials to the presidency. He holds a PhD in political science and government from the University of Paris and had been active in the movement for restoration of democracy in Masawa. He enjoyed the almost total loyalty of his tribe, the Waldesi, which is the largest tribe in the country, constituting 30 percent of the population. Besides the Waldesi, Masawa also has three other major and sixteen minor tribes. The three other major tribes are the Mokoti (18 percent), Lemata (15 percent), and Simoki (11 percent). The remaining 27 percent of the population is made up of members of the smaller tribes, none of which individually constitutes more than 5 percent of the population.

Dr. Sabankwa enjoyed considerable support from the Simoki and several minor tribes at the time of his election. After more than fifteen years in office, however, that support has eroded, and rumblings of discontent have been heard, even from Sabankwa's own Waldesi tribespeople, especially those living in urban areas. Much of the discontent is clearly the result of the economic difficulties the country is facing, which have led to considerable difficulties for both the urban and rural populations. Reactions, however, tend to be more pronounced in the densely populated and politically conscious urban areas.

Most of Masawa's economic difficulties began before the election of Dr. Sabankwa. The country had little in the way of industrial or technological development when it attained independence, and the annual per capita GNP was $160. Much of the agriculture was conducted along primitive lines and was largely dependent on seasonal rainfall, which tended to be erratic. In the initial years of independence, Masawa's rulers sought to adopt a centralized planning approach to economic development, assigning a key role to the government in nearly all aspects of economic activity. The public sector accounts for 90 percent of industrial production, and all key infrastructure projects are run by government agencies. Masawa has a large number of highly paid civil servants who administer the wide range of economic and other controls imposed by the government. Although private enterprise is officially permitted, there are a number of bureaucratic disincentives for entrepreneurship. A typical new venture in the private sector needs separate approvals from thirty-two different government agencies and departments.

As in many other countries of the developing world, the state-owned industrial enterprises of Masawa have had losses for a variety of reasons, including inefficient management, overstaffing, administered prices of products, and outmoded technology. The government has guaranteed most of the debt taken on by the enterprises and has had to resort to substantial deficit financing to make good on these obligations.

(continued)

Case Study 6.1 *(continued)*

The government of Masawa has faced a major budget deficit every year for the past eleven years; for several reasons, the deficit has become a permanent feature of the government's finances. Government expenditures have been rising rapidly in five areas: defense, oil imports, administrative expenses of the government, subsidies to industrial enterprises, and price subsidies for essential consumption items, especially food. On the other side, revenues have been stagnant, principally because of the absence of strong measures to secure better tax compliance by the vast majority of taxpayers. The government has, therefore, resorted to large-scale deficit financing, which has pushed the inflation rate progressively higher every year. In 2011, Masawa experienced 93 percent inflation, and there were indications that this number would increase by another 40 percent in 2012.

Imports have been increasing steadily over the past seven years, while exports are stagnant, because the world market for Masawa's principal exports continues to be sluggish. The exchange rate of Masawa is overvalued by about 70 percent, and there is a large premium on the black market for foreign currencies. The country has suffered considerable flight of capital as wealthy industrialists lost faith in the political and economic stability of Masawa.

The external debt of Masawa, largely to official creditors, is well above the level considered dangerous for sustaining the debt-service schedule. The country has no access to the international capital market, having defaulted on the amortization of earlier loans, taken primarily by state-owned corporations. Foreign exchange reserves are at a dangerously low level and are sufficient to finance only two weeks of imports.

Dr. Sabankwa calls a meeting of his cabinet to discuss the question of accepting an International Monetary Fund structural adjustment loan in order to tide the country over the immediate problems on the balance of payments front and to improve future prospects. The finance minister briefs Dr. Sabankwa and the cabinet ministers on the pertinent issues.

The IMF is willing to extend a $3 billion loan to Masawa under its structural adjustment lending program, but it wants Masawa to draw up a set of concrete economic measures to restructure the economy. Although several measures have been recommended by the IMF, five are the most important:

1. The government should initiate a phased reduction of official subsidies on food.
2. Masawa should devalue the exchange rate by 40 percent.
3. The government should take steps toward privatizing state-owned enterprises.

4. The level of imports should be reduced.
5. The government should reduce its administrative expenses by cutting the government staff and salaries.

While these measures seem sensible and useful, effective implementation of them would create many practical difficulties. First, cutting food subsidies would be an extremely unpopular measure that might spark civil disturbances, especially in the urban areas. Those most affected would be the urban poor, who are already under great economic hardship. Devaluing the exchange rate also has ominous implications. Politically, it might be viewed as a weakening of the economy, providing another reason for opposition groups to attack the government's handling of the economic situation. Further, the costs of imports would rise and contribute to an increase in the already high inflation rate. Privatization would also be difficult, since there are few people in Masawa with the managerial or technical expertise to take over the operations of these enterprises. Further, there is bound to be strong opposition from the trade unions to any move for privatization.

Reducing the level of imports would be a feasible option, but it would hurt the growth rate considerably, because imports of essential industrial equipment and machinery would have to be curtailed. A very large cut in imports might not even be possible because of the inelastic level of defense and oil imports. Reducing government staffing may create ill feelings in a crucial time.

Dr. Sabankwa fears that these steps, if implemented, would generate political unrest that would lead to the fall of his government. As he mulls over these issues, he wonders whether a compromise solution can be found.

DISCUSSION QUESTIONS

1. What would be your position if you were a member of Dr. Sabankwa's cabinet?
2. Should Dr. Sabankwa accept the IMF plan as it exists or should he insist on some modification? If modification is needed, what changes should he suggest? What arguments can Dr. Sabankwa make to convince IMF officials to agree to these modifications in the structural adjustment plan?

CHAPTER 7

Analyzing National Economies

"There is no substitute for knowledge."
—W. Edwards Deming

CHAPTER OBJECTIVES

This chapter will:

- Describe the importance of national economic analysis and identify the major indicators used in this analysis
- Describe the sources of data and research tools that can be incorporated in national economic analysis
- Discuss the results of analysis as inputs to developing an international marketing strategy

---

While W. Edwards Deming was a noted quality expert, the quote at the beginning of this chapter still serves as an important introductory statement for international business. Whether the aspiring international business is large, midsize, or small, the analysis done before venturing into foreign markets is crucial for success. Sometimes equally important is the level of ongoing analysis that is undertaken once the international venture has commenced. The analysis of national economies is an ongoing process; the nimble business is one that can respond to changes on the ground in all of its markets of operation. In order to respond in a timely manner, a solid foundation of understanding of the various markets is vital.

THE PURPOSE AND METHODOLOGY OF COUNTRY ANALYSIS

Targeting a new country either as a market or as a manufacturing location must be preceded by a detailed analysis of the country's past, present, and future economic situation. This analysis is extremely important for a multinational corporation, because the nature and state of an economy's development are crucial factors in determining a country's suitability as a new market or manufacturing location. Emerging trends also must be analyzed to develop an estimate of how the corporation should respond.

Country analysis takes many forms, depending on the type of information sought, the objectives, the required depth and detail, the time frame being considered, and so on. In general, four broad categories serve as starting points:

1. Leading economic indicators at a particular point in time
2. Trends in different economic indicators
3. Trends in various specific sectors
4. Analysis of specific areas or sectors of the economy

The methodology for analysis of a country's economic prospects and its potential varies according to the purpose of the analysis and the MNC's situation. If the MNC has a local subsidiary in the country and the object of the analysis is to plan for further expansion or diversification into new industries, a two-tier analysis is carried out. At the first tier, the local subsidiary gathers and processes all the available local data and passes on the resulting information, along with its own assessment of the situation and prospects, to the home office abroad. The home office, which is the second tier, then examines the information and the subsidiary's recommendation and makes its own assessment, keeping in mind its global corporate and strategic goals, as well as the opportunities and constraints worldwide. The management of the local subsidiary is often closely consulted while the home office views are being formulated, because some strategic considerations may not be put on paper for security and confidentiality reasons. The home office usually has an independent economic research division or economic analysts to generate independent information that is compared with and used to support or contest that supplied by the subsidiary.

If a country is totally new to an MNC, the methodology is different. Some corporations hire consultants who are experts on a particular country to do a comprehensive economic analysis. Information is also gleaned from the materials available publicly, such as government publications, country studies, and commercial publications. Local consultants are sometimes employed by MNCs because of their deeper understanding of the local environment and better access to relevant information. Another option is the use of international consultants who utilize local associates. The local associates provide vital contacts and sources of information, while the international consultants integrate and analyze the data and prepare the formal report on the country being studied.

PRELIMINARY ECONOMIC INDICATORS

Regardless of the methodology employed by the MNC in its economic analysis of a country's potential as a location for industrial production or as a market for its products or services, there are certain general economic criteria that are almost invariably considered. A discussion of the most important of these criteria follows.

SIZE OF THE ECONOMY

The size of the economy is a basic measure of a country's potential as a market for an MNC's products. It is generally measured by the **gross national income (GNI)**, which is the sum total of goods and services produced in an economy, including the net transactions it has with the external (foreign) sector. The GNI is an important measure because it shows the total level of economic activity in a country. An alternative measure is the **gross domestic product (GDP)**, which indicates the gross amount of goods and services produced within the country. The GDP does not take into account the contribution of the external sector to the economy.

INCOME LEVELS

Income levels of the citizens of a country are a very important economic indicator for an MNC. To a significant extent, the prevailing income levels influence the nature of the potential a country offers as a market for different types of goods. The broadest measure of the income levels enjoyed by a population is per capita GNI. Per capita GNI is determined by dividing the total GNI by the total population.

Per capita GNI varies greatly from country to country. Industrialized countries that have a high gross national product and relatively small populations tend to have a high per capita GNI. On the other hand, less-developed countries have a low GNI but relatively large populations, which results in a very low per capita GNI.

The World Bank has formulated four categories of countries based on their per capita GNI:

1. *Low-income* countries, with a per capita GNI of US$1,025 or less
2. *Lower-middle-income* developing countries, with a per capita GNI between US$1,026 and US$4,035
3. *Upper-middle-income* countries, with a per capita GNI between US$4,036 and US$12,475
4. *High income* countries, with a per capita GNI exceeding US$12,476

Countries with a low per capita GNI would not have a very large potential as a market for such goods as automobiles and air conditioners, which are considered necessities in developed countries but are luxuries in developing countries. On the other hand, countries with a low per capita income are likely to have lower labor costs and could prove attractive to MNCs as sites for manufacturing facilities.

INCOME DISTRIBUTION

Although the per capita GNI statistics provide a broad indication of the income levels of different countries of the world, this information is by no means adequate for assessment of a country as a potential market. GNI per capita is actually a very broad measure that does not take into account the distribution of income within a country. Moreover, it provides no information on the size of market segments that would be potential targets for an MNC marketing effort. For example, a small country such as Kuwait has a very large per capita GNI because of a high GNI and a very small population, but it is not a very large market for automobiles because of the limited number of people who would purchase autos. On the other hand, a very low per capita GNI of a country might mask the significant purchasing power of a particular segment of its citizens.

In most developing countries there are sharp inequalities of wealth, and a large percentage of the country's total wealth is concentrated in the hands of a fairly small percentage of the population. This segment has significant purchasing power and offers considerable potential for different types of goods and services marketed by MNCs. This situation is particularly true in countries where the low per capita GNI occurs because of a very large low-income population. Thus, a country may have a large GNI, but its per capita GNI is low because of its large population.

In countries where there is substantial purchasing power in the hands of a small percentage of the population, it should be kept in mind that the absolute size of this wealthy segment may be considerable because it is a percentage of a very large absolute number. Thus, if a country has a population of 400 million and only 5 percent of its citizens are wealthy enough to qualify as a potential market segment for an MNC, the total market would still be 20 million people, which is the size of the entire population of some industrialized countries.

The degree of income distribution also provides other important clues to the economy in general and different market segments within it in particular. A more even income distribution would generally be found in the developed or industrialized countries, which would offer large potential for standardized mass-consumption products. The size of the very-high-income group in the total population would reveal the country's potential as a market for luxury goods, such as designer clothes and luxury automobiles.

Less-developed countries would show a very large percentage of very-low-income groups that usually would not offer an immediate market for most products promoted by MNCs. The size of the wealthy segments, on the other hand, would be a factor in determining the market size.

Another important indicator of market potential is the size of the middle-income groups within the overall income distribution. In the developed countries, the middle-income groups are usually the largest proportion of the population, which implies the existence of big markets for a wide range of mass-produced consumer products. The middle class is relatively small in most less-developed economies, which limits their potential as a market for a wide variety of consumer goods.

Traditionally, trends and income distributions tend to move relatively slowly because they reflect basic socioeconomic structures and patterns that are fairly resistant to change. In less-developed countries, however, these patterns have been changing at a relatively rapid pace over the past four or five decades. An important trend has been the emergence of a large middle class with substantial purchasing power and a positive attitude toward utilizing that power for the purchase of consumer goods.

PERSONAL CONSUMPTION

In addition to the income distribution patterns prevalent in a country, the prevailing consumption patterns influence a country's potential as a market. While income distribution statistics provide information on how and to whom income accrues, data on personal consumption indicate how this income is spent on goods and services. Personal-consumption data indicate the buying habits of the citizens of a particular country: what they buy, in what quantities, in which parts of the country, and so on. This information is vital for an MNC because it indicates patterns of consumer behavior and therefore sets parameters for marketing efforts. Thus, a country where the consumers spend a large proportion of their income on food and shelter offers no potential market for luxury goods such as VCRs. On the other hand, the same country may provide markets for inexpensive goods that meet the basic necessities of life. Although characterized by low consumption levels, a country may have substantial market segments comprised of persons with considerable discretionary income. Many MNCs develop marketing strategies on the basis of consumption patterns. Thus, patterns of consumption give important clues to an MNC regarding the possibilities for marketing different types of goods in a particular country.

GROWTH AND STABILITY PATTERNS

The size of the economy, income levels and distribution, and personal consumption are static indicators, inasmuch as they represent the position of a country at a particular point in time. An MNC contemplating long-term involvement in a country either as an exporter to that country or as a direct investor must also concern itself with a country's prior, current, and projected economic trends.

The growth rate of a country's economy, for example, must be watched carefully. Past growth trends show how the economy has been moving and the rate at which it is contracting or expanding. Projected growth rates indicate how it may do in the future. The growth trends generally have a direct relation to the market size for different products and services in a country. A fast growth rate would indicate rapid industrial development.

Countries seeking rapid rates of growth aim to achieve this largely by increases in industrialization levels, by the modernization of existing industries, and by the introduction of new industries and new technologies. Such countries are likely to welcome MNCs as direct investors in production facilities. Moreover, countries that have achieved a rapid growth rate over the past few years are usually the ones that have opened up their economies to external technologies, have pushed their export efforts, and have increased the competitiveness and efficiency of their domestic economies. Such countries are likely to prove to be potential winners as markets for MNCs because they would be expected to have increased levels of income.

Rapidly growing economies are also characterized by the development of a professional middle class, which evens out the distribution of income relative to that in previous years and provides a market base for an MNC's consumer products.

Growing economies also offer enhanced markets for capital goods, technology, and related services. Therefore, MNCs closely monitor future growth trends to identify potential countries for export marketing and direct investment activities. The absolute growth rate and the growth rate per capita are related in this context. The absolute growth rate indicates the overall level of economic activity and gives the broadest indication of its enhancement to a country's markets. Growth rate per capita indicates achievement not only on the economic front but also, indirectly, on the population front. If the growth per capita is rapid, the country can be considered to have surmounted one of the most important economic problems that afflict most developing countries: overpopulation.

Actually, per capita GNI is also an important indicator because of its future implications. A high per capita GNI would imply an increased availability of resources to invest that could be further deployed for accelerating economic growth and improving the living standards of the population, which would represent a real change in the economic profile of the country as a market for goods and services and as a location for overseas production. If the growth rate is matched or exceeded by the population growth, the economic benefits of progress would be lost.

POPULATION

The population of a country represents an important economic statistic. It is an important factor in influencing the size of market potential for a large number of goods and services, especially goods for personal consumption.

Population density (the number of persons living per square mile) is a particularly relevant factor. A high population density could have both negative and positive implications. On the one hand, it may imply overcrowding, overpopulation, and pressure on the resource base of a country. On the other hand, it may also imply reduced transportation costs in marketing products, availability of large numbers of consumers, and an easily accessible pool of labor.

Geographical distribution of the population is also important. Areas of high population concentration within a country generally offer wide market potential and great possibilities of servicing the labor requirements for an overseas manufacturing facility.

The educational level of the population is also extremely important. Consumption patterns, living standards, and so on vary considerably with level of literacy. A country with a high level of literacy is likely to offer great potential for an MNC's products because individuals are likely to have a broad outlook on the types of products they consume and would, in general, be willing to accept new products and services that an MNC might offer. For some types of products (books and other intellectual media, software, and so on), literacy levels are critical factors. Moreover, they also determine what sort of advertising strategy the MNC should pursue to promote its products locally. Literacy levels also indicate the potential of finding local skilled labor and local managers for a company's operations.

In general, literacy levels directly correlate with levels of per capita income. While developed countries have high literacy levels, ranging from 95 percent to 100 percent, less-developed countries have levels that drop to as low as 40 percent.

The rate of population growth is another trend worth watching. A growing population indicates an expanding market in countries where the density of population is low and per capita incomes are rising. A high population growth rate in countries already over-populated indicates growing economic difficulties that could be manifested in severe shortages of available resources, heavy pressures on the infrastructure and services system of a country, fiscal difficulties for the government, shortages of capital for investments, increasing numbers of people living in poverty, and ever-increasing prices.

The age structure of a population should also be considered. In developed countries, large proportions of the population tend to be over the age of eighteen, and there are a sizable number of people in the over-sixty age group. Less-developed countries, however, are characterized by fairly young populations, where persons younger than eighteen are the dominant segment. Relatively young populations imply possibilities for higher popu-lation growth over the next few years, particularly in countries where birth control is not practiced widely. Moreover, such countries are also characterized by high dependency burdens, meaning that the income-earning members of the population have to support a large number of nonearning members on a per capita basis. Dependency burdens have important economic implications, inasmuch as they affect the amount of discretionary income people may or may not have after taking care of the essential needs of their depen-dents and themselves. Most countries with high dependency burdens have low levels of discretionary income, which limits their potential as markets for an MNC's products.

SECTOR ANALYSIS

It is also important to analyze different sectors of the country's economy, to identify the particular areas that could offer business opportunities. The state of development of a particular sector of the economy can provide clues to its product needs and the possibili-ties of providing necessary imports and support for the establishment of a manufacturing operation by an overseas corporation. For example, an MNC contemplating the establish-ment of an automobile plant in a developing country would have to assess the engineering sector in general and the automotive industry in particular, to determine the degree and availability of local support by way of ancillary and spare parts manufacturers, skilled labor, and locally trained production personnel.

On a broader level, sector analysis suggests the state of a country's overall economic development. From a macroeconomic standpoint, economic activity is divided into three broad categories. The **primary sector** incorporates traditional economic activities, such as agriculture. The **secondary sector** comprises primarily manufacturing and industrial activity. The **tertiary sector** refers to services and related industries.

Industrialized and developed countries are characterized by a high proportion of their economic activity in the secondary and tertiary sectors. For example, many developed countries typically have a very low percentage of GNI produced by the primary sector, while many developing countries often depend heavily on that same sector.[1] A high concentration of economic activity in agriculture implies that the country is over-dependent on one type of economic activity, has little industrial development, and is likely to have low levels of per capita income, relatively high rates of unemployment, and an unsteady economic performance. For an MNC, such data suggest that these countries do not offer good potential for expensive products but may prove reasonably good locations for setting up processing plants for raw materials and agricultural produce, because costs of material inputs and labor would be quite low. On the other hand, they may lack the infrastructural facilities required for large-scale industrial plants.

A highly developed country would have its economy dominated by the industrial and services sector. For an MNC, this economy would provide opportunities to market a wide range of industrial products and allow the establishment of almost any type of manufacturing operation. At the same time, such economies are likely to be characterized by strong competition from both domestic and international corporations.

INFLATIONARY TRENDS

Local inflationary trends must also be closely watched. **Inflation** is the increase in prices over time measured against a certain benchmark, usually known as the base year. Different indices, consisting of different commodities at different market levels, are constructed to gauge the overall degree of price increases in a country. High inflation can have severe economic consequences. Generally, income levels do not keep pace with inflation, which reduces the purchasing power of consumers and erodes their potential as a market segment, especially for products that have relatively high income elasticity, such as nonessential goods and services. High inflation would also have severe implications for local manufacturing operations, because prices of inputs would increase and pressures would rise to increase wage levels.

Increased inflation in a particular overseas manufacturing location would also have serious effects on the competitiveness of the products produced in that location if they were to be exported to overseas markets. Moreover, in real terms, local inflation would devalue the local currency against the MNC's home currency (if the local rate of inflation exceeds that prevailing in the MNC's home country). As a result, the value of the profits to be repatriated to the home country would go down in home currency terms. High inflation in overseas locations also could prompt restrictive measures by the government, which could hamper operations of the MNC or erode their profitability.

During the 1980s and 1990s, many countries experienced **hyperinflation**, a situation in which inflation occurs in hundreds of percent or even thousands of percent per year. A number of Latin American countries, such as Brazil, Argentina, and Bolivia, have experienced hyperinflation. A more recent example is Zimbabwe, where inflation levels hit 600 percent during 2004.[2] In such situations, MNCs have to be extremely cautious in initiating new ventures and managing existing ones in order to avoid losing their profits.

External Financial Position: Extent of Debt

The external financial sector of a country is another extremely important variable that has to be considered very carefully by MNCs while they are evaluating the country as a site for potential investment or marketing efforts.

The primary indicator of the strength of a country's external sector is its balance of payments position. The balance of payments (BOP), as was discussed in Chapter 4, is an annual record of all the external transactions of a country. A strong BOP position implies that a country can meet its external obligations. Such countries are ideally suited for investment by MNCs. They are not likely to have substantial import controls, because they are in a position to pay for imports with their current earnings of foreign exchange. A strong BOP position is also likely to foster a lenient policy toward foreign direct investment, because the country is able to generate the necessary foreign currency resources to permit conversion of local currencies into foreign currencies for repatriation of MNC profits.

A country facing BOP difficulties, in contrast, is likely to impose restrictions on imports in order to conserve foreign exchange resources. In such countries the chances of greater restrictions on repatriation of profits by MNCs could also be high. As a result, an MNC may find it more difficult to do business there.

Analysis of current and future trends is perhaps more important in this area than in any other, as the balance of payments scenario changes quite rapidly. All too often a country that had an excellent BOP position and was encouraging foreign investment and imports has its external position deteriorate within a few years to such an extent that it is compelled to clamp down on imports and restrict foreign investment. Obviously, plans of many MNCs involved in such countries would be completely upset by such a policy reversal. It is therefore extremely important that an MNC keep an ongoing watch on the emerging trends in the BOP and make timely adjustments if the MNC foresees major changes in this area.

The volatility of the BOP of a country is generally higher if the composition of its exports is not diversified. It is imperative that the composition of exports of the potential investee country be analyzed closely. Countries that depend on the exports of one commodity are generally prone to greater instability in their export revenues, because a decline in the prices and demand for that commodity in the international markets could jeopardize the whole BOP. This situation occurred in oil-exporting countries such as Mexico and Venezuela when oil prices dropped steeply in the early 1980s. Over the last decade, this problem has also hindered the development efforts of the African nation of Ghana, which has attempted to diversify its export base away from cocoa, timber, and gold but has experienced BOP problems over this same time period.

EXCHANGE-RATE LEVELS AND POLICIES

Exchange-rate trends are another vital consideration for MNCs contemplating overseas direct investment. An appreciation of the exchange rates in the country under consideration would increase the home currency value of the revenues generated in that country by the MNC. In contrast, a depreciation of the currency of the investee country would have the opposite effect. The MNC must carefully monitor the direction of the future movements of exchange rates, but forecasting exchange rates is an extremely difficult proposition because many factors are involved. For many countries, however, an estimate of the future trends can be attempted on the basis of such economic fundamentals as BOP prospects, import and export trends, levels of overseas borrowings, debt service burden, local trends, and trends in inflation.

In many countries, especially LDCs, exchange rates are controlled and administered by authorities under various types of official arrangements. While some countries allow free conversion of their currency to other nations' currencies, others have their rates determined on the basis of a currency basket (see Chapter 4). Many countries also have dual or multiple exchange rates that are prescribed according to the type of transaction. Some countries also have different rates for repatriating profits out of the country. MNCs must be very careful in evaluating the exchange-rate arrangements and regulations of the potential investee country and should assess how they are likely to impact the translation of revenues from the local currency to the home currency.

Many countries also follow preset exchange-rate policies that, by administrative actions, are aimed to bring the exchange rate to the level desired by the monetary authorities. On other occasions, the policy could maintain the exchange rate within a certain bandwidth. For example, the Chinese government has purchased large amounts of US dollars in the effort to keep the yuan floating within a narrow band relative to the dollar in recent years.[3] Policies to attain exchange-rate objectives may or may not be announced. When they are not announced, they must be estimated and appropriate action taken. The MNC must seek the assistance of its own or external experts to gauge the policy direction from the prevailing trends over a certain time period.

BANKING AND FINANCIAL MARKETS

Finance is a crucial resource to any business operation, and MNCs must carefully evaluate the banking and financial market structure of the target country. The banking sector must be well developed and able to provide the needed working capital and term financing for meeting the MNC's operational requirements within the investee country. Moreover, the financial market structure must provide opportunities for raising funds to meet the cost of operations. The MNC must also evaluate the costs of funds in local markets and assess whether it would be cheaper to raise funds locally or to bring them in from abroad. The host country, however, may have regulations that prohibit, restrict, or require the sourcing of funds from abroad or the local market.

COMPARISON OF SIMILAR ECONOMIES

Typically, an MNC has a global perspective and will analyze several countries as potential sites of direct investment or export marketing. Choosing the best option involves many considerations, including a comparison of the economic structure and performance of different countries. There are several difficulties, however, in comparing economic data across countries. For one, each country publishes data in its own currency, which must be translated into a standard international currency to permit any sort of comparison, and straight translation into an international currency may not yield accurate figures. Exchange rates of one country could be officially fixed at a value much higher than the actual market rate, which could artificially inflate certain crucial country data and provide misleading information. This has been the case in Zimbabwe for the past few years.

Moreover, data standards vary greatly across countries in breadth and coverage. Some countries, especially the industrialized ones, have sophisticated data-collection and processing systems at their disposal, while many developing countries may not be able to gather even the basic data. The data also vary considerably in their timing. At a particular point in time, data for the same period may not be available for a set of countries to be compared. The reliability of data is also not always certain. Political leaders in certain countries sometimes manipulate official data to present a better picture of the economy than is actually the case, in order to preserve their own support at home and abroad. Some data often are not comparable at all. If the basis of the computation for personal income or the definition of the level of income differs across two countries, for example, then the numbers for these two indicators cannot be compared accurately. Because the computational basis does differ, any comparative analysis has to make the necessary adjustments in the nominal figures published by the sources of each country.

TAX SYSTEMS

A very important constituent of the analysis is the prevailing tax system. Taxation levels have a crucial effect on MNC operations, because high tax rates can take a substantial proportion of MNC earnings in overseas locations. Complicated and cumbersome tax procedures and systems also can make it extremely difficult for an MNC to organize and manage its international accounting system.

Tax systems and tax rates vary considerably across the world. Some countries have taxes on production levels, which are based on the quantity of goods produced by the company; such taxes, known as "excise duties," are collected at the production site of goods. In other countries, industries are subject to a value-added tax (VAT).

Countries often indicate their attitudes toward foreign investment and economic activity by the design of tax provisions that concern foreign business entities. Some countries eager to attract foreign investments have liberal tax requirements and often provide incentives for foreign investors that lower their tax rates below those of domestic industries, but many other countries tax overseas business entities at differential rates that are higher than those levied on domestic business entities. Additional taxes often are levied in some countries on the repatriation of profits by overseas investors.

The tax consideration, therefore, weighs quite heavily in any economic analysis by an MNC of a targeted country. Some countries may have a **double taxation avoidance treaty** with an MNC's home country, which is a treaty whereby an MNC's revenues would not be taxed in the overseas location in return for the same tax treatment for the overseas country's companies in the MNC's home country. Such countries would obviously provide the best tax environment for an MNC's operations.

FISCAL AND MONETARY POLICY SITUATIONS

The fiscal and monetary situation of any country is a key indicator of its economic health and the direction of future economic trends. The fiscal situation generally refers to the position of the finances of a government, whether it is able to match its expenditures with the revenues it generates, how those revenues are generated, and the effects of the fiscal policy on the country's general economic situation. The monetary situation, on the other hand, refers to the picture of the economy as seen from the perspective of the money supply and other monetary aggregates and their influence on the general economic situation.

There is considerable debate on what constitutes a good local fiscal and monetary situation and what an appropriate fiscal policy is. Generally, the debate revolves around the size of the budget deficit or surplus and how a deficit is financed. It can be safely argued, however, that a stable fiscal policy and situation would imply a scenario in which the government is able to incur sufficient expenditures to maintain a desirable rate of growth in the economy without building up too much public debt or fueling inflationary expectations. Countries with large budget deficits that are financed by the creation of more money tend to be inflationary and could disrupt the real rate of economic growth. A country with large fiscal deficits financed by government borrowings could be a dangerous place to invest. The size of the deficit and the level of government borrowing must be examined in the context of the total size of the GNI. A large absolute deficit may be disastrous for one country but manageable for another.

Any analysis has to bear in mind the current and indicative future effects of the continued deficits of a country. The economies of some countries may already be stretched, and a slight increase in the fiscal deficit may trigger immediate inflationary trends. On the other hand, there could be larger economies in which deficits would not make such a large, immediate difference. Large deficits may also signal higher taxes, lower subsidies, and lower government expenditures, which could slow down the economy, depress prices, and possibly shrink the market for the MNC. Not only is it important for an MNC to watch the level of the fiscal deficit; it is also important that the MNC consider how the government has been handling the situation and what economic consequences have emerged out of the effort.

The monetary situation is reflected to a large extent in the level of the money supply in relation to the total size of the economy. An excessive money supply in theory, and to some economists in practice, pushes up prices, as too much money chases too few goods. Inflation, therefore, is often attributed to an excess money supply.

Central banks generally take this view and often try to control the level of inflation in a country by adjusting the level of money supply through a series of monetary measures, some of which have a direct bearing on an MNC's profitability. For example, if a central bank fears that there is excess liquidity in the economy, it may decide to raise the level of interest rates in the banking system, making it more expensive to borrow money from banks and thus eliminating the incentive for loans. Central banks in some countries even place restrictions on the volume and purposes for which credit can be extended by banks to their customers. When the authorities choose to follow a tight monetary policy, the MNC may find itself squeezed for liquidity to finance its operations. Interest-rate hikes also tend to slow down economic activity, which could adversely affect export sales or the sales of local manufacturers being contemplated by an MNC. These fears can be abated as the diversity of the MNC's operating areas increases.

Fiscal and monetary policies also interact in a number of ways with the external payments situation and the exchange rates. Trends in fiscal and monetary policies also provide clues, although no definitive answers, to the future movements of exchange rates between countries. Thus, an MNC must also carefully analyze the fiscal and monetary situations and the policy stances taken in this context by the authorities.

ECONOMIC PLANNING: IDEOLOGY AND PRACTICES

After the fall of communism in eastern Europe, the importance of central economic planning decreased. It is still helpful to discuss this type of economic planning, however, since some countries still cling to this form of economic governance. In countries such as these, the economy is expected to be directed by the government through a central planning authority, which formulates broad plans for the entire economy over the medium to long term. Typically, the length of an economic plan is five years. In most countries where economic planning is used, the nation's entire economic development is strongly influenced by what is decided by the planners. For example, plans dictate which areas of industry, agriculture, or services will be emphasized or what the level of government expenditures will be in each of these sectors. Some plans even spell out specific projects in the public or government sectors that will begin during a particular plan period. In China, for example, state planning focused on rural, entrepreneurial activity during the 1980s, only to be replaced with export-oriented investment in large cities in more recent times.

The development expenditures to be incurred are laid out for different areas or provinces of a country. Thus, the plans provide a blueprint of the overall economy. Although in several instances plans are not adhered to fully, there is no doubt that they provide excellent insights into the direction an economy is likely to take, the activities that are likely to be encouraged, and the host government's economic priorities.

The MNC considering investment in a planned economy has to place some importance on the plan in order to position itself at the best strategic point, where it maximizes its own objectives and fits in best with the host country's economic priorities. Thus, a country aiming to double the production of steel in a particular plan period but lacking the capability or the know-how to do so on its own presents an excellent opportunity for MNCs who are in the business of setting up steel plants or other activities that are spin-offs of such projects.

COMPETITION

The element of competition is ever-present in most countries, and if they are open to one multinational corporation, they are open to others. The strengths of the competing multinationals; their marketing, production, and management strategies; their shares of the market; and the history of their emergence in the local markets must be analyzed, both to draw lessons and to prepare a competitive strategy to enter and penetrate the overseas market. Competition can also arise from local manufacturers as well as state-owned entities. In fact, local competitors often have considerable influence with the host governments and are able to carve out privileges for themselves to secure their own market position. This is particularly true where the local competition consists of government-owned enterprises.

MARKET DEMAND FORECASTING

PURPOSES

Market demand forecasting is usually a secondary stage in the analysis of a country as a potential market and is attempted after the overall macroeconomic environment and business climate are found conducive to a marketing effort. The basic objective is to obtain reliable, current information to fashion a successful marketing program. This data can also be used to weigh the costs of exporting products to foreign countries against the prospective benefits of manufacturing these goods in those markets.

The methodology in gathering data is to first estimate the demand for potential sales of a type of product an MNC wants to sell in the country in its entirety, then to estimate its potential share of that market. Through such a process, the firm will be better able to predict the costs, sales, and profits associated with marketing the product in the new area.

Data are gathered and processed in several stages. At the first level, the MNC may survey existing information regarding market size and historic demand within an individual country market. Next, the company might expand its research to in-depth study in order to identify specific demand, supply, and consumer characteristics within the market. Third, the company must evaluate these data to develop the most appropriate match of its resources within the network of existing opportunities. It can also use this information in its ongoing operations to change strategies in existing markets; to develop, design, package, and promote products in future markets; and to control operations by giving the company a measure of potential market share.

DATA COLLECTION AND SOURCES

The market researcher will first attempt to gather information or data from existing published sources, which is the least expensive method of gathering demand data. Sources of such information are numerous. In the United States, the Department of Commerce and the International Trade Administration provide a great deal of information regarding markets in other countries.

Organizations such as the World Bank, the Export-Import Bank of the United States, and the International Monetary Fund provide other sources of data. The **Organization for Economic Cooperation and Development (OECD)** publishes information on a full range of economic trends, providing data on production and productivity by industry classification, the structure and composition of the labor force, market consumption patterns, economic divisions within the country according to industrial sectors, relative profit shares and price structures in industries, costs of wages and labor, and financial indicators, inflation, and interest rates. In addition, the OECD provides a full range of information regarding each country's level and composition of foreign trade and official levels of reserves. The range and depth of these statistics are impressive, and they provide a great deal of valuable information for the market analyst. They are limited, however, to the OECD countries, which generally have highly developed statistical bases. Additional information regarding market behavior can be obtained from international trade associations, business groups, service organizations, chambers of commerce of individual countries, foreign groups, and the governments of other countries. Much of this information is available on the Internet free of charge.

Many governments publish such data in annual statistical yearbooks, and some private firms make a business of providing such information services to companies or individuals requesting information about specific countries. These companies provide information on a large number of indicators, such as population, GNI, export composition, basic goods and energy production, balance of payments information, media availability and usage, plus information on history, problems, and the nuts and bolts of doing business in these countries.

Other firms develop and publish indexes of market potential by identifying possible markets in three forms: according to size as a percentage of world consumption, according to intensity or degree to which consumers hold purchasing power, and according to historic growth patterns with a concentration on the past five years to identify past and potential trends. The objective is for the marketer to be able to see recent patterns in growth and make predictions about future growth areas by correlating the market characteristics and factors with detailed data on consumer and buying behavior. Thus, the next level of involvement in marketing research is a detailed country investigation of existing data gathered by others.

Primary Research

A firm may decide to conduct its own primary research either through its own resources or through the services of an agent, consultant, or specialty firm. While collecting detailed data on consumer demand levels is arduous, this process is even more difficult in overseas markets for a number of reasons.

First, the physical distance between countries makes it difficult to conduct research on site. Second, collecting takes more time abroad than it does at home, thus creating time lags and reducing the timeliness of the information.

Gathering information from consumers in foreign locales is also fraught with problems based on cultural differences. For example, US consumers think nothing of responding to surveys regarding buying behavior, habits, preferences, and use of goods. There may be cultural barriers in other countries to participating in such personal question-and-answer sessions, especially with interviewers of the opposite sex.

In addition, barriers frequently arise in the form of language and comprehension problems, where translations are either inaccurate or inappropriate or literacy levels are low. Similarly, researchers may encounter difficulty in developing a sample that is significantly representative of the population. For example, in many less-developed countries, the telephone is not as ubiquitous as it is in industrialized countries; fewer families own phones, and telephone books, when published, are often inaccurate. For this reason, researchers cannot use random samples gleaned from phone directories or the Internet, as they do in the United States.

Consequently, when researchers evaluate primary data, they must be sure to regard those results with a healthy amount of skepticism and within a cultural framework or perspective similar to that of the target country. They must also have an open mind in analyzing the results of such research and consider all possible explanations for buyer behavior.

Areas of Research

To evaluate total market potential, international marketers use a number of forecasting methods, which fall into four categories, depending on their types and treatment of data. Some methods analyze existing consumption patterns within the country under scrutiny; others look at historical market data regarding past market activities; others use data from comparable countries; and some attempt to find correlations between a number of descriptive factors and market demand.

All these methods suffer from some basic shortcomings in many potential market areas, generally the less industrialized countries of the world. Difficulties arise for the following reasons:

- Sales data are often sparse; therefore, the forecaster has no actual data on which to base projections of potential market share and must use other arbitrary determinations of demand, such as apparent consumption, which is a measure of local production plus imports adjusted for exports and domestic inventory variations.
- Data may be available for some but not all variables being used in market demand analysis models, so the researcher may not have information on enough variables to construct or use a viable computer model.
- Data availability may vary among countries; that is, some or all data may not be available for each country under consideration.
- Existing data may be out of date.

Given these caveats, marketers still find that the tools they have developed to estimate market demand are effective in assisting firms in the decision-making process.

TRADE ACTIVITIES

Market analysts look at existing patterns of consumption of goods and services to get a feel for prospective sales of their goods within that market, as well as its basic need levels. Some of this information can be gleaned from a look at the composition of the home country's exports to the target market. In the United States, for example, information regarding estimated US exports and imports in foreign markets according to product types is published by the Department of Commerce. Alternately, or in addition to looking at export competition within its own sphere, the firm also examines the total composition of imports for the foreign market from all world competitors. This international information, organized according to North American Industry Classification System (NAICS) code, is available from supranational organizations, such as the United Nations and the OECD.

These kinds of import-export analyses are not, however, definitive because they present a static historical perspective. The company has no assurance that the target country

- Will continue to import the same levels or types of goods
- Will not mount efforts to increase its own local or nationalized production and displace imports or foreign subsidiary production
- Will not have political, economic, social, or legal problems in its future that lead to the imposition of trade barriers or limits on imports

INPUT-OUTPUT TABLES

Another method of looking at current consumption of goods and products in foreign markets is through the construction of input-output tables, which systematically organize usage flows of countries' input and output goods. These complex tables are constructed so that all industrial sectors are displayed along the vertical and horizontal axes. In these tables, output or production for one industry becomes input or demand for another. For example, in the manufacturing of cars or trucks, the vehicles are outputs for the automobile manufacturer, but require inputs from such basic sectors as steel or aluminum. Similarly, construction output of houses, roads, and buildings requires inputs of concrete, lumber, hardware, and other basic building materials. These tables show the relationships among volumes of goods sold among sectors and their interdependence or their independence from one another. If this information is analyzed in light of expectations regarding future economic trends in the nation, the forecaster can make some judgments about potential changes in demand for goods in that country. Input-output tables are particularly helpful if the analyst predicts a period of economic growth for the nation, in which case the analyst can attempt to predict in which sectors that growth will translate into market demand.

Most developed, industrial countries publish input-output tables as a matter of course. Increasing numbers of developing countries are publishing such tables as an aid to promoting growth in their economies through accurate prediction of demand in appropriate sectors. While they are useful tools, these tables suffer from several limitations. One problem has to do with the reliability, breadth, and comparability of data among countries. Not every country has a complete and accurate set of data about production inputs and outputs. Another problem is that information may be dated.

Input-output tables also suffer from their assumption of fixed relationships between two industries. Thus, they give a static picture of interactions between industries and use fixed coefficients to account for increases in demand for inputs from increases in production. They also do not take into account increases in production efficiencies, the use of new production processes, or other possible dynamics, such as new technological developments.

HISTORICAL TRENDS

Another basic method of examining and predicting market trends in a potential market is based on an analysis of past activity within the country. It is crucial in methods based on past usage that the data used are complete, broad, and reliable. The data set should include accurate figures for local production and inventory levels and for the country's imports and exports. Thus, an analyst can determine the country's apparent consumption or market demand, which is figured from local production plus imports, total goods adjusted for exports, and fluctuations in inventory levels.

The analyst then determines the historical trends revealed by this information and extrapolates through a time series analysis to determine future trends. The crucial assumption made in this analysis is that past trends will continue to be in effect in the future and that consumer behavior, values, and buying activity will continue as they have in the past. This method is sometimes used in conjunction with a comparison of historical trends experienced by other, comparable nations in tandem with growth predictions for the target market country's GNI or levels of production.

COUNTRY COMPARISONS: ANALYSIS BY ANALOGY

The use of data from one country to predict market demand patterns for another country is referred to as analysis by analogy. This process makes a crucial assumption that products in new markets move along a universal path according to a country's level of development. Using this method, analysts identify comparable countries as those that are reasonably similar in market and in economic, political, and developmental structures and stages. The market researcher then looks at the consumption patterns for the product in relation to changes in the country's growth. For example, the researcher might plot consumption with changes in personal income and increasing development in one country, ascribe this predicted relationship to the fortunes of another country, and make predictions about product use based on expectations of increases in personal income.

Analysis by analogy must also be used with caution. The use of blind, absolute analogy is dangerous because no two countries are exactly similar. They differ according to non-quantifiable but significant factors, such as cultural traditions, values, and tastes. They may also differ in levels of technology, the path their developmental growth takes, and the pricing of goods. Another key problem is the assumption that demand relates to a specific variable, such as personal income or aggregate GNI within a nation. In fact, other variables, such as pricing, may have as much as or even more of an effect on market demand for the product. This method also explains a static, not dynamic, relationship between demand behavior and the economic situation and cannot account for changes to be expected in the countries under comparison.

REGRESSION ANALYSIS

To deal with the need to account for the potential effects of a number of variables on market demand, some analysts use a statistical technique called regression analysis to identify significant relationships between market demand and other variables, such as economic or population indicators. This method uses data collected from several countries on a historical basis for market demand levels and one or several other economic indicators, such as growth or price levels. One of the most widely used indicators is that of economic growth as calculated by GNI. In regression analysis the relationship between the variables is characterized as a formula, $Y = a + bx$, where Y represents total market potential, a is equal to actual use, and bx is a function of consumer use of the product times the selected indicator. For example, statisticians may find a correlation between increases in GNI or country wealth (b) and purchases (a) of luxury or non-necessities, such as appliances, designer clothing, automobiles, or leisure items.

While this linear method is helpful and can examine the relationship of several variables at once through expansion of the formula (e.g., $Y = a + bx1 + bx2 \ldots bxn$), it is also not without its limitations. For example, while it uses specific indicators as variables, these do not account for consumer differences in tastes or for product changes. This is also a situation that uses static information to provide a snapshot of the existing situation. The regression model also does not account for the achievement of a saturation level where demand increases to a certain point, then levels out.

INCOME ELASTICITY

The most common and most frequently used variable affecting market demand is (not surprisingly) personal income levels. Thus, the forecasting method that uses income elasticity looks at the relationship between two crucial variables: demand for a specific product and individual income levels. It analyzes the relationship between changes in the levels of both demand and income, which is accomplished by dividing the percentage change in product demand by the percentage change in income. If there is an increase or decrease in demand, the demand is considered to be elastic, and the ratio of the two is equal to or greater than one.

If a change in income yields less than an equal change in demand for a product, it is said to be inelastic and the value of the ratio is less than one. Frequently, elasticity follows the dictates of common sense. Food, for example, is a basic necessity and therefore demand is generally inelastic for food products; that is, regardless of changes in income, consumers maintain an even level of demand for food products. On the other hand, items that are considered luxuries are often highly elastic, and a correlation would be found between increases in demand for items such as televisions or radios and increases in income levels.

For example, sales of a luxury item such as a DVD player are likely to be highly elastic, perhaps reaching 2.5. Such elasticity would mean that for every unit of increase in average individual income, demand for DVD players would rise two and a half times. This demand elasticity will eventually level out, however, once a certain income level is reached and the market for DVD players becomes saturated.

To use income elasticity analysis in forecasting foreign market demand, the market researcher must be able to accurately determine current demand levels for a given product in a country and develop reasonable expectations of forecasts of average per capita income changes in that country. Then, using elasticity found for the same items in similar countries, the researcher can estimate foreign demand as a function of the foreign increase in income plus the elasticity for the product, as seen previously. Thus, an expectation of a foreign increase in income of one-quarter (0.25) multiplied by a high elasticity given for a product (such as 2) will yield an expectation of an increase in demand of 0.5, or 50 percent, in the foreign market.

Income elasticity, like other market estimation procedures, raises warnings. Again, the method holds the relationship out as being static; elasticity is represented as a constant value and does not allow for the dynamics of the market.

The methodology also does not account for the importance of prices in the demand equation, even though they can have a direct effect on demand, in that lowered prices often lead to increased demand or higher prices to lowered demand because of shifts of consumer purchases to lower-priced substitutes. The formula also does not account for differences in individual tastes for products and the proportion of demand generated by these preferences. Those utilizing income elasticity analyses should keep in mind that high elasticity does not equal high demand volumes. It merely signifies the relationship between income and demand for goods. Generally speaking, goods with high elasticity would be more likely to be low-volume, high-priced goods, while high-sales-volume products are often those that are income inelastic.

METHODS OF ESTIMATING MARKET SIZE AND SHARE

Once the market researcher develops suitable market data, there are a number of methods available to estimate market size and probable share of that market. Three of these methods are the market buildup, chain ratio, and analogy methods.

MARKET BUILDUP

In the market buildup method, the marketing firm gathers data from a number of small separate segments within the overall market and estimates its potential market sales in each segment. These estimates are added to develop an aggregate market total. In evaluating market potential, the marketer must take into consideration differences between segments in consumer tastes, demographics, and competition and must be careful not to assume that similar market segment sizes provide similar market opportunities.

CHAIN RATIO

The chain ratio method is used for consumer products. It consists of a string of estimates regarding target market size and attributes. It is rough, and it varies according to the accuracy of the assumptions, data, and variables used. Still, if a firm knows its markets well and has high-quality data, this method can be useful in predicting sales levels.

As an example, assume that a US brewing company, such as Samuel Adams, decides to market its beer, brewed in glass-lined tanks in Boston, Massachusetts, to a particular target market in Canada. Samuel Adams analysts would use the chain ratio method of estimating sales as follows: First, they would multiply the number of people in the target market by the estimated percentage of people who drink beer. This number would then be multiplied by the number of beer drinkers who drink imported beer times the estimated number of bottles of beer drunk per week by the average Canadian beer drinker. This number, multiplied by fifty-two weeks per year, divided by twenty-four bottles per case, yields a case volume, which is multiplied by the price per case of beer to yield a total dollar volume of imported beer sales in the Canadian target market. In this way, Samuel Adams would have an estimate of the total imported beer market in Canada and the challenge that faces it in penetrating that market.

Analogy with Known Data

Another method used to estimate market size and share works through analogy with known data from existing markets. The analogy method relates hard data about market size and penetration in one country to unknown information in another. Assume, for example, that Samuel Adams believes that its market share in the United States would correlate to possible market share in Canada according to the variable of total population. (It could also use another market indicator, such as per capita income.) If MUS = market demand in the United States, MC = market demand in Canada, VUS = population of the United States, and VC = population of Canada, the formula that would yield an estimate of Samuel Adam's market share in Canada would be as follows: If

$$\frac{MUS}{VUS} = \frac{MC}{VC}$$

then

$$MC = \frac{MUSVC}{VUS}$$

If the countries are dissimilar but the marketer has a fair estimation of the relative proportion of the total population fitting the buying criteria, the marketer can adjust the formula to reflect that proportion by multiplying the ratio against the total.

Designing Initial Market Strategy

Firms use the tools and procedures for identifying economic trends and market demand to develop an overall marketing plan, which incorporates the firm's objectives into a strategy for approaching new markets successfully or for evaluating existing operations in foreign markets. One method of viewing the existing situation in foreign markets is to compare estimates of market demand and company share with actual company performance. Through such a comparison, the firm can identify competitive gaps in the market between its potential and actual shares of markets, which it can actively attempt to narrow through increases in sales and expanded market coverage.

If sales are lower than estimated potentials, the company may be missing competitive opportunities because of underuse of its products by consumers, limitations in the product line, or gaps in the coverage of the entire market, either by being too thinly spread across the market or by not focusing intensively enough on the most lucrative market segments or geographic areas. The company also may be missing an opportunity to increase market share at the expense of its competitors. By aggressively targeting the portion of the market covered by weak competitors, it may be able to increase its market share to its full potential.

In sum, through judicious use of these forecasting techniques, the company should be able to develop, hone, and coordinate its overall marketing plan to maximize opportunities that exist in new markets, develop and implement effective operating strategies, penetrate new markets, and gain market share. Market researchers must be sure, however, not to use such techniques blindly or alone. Instead, they must be tempered with common sense and should be utilized in concert with other sources of information or analysis, such as expert opinions, field visits, and in-depth research to verify initial findings.

If the company is absolutely intent on marketing in the new country and expects to reap large benefits in terms of increased sales and profits, it might be wise to spend resources to conduct primary research in that market area, in order to be more certain of consumer tastes, preferences, and buying behavior. Conducting this research, however, is difficult and expensive. These costs must be balanced against expectations of high demand and growth of markets and market share.

All this market information must be integrated into the company's overall strategic marketing plan for all markets in all countries. At this stage, the company must decide on the level of standardization that it will find most appropriate among the marketing programs. Through standardization, the company can realize economies of scale by using similar strategies for penetrating geographically diverse markets. This is often referred to as the geocentric approach. This approach implements the strategy that best fits the various markets in which a company operates. In other situations or with other aspects of the *marketing mix*, the company may prefer to adapt its marketing program to the cultural and market differences specific to the separate marketing environments. This is often referred to as the polycentric approach. This strategy is typically more costly given the customization to each different target market that a company serves. Sometimes, companies opt for the ethnocentric approach, which uses the same methods developed in the home market for each subsequent foreign market the company enters.

Similarly, the company must make sure that its collection process for market data takes place on an ongoing basis and is coordinated in a systematic, timely, and centralized way. For this reason, many international marketing firms develop and maintain extensive marketing information systems, which contain the economic models used by market planners in the company and different levels of available market data obtained from a variety of sources, especially the field-level offices in different countries. The key to the effectiveness of the system lies in continuous updating of all market information, so that the information is accurate, relevant, cost-effective, and convenient to use. An effective marketing information system provides the marketing firm with the tools to develop a comprehensive, strategic global marketing plan that not only identifies which markets hold the greatest potential for the firm but also gives the firm a perspective on the best methods of entering the new markets.

The information provided by a company's marketing information system and the strategic plans devised on that basis are essential not only to MNCs' continued growth and expansion but also to their very survival. International markets are becoming increasingly competitive, and often the quality of information a particular company has is likely to determine whether it is a winner or a loser.

SUMMARY

Country analysis must be viewed as a prerequisite for making decisions about expanding operations internationally, regardless of whether the planned venture is simply exporting or establishing a new manufacturing location. To assess the suitability of a new target country, a company needs analysis of general economic data, such as country size, current stage of development, income distribution levels, personal consumption patterns, economic growth, and country stability. Understanding the target country's composition and mix of primary (agriculture), secondary (manufacturing), and tertiary (services) sectors is important in determining whether the country has sufficient skills and resources to support the new venture. Inflation trends, balance of payments, and foreign exchange rates and policies are also important factors for determining the suitability of a country. Special consideration also must be given to the tax structure of the targeted country. After performing this type of analysis on numerous countries, the MNC can select the location that best serves its project.

The fiscal and monetary policies of a country provide key information on the general health of the national economy. Also, economic plans developed by the central government help to identify the country's future growth directions. The presence of multinationals and the current level of competition provide further information about the target country's suitability for expansion.

Market demand forecasts must be prepared using secondary data, which comes, for example, from the Department of Commerce, world organizations such as the World Bank and the International Monetary Fund, or the target country itself. Primary data such as consumer surveys gathered by the MNC itself may also be considered when developing market demand forecasts. Four general methods are used to develop total market potential: analysis of existing consumption methods, use of historical data from past market activities, use of data from comparable countries, and development of correlations between a number of descriptive factors and market demand. Market size and share can be estimated by using market buildup, chain ratio, and analogy methods.

The quality of information and the strategic decisions developed from that information are critical to the MNC's survival and expansion.

DISCUSSION QUESTIONS

1. Why is country analysis important to the international businessperson?
2. If you are a manufacturer of toys interested in beginning export operations, which economic indicators would you choose to analyze country opportunities? How would these indicators change if you were considering building a computer manufacturing and assembly plant overseas?

3. What information results from a market demand forecast? Describe the general process of forecasting market demand.
4. What data problems occur when conducting a forecast?
5. Discuss alternative analysis techniques that can be used to estimate market demand.

NOTES

1. World Bank Group, "Country Profiles."
2. Obinna, "Zimbabwe: Pensioners Hurt by Record Inflation."
3. Yahoo Finance, "Currency Converter."

BIBLIOGRAPHY

Cateora, Phillip R. *International Marketing*. Homewood, IL: Irwin, 1987.
Devarajan, Shantayanan, et al. "Making Services Work for Poor People." *World Development Report*. New York: Oxford University Press, 2004.
International Monetary Fund. *International Financial Statistics*. July 2003.
———. *World Economic Outlook*. April 2003.
Obinna, Anyadike. "Zimbabwe: Pensioners Hurt by Record Inflation." *IRIN Humanitarian News and Analysis*, 26 December 2003. www.irinnews.org/report.asp?ReportID=38601&SelectRegion=Southe rn_Africa&SelectCountry=ZIMBABWE.
Organization for Economic Cooperation and Development. *Historical Statistics, 1960–2003*. Washington, DC: World Bank, 2004.
World Bank. www.data.worldbank.org//news/newest-country-classifications-released.
World Bank Group. "Country Profiles." 2004. http://web.worldbank.org/WBSITE/EXTERNAL/COUNTR IES/0,,pagePK:180619~theSitePK:136917,00.html.
Yahoo Finance. "Currency Converter." http://finance.yahoo.com/currency.

GLOBALIZATION AT THE CROSSROADS: WORLD OIL DEMAND AND THE EDGEWORTH BOX

World oil demand has been impacted by the world financial crisis of 2008 and environmental concerns. The financial crisis caused a slowdown in global economic growth in the OECD countries and these same countries are focusing more on the environmental effects of carbon pollution, which has been linked as a primary component of greenhouse gases that contribute to global warming. In contrast, the developing countries of eastern Europe, Africa, Asia, and Latin America (i.e., the BRICs and MINTs) are the main drivers of world economic growth. International oil companies (IOC) must now shift to more efficient, clean, and therefore complex refineries in the OECD countries, while working with the governments and the national oil companies in the developing countries. The developing countries have realized that stable sources of energy are necessary to contribute to the long-term economic growth and economic stability of their economies. They are also aware that economic growth and the associated increased energy consumption will lead to more greenhouse gas emissions.

The national oil companies (NOC) are often the legal owners of the underground natural resources, such as oil, gas, and minerals, unlike in the United States, where there is private ownership of the land and the underlying natural resources. The national oil companies need the expertise of the International Oil Companies, such as Exxon-Mobil, British Petroleum, and Shell. The international oil companies, as specialists in the exploration, development, and production of oil fields, are therefore partners in the process of bringing the oil to the market. Conversely, for the international oil company, their concern is bringing the production to the market whereby they are not necessarily motivated by the long term economic development of the country in which production is taking place. The national oil companies often not only have financially driven profit motivations, but are also tasked with economic development, social, and environmental goals. The national oil companies, especially in countries such as Brazil, Russia, India, China, are not only in charge of bringing or supervising the extraction of the natural resources, but also need to be concerned with the refining and distribution of the finished products (such as gasoline, fuel oil, diesel).

What type of model can be developed that can help us understand the complexities of dual motivations of both the international oil companies and the national oil companies? The international oil companies are most interested in the profit motivations of the oil and the refined products, but not necessarily with the underlying social, economic, and environmental secondary tasks of the national oil companies. Often the International oil companies do not own the natural resources or the distribution in the source country, while the national oil companies do not own the distribution resources in the destination country. Can dual branding of the oil and gas products assist in stabilizing oil and gasoline prices, while providing for an optimal solution of the distribution of the oil and gas.

The Edgeworth Box is a graphical representation of a two good and two entity economy. Let us look at a two good and two entity economy in which the goods are oil and gas, while the two entities are a national oil company and an international oil company. Each entity is endowed with a predetermined set of goods, which they are able to produce efficiently. The national oil company is endowed with oil and the international oil company is endowed with gasoline. One producer may have a competitive advantage in the production of the oil while the second producer may have a competitive advantage in refining of the oil into gas. An additional competitive advantage is the presence in highly industrial countries where the largest consumers of oil happen to be. As is shown in Figures 7.1 through 7.3, a shift in the indifference curve into the area of the negotiation space will allow for a Pareto improvement. The shift in the indifference curve can be owing to negotiations for gasoline refining capability and joint venture agreements. When the two different goods are traded between the two entities, a different allocation of the two goods is achieved. A Pareto superior outcome is where you are able to devise a tariff schedule where different prices are charged to different consumers, and you are able to make each one better off, while obtaining a greater amount of the good, such as lower gasoline prices. When an efficient allocation of the goods is achieved, it is said to

Figure 7.1 **Edgeworth Box: Initial Conditions**

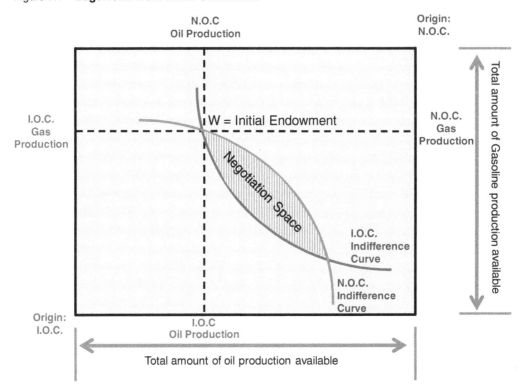

be a Pareto optimal solution. A Pareto optimal solution is where you make someone else better off without making anyone else worse off. Ideally, there will be an optimum Pareto efficient set where the benefits for both are at a maximum.

QUESTIONS FOR DISCUSSION

1. *Research the top national oil companies and international oil companies. How do these largest producers stack up in terms of geographic presence and market supply?*
2. *Research the initial total endowments in billions of barrels of oil for both the OPEC country oil producers and non-OPEC country oil producers.*

Figure 7.2 **Edgeworth Box: Indifference Curve Shift Allowing Pareto Improvement**

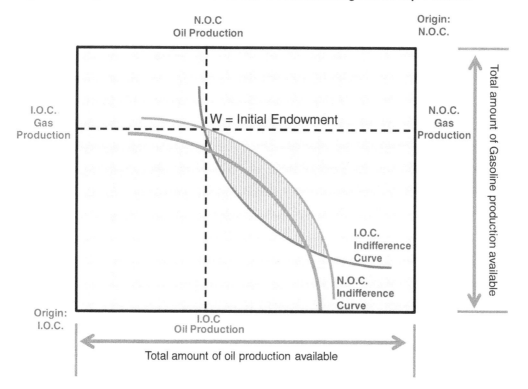

3. *Position the United States as an oil producer as well as an oil consumer (in number of barrels daily). Discuss how the Edgeworth Box can be used to illustrate oil trade between the US and the following three countries combined together: Saudi Arabia, Nigeria, and Venezuela.*

4. *What might the projected growth in world population over the next thirty years imply about the price and supply of oil?*

Figure 7.3 **Edgeworth Box: Pareto Optimal Solution**

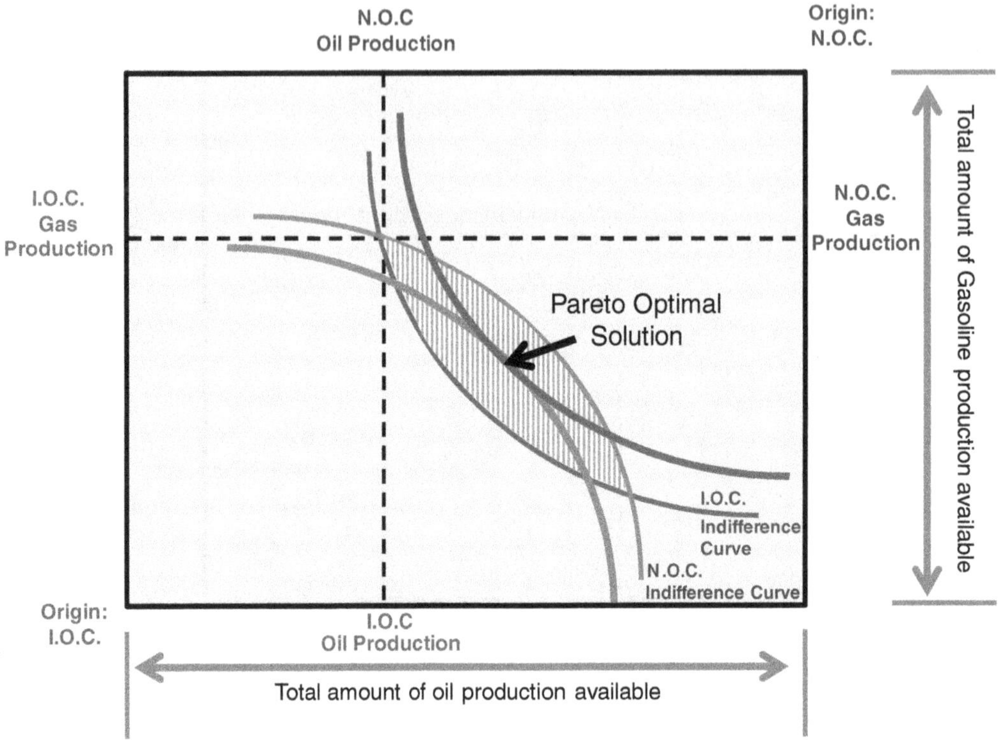

CASE STUDY 7.1

CASE STUDY 7.1

THE REPUBLIC OF MAZUWA

It is only 8 AM, but nearly all the top managers are already at work at McBride and Mackers corporate headquarters in Minneapolis, Minnesota. The company is a leading consulting organization specializing in market research, especially in the area of international marketing. Founded in 1965, the company has established an enviable track record in international marketing research and counts a number of top corporate names among its clients.

The company was founded by Walter McBride, a graduate of Columbia University, where he received an MBA with a major in marketing. Three years after establishing his firm, McBride was joined by Jim Mackers, a practicing management consultant with one of the large accounting firms. The firm has grown steadily over the years, and by 2012 total billings were about $4 million.

In the 1960s and most of the 1970s, much of the company's business involved doing marketing research for companies looking for business opportunities in Latin America, especially Brazil, Chile, and Argentina. In the 1970s, as the focus shifted to the Middle East, the company earned substantial revenue from undertaking consulting contracts for business opportunities in that region.

The company has recently won a contract for doing a market study for Peitra Inc., a large diversified manufacturer of consumer goods that is looking at the Republic of Mazuwa as a potential export market. McBride and Mackers has little experience with Africa, and its only connections are some minor research projects done for North African countries in conjunction with studies on Middle Eastern markets. It won the contract primarily on the basis of its excellent record in other markets and its competitive bids.

Having received the contract, the company has to come up with a strategy to analyze the Mazuwan economy. As a first step, the firm sends a preliminary study team to Mazuwa to get a sense of the situation there and to report back to headquarters with its recommendations on the best possible way to look at the country's economy and study it as a possible market for export of the client's products. In the meanwhile, back at the head office, other members of the project team put together a market fact sheet on the essential features of the Republic of Mazuwa (see Table 7.1).

Table 7.1 **Essential Features of the Republic of Mazuwa**

Country data sheet

Population	38 million
Area	267,000 square miles
Per capita GNP (annual)	US$450
Ratio of urban/rural population	60 percent rural; 40 percent urban
Foreign debt (commercial credits)	US$3 billion
Debt service rate (debt service/exports)	42 percent
Main exports	Copper, coffee, unfinished leather
Main imports	Petroleum and petroleum products, fertilizers, arms
Main industries	Agro-processing, mineral extraction, small industrial goods
Balance of payments	Average debt of US$410 million over the past three years
Total export volume	US$740 million (2010)
Total import volume	US$1,190 million (2010)
Form of government	Military dictatorship with provincial councils headed by presidential appointees

(continued)

Case Study 7.1 *(continued)*

The study mission returns after a four-day stay in Silvata, the main business center and port of Mazuwa. They also visited the capital city of Kilbanga and met with government officials in the Ministries of Finance and Trade and the Bureau of Statistics. Shortly after their return, they prepare a brief but well-documented summary of their findings, which is circulated to the policy committee, which comprises all the top managers of the company. McBride calls an urgent meeting to discuss the findings and to make a decision on the best strategy to adopt.

Five top managers attend the meeting; McBride, as president of the company, is in charge of corporate policy and overall management of the company; Mackers is executive vice president and in charge of day-to-day operations, with personal responsibility for the management consulting division; John Waters, an MBA from Stanford and head of the marketing research division, with the title of senior vice president; Gilbert Harris, head of financial advisory services, a CPA by profession and a senior vice president; and Robert Ponsford, senior vice president and head of the management information systems consulting division. Cynthia Peters, vice president of the marketing research division, and Deborah Seidman, assistant vice president in the division that did the preliminary study, are also invited to attend.

The meeting begins at 8:30 AM; McBride calls it to order and begins the discussion.

McBride: Good morning and welcome to the meeting. It's nice to see all of us together at once. Most of you are usually several thousand miles apart most of the time. You have already had a look at the preliminary report by Cynthia and Deborah. It is a good job; thanks to both of you. We will do this as quickly and smoothly as possible. I'll shoot off any comments to begin with, and then everyone can make his own comments in turn. We'll give Cynthia and Deborah time to respond to the comments and answer any questions. I'll conclude by summarizing the issues, and then we'll make a decision.

As you have read in the summary, Mazuwa is, by any standards, a difficult country to do research in, in the best of circumstances. Most of the data are available only through government sources, and most of the official figures are fairly unreliable. Further, whatever data we get are dated, and by the time we do the numbers at our end, I am not sure we'll be able to make much of a contribution to the client's marketing plans. I am therefore forced to rethink the whole project and am inclined to tell our client quite clearly that there is little we can do for them in Mazuwa, at least at this stage. I am being pessimistic, but the picture drawn by Cynthia and Deborah does not appear very encouraging.

Mackers: Walter, I think you are really being overcautious. We have created marketing plans for new countries in the past and made a success of it. In the Middle East we had all kinds of cultural and language problems, not to mention dealing with the arbitrary system of administration. I know Mazuwa's data are dated and extremely difficult to gather, and some of the data could be pretty unreliable. However, I think we should make a go of it and tell our client that this analysis is based on this type of data and must therefore be treated with that amount of caution. Anyway, if we don't go ahead with this project, I am sure someone else will, since Peitra, our client, is interested quite seriously in expanding into Africa. I know there is a risk of us spending a lot of time and effort on this and not being able to come up with any useful information at all, but then we are in this business, and having gone international, there are some risks we have to take.

Waters: I have been rolling this around in my head ever since Peitra first approached us. The more I think about it, the more convinced I get of the feasibility of this project. All we really have to do is to put enough effort and commitment into the exercise. I propose that we send three of our best analysts down to Silvata and Kilbanga and have them pick up these data firsthand from the government and the chamber of commerce. Their presence will allow for a thorough recording, analysis, cross-referencing, and verification of the data. While they are there, any doubts and discrepancies can be discussed with local officials, who, on the first visits, were quite helpful and open, much to our surprise. I am aware that nearly all the records are maintained manually and that computer-savvy employees are few and far between, but with our analysts on the spot, we can overcome these problems and come out with a good information set that we can use to put together what I would call a pioneering marketing research effort for our client.

Harris: I agree with John that the project is doable and that we can come out with a fairly decent report on the business possibilities for Peitra in Mazuwa, but I think we need to take a different approach to doing this. Putting a team of three of our best analysts in this area is going to add up to enormous costs, and we will have a hard time justifying the expense to our clients. Moreover, our people are needed in other, much higher-value contracts, and taking them away for an extended period of time could hurt business at that end. My thought in this matter would be to get hold of a local research firm. I know there are a couple of good business consulting groups in neighboring Dolawi, who could gather the data and send them to us for less than half the cost. Obviously, we will not have the quality and reliability of the data that our own analysts would generate, but then, that's the trade-off we will have to make.

Peters: As the person who has been down at the field level, I can only testify that the difficulties are real and challenging but are not insurmountable. What will

(continued)

Case Study 7.1 *(continued)*

be critical is the strategy we adopt. Perhaps we can look at a few country studies done on other, similarly placed African countries and see how such situations have been approached before. There must be some information available from secondary services. Mazuwa has had a number of World Bank loans, and I am sure there must be considerable economic data available at the major international development institutions. Our preliminary findings would certainly benefit from access to this type of information.

McBride: Thanks, Cynthia. There have been a number of different views on this, and it appears that most of us really want to do this. I had objections previously but given the good work here, I believe this should be pursued. However, while devising a strategy on how to do this project, I want the following to be kept in mind. First, we don't want to be seen giving wrong information to our clients. Second, the project shouldn't cost us more to do than we are being paid; loss leaders are okay but not at this point in the company's financial situation. Third, I do not want this project delayed. We have built a reputation for timely delivery after years of sustained efforts; let's keep it that way.

DISCUSSION QUESTIONS

1. If you were present at the meeting, what would be your position?
2. Prepare a strategy for doing a study for the client, keeping in mind the considerations established by Walter McBride.

CHAPTER 8

International Law and Global Orientations

"If you had to live your life over again, do it overseas."
—Henny Youngman

CHAPTER OBJECTIVES

This chapter will:

- Briefly describe how legal systems differ between countries
- Discuss the legal concepts that are important in the international business environment
- Identify current US laws that influence international trade and multinational corporations
- Examine the importance of intellectual and industrial property rights
- Define the methods for resolving international business conflicts and the legal organizations that are available in the international arena

---

PUBLIC AND PRIVATE LAW

International transactions are complex and tend to be risky. Consequently, disputes often arise between business partners. To the international businessperson, however, the normal recourse to national law is not always available, because host-country laws often discriminate in favor of their citizens. Moreover, there is no international body of law that governs international transactions. Thus, when people refer to the study or the conducting of **international law**, they are merely referring to the laws that govern the activity

245

of nations in their relationships with one another. These laws collectively are referred to as the public law of nations, which reflects individual countries' methods for dealing with other nations of the world. Public law is based not only on written law but also on unwritten customs and conventions.

Public law, that is, the manner in which nations interact according to a legal framework, differs from private law. **Private law** applies not to nation-states but to individuals within those nation-states. These parties enter into agreements called contracts in order to establish a set of rules and regulations regarding their mutual interests and interactions. Their contracts stipulate the terms of their agreements regarding what is to be exchanged, when, where, and for what price in what currency. This private law is still affected, however, by the rules and regulations emanating from public law—overall stipulations regarding permissible behavior between the contracting parties. For example, despite having contracts to the contrary, private citizens may be prohibited by the laws of their countries from buying goods that a nation has barred for importation, because of public policy or national economic goals.

DIFFERENT LEGAL SYSTEMS

The legal systems of different countries are based in one of four legal traditions or foundations: civil, common, bureaucratic, and religious law. **Civil law**, which traces its origins from ancient Roman law and, more recently, the Napoleonic Code, is practiced in most European nations and the former colonies of those countries. Civil law is a body of law that is written essentially in the form of statutes and is constructed and administered by judicial experts in government. A hybrid of civil law is practiced, for example, in Japan. Under the hybrid systems, government experts are involved in the development of new statutes, but before even being proposed, these potential laws generally achieve political consensus. Law is seldom modified or amended in civil law systems.

Common law, which is practiced in Great Britain and its former colonies, for example, the United States, is more susceptible to challenge, change, and amendment. The common law system is based not on federal administration but on judicial interpretation of the law as well as on customs or usages existing within the nation. Under common law, decisions made by the court are based on preceding judicial judgments (i.e., precedence) rendered by prior courts.

Bureaucratic law, which is practiced in many communist countries as well as dictatorships, is law that is set by the country's current leadership. This law is subject to change rapidly when the regime changes. In the summer of 2003, the citizens of Hong Kong feared that the Chinese government would impose an anti-subversion law on the island, as is in place on the mainland. This law, which could have been used to quell future protests in Hong Kong, contradicted the concept of "one nation, two systems" that has existed between China and Hong Kong since China took over possession of the island from Great Britain in 1997. While the Chinese government eventually backed off on its implementation of an anti-subversion law in Hong Kong, this is an example of how bureaucratic law can suddenly change the operating environment in a formerly open society.

The countries that adhere to **religious law** are primarily Muslim. In these nations, religious law is generally mixed to an extent with other forms of law, such as civil or common law. In some countries, such as Saudi Arabia, religious precepts referred to as the sharia (one translation of which is "way to follow") govern all behavior and are administered by the government and Islamic judges. A system such as this is also known as a **theocracy**.

INTERNATIONAL TREATIES FRAMEWORK

These legal traditions and systems provide each nation with its own public law and a framework for conducting both its relationships with other countries and its citizens' relations with private citizens from other nations. This framework, a law of nations, is formalized for individual countries through their agreements, which are developed either individually or within a bloc with other nations. These agreements outline rules and regulations to be observed by the parties with regard to economic and commercial matters. The most important of such accords are treaties; those that are considered less important are called protocols, acts, agreements, or conventions.

These agreements are binding on the parties that enter into them. If there are only two nations involved, the agreement is termed a bilateral treaty; if there are more than two nations involved, the agreement is termed a multilateral treaty. Treaties are entered into primarily to facilitate the conduct of commerce between nations. They determine the rules to be followed, define the rights and obligations of each party, and provide for the enforcement of judgments when the terms of the treaties are violated.

There are many different kinds of treaties entered into by nation-states. The most fundamental provide the basis for conducting business between nations by allowing the citizens of the counterpart country to participate in business activity in the home country through trading, investing, or operating or owning a business. Such treaties, known as treaties of friendship, commerce, and navigation, stipulate fundamental parameters to be observed by citizens within each nation while interacting with those from the other and establish guidelines for doing business across borders. Thus, they address such issues as the entry of people, goods, ships, cargoes, and capital into countries. They also establish guidelines regarding the acquisition of property by foreign nationals, as well as the protection of their own citizens and their property abroad. Similarly, they address flows of resources between countries in the transfer of funds or currencies between the two nations.

Tax treaties allow for countries to establish criteria for determining which country has jurisdiction over income earned, how double taxation is to be avoided, and how the countries can cooperate to reduce the evasion of taxes by each other's citizenry.

Legal Concepts Relating to International Business

Sovereignty

Even casual examination of international law requires the definition of the concept of **sovereignty**, which is the principle that individual nations have absolute power over the governing of their populaces and the activities that occur within their borders. To be considered a sovereign entity, a nation must be independent, have a permanent population and well-defined boundaries, possess a working economy and government, and have the capacity to conduct foreign relations. To be sovereign and conduct relations with other nations, the country must be recognized as such by those other nations. Recognition is the official political action taken by the countries of the world to accept the status of a country as a legal entity and a full-fledged member of the political and economic system of the world. One example of a nation *not* recognized as sovereign is Northern Cyprus, which Turkish-Cypriots have occupied since 1974 and which is officially recognized as a nation only by the Republic of Turkey.

Sovereignty has been in the news lately in two ways. Firstly, protesters claim that increased globalization entails a surrender of sovereign rights to the global marketplace. Secondly, the EU sovereign debt crisis exposed the flaws of sovereign entities being managed by one central bank and one currency.

Sovereign Immunity

Sovereignty implies that a nation can impose laws and restrictions, levy taxes, and circumscribe business activities. A manifestation of this sovereign power is the doctrine of **sovereign immunity**, which is the principle that a sovereign state enjoys immunity from being held under the jurisdiction of local courts when it is party to a suit unless the state itself consents to be a party to that suit. Therefore, courts have no jurisdiction to hear claims against a sovereign nation.

In an attempt to clarify this situation, the United States passed the Foreign Sovereign Immunity Act (FSIA) in 1977. This law stipulated that, in the eyes of the United States, a foreign nation waives its right to sovereign immunity when it or its agency engages in a commercial activity. The FSIA focuses on the nature and the purpose of commercial activity undertaken and covers business activities that take place in the United States, are performed in the United States but involve activities elsewhere, or have a direct effect on the United States, even if performed outside the country's borders.

Act of State

The **act of state doctrine** is a legal principle that refers to claims made by foreign parties whose assets or belongings have been taken by the state in public actions. This doctrine holds that sovereign nations can act within their proper scope in confiscating these assets. To be an act of state, however, the activity must satisfy several conditions. It must be an exercise of foreign power, conducted within a country's own territory, with a degree of consequence calculated to affect a foreign investor or party, and it must be an action that is taken by the state in the public interest.

Because acts of state are considered to be within the rights of sovereign entities, judicial bodies in other countries have no standing to consider the legality of such actions. The biggest issue in these actions arises in regard to foreign owners being compensated adequately for the loss of these assets. Although international law and convention require that owners be paid appropriately for their confiscated or nationalized assets, the definition of "appropriate" varies according to each party's opinion and judgment. This problem is a major concern when investments are expropriated by developing nations, especially because some of these countries have repudiated the classical principles of compensation for expropriation, citing the country's overriding development goals.

EXTRATERRITORIALITY

Extraterritoriality refers to the application of one country's laws to activities outside its borders. Such a transnational reach across borders comes into play when a government seeks to restrict, limit, or direct business activities, such as monopolistic practices, the collection of taxes, or allowable payments for corrupt practices. The United States, in particular, attempts to extend its regulatory and legal reach across national borders in all these areas, although it is not always successful. One such attempt by the United States began in the early 1980s, when President Ronald Reagan decided to impose economic sanctions on the Soviet Union to protest Soviet pressure on Polish officials to impose martial law and crack down on leaders of the Solidarity trade union.

The sanctions prohibited American companies and their foreign subsidiaries and affiliates using US licenses from selling equipment or technology to the Soviet Union for the transmission or refining of oil and gas. The sanctions, targeted at the Soviet Union's construction of a 2,600-mile natural gas pipeline from Siberia to Western Europe, raised a storm of controversy in the United States and Europe. At the center of the controversy were technological licenses issued by General Electric to foreign affiliates in Scotland, France, Italy, and Germany, which the US government forced General Electric to cancel. Protests by the licensees were made on the grounds that the sanctions violated international legal principles of the sanctity of valid contracts between parties and on the impropriety of the US attempt to use extraterritoriality. When licensees appealed to their national governments, European leaders rejected the sanctions out of hand, arguing that President Reagan had no right to extend US laws beyond US territory, and instructed the licensees to continue their operation.[1]

AREAS OF CONCERN TO MULTINATIONAL CORPORATIONS

US TRADE LAWS

One area in which nations use their legal systems to affect international commerce is trade law. One aspect of this legal jurisdiction is the granting of licenses allowing US concerns to export goods. Through the issuing of such licenses, national governments control how and to what degree national resources will be allocated to foreign users through the export of commodities, services, and technology. Other methods of controlling trade are the imposition of tariffs in the form of customs duties on imports and exports, and nontariff barriers that slow exchanges of goods and services by increasing the complexities of international commerce.

In addition to these controls on trade and international trading agreement participation under the World Trade Organization (WTO), the United States also has specific trade laws designed to protect US citizens from the unfair trade practices of other nations, including subsidies and pricing practices with countervailing and antidumping laws.

COUNTERVAILING DUTIES

Countervailing duty law is designed to provide for the imposition of tariffs to equalize prices of imports that are low because of subsidies provided by home governments to encourage trade. These subsidies can include financial help from a government, such as loans with special interest rates; providing input goods, raw materials, or services at preferential rates; forgiveness of debt; and assuming costs of industry manufacturing, production, or distribution.

Before countervailing duties are levied, many legal steps must be taken. The legal proceedings follow two paths: determination of injury to an industry or firm, and findings that imported goods have been subsidized. In the first situation, the US government, through the efforts of the International Trade Commission (ITC), must decide that the existing or potential domestic industry has been injured by the practices of foreign exporters. Proceedings can be initiated by the government itself or through the petition of private parties (usually the injured industry). If the country concerned is a member of a regional trade area (such as NAFTA), then the proceedings are typically officiated by the tribunal associated with the regional trade agreement. If the aggrieved parties are more than two, the WTO would typically administer the complaint and render a verdict.

After an action is initiated and a case is brought before the ITC, efforts are mounted along the second path to determine whether or not the goods being imported into the United States are subsidized. If it is found that prima facie subsidization exists, sales of those goods by the foreign interest are suspended in the United States, and the party must post a bond for the amount of the estimated subsidy. Within seventy-five days after a determination is made, the administering authority makes a final decision regarding the existence and the amount of the subsidy.

Following the finding of a subsidy, the ITC makes its final determination of injury. If both authorities rule affirmatively regarding subsidies and injury, then a countervailing duty is levied on goods brought into the United States in the amount of the subsidization. The conduct of such cases is a lengthy, arduous, and expensive process that involves many teams of lawyers representing the domestic industry and the countries in question. For example, the softwood lumber dispute between the United

States and Canada (see Chapter 2) ran for more than two decades under the auspices of the NAFTA tribunal.

Antidumping Laws

US **antidumping laws** also protect American industries and companies against the unfair practices of parties in other nations as they relate to pricing practices, specifically, **predatory pricing**. Through such a practice, a foreign competitor attempts to capture a large share of a target market by cutting prices below those charged locally. Once such a share is attained and domestic competition is eliminated, the exporter can freely raise prices to prior or even higher levels. This practice is considered predatory if the seller is charging a price that does not reflect the fair value of the goods and is counterbalanced by higher prices charged in domestic or other markets.

The legal process of imposing duties on such dumped goods is similar to that in countervailing duty cases. The initiation of the case is the same, and the ITC is charged with determining both preliminary and final findings of injury to the domestic industry. Meanwhile, the administrative agency attempts to determine whether or not the goods are being sold for less than their fair market value. If the final findings of both determinations are affirmative, dumping duties equal to the amount of actual fair market value above the price charged in the US market are assessed on the foreign goods in question. The duty remains in effect only as long as and to the extent that the dumping practice continues.

Antitrust Laws

One special area of legal concern for practitioners of international business is the application of antitrust laws by the United States to the activities of those engaging in international commerce. US antitrust laws are based on free-market economic principles of competition. Thus, antitrust laws in the United States were enacted to prevent businesses from engaging in anticompetitive activities and to challenge the growth of monopoly power in industries.

The United States is noted in the international legal community for strict enforcement of these laws and for transnational application of these restrictions. The United States attempts to enforce antitrust statutes through the use of extraterritoriality and the imposition of its laws on the activities of US business concerns in other nations. US justification for such activity is that the United States rightly has extraterritorial reach if the action being disputed or acted against has the effect of materially affecting commerce in the United States.

The two main US laws covering the antitrust area are the Sherman Act and the Clayton Act. The **Sherman Act** was instituted in 1890 with the goal of preserving competition in both US domestic and export markets. It prohibits anticompetitive or monopolistic activities by business entities. Some such anticompetitive practices are trust-building, agreements to fix prices or allocate markets by industry participants, and agreements to engage in monopolistic activities in the United States or with foreign nations.

The antitrust purview was extended by the adoption of the **Clayton Act** of 1914, which prohibits the acquisition of the stock or assets of another firm if the effect of that acquisition is the reduction of competition within the industry or the creation of a monopoly. This law has been interpreted by US courts to affect activity in international markets, because it requires only that the effect of the acquisition or merger be felt in the US market; there are no geographic constraints as to the physical locale where these acquisitions were made. Thus, the statute would cover horizontal mergers between industry competitors, vertical mergers between producers and suppliers or distributors, and mergers that have the effect of eliminating potential competition in markets.

The **Webb-Pomerene Act** of 1918 allows some American firms to seek exemptions from the application of these antitrust laws if they join together to gain access to foreign markets by exporting their goods. Under the Webb-Pomerene Act, firms are given specific exemptions from antitrust law and are allowed to join together to agree on prices and market allocations if such activity does not have the effect of reducing competition within the United States. Similarly, in 1982 Congress passed the Export Trading Company Act, which provided some guidance for these companies to facilitate international trade by acting as middlemen between potential buyers and sellers of export goods. Frequently, these **export-trading companies (ETCs)** trade simultaneously in products that compete against each other and represent competing firms. The purpose of the 1982 law was to provide an exemption from antitrust law so that US firms could combine resources in pursuing these export activities, as long as competitiveness in domestic US trade remained unaffected.

Over the years, antitrust legislation similar to the United States laws has been passed in the European Union, United Kingdom, Australia, China, India, and elsewhere. While there are some differences in the various international laws, most are similar in spirit to the legislation passed in the United States.

FOREIGN CORRUPT PRACTICES

In the 1970s questions about and interest in unethical behavior mushroomed as the events of Watergate unfolded. This interest was magnified by revelations that the Lockheed aerospace firm had made enormous payoffs to Japanese premier Kakui Tanaka for his help obtaining security contracts. It appeared also that other firms in such industries as construction, arms, aerospace, and pharmaceuticals routinely made payments to facilitate contract awards, sales orders, or project clearance by foreign regulatory agencies. In response to these revelations, the **Foreign Corrupt Practices Act (FCPA)** was enacted in 1977 to deal with payments abroad.

The FCPA contains three major provisions regarding the payment of bribes and payoffs. First, it sets standards for accounting for all businesses, so that enterprises keep accurate books and records and maintain internal controls on their accounting procedures and systems. Second, it prohibits the use of corrupt business practices, such as making gifts, payments, or even offers of payments to foreign officials, political parties, or political candidates, if the purpose of the payments is to get the recipient to act (or not act) in the interests of the firm and its business dealings. Third, it establishes sanctions or punishments for such behavior. For example, violation of the corrupt practices sections of the act could result in fines of up to US$2 million for criminal cases.

Under the terms of the act, the word "corrupt" is used to denote activity in which it is clear that the payment or offer is being made with the purpose of inducing a public official to use his or her power wrongly in providing business for a firm or in obtaining special legislative or regulatory treatment for a company. The act also differentiates between bribes and payments made to facilitate international business by exempting payments made to minor officials in foreign bureaucracies. These payments, often called "grease," are routinely paid to smooth the path of business for international firms. For example, a payment may provide for faster service or red-tape clearance. These payments are considered a legitimate cost of doing business but must be accounted for appropriately. There are those who oppose making such payments illegal and defend them as being a reasonable cost of doing business, especially in foreign environments with different cultural patterns, values, and mores. They criticize the law for being expensive in its compliance and reporting requirements and cite difficulties in making the necessary distinctions between facilitative payments and customary business expenses, such as entertainment of potential customers. These critics also believe that the law has worked to the detriment of American business by causing the loss of enormous volumes of business, especially to firms from other countries in which such payments are considered routine and ordinary operational costs.

The position of the United States and its laws regarding these payments differs from that of many other countries of the world, where such practices as making payoffs and paying bribes are considered ordinary costs of doing business in international settings. In Germany, for example, such payments have historically been considered customary and have been accounted for as tax-deductible special expenses, just as they have been in the United Kingdom. Similarly, France and Japan have no restrictions on making such payments to facilitate the development of business. The question remains, however, whether these allowances for such payments put French, Japanese, German, and British firms at a competitive advantage over American firms.

TAX TREATIES

An area of particular interest for sovereign nations that affects international firms and their operations is that of taxation. Tax procedures and policies can have significant effects on the well-being and health of firms. They can discourage growth, investment, and the pursuit of profits by being onerous, or they can stimulate economic development and growth by providing incentives for firms and individuals. Taxation policies and laws differ around the world; rates vary considerably, as do types of taxes. Some countries, for example, allow for a lower tax on capital gains than on regular gains, to provide incentives for long-term savings and investment, while others tax all gains at the same rate.

In general, income taxes are a form of **progressive taxation**; that is, the larger one's income, the higher the tax rate. European countries levy a **value-added tax (VAT)** only on the value that is added to products as they progress from raw materials to consumer goods. The VAT has the benefits of being relatively easy to collect and administer as well as being easily raised or lowered according to the country's economic needs, but it has the disadvantage of not being progressive. Consequently, both low- and high-income members of society are taxed at the same rate because their total tax obligations may differ only according to their purchases, not according to their levels of income.

Taxes are levied not only to produce income or revenue for nations but also to affect public policy. For example, some taxes are intended to discourage the consumption of certain items. These so-called **sin taxes** (or **excise taxes**) are often levied on such goods as alcoholic beverages and tobacco products. Other tax policies provide incentives for firms to engage in particular activities. One such incentive in the United States encourages export activities by providing tax breaks for companies exporting as foreign sales corporations.

Countries differ greatly in the focus, provisions, regulations, levels of compliance, and enforcement of their tax policies. These differences can lead to significant problems for the multinational firm conducting business across the boundaries of different taxing authorities that vary in their determination of who is taxed on what property, what income, and at what rate. The question then becomes to which taxing authority must multinational firms or employees of that multinational firm remit taxes. The solution is one that recognizes both the concept that all sovereign nations have the authority to tax and the concept that corporations and individuals should be spared from having undue or double tax liabilities.

In consequence, nations around the world enter into tax treaties that generally provide for credits in the home country for taxes paid in the host country by corporations or individuals. Thus, the entity is not taxed twice on the same income or property. For example, the United States taxes personal income not according to the residence or site where the income was earned but according to the nationality of the taxpayer. Therefore, expatriates working abroad are liable for taxes on income earned in those foreign settings. Tax law, however, provides a break for these individuals by allowing them exemptions from taxes for housing allowances for foreign residences and income tax relief on a portion of their income earned abroad, since they pay taxes in foreign jurisdictions. As of 2012, the maximum exemption for foreign-earned income per year was US$95,100.

Tax conventions or treaties between nations define the basis for taxation, such as the site of the official residence of a firm or person or the location of operations for that firm. The agreements also define what constitutes taxable income and provide for the mutual exchange of information and assistance to increase compliance with and enforcement of tax laws in order to decrease tax evasion.

Intellectual and Industrial Property Rights

Another crucial area of concern for multinational firms involved in R&D and advanced technology is the protection of such intangible assets as know-how, processes, trademarks, trade names, and trade secrets. These assets generally find protection under legal systems that provide for the creation of patents and copyrights. The dangers involved with such assets are that they could be stolen, used, copied, and sold without proper authority or compensation. As is discussed in Chapter 6, the Trade-Related Aspects of Intellectual Property Rights (TRIPS) was signed during the Uruguay Round of trade negotiations and is a part of the World Trade Organization's basic framework. Following is a more detailed discussion of intellectual property and highlights of some of the major agreements of the past concerning this topic.

Patents are rights granted by governments to the inventors of products or processes for exclusive manufacturing, production, sale, and use of those products or processes. Patents are the equivalent of the legal ceding of monopolistic power over the subject matter of the patent. They are intended to stimulate the creation of new technology and inventions by providing creators with assurances of gain from the potential benefit from their endeavors. Patents protect the subject from infringement of rights only in the country in which they are registered. Consequently, a multinational firm marketing its products or processes in a number of countries must make sure that its patents are protected in all existing as well as potential market areas.

Trademarks and Trade Names

Trademarks and **trade names** are designs, logos, and names used by manufacturers to differentiate and identify their goods with customers. They are considered an integral part of the total product, which is the entire image and package surrounding the product being marketed. Trademarks and trade names have an indefinite life and can be licensed to others, as long as they retain their brand distinction and do not pass into generic descriptive use, as happened, for example, with aspirin. Goods that use false trademarks are **counterfeit** products, and producers and sellers of such goods are subject to prosecution under trademark laws of individual countries. Trademarks are generally not considered infringed on when they are imitated ("knocked off"), as long as the imitation goods are not characterized as the original merchandise.

The inappropriate use of trade names and trademarks creates legal conflicts around the world. In a well-known case, rap star Missy Elliott's clothing line ran into trouble in Denmark. The logo on the clothes was too similar to that of the country's queen. The shoes, bags, and shirts in the collection carry a logo that consists of a crown on the top of the word "respect," and Missy Elliott's initials, "M.E." Queen Margrethe II's logo consists of a crown on top of the characters "M-2-R," with the "R" standing for the Latin word for queen (*regina*). Clothing maker Adidas-Salomon AG was forced to withdraw the line from Danish stores after the royal court said that the logo infringed on the queen's copyright.[2]

Patent Laws and Accords

Different countries around the world have different criteria for the proper registration and granting of patents. A multinational firm must take care to comply with the different requirements of each country. For example, the lifetime of a patent may vary from country to country; nations may have different requirements about products or processes having published descriptions, whether they worked or were used prior to patent application, and whether a product is substantially different from previously patented goods. The countries may also differ in the procedures used to resolve conflicts when more than one inventor claims the rights to the same patent. Consequently, ensuring protection of patents can be a complex, lengthy, involved, and expensive process for firms engaged in commerce in a multitude of markets.

The United States, for example, has historically had a **first to invent** patent-granting policy that requires that any new patent filing be new, useful, and unobvious. Interestingly, what is at first deemed obvious is overturned in 30 to 40 percent of the cases.[3] In March 2013, the US changed to the more common **first to file** patent granting policy. Japan, on the other hand, allows patents for minor modifications. This policy has tended to flood Japan's patent office with new filings. This large amount of patent filings delays the process for getting new patents approved and could also prove detrimental to the level of innovation in the country. In Europe, patents granted by the European Patent Office must be registered and enforced nationally.

These complexities and intricacies have led to the emergence of international agreements regarding the mutual recognition of patents on goods and processes of member countries. The largest of these is the **Paris Convention**, which provides for the protection of patents and trademarks. This convention, also called the Paris Union, was established in 1883. Under its terms, members agree to recognize and protect the patents and trademarks of member countries and allow for expedited (that is, a six-month priority period) registration for enterprises having filed in home countries that are members of the union. Similar patent agreements exist between the United States and Latin American countries in the Pan American Convention of 1929 and in sub-regional groups, such as the European Community and Sweden and Switzerland. In these nations, filing for patents in one of the member countries automatically confers protection in all member countries. Notably absent are many Asian nations whose compliance is mandated under TRIPS.

Trademarks are generally used without consent when a product with a worldwide reputation is not registered in all potential markets. Thus, with its reputation at stake, a multinational firm is faced in such situations with either having to litigate to regain use of its trademark or trade name or having to buy back that identifying symbol or name. While registration of all trademarks and trade names prevents these problems, such action becomes very expensive, especially if the firm markets several product lines in many markets where registration requirements differ substantially. For example, in some countries trademarks are registered only after they have been used, while in others, they cannot be used until they are registered.

To deal with these problems, cooperating international entities have made attempts to synchronize registration processes in recent years. The **Madrid Agreement of 1991** provides for the protection of trademarks in a centralized bureau in Geneva, the International Bureau for the Protection of Industrial Patents, which is a part of the **World Intellectual Property Organization (WIPO)**. Currently, 185 countries are members of WIPO. Registrations under this agreement have the benefit of being effective in many nations and potentially all members of the Madrid Agreement. Once the trademark is properly registered in its home country, an application may be made for international registration, at which point the trademark is published by the international bureau and communicated to the member countries where a firm is seeking patent protection. It is then up to the member countries to decide within twelve months whether or not they wish to refuse acceptance of the mark, and, in that case, they must outline the grounds for such refusal.

COPYRIGHTS

Copyrights give exclusive rights to authors, composers, singers, musicians, and artists to publish, dispose of, or release their work as they see fit. The people in the music business face problems with the illegal use of their material—**piracy**, which is the unlawful duplication of copyrighted material including sound recordings to make bootleg tapes and records. A major area in which copyrights are routinely infringed is computer software. Many developing countries are known to illegally copy computer software and sell it at reduced prices in the local markets. This was a primary reason for the inclusion of intellectual property protection in trade agreements under the WTO.

Copyright protection is sought by creators of works of art, literature, and music to ensure that no one wrongly reaps the benefit of their creative efforts through the sale, use, or licensing of those works. Copyright protection is divided into two categories: that which protects the right of creators to economic benefits or returns from their work and that which protects the creators' moral right to claim title to the work and to prevent its being altered without consent or published without permission.

International copyright protection is covered under the **Berne Convention of 1886** for the Protection of Literary and Artistic Works, which has 150 signatory countries. To be covered under the Berne Convention, material must be published or generally made available in a member country. The author or artist need not be a citizen of that member country to be afforded copyright protection. Thus, artists from nonmember countries, such as the United States, gain coverage by publishing simultaneously at home and abroad.

A similar agreement that also provides for international copyright protection is the **Universal Copyright Convention (UCC) of 1952**, sponsored and administered by the **United Nations Educational, Scientific, and Cultural Organization (UNESCO)**. Members of the UCC are accorded national status within each other's borders; that is, non-citizens holding copyrights are entitled to the same protection against copyright infringement as national citizens. Many members of the Berne convention are also signatories of the UCC.

OPERATIONAL CONCERNS OF MULTINATIONAL CORPORATIONS

WHICH NATIONALITY?

In the world of international commerce, there is no such entity as an international corporation; rather, the multinational firm consists of connected groups of individual operating units organized to operate within a variety of nations. The nationality of each corporation depends not on its own choice or determination but on the laws within the nation of operation. In some countries, a corporation need only be incorporated within the national boundaries; in others, it must have a registered office on domestic soil; in still others, it must be managed and operated within the country. Some nations allow for corporate dual citizenship.

The determination of nationality is a crucial matter, because it has the potential to affect all business operations. For example, multinational corporations may seek protection or assistance from their national governments or domestic courts of law in disputes with host countries. Nationality also determines tax liability and entitlement to government-sponsored incentive programs and tax breaks, as well as the degree of liability carried by the directors of a corporation. The determination of what constitutes a corporation also tends to differ among countries. All these factors imply that the multinational concern must seriously consider the form of organization it wishes to adopt in a particular country. The choice of form will depend on the strategic objectives of the corporation in a particular country and how the corporation believes it can best serve those objectives.

LOCAL LAWS AND ORIENTATIONS

Local laws affect the welfare and day-to-day operations of a firm. The labor laws of a nation, for example, affect the multinational corporations' use of labor. Some of these laws stipulate minimum wages, standards for working conditions, requirements for levels and types of fringe benefits, and timing and duration of holidays and vacations. In some countries management is considered fully liable for workers' safety and faces possible criminal prosecution for workers' injuries or deaths suffered on the job.

Some nations have requirements that multinational firms employ certain percentages of local labor within their operating and managerial classes of employees; some nations stipulate hiring and firing procedures and levels of severance pay when employees are terminated. All nations have national policies regarding contributions to the labor pool through immigration. They regulate or place limits on the number of foreigners or **guest workers** and the length of employment and sometimes the types of jobs or positions they are allowed to hold.

Individual nations also impose standards on product safety and put into place testing requirements and compulsory regulatory processes for gaining product approval. In the United States, the Consumer Product Safety Commission evaluates the safety of various products and sometimes recommends that unsafe products be taken off the market. Similarly, the Federal Drug Administration tests and evaluates new pharmaceutical products to determine whether or not they are safe to be used by the public. Internationally, more and more attention is being paid to the development, enforcement, and standardization of product safety laws. In recent years, businesses, politicians, and trade groups in the developed world have sometimes been successful in requesting that these standards be included in trade agreements.

Local laws also affect the operations of multinational firms when they involve controls on wages, prices, or currency transactions. Wage and price controls are generally imposed as part of efforts to encourage and stimulate economic development by keeping the incomes of workers up (through minimum wages) or their costs down (through limits on prices). Such controls are also used to bring down inflation, lower import volumes, and raise exports to bring the balance of payments into equilibrium.

Similarly, some countries put limits on currency exchanges because they wish to increase their store of hard currency. These nations often set limits on the amounts of local currency that can be exchanged for hard currency and on amounts paid for goods or profits that can be repatriated by multinational firms.

RESOLVING BUSINESS CONFLICTS

The problem of business conflicts is particularly complex in the arena of international business, primarily for three reasons. First, the contracting parties are generally not as familiar with each other as are parties from the same country, and they are subject to the jurisdiction of their own countries and laws. Thus, an injured party cannot claim redress in the domestic courts against the defaulting party if the latter is based in a foreign country.

Second, international transactions operate in a relatively uncertain environment and face the risks of fluctuations in prices and exchange rates, changes in laws and regulations, transit risks, and so on. The possibilities of transactions not being completed to the satisfaction of both parties are higher than in a domestic environment.

Third, business ethics, practices, and cultures vary considerably across countries. Language is often a barrier, and there is always a distinct possibility of a misunderstanding because of a communications gap between the two parties. Communications are also hampered by the fact that the parties can be at a great distance from each other during the life of the transaction.

CONTRACTS

It is essential that conflicts in international business be avoided to the extent possible. One of the best ways to avoid conflicts in international business is to have a clearly drafted contract, with all terms and conditions well understood by both parties. A contract is defined as a promise or set of promises, for the breach of which the law gives a remedy, or the performance of which the law in some way recognizes as a duty. An international commercial contract spells out the details of the transactions, the obligations of the two parties, the consideration involved, and so on.

The international businessperson must be aware of the possibility of conflict. Therefore, five specific steps should be taken when signing contracts with overseas parties:

1. The contract provisions must be unambiguous and clear and cover every relevant aspect of the transaction.
2. The applicable law used in the contract should be understood by the company.
3. The contract should stipulate the relevant jurisdiction where potential disputes will be settled. This is known as the **choice of forum**.
4. Risk transfer must be clearly outlined in the contract, especially where the contract involves sale and purchase of goods. The contract should state clearly the stage at which the risk of loss of the goods passes from the seller to the buyer.
5. The contract should contain some provisions for dispute resolution without resorting to arbitration or litigation.

RESOLVING DISPUTES

Despite the insertion of all precautionary clauses into a contract, disputes may emerge. Usually, the method adopted to deal with such situations is either arbitration or litigation, but there are some interim dispute resolution methods that are quicker and less expensive: adaptation, renegotiation, and mediation.

Adaptation

Provisions can be inserted into a contract to enable the agreement to be adapted to changing circumstances over the life of the transaction, which is particularly important when the contract involves a long-term commitment by both parties. There are several issues for which the adaptability of a contract is desirable so that both parties enjoy some flexibility in the performance of their respective obligations. Typically, in long-term contracts, flexibility is sought in such issues as prices and delivery schedules. Most contracts contain a **force majeure clause**, which absolves the parties of their obligations under the contract if they are prevented from carrying them out by circumstances beyond their control.

Renegotiation

If a dispute arises during the life of the contract over some provisions, the two involved parties can renegotiate the contract. In certain instances, the contract itself contains a proviso to the effect that under certain circumstances, if the parties differ, they will renegotiate certain parts of the contract. Renegotiation has obvious advantages. Apart from saving court fees and other charges involved in formal dispute-resolution procedures, renegotiation can be an ongoing process that need not disrupt the continued progress of business under the contract.

Mediation

Mediation is a method of dispute resolution using the offices of a third party known as the mediator. The actual mediation proceedings are generally less formal and rigid than arbitration, but the nature of individual mediation proceedings does vary. Mediation, if carried out in a non-confrontational and relatively cooperative manner, can be an effective way to resolve commercial disputes without resorting to the long and relatively difficult methods of arbitration and litigation. What is important is the cooperation of the two parties in the mediation proceedings, because they are not bound by the verdict of the mediator, whose role is essentially to moderate and balance the discussion and suggest ways to reach a common ground on a mutually agreeable basis. Of course, mediation can become a long and tedious process if both parties adopt a confrontational approach and especially if the issues involved are complex and the mediator is relatively unfamiliar with them at the outset.

In summary, the international businessperson operating in overseas environments is faced with a multitude of complex, differing, and sometimes conflicting bodies of law regarding allowable forms of ownership and business activities. Thus, it is crucial that the firm ensure adequate coverage by its own legal staff or by retaining effective local counsel. In doing so, the company can take the greatest amount of precaution to avoid problems that can arise in international legal disputes.

LOCAL COURTS, LOCAL REMEDIES

If disputes are not resolved by the informal methods, parties to the contracts have at least two possible paths of dispute resolution to pursue, commercial litigation and international arbitration, which assume that other methods of dispute resolution have been ineffective. Before these methods can be used, another established rule of international law holds that recourse to international legal forums is pursued only after the parties have exhausted local possibilities for achieving relief. These local remedies include the use of local courts or action by national governmental and administrative bodies. This rule applies only to actions between private parties, however, and not to those between states and individuals, because a state cannot be said to have local remedies to exhaust. The exhaustion rule protects the interests of both the foreign national and a host state. By respecting the sovereignty of states and the primacy of national jurisdiction in international disputes, the rule gives the states the necessary flexibility to regulate their internal affairs. At the same time, the rule requires states to recognize their international responsibility to offer justice to foreign nationals. Thus, the rule protects the interest of the multinational by promising either effective local remedies or a remedy in an international forum.

THE PRINCIPLE OF COMITY

The principle of sovereignty provides for international etiquette in the form of countries' reciprocal respect for each other's laws and powers regarding the actions of citizens abroad. This is the **principle of comity**, under which each nation defers to another's sovereignty in the protection of the rights of foreign citizens under their own legislative, executive, and judicial systems. The provision of comity is discretionary for each government and stems not from law but from tradition and good faith. It accounts for the international convention that provides immunity from the laws of the visited country for another nation's diplomats. The expectation is that in *reciprocity* the governments of foreign nations will similarly provide for diplomatic corps members working abroad.

LITIGATION

The litigation of international disputes involves the use of courts to apply both domestic and international law to resolve conflicts between parties. In the event that litigation is necessary, parties look to the courts of the host country, the home country, or even a third country for a resolution.

Litigation through court systems has the disadvantage of being a lengthy and involved process that can use a vast amount of a firm's resources in the form of time and expenses. For example, obtaining evidence from one country while in another is an intricate process involving **letters rogatory**, which provide the means for courts of different countries to communicate with one another. Domestic lawyers obtain letters rogatory by petitioning the district court where the action is pending to issue letters to the appropriate judicial counterpart in the foreign country. The letters, couched in standard polite language, request the provision of certain evidence necessary to try the case in home courts. Generally, under the principle of comity, courts will grant such requests. Obstacles and refusals do arise in foreign environments when national interests or principles are involved, as is the case when US courts seek evidence in antitrust suits intended to extend judicial extraterritoriality.

Another problem with litigation is that even if a party receives a judgment in its favor, it may have difficulty enforcing that judgment, particularly if the court used for settlement of the dispute does not have jurisdiction over the losing party. **Jurisdiction** is the capacity of a nation to prescribe a course of conduct for its citizens and to enforce a rule of law on its citizens. To enforce any legal rule, both jurisdiction to prescribe and jurisdiction to enforce that rule must be present. Because of these complexities and in the interest of expediency, those involved in disputes of an international nature often turn to arbitration, a quicker and easier method of resolving such conflicts.

INTERNATIONAL ARBITRATION

In arbitration, parties to a dispute agree to take their case to a third party in the form of an agency of independent arbitration. They submit whatever documents of evidence they feel are relevant and agree to accept the judgment of the arbitrators, waiving their rights to appeal through court systems.

Arbitration has several advantages over litigation. It is a speedier process than court procedures; the parties have a say in the choice of expert arbitrators, as compared to arbitrary judicial assignments; and the parties can have private adjudication. Results are achieved faster and less expensively in arbitration, because the proceedings are less complex and less formal than in litigation. The main drawback of international arbitration is that its use precludes further appeals, because there is no parallel in arbitration to appellate courts within judicial systems.

The use of arbitration by international parties is backed by laws and governmental treaties that allow for the recognition and enforcement of awards made through arbitration. The United States is a signatory to many treaties providing for the recognition of arbitration, including the multinational treaties on arbitration in the New York Convention of 1958, the Inter-American Arbitration Convention of 1975, and the New York Convention on the Recognition and Enforcement of Foreign Arbitral Awards of 1970. This last treaty was signed by 145 countries, and it lends uniformity and credibility to the practice of international arbitration and provides for each country's recognition of arbitration awards and agreements. It also prevents the parties from adjudicating disputes that they agreed to arbitrate.

To provide for arbitration rather than litigation of potential disputes between parties to an international contract, the terms of the contract must include a clause regarding the arbitration of potential disagreements. Arbitration clauses in international contracts must cover several important points of agreement between the parties, including the following:

- The determination of the scope of the arbitration
- The nature of potential disputes to be covered
- Whether the arbitration findings are protected by national treaties
- The language to be used in the conduct of the arbitration

More important, arbitration clauses in contracts between international parties include a choice of law under which to conduct the arbitration. Because each party usually prefers the procedural and substantive law of its own country to govern the proceedings, frequently the law of a third country is chosen as a compromise. Similarly, the contract clause often includes a choice of forum for the arbitration, which might be stipulated as an existing institutional framework, such as a major international arbitration center. One such center is the **London Court of International Arbitration**, which has dealt with disputes regarding private international commercial transactions since 1982. As of October 2012, the organization had in excess of 1,600 members from more than eighty countries.

Other alternatives in the choice of arbitration forums are available. The parties can designate the use of a specific private commercial arbitration firm or the creation of a commission to arbitrate the dispute. Many public entities choose the latter course because the commissions are composed of an equal number of arbitrators chosen by each side, to ensure proper airing of each party's position. Stipulating the choice of forum often has the advantage of simultaneously ensuring a choice of law under which there are minimal amounts of judicial interference prior to, during, and after the proceedings and few complex procedural requirements for conducting the arbitration. In England and France, for example, there have historically been statutes covering arbitration laws that allowed for judicial intervention in the process. These laws also have allowed for very narrow scopes of discovery and limited powers ceded to the arbitrator to force the production of evidence.

International Centre for Settlement of Investment Disputes

When the contract being disputed involves investments in foreign countries, the parties can seek adjudication through the **International Centre for Settlement of Investment Disputes (ICSID)**, which is affiliated with the World Bank, as is briefly discussed in Chapter 6. This forum was established in 1966 through an international convention to settle disagreements arising between states and foreign investors, especially in cases of acts of state that result in the nationalization or expropriation of investors' assets.

The role of the ICSID is not to develop rules and regulations regarding host country–investor relationships but to establish a methodology and forum for disputing parties to resolve their differences. To use the ICSID, all parties must agree to refer their dispute to it and accept that forum's ruling as final and binding. In addition, all signatory countries to the convention must accept the decision as binding. Signatories to the ICSID convention include most industrialized countries and many less-developed nations.

Most Latin American countries, however, do not subscribe to the ICSID, believing that its provisions infringe on their sovereign rights. These nations subscribe to the **Calvo doctrine**,[4] which is the belief that when foreign interests choose to enter a nation and conduct business within that country, they are implicitly agreeing to be treated as if they were nationals and thus are subject to the laws and decisions of the sovereign nation; they thus have no legal recourse outside that nation.

Disputes between states can be submitted for adjudication to the international court associated with the United Nations, the **International Court of Justice** at The Hague. All members of the United Nations by definition have access to this international court. The purpose of the court is to make judgments about disputes between nations that have chosen to submit to its jurisdiction. Problems or disagreements experienced by private individuals or corporate entities can be brought before the court only if they are sponsored or put forward by one of the court's member states. As with arbitration, the parties in the action must agree to submit to the jurisdiction of the court, but once a judgment is reached, there is no overriding international method of providing for the enforcement of that decision, save through sanctions imposed by individual nations or other international pressures brought to bear on the transgressing party.

In the European Union, members can seek redress of disputes through the **European Court of Justice**, which not only rules on the constitutionality of EU administrative activities but also provides recourse for legal questions referred to it by any court in a member country. The judgments of the European Court of Justice have the force of law in the EU and are binding on individuals, corporations, and governments. The purpose of the court is to provide for uniformity in the development of a legal process within the entire community. There are fifteen judges at the European Court of Justice, who serve six-year terms.

Dispute settlement under trade agreements is generally achieved through consultations and negotiations between the parties. If terms cannot be reached, the disputes are sometimes taken to councils for consideration. Under the auspices of the WTO, such a council can be appointed to hear disputes and render an advisory opinion. Should one of the parties choose to ignore that advice, the complaining country is allowed to suspend its trade obligations with the other party of the suit.

Summary

The operations, profit, and welfare of the modern multinational corporation can be profoundly affected by differences in international legal systems or even the imposition of domestic laws on the operations of a firm in a foreign environment. These laws can be in the areas of antitrust activity, protection of intangible property rights, taxation, corrupt practices, and all aspects of ongoing business operations for the multinational firm.

While treaties, trade agreements, and conventions among countries provide some international framework for a legal system, disputes continue to arise between parties in commerce. Some of these disputes can be avoided through the judicious writing of clear, unambiguous contracts that provide for these potential pitfalls. Some conflicts still occur between private parties, between nations, or between nations and individual interests. The resolution of these conflicts involves the answering of questions regarding legal jurisdiction, statutory interpretation, and the enforcement of judgments by judiciaries or third-party arbitrators in either national or international forums.

Discussion Questions

1. Is there a single body of international law that governs all countries in the world?
2. What are the differences among civil law, common law, and religious law?
3. Why are international treaties important to conducting international business?
4. What is the doctrine of sovereign immunity?
5. What is extraterritoriality?
6. What is predatory pricing?
7. How do antidumping laws protect domestic manufacturers?

8. What are antitrust laws?

9. What US law was enacted to control bribery and payoffs in international business? Why were bribes being paid? How do other countries view the practice of bribery?

10. What techniques can be used to resolve business disputes rather than resorting to litigation?

11. How is arbitration similar to or different from litigation?

12. What is the International Court of Justice?

NOTES

1. Felton, "Congress May Weigh Limits on President's Authority to Impose Trade Restrictions."
2. Teng. "Queens Royal Monogram: Reasons for Protection."
3. *Economist*, "Monopolies of the Mind."
4. Named after Argentine diplomat Carlos Calvo (1824–1906).

BIBLIOGRAPHY

Brand, Ronald A. "Private Parties and GATT Dispute Resolution: Implications of the Panel Report on Section 337 of the U.S. Tariff Act of 1930." *Journal of World Trade* (June 1990): 5–30.

Brown, Jeffrey A. "Extraterritoriality: Current Policy of the United States." *Syracuse Journal of International Law and Commerce* (Spring 1986): 493–519.

Carroll, Eileen P. "Are We Ready for ADR in Europe?" *International Financial Law Review* (December 1989): 11–14.

Chard, John S., and Christopher J. Mellor. "Intellectual Property Rights and Parallel Imports." *World Economy* (March 1989): 69–83.

David, Rene, and John E.C. Brierley. *Major Legal Systems in the World Today*. 3rd ed. New York: Macmillan, 1978.

Economist. "Monopolies of the Mind." November 11, 2004.

Felton, John. "Congress May Weigh Limits on President's Authority to Impose Trade Restrictions." *Congressional Quarterly* (November 1982): 2882–2884.

Fox, William F. *International Commercial Agreements*. Netherlands: Kluwer Law and Taxation Publishers, 1988.

Getz, Kathleen A. "International Codes of Conduct: An Analysis of Ethical Reasoning." *Journal of Business Ethics* (July 1990): 567–577.

Greer, Thomas V. "Product Liability in the European Economic Community: The New Situation." *Journal of International Business Studies* (Summer 1989): 337–348.

Kruckenberg, Dean. "The Need for an International Code of Ethics." *Public Relations Review* (Summer 1989): 6–18.

Litka, Michael. *International Dimensions of the Legal Environment of Business*. Boston: PWS-Kent, 1988.

McGraw, Thomas K. *America Versus Japan*. Boston: Harvard Business School Press, 1986.

Teng, Simon. "Queens Royal Monogram: Reasons for Protection." *IP Frontline*. February 18, 2005. www.ipfrontline.com/depts/article.aspx?id=2159&deptid=3#

GLOBALIZATION AT THE CROSSROADS: THE UNIFIED EUROPEAN PATENT

Imagine that you have just created a fantastic new invention and would like to assure your protection as inventor throughout the continent of Europe. This would currently entail registering and enforcing your patent protection in all EU member states. This can be a painstaking process and very costly for small to mid-sized companies. Discussions for the creation of a unified patent for all of Europe have been in process (on and off) since 1973. After much delay, in 2013 it was announced that significant progress had been made toward the unified patent. From the inventor's point of view, the unified patent could save significant time and money relative to the national system which has been in place for many years. In the future, there may be a choice of either registering a patent country by country, or as a unitary patent providing protection across all signatory states. There are some crucial points of debate, as Italy and Spain have opted out in objection to the inclusion of only English, French, and German as unified patent languages. Also there has been much discussion of the cost for the unified patent not exceeding the traditional cost of filing national patents in four or five countries, which is the norm currently. On the plus side, the unified patent provides protection throughout the EU, but on the downside, should the to-be-established Unified Patent Court rule against a patent holder, the patent would be wiped out in all twenty-six countries at once, which in a first to file system could prove highly problematic.

Questions for Discussion

1. Research the current progress of the EU unified patent debate. Has there been further progress to reaching the intended goal?
2. Have there been any roadblocks to the unified patent and what have they been?
3. What are some other possible problems and benefits of a unified EU patent?
4. What might a unified patent bode for competitiveness in Europe?

Case Study 8.1

CompuSoft Systems Inc.

It was a fairly thorough and well-drafted international sales and service agreement that CompuSoft Systems Inc., of Palo Alto, California, had entered into with Los Santos Services, a large computer software reseller in the Latin American country of Cartunja. As Ken Rossi, marketing director of CompuSoft, read the email message from Dom Simoes, executive vice president of Los Santos, he regretted the decision to sell to Cartunja, even though the agreement had been hailed three years ago,

(continued)

Case Study 8.1 *(continued)*

upon its signing, as a major step forward in international market expansion in Latin America. "It's time to call in the attorneys," thought Rossi as he reread the email to let the implications of its contents sink in fully.

CompuSoft Systems began in 1991 as a small venture-capital enterprise, put together by a group of four young, technically qualified professionals. Mitch Holland had a PhD in electrical engineering and had worked for four years with a large software development company in California's Silicon Valley. Tom Heilbroner held an MS degree in electronics and systems development from the University of Stanford and had been with the management information systems division of a New York City–based multinational corporation for three years, developing specialized software and networking systems for the internal use of the company. Peter Daniels was a certified public accountant, had worked in the consulting division of a large accounting firm for three years, specializing in the development of computer-based accounting systems. Ken Rossi had a master's in business administration in accounting from Yale and also held an electrical engineering degree from Virginia Tech.

Like many Silicon Valley firms, CompuSoft had done extremely well. It had grown rapidly, and by 1999 sales had reached $640 million. The company was able to carve a small but significant niche in the accounting software market, and its wide range of accounting software applications packages had gained acceptance with a large number of US companies. CompuSoft's products were known for their reliability and quality, but further market expansion seemed difficult, given the growing intensity of competition, especially from the larger and financially stronger software companies who offered aggressively priced products. Further, the market for accounting software in the United States appeared limited, and overall market growth was leveling off.

In the face of these circumstances, CompuSoft concluded that the time was ripe for a shift in its strategy, and in 2010, the company decided to go international. None of the senior management had any international business experience, and initially there were some doubts about the wisdom of this move. It was felt, however, that the company need not take on the responsibility of marketing its products overseas itself since this could easily be done through a local agent in a foreign country with whom the company would enter into a comprehensive agreement that would include all promises necessary to protect it from difficulties in the future.

Latin America was chosen as the first region for the international marketing effort of CompuSoft, and agreements were signed with three local software retailing companies in three countries, including Cartunja. The company hired a top San Francisco law firm specializing in such agreements to draft and negotiate the contracts with the local selling agents.

Under these contracts the local selling agents were to market CompuSoft's software packages in sealed covers, supplied in a fully finished form by the company. The agents were not permitted to make any alterations, modifications, or changes in either the contents of the software or the external packaging. Another important provision of these agreements was that the reseller would advise each buyer in writing of the copyright to the software, and a statement of the restrictions on the use of the software was printed on the external cover of the software package. In addition, another leaflet defining the rights and obligations of the holder of the copyright (CompuSoft) was included in the package. The local agents also agreed to make all efforts to ensure that the copyrights of CompuSoft Systems were not violated in their respective countries.

For the first two years, things appeared to go well. The company had made considerable effort to adapt its accounting software to the needs of Latin American corporate customers, and the programs were an immediate success with local companies. The local agents also pushed the products because they were keen to maximize the attractive benefits of the graduated commission system put together by Rossi.

The first hint of problems came up in January 2012, when Simoes called Rossi to say that Los Santos would be lowering the estimates of sales to Peseta National Bank, a leading state-owned bank in Cartunja, which had 274 branches in thirteen cities and townships all over Cartunja. Similarly, the estimated sales to eleven other state-owned banks were down by 60 percent. No reasons for the declines were given, except that the bank officials had informed Los Santos that their original interest in this software was only of a preliminary nature, and, on closer examination, they found that they were not ready to modernize their accounting systems using such sophisticated programs. The news came as a setback to CompuSoft's executives, who sensed that the reason given by the banks was not the real one. There was no competing product in Cartunja, and the banks badly needed to modernize their systems, having come under considerable criticism from the finance ministry and external auditors for having large arrears in the reconciliation of accounts between different branches and the corporate head offices. Further, Peseta National had already acquired the package from Los Santos, and it had been installed and running smoothly for the past four months. CompuSoft had also conducted a six-week training program, free of cost, for the accounting and systems personnel of Peseta National. The personnel were quite comfortable with the software and reported no problems. Therefore, in February 2013, Rossi called Simoes and asked him to dig further and find out what was really happening.

In the first week of March, Simoes called back with a startling answer; it

(continued)

Case Study 8.1 *(continued)*

appeared that the management information systems division of Peseta National had copied the software and was busy installing it at seventy of its branches. Further, he learned that Peseta was likely to pass the program on, along with installation services, to eleven other state-owned banks. It was a clear violation of the copyright. CompuSoft's top management was, expectedly, disturbed. They called Simoes and asked him to take every possible step to stop Peseta National Bank from further infringing the copyright.

The fax on Rossi's desk was a reply from Simoes. In effect, it said that Peseta National Bank and the eleven other banks in question are 100 percent state-owned institutions, and any legal action against them would be tantamount to legal action against the government. Further, if Los Santos instituted a suit against Peseta National, it might lose substantial orders that it was negotiating with other state-owned enterprises. Given the power of the government, a suit would hurt Los Santos in its other lines of business and build an adversarial relationship with the government. It would therefore be better if CompuSoft would initiate action against Peseta National Bank directly.

"This is a real big one," thought Rossi. "If we do go ahead and fight it out, the government may ban our products from official purchases. If we don't, everybody in Cartunja and everywhere else in Latin America will merely copy our software, and our entire international expansion effort there would fall apart."

DISCUSSION QUESTIONS

1. What should CompuSoft Systems Inc. do in this situation and why?
2. Suggest a strategy to deal with the situation, keeping in mind the possible international legal issues.

CHAPTER 9

Sociocultural Factors

"Over-generalization is the enemy of science."
—John Kenneth Galbraith

CHAPTER OBJECTIVES

This chapter will:

- Define the term "sociocultural" as a combination of societal, political, and cultural norms and responses and discuss their influence in international business
- Discuss how attitudes and beliefs influence human behavior, especially attitudes about time, achievement, work, change, and occupational status
- Present the influence of aesthetics and material culture within different societies
- Examine how communication, both verbal and nonverbal, may serve as a barrier to international business operations
- Investigate the importance of social status and the family within different cultures and their effect on the business environment
- Identify the role of multinational corporations as agents of change in the international community

---

SOCIOCULTURAL FACTORS AND INTERNATIONAL BUSINESS

Multinational corporations operate in different host countries around the world and have to deal with a wide variety of political, economic, geographical, technological, and business situations. Moreover, each host country has its own society and culture, which are different in many important ways from almost every other society and culture, although there are some commonalities. Although society and culture do not appear to be a part of business situations, they are actually key elements in shaping how business is conducted, from what goods are produced and how and through what means they are sold, to the establishment of industrial and management patterns and the determination of the success or failure of a local subsidiary or affiliate.

Society and culture influence every aspect of an MNC's overseas business, and a successful MNC operation, whether it involves marketing, finance, operations, information systems, or human resources, has to be acutely aware of the predominant attitudes, feelings, and opinions in the local environment. Differences in values and attitudes between the management at the parent offices and expatriate managers at the subsidiary or affiliate level, on the one hand, and local managers and employees, on the other, can lead to serious operational and functional problems, which arise not because there are individual problems but because of the important differences between the societies and cultures. Society and culture often mold general attitudes about fundamental aspects of life, such as time, money, productivity, and achievement, all of which can differ widely across countries and lead to differing expectations between the management in the home office and local employees of subsidiaries and affiliates.

While some sociocultural differences are obvious, others are relatively subtle though equally important. It is often difficult for international managers to catch on to these subtle differences if they have not lived or worked in cultures other than that of the home country. Cultural differences can be profound, but expatriate managers who make some attempt to understand them can ensure that these gaps do not materially affect the performance of business.

MNCs have realized, sometimes through costly blunders, that sociocultural factors are vital ingredients that make up the overall business environment and that it is essential to appreciate these differences and their influences on business before attempting to set up an operation in a host country.

Society, Culture, and Sociocultural Forces

There are many definitions of culture. In general, **culture** can be defined as the entire set of social norms and responses that dominates the behavior of a population and makes each social environment different. Culture is the conglomeration of beliefs, rules, techniques, institutions, and artifacts that characterize a human population. It consists of the learned patterns of behavior common to members of a given society—the unique lifestyle of a particular group of people.

The various aspects of culture are interrelated; culture influences individual and group behavior and determines how things are done. Features of culture include religion, education, caste structure, politics, language differences, and production.

Society refers to a political and social entity that is defined geographically. To understand society and culture, we must relate one to the other—hence the term "**sociocultural.**" To be successful in their relationships with people in other countries, international managers must study and understand the various aspects of culture.

How should one begin? With as broad a concept as culture, it is necessary to utilize some type of classification scheme as a guide to studying or comparing cultures. Table 9.1 outlines Murdock's list of **cultural universals** that occur in all cultures.[1] While this

Table 9.1 **Murdock's List of Cultural Universals**

Age grading	Games	Music
Athletic sports	Gestures	Mythology
Bodily adornment	Gift giving	Numerals
Calendar	Government	Obstetrics
Cleanliness training	Greetings	Penal sanctions
Community organization	Hairstyles	Personal names
Cooking	Hospitality	Population policy
Cooperative labor	Housing	Postnatal care
Cosmology	Hygiene	Pregnancy usages
Courtship	Incest taboos	Property rights
Dancing	Inheritance rules	Propitiation of supernatural beings
Decorative art	Joking	Puberty customs
Divination	Kin Groups	Religious rituals
Division of labor	Kinship nomenclature	Residence rules
Dream interpretation	Language	Sexual restrictions
Education	Law	Soul concepts
Ethics	Luck/superstitions	Status differentiation
Ethno-botany	Magic	Supernatural beings
Etiquette	Marriage	Surgery
Faith healing	Mealtimes	Tool making
Family feasting	Medicine	Trade
Fire-making	Modesty of natural functions	Visiting
Folklore	Mourning	Weather control
Food taboos		Weaving
Funeral rites		

Source: Murdock, 1945.

schematic is limited by its one-dimensional approach, it provides an initial guide and checklist for the international firm and manager. For example, the international firm selling contraceptives must be aware that it is dealing with the family customs, population policy, and sexual restrictions of different cultures. Since many individuals base their decisions regarding contraception on religious beliefs, the seller must also consider this aspect of various cultures in the plan.

Students often experience cultural differences when they first travel abroad. The things that cause cognitive dissonance during these trips often represent the things typically taken for granted at home. These things taken for granted often help to identify elements of culture. Students should keep in mind that observing culture can often resemble observing an iceberg. What lies beneath the surface may be more meaningful than things visible to the naked eye (see Figure 9.1).

ELEMENTS OF CULTURE

The number of human variables and different types of business functions preclude an exhaustive discussion of culture here. Instead, we have broken down the broad area of culture into some major topics to facilitate study.

Figure 9.1 **Iceberg Theory of Culture**

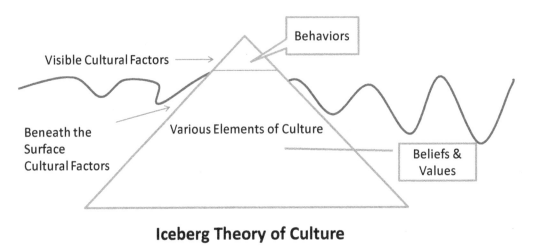

Iceberg Theory of Culture

Source: Adapted from Hall, 1976.

ATTITUDES AND BELIEFS

In every society there are norms of behavior based on the attitudes, values, and beliefs that constitute a part of its culture. The attitudes and beliefs of a culture, which vary from country to country, influence nearly all aspects of human behavior, providing guidelines and organization to a society and its individuals. Identifying the attitudes and beliefs of a society, and how or whether they differ from one's own culture, will help the business-person more easily understand people's behavior.

ATTITUDES ABOUT TIME

Everywhere in the world people use time to communicate with one another. In inter-national business, attitudes about time are displayed in behavior regarding punctuality, responses to business communications, responses to deadlines, and the amounts of time that are spent waiting in an outer office for an appointment. For example, while Ameri-cans are known to be punctual, other cultures give less importance to being on time. In terms of business communications, Japanese companies may not respond immediately to an offer from a foreign company. What a foreign company may see as rejection of an offer or disinterest may simply be the lengthy time the Japanese company takes to review the details of a deal. In fact, the US emphasis on speed and deadlines is often used against Americans in foreign business dealings in which local business managers have their own schedules.

ATTITUDES ABOUT WORK AND LEISURE

Most people in industrial societies work many more hours than are necessary to satisfy their basic needs for food, clothing, and shelter. Their attitudes toward work and achievement are indicative of their view of wealth and material gain. These attitudes affect the types, qualities, and numbers of individuals who pursue entrepreneurial and management careers as well as the way workers respond to material incentives.

Many industrial psychologists have conducted research in this area to determine what motivates people to work more than is necessary to provide for their basic needs. One explanation is the **Protestant ethic**, which has its basis in the Reformation, when work was viewed as a means of salvation and people preferred to transform productivity gains into additional output rather than additional leisure. Europeans and Americans are typically considered to adhere to this work ethic because they generally view work as a moral virtue and look unfavorably on the idle. In comparison, in places where work is considered necessary only to obtain the essentials for survival, people may stop working once they obtain the essentials.

Today, few other societies hold to this strict basic concept of work for work's sake, and leisure is viewed more highly in some societies than in others. It has been argued that many Asian economies are characterized by limited economic needs that reflect the culture. Therefore, it is expected that if incomes start to rise, workers would tend to reduce their efforts, so personal income would remain unchanged. The promise of overtime pay may fail to keep workers on the job, and raising employees' salaries could result in their working less, a phenomenon that economists have called the **backward-bending labor supply curve**. In contrast, the pursuit of leisure activities may have to be a learned process. After a long period of sustained work activity with little time for leisure, people may have difficulty in deciding what to do with additional free time.

These attitudes, however, can change. The demonstration effect of seeing others with higher incomes and better standards of living has motivated workers in such cultures to put in longer hours to improve their own financial status and material well-being. Additionally, attitudes about work are shaped by the perceived rewards and punishments of the amount of work. In cultures where both rewards for greater amounts of work and punishments for lesser amounts of work are low, there is little incentive for people to work harder than absolutely necessary. Moreover, when the outcome of a particular work cycle is certain, there is little enthusiasm for the work itself. Where high uncertainty of success is combined with some probability of a very positive reward for success, one finds the greatest enthusiasm for work.

ATTITUDES ABOUT ACHIEVEMENT

Cultural differences in the general attitude toward work are also accompanied by significant national differences in achievement motivation. In some cultures, particularly those with highly stratified and hierarchical societies, there is a tendency to avoid personal

responsibility and to work according to precise instructions that are received from su-
pervisors and followed to the letter. In many societies, especially where social security is
low and jobs are prized, there is both a tendency to avoid taking risk and little innovation
in work or production processes. In such cultures, the prospect of higher achievement is
not considered attractive enough to warrant taking avoidable risks. In many industrial
societies, however, attitudes toward personal achievement are quite different. Personal
responsibility and the ability to take risk for potential gain are considered valuable instruments in achieving higher goals. In fact, in many cultures the societal pressure to achieve
is so intense that individuals are automatically driven to attempt ambitious goals.

Attitudes among workers and managers often influence the types of management that
has to be utilized to achieve corporate goals. In a culture that emphasizes risk-taking,
personal responsibility, and individual decision-making, a decentralized management
system would be appropriate. In a culture where there is a tendency to put in only adequate amounts of work and where achievement is not a valued personal attribute, the
company will follow a more centralized management system, with only limited delegation
of decision-making authority.

Attitudes About Change

The international manager must understand what aspects of a culture resist change, how
those areas of resistance differ among cultures, how the process of change takes place in
different cultures, and how long it will take to implement change. There are two conflicting forces within a culture regarding change. People attempt to protect and preserve their
culture with an elaborate set of sanctions and laws invoked against those who deviate
from their norms. Differences are perceived in light of the belief that "my method is right;
thus, the other method must be wrong."

These contradictory forces suggest the public's awareness that the cultural environment
is continually changing and that a culture must change in order to ensure its own continuity. In other words, to balance these attitudes, the manager must remember that the closer
a new idea can be related to a traditional one when illustrating its relative advantage, the
greater the acceptance of that new concept. Usually cultures with centuries-old traditions
that have remained closed to outside influences are more resistant to change than other
cultures. The level of education in a society and the exposure of its people to knowledge
and the experience of other cultures is an extremely important determinant of its attitude
toward change. The influence and nature of religious beliefs in a society also influence
attitudes about change.

Attitudes About Jobs

The type of job that is considered most desirable or prestigious varies greatly across different cultures. Thus, while the medical and legal professions are considered extremely
prestigious in the United States, civil service is considered the most prestigious occupation

in several developing countries. The importance of a particular profession in a culture is an important determinant of the number and quality of people who seek to join that profession. Thus, in a country where business is regarded as a prestigious occupation, the MNC will be able to tap a large, well-qualified pool of local managers. On the other hand, if business is not considered an important profession, much of the country's talent will be focused elsewhere.

There is great emphasis in some countries on being one's own boss, and the idea of working for someone, even if that happens to be a prestigious organization, tends to be frowned on. In many countries, however, MNCs are able to counter the lower prestige of business as a profession by offering high salaries and other forms of compensation. Some MNCs, in fact, have succeeded in luring some of the best local talent away from jobs that are traditionally considered the most prestigious in those countries. In most cultures, there are some types of work that are considered more prestigious than others, and certain occupations carry a perception of greater rewards than others, which may be because of economic, social, or traditional factors.

DOES RELIGION AFFECT COMMERCE?

International business is affected by religious beliefs in many ways, because religion can provide the spiritual foundation of a culture. Business can bring about modernization that disrupts religious traditions, and international business can conflict with holy days and religious holidays. Cultural conflicts in the area of religion can be quite serious. For example, an MNC would have problems with a subsidiary where employees traditionally enjoy a month-long religious holiday.

Religion can also impose moral norms on culture. It may insist on limits, particularly the subordination of impulse to moral conduct. Islamic finance is a variant of international business in Muslim countries that ban the assessment of risk and look unfavorably on excessive risk-taking or speculative endeavors, given their religious beliefs. Another example of business conflicting with religion is the development of a promotional campaign for contraceptives in any of the predominantly Roman Catholic countries.

In certain countries, religion may require its followers to dress in a particular manner or maintain a certain type of physical appearance, which may conflict with the MNC's appearance and presentation norms. Certain products manufactured by the MNC or some ingredients used in manufacturing may be taboo in some religions. For example, beef and tallow are taboo in the Hindu religion and cannot be used as ingredients in soap manufacturing in India. Similarly, pork products cannot be sold or used in manufacture in Muslim countries because pork is religiously impure according to the tenets of Islam.

In many religions, the general philosophy of life is completely different from that in the Western world. Some Asian religions, for example, teach that nothing is permanent and therefore the world is an illusion. To followers of such beliefs, time is cyclical—from birth to death to reincarnation—and the goal of salvation is to escape the cycle and move into a state of eternal bliss (nirvana). These religious beliefs directly affect how and why people work; for example, Buddhists and Hindus are supposed to eliminate all desires and therefore may have little motivation for achievement and the acquisition of material goods.

AESTHETICS

Aesthetics pertains to the sense of beauty and good taste of a culture and includes myths, tales, dramatization of legends, and more modern expressions of the arts: drama, music, painting, sculpture, architecture, and so on. Like language, art serves as a means of communication. Color and form are of particular interest to international business because in most cultures these elements are used as symbols that convey specific meanings. Green is a popular color in many Muslim countries but is often associated with disease in countries with dense, green jungles. In France, the Netherlands, and Sweden, green is associated with cosmetics. Similarly, different colors represent death in different cultures. In the United States and many European countries, black represents death, while in Japan and many other Asian countries, white signifies death.

In many countries physical contact in public by persons of opposite sexes is not considered proper, and exposure of the human body is treated as obscene. MNCs must be exceptionally careful in designing their advertising programs, the packaging of their products, and the content of their verbal messages to ensure that they do not offend the aesthetic sensibilities of the country they are operating in.

MATERIAL CULTURE

Material culture refers to the things that people use and enjoy and includes all human-made objects. Its study is concerned with technology and economics. Material cultures differ very significantly because of tradition, climate, economic status, and a host of other factors. Material culture is an extremely important issue to be considered by an MNC. Almost everything a society consumes, or, in other words, whatever the MNC sells, or hopes to sell, is determined by the material culture of the population. For example, selling humidifiers in a tropical country would be a failure because they are not needed by the local people and are simply not a part of the material culture. Alternatively, selling American-style barbecues would be a failure in parts of the world where outdoor cookery is not a part of popular material culture.

Technology is an important factor that affects the material culture of a society. As more and more new products and processes are made available by technology and become familiar to the population, they ultimately become a part of the material culture. One example is the cell phone, which has become an integral part of the material culture of most industrialized societies. Therefore, a US multinational might target France or Australia as a major market for selling cell phone accessories. There would not, however, be much of a market for this product in the nations of sub-Saharan Africa, at least at present, because cell phones are not as large a part of the material culture in these countries.

Tradition also determines material culture to a considerable extent. The French, for example, prefer drinking wine, while Germans prefer drinking beer, the distinction being largely traditional, but critical for a company aiming to establish a market for alcoholic beverages in these countries.

A country's particular physical and geographic circumstances also play an important part in influencing its material culture. Space limitations in Japan prevent the use of large domestic appliances, such as large-capacity deep freezers or refrigerators, and preclude a real estate market featuring rambling suburban homes, even though the economy may be prosperous enough to pay for these luxuries. Thus, suburban homeowner living is not a part of the material culture of Japan, and this affects the type of products the Japanese middle class will or will not buy. For example, sales of lawn mowers, backyard pools, and playgrounds are likely to be extremely low in Japan, while sales of compact, sophisticated appliances and luxuries that can be accommodated in small apartments are likely to be very high.

LITERACY RATE

The literacy rate of a potential overseas market or facility is used by many areas of the international business firm. The marketer uses it to determine the types and sophistication of advertising to employ. The personnel manager uses it as a guide in estimating the types of people available for staffing the operation. Literacy rate numbers, however, rarely provide any information about the quality of education.

Countries with low literacy rates are less likely to provide the MNC with all the qualified personnel it needs to staff its local operation and will necessitate the transfer of a large number of expatriate managers. Literacy rates must be used with caution, however, because they often hide the fact that a country with a low literacy rate but a very large population may have a large number of qualified professionals, who as a percentage of the population may be very small but form a fairly large absolute number by themselves. Literacy rates generally have a more direct bearing on the general level of education and abilities of the workers at the lower levels, because much of the population that suffers from illiteracy is at the lowest economic level in society.

EDUCATION MIX

When considering education as an aspect of culture, an MNC should not only look at literacy rates and levels of education but also try to understand the education mix of a certain society; that is, which areas are considered important for concentrated education? For example, a combination of factors caused a proliferation of European business schools patterned on American models. First, increased competition in the European Union resulted in a demand for better-trained managers. Second, Europeans began establishing their own business schools after they were educated at American business schools and returned home. Third, the establishment of American-type schools with faculty from the United States was frequently accomplished with the assistance of American universities.

This trend toward specialized business education is slower in less-developed countries. Historically, higher education in LDCs has focused on the humanities, law, and medicine; engineering has not been popular, with the exception of architectural and civil engineering, because there were few job opportunities in that field; and business careers have lacked prestige. As income levels in developing countries increase, so will the desire for expanded educational offerings.

Brain Drain

Brain drain is a phenomenon experienced by many developing nations, especially China and India. Because governments overinvested in higher education in relation to demand, developing nations have seen rising unemployment among the educated. These unemployed professionals must emigrate to industrialized nations to find appropriate work, which effectively represents a loss to the country that has spent substantial amounts of scarce public resources to finance professional education. The brain drain creates a cultural diaspora abroad, something also of interest to multinational firms desiring to target ethnic groups in advertising campaigns.

Communication and Language

Communication and language are closely related to culture because each culture reflects what the society values in its language. Culture determines to a large extent the use of spoken language—specific words, phrases, and intonations used to communicate people's thoughts and needs. These verbal patterns are reinforced by unspoken language—gestures, body positions, and symbolic aids.

Spoken language becomes a cultural barrier between different countries and regions. In China for example, verbal language can consist of many dialects and different colloquialisms and may be totally different from the written language. There is no way to learn a language so that nuances, double meanings, and slang terms are immediately understood unless one also learns other aspects of the culture.

Languages delineate culture. In some European countries there is more than one language and, hence, more than one culture. For example, French and Dutch are spoken in Belgium; German, Italian, French, and Romansh are officially spoken in Switzerland. Different cultures exist within each country. One cannot conclude, however, that where only one official language exists, there will be only one culture. The people of both the United States and Great Britain speak English, but each country has its own multifaceted culture.

An example of the problems facing an international firm that must respond to the language aspects of a culture involves the sort of computer hardware marketed in Canada. Although the Canadian government is officially bilingual, English remains the dominant language; French is dominant only in Quebec. After years of heated national debate about the country's official language, a joint government-industry committee has come up with

Canada's first national standard for computer keyboards with both English and accented French letters. Many English speakers resent the government's move to promote French. Hence, selling keyboards with both English and accented French letters could prove to be an obstacle in the English-speaking provinces of Canada.

Where many spoken languages exist in a single country, one language usually serves as the principal vehicle for communication across cultures. This is true for many countries that were once colonies, such as India, which uses English. Although they serve as national languages, these foreign substitutes are not the first language of the populace and are therefore less effective than native tongues for reaching mass markets or for day-to-day conversations between managers and workers. In many situations, managers try to ease these communication difficulties by separating the workforce according to origin. The preferred solution is to teach managers the language of their workers.

When communication involves translation from one language to another, the problems of ascertaining meanings that arise in different cultures are multiplied many times. Translation is not just the matching of words in one language with words of identical meanings in another language. It involves interpretation of the cultural patterns and concepts of one country into the terms of those of another. It is often difficult to translate directly from one language to another. Many international managers have been unpleasantly surprised to learn that the nodding and yes responses of their Japanese counterparts did not mean that the deal was closed or that they agreed, because the word for yes, *hai*, can also simply mean "it is understood" or "I hear you." In fact, it is typical of the Japanese to avoid saying anything disagreeable to a listener.

Many international business consultants advise the manager in a foreign country to use two translations by two different translators. The manager's words are first translated by a nonnative speaker; then a native speaker translates the first translator's words back into the original language. Unless translators have a special knowledge of the industry, they often go to a dictionary for a literal translation that is frequently erroneous or simply makes no sense.

Nonverbal language is another form of communication. Silent communication can take several forms, such as body language, space, and language of things. Body talk is a universal form of language that has different meanings from country to country. Usually, it involves facial expressions, postures, gestures, handshakes, eye contact, color or symbols, and time (punctuality). The language of space includes such things as conversational distance between people, closed office doors, or office size. Each of these has a different connotation and appropriateness in different cultures. The language of things includes money and possessions.

GROUPS: FAMILIES AND FRIENDS

All populations of men, women, and children are commonly divided into groups, and individuals are members of more than one group. Affiliations determined by birth, known as **ascribed group memberships**, are based on sex, family, age, caste, and ethnic, racial, or national origin. Those affiliations not determined by birth are called **acquired group memberships** and are based on religious, political, and other associations. Both ascribed and acquired group membership reflects one's place in the social structure. Employment, manners, dress, and expectations are often dictated by each culture to its members. Group rituals, such as marriage, funerals, and graduations, also form a part of the societal organization.

In some societies, acceptance of people for jobs and promotion is based primarily on their performance capabilities. In others, competence is of secondary importance. Whatever factor is given primary importance (seniority, sex, and so on) will determine to a great extent the workers who are eligible to fill certain positions and what their compensation will be. The more egalitarian or open a society, the less difference ascribed group membership will make.

Three types of international contrasts indicate how widespread the differences in group memberships are and how important they are as business considerations. These contrasts involve sex, age, and family. Differences in attitudes toward males and females are especially apparent from country to country. The level of rigidity of expected behavior because of one's gender is indicative of cultural differences. Often, these differences are clearly reflected in education statistics; boys get access to education more than girls, although many countries have instituted or have plans to institute additional educational opportunities for females.

In many countries age and wisdom are correlated. Where this is so, advancement is usually based on seniority. In the past, this has been a common practice in Japan. In contrast, in many countries retirement at a particular age is mandatory and relative youthfulness may be an advantage in moving up in an organization. Barriers to employment on the basis of age or sex are undergoing substantial changes around the world, and data collected about these trends that are even only a few years old are not considered reliable.

Kinship, or family associations, plays a more active role as an element of culture in some societies than in others. Individuals may be accepted or rejected based on the social status of their family. Because family ties are so strong, there is a compulsion to cooperate closely within the family but to be distrustful of links involving others outside the family.

In some countries, the word "family" may have very different connotations. In the United States, we have come to depend on the nuclear family—mother, father, and children—as the definition of family. In other societies, the extended family is the norm. A vertically extended family includes grandparents and possibly great-grandparents as part of a single family, while horizontally extended families include aunts, uncles, and cousins.

The impact of the extended family on the foreign firm derives from the fact that it is a source of employees and business connections. Responsibility to a family is often a cause of high absenteeism in developing countries where workers are called to help with the harvest. Motivation to work also may be affected in cultures where workers are responsible for the welfare of their extended families. When additional income means additional mouths to feed and further responsibility, workers may reduce output if they are given an increase in salary.

The international firm may be directly affected by the cultural aspect of group and social organizations. Even if individuals have qualifications for certain positions and there are no legal barriers to hiring them, social obstacles may make the international firm think twice about employing them. Class structures can also be so rigid within one type of group that they are difficult to overcome in other contexts. For example, in a society where caste structures are deeply ingrained, serious problems could arise if these caste levels are not considered in determining work groups, supervisor roles, and managerial promotions; if individuals in a lower caste are placed higher within the corporate hierarchy than members of higher-caste groups, internal tensions may arise.

GIFT-GIVING AND BRIBERY

Gift-giving is a custom that has great value in some business environments. It is important not only to remember to bring a gift, but also to make certain that the gift you have chosen is appropriate. In other cultures, gift-giving is not expected or encouraged, and the international businessperson must be familiar with the appropriate behavior in each environment.

Gift-giving is viewed as a different and separate activity from **bribery**, at least in the United States. During the 1970s many large international companies were faced with serious problems after they were caught paying bribes to government officials to obtain large contracts from foreign business firms. While much of the criticism was vented against multinational companies, especially those from the United States, it is important to note that the practice was widespread. In 1977, however, the United States passed the Foreign Corrupt Practices Act, making illegal certain payments to foreign officials by US executives of publicly traded firms. The legislation has been controversial and often called inconsistent. One such inconsistency is that it is clearly legal to make payments to people to expedite their compliance with the law, but illegal to make payments to other government officials who are not directly responsible for carrying out the law. It is important for the international business executive to identify the thin line between complying with foreign expectations and offering bribes, a form of corruption.

OTHER THEORIES OF CULTURE

CULTURAL CLUSTER APPROACH

Some theorists have attempted to group cultural patterns based on geographical similarities. One such theory is the **cultural cluster approach**. This approach groups cultures together based on where people are located in the world as follows:

- Nordic countries—Denmark, Finland, Norway, Sweden
- Germanic countries—Austria, Germany, Switzerland
- Anglo countries—Australia, Canada, Ireland, South Africa, United Kingdom, United States
- Latin American countries—Argentina, Chile, Colombia, Mexico, Peru
- Arab countries—Bahrain, Kuwait, Oman, Saudi Arabia
- Far Eastern countries—China, Hong Kong, Indonesia, Philippines

A quick glance at the groupings above reveals many differences among the groups themselves, and there are certainly differences within individual countries as well. Few academic cultural theorists would agree that all of the citizens of the United States are culturally the same, so attempting to classify the members of other countries in this manner would appear to be problematic at best. These types of classifications are often too general and have little practical use in a business environment. In the words of economist John Kenneth Galbraith that begin this chapter, "over-generalization is the enemy of science." This is a key point to remember when considering various cultural theories.

Other cultural classifications move away from geography and examine factors that are present for individuals rather than trying to classify large groups of people in the same manner. Two theories discussed here are Hall's low-context, high-context approach and Hofstede's five dimensions of culture.

HALL'S LOW-CONTEXT, HIGH-CONTEXT APPROACH

Edward Hall's low-context, high-context approach categorizes individuals (and societies) in terms of how they communicate and what is required in order to successfully communicate in a given society. In a **low-context culture**, the words used by the speaker explicitly convey the speaker's message to the listener. This is similar to interacting with a computer. If information is not explicitly stated, the meaning can be distorted. In low-context cultures, behavior and beliefs may need to be spelled out clearly, and the society in question is very rule-oriented. In codified systems such as this, knowledge is easy to transfer between individuals and groups, as there are written directions for what is expected in a given situation. Low-context communication is prevalent in groups that have been together for a short period of time and are engaged in small or specific tasks. Communication among employees at large corporations is typically categorized as low-context, as is that in sports groups, where the rules of engagement are clearly laid out. Among nations, the United States has historically been the example of the low-context approach to communication. In low-context cultures, the information content in advertising should be higher than that in high-context cultures.

The second societal grouping is the **high-context culture**. In these groups, the context in which a conversation occurs is just as important as the words that are actually spoken. To be successful in this form of communication, an individual or company must understand certain cultural clues that are being communicated along with the spoken words. Groups exhibiting the high-context approach typically have been together for a long period of time, and there is more internalized understanding of what is being communicated than in low-context cultures. Much of the knowledge in these settings is situational, and thus there is less written or formal communication. In high-context cultures, it is harder to transfer knowledge outside of the group, given the lack of codified rules of engagement. Some examples of high-context cultures are family gatherings, small religious congregations, or a party with friends. On a national level, prior studies have shown that the citizens of Japan and France typically exhibit behavior that is closer to the high-context approach. In terms of marketing strategies, the information content is less for high-context cultures than for low-context cultures, as less information needs to be conveyed.

To date, there has not been much statistical evidence in support of national cultures clearly exhibiting one approach or the other, but there has been some validation of this theory at the individual or situational level. In other words, the context in which specific communication takes place depends on the group that is involved, and it is hard to apply this theory at the national level.

HOFSTEDE'S FIVE DIMENSIONS OF CULTURE

Other theories of culture better lend themselves to comparison across cultures than does Edward Hall's theory. **Hofstede's five dimensions of culture** is one example of such a theory. The five dimensions of culture as theorized by Hofstede are social orientation, power orientation, uncertainty orientation, goal orientation, and time orientation. These dimensions, as well as the extremes for each, are discussed below.

Social Orientation

The first of Hofstede's five dimensions is social orientation. This orientation reflects a person's beliefs about the relative importance of the individual and the groups to which that person belongs. One extreme is individualism. This form of social orientation is exhibited primarily by Western societies and others that follow a free-market-based system. Individualistic people or countries tend to put themselves ahead of the group as a whole. The other extreme is collectivism. This form of society prefers group consensus rather than individual effort or decision-making. Many of the former communist countries have historically exhibited this form of social orientation.

Power Orientation

The next of the five dimensions is power orientation. This dimension refers to the beliefs that people tend to hold about the appropriateness of power and authority differences in hierarchies such as business organizations. One extreme of this dimension is power respect. Individuals in these cultures tend to accept power based on the position and do not question authority as much as do individuals in other cultures. Some examples of power-respect cultures are Brazil, France, Italy, Japan, and Spain. Other societies tend to be power-tolerant cultures. These cultures are more often willing to question authority. Some examples of power-tolerant cultures are Denmark, Israel, the United Kingdom, and the United States.

Uncertainty Orientation

The third of Hofstede's cultural dimensions, uncertainty orientation, refers to the feelings that people tend to have regarding uncertain and ambiguous situations. Some cultures exhibit uncertainty acceptance. These cultures tend not to be bothered by change. Some examples of societies that typically represent this category are Canada, Denmark, and the United States. The other extreme in the uncertainty-orientation category is uncertainty avoidance. Societies that are more hierarchical tend to exhibit an avoidance of uncertainty and thus embrace rigid, rules-based systems. Recent studies have shown that former Soviet bloc countries, where employment was certain in a centrally planned system, have yet to completely accept the ambiguity that comes with a free-market economy; these countries tend to avoid uncertainty.[2]

Goal Orientation

Another of Hofstede's five dimensions, goal orientation, deals with the manner in which people are motivated to work toward different goals. Sometimes in the developed world, we tend to think that all societies have similar aggressive goals regarding achieving material possessions. This aggressive goal behavior is seen in countries such as Germany, Japan, and the United States. Other countries exhibit passive goal behavior and tend to place a higher value on social relationships and the quality of life. Many of the Nordic countries exhibit these passive goal beliefs. In a recent study comparing the quality of life in different countries in the world, all of the Nordic countries (Denmark, Finland, Iceland, Norway, and Sweden) were in the top ten in this category.[3]

Time Orientation

The final of Hofstede's five cultural dimensions is time orientation. This category deals with the extent to which members of a culture adopt a long-term outlook versus a short-term outlook regarding life, work, and other issues. Some cultures tend to exhibit a future-oriented viewpoint, and individuals within these cultures value things such as dedication and perseverance, while other cultures tend to have a shorter-term outlook. Two long-term-oriented cultures are China and Japan. Short-term-oriented societies tend to look to the past and the present more than to the future; individuals within these cultures have a respect for traditions. Some examples of short-term-oriented cultures are Pakistan and parts of Western Africa.

Time orientation has an effect on a consumer's response to marketing content. Those with a past orientation have little use for marketing information. Individuals who are focused on the present will typically exhibit favorable responses to marketing as an aid to their current consumption. Individuals with a future orientation will typically view marketing as an aid in their future planning.

One benefit of Hofstede's approach is that numerous studies have been undertaken to validate his findings. Hofstede's original study was of IBM employees between the ages of thirty and thirty-four, and subsequent studies have been implemented via behavior-oriented questionnaires designed to determine where individuals rank on each of these five cultural dimensions.

CORPORATE DIVERSITY INITIATIVES

What is apparent is that few cultural theories have proved to be effective over entire populations within a specific country. It is helpful, however, to be aware of these approaches in a multinational business environment, as they could aid the successful business manager in managing day-to-day employee issues.

The goal of cultural studies in a business environment is to achieve cultural convergence, which involves a business leader's attempt to avoid using only self-reference criteria when making judgments involving businesses or individuals in different countries. Successful managers for a multinational firm will not only attempt to understand the diverse foreign cultures where the business is involved, but also modify and adapt their behavior to become more compatible with the local culture. This process which is known as **acculturation**, calls to mind the old adage "When in Rome, do as the Romans do." As the Danish philosopher Søren Kierkegaard said, "The first thing to understand is that you do not understand." Prior to entering a foreign market, multinational corporations must first realize that the cultural norms observed in other markets may not be the same as those observed in the multinational firm's home country. Thus, understanding these cultural differences is a requirement for successful entry into a foreign market.

Throughout much of the developed world, corporations have commenced diversity initiatives in an effort to root out insensitivity and to better understand the cultural backgrounds, beliefs, and habits of both employees and customers of multinational firms. The "identity wheel" is one method whereby individuals can identify certain characteristics that define their personality and make up their identity. Religious beliefs, economic status, familial history, sexual orientation, and other facets of an individual's identity vary considerably even within a single company. The better a company understands the diverse backgrounds of its employees and customers the easier it is to provide products and services that cater to diverse needs. Figure 9.2 provides an illustration of an identity wheel for a hypothetical individual.

Rather than making the assumption that an individual's identity primarily comprises only a few factors (as in Samuel Huntington's *Clash of Civilizations*, which made this claim regarding fervent religious beliefs resulting in cultural clashes, given the singular importance of religion as theorized by this view), the identity wheel assumes that a person's identity is multifaceted. Smart organizations seek to understand and appeal

Figure 9.2 **The Identity Wheel**

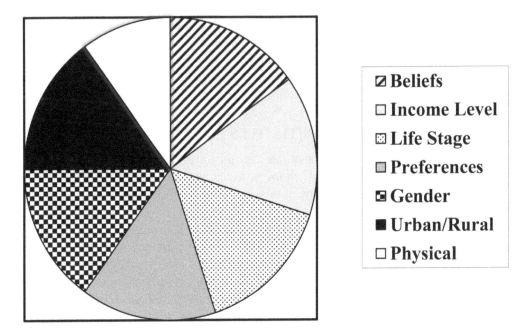

to the components of their customers' identity in order to gain market share over their competitors.

MANAGEMENT OF CULTURAL CHANGE

Managers must understand what aspects of a culture will resist change, how those aspects will differ among cultures, how the process of change takes place in different cultures, and how long it will take to implement changes. They must also consider that change may occur in different ways: their organization may act as an agent of change, influencing the foreign culture; it may be somewhat changed itself; or it may both create change and be changed at the same time.

In deciding how much change an organization will assume and how an organization may attempt to influence its host environment, a manager must consider the value system of the organization and its strategic mission, goals, and objectives. In addition, the costs and benefits of change need to be outlined, because the costs of change may far outweigh the benefits reaped from change.

If it is determined that some change is necessary in the foreign locale, the international manager should remember that resistance to change is low if the amount of change is not too great. If too much change is perceived by individuals within a certain culture at the outset, resistance will be stronger. In the same vein, individuals will be more apt to allow and accept change if they are involved in the decision and participate in the change process. Also, people are more likely to support change when they see personal or reference group rewards.

To ease the problems associated with change, the international manager must find opinion leaders and try to convince those who can influence others. The international firm should also time the implementation of change wisely. Change should be planned for a time when there is the least likelihood of resistance. When considering timing, all elements should be considered to avoid conflict, such as political disturbances or religious holidays. Moreover, the international manager needs to look toward the home office for possible areas of change that will improve the potential for acceptance and success within the foreign environment.

SUMMARY

When businesses cross over national borders, they face a diversity of societies and cultures quite different from their own. "Society" refers to a political and social entity that is geographically defined and is composed of people and their culture. "Culture" is a set of social norms and responses that conditions the behavior of a population. The term "sociocultural" describes how society and culture relate to each other.

In the study of culture, the major topics are attitudes, beliefs, religion, aesthetics, material culture, education, language, and social organizations. Attitudes and beliefs, including attitudes about time, achievement and work, change, and the importance of occupation, influence human behavior by providing a set of rules and guidelines. Religion provides the spiritual basis for a society by imposing moral norms and appropriate behavior. Aesthetics include various forms of artistic expression. Material culture refers to objects and possessions and focuses on technology, while nonmaterial culture covers a set of intangibles. Communication and language can be silent, as well as spoken or written, and may be a barrier to an international organization. Silent language includes body language, gestures, color, and symbols.

Societal organizations take a number of different forms and indicate the level of social stratification within a society. Social groups are either ascribed (determined by birth) or acquired.

Business customers differ from one country to another and must be understood before an MNC begins any negotiations or business dealings outside its own culture. Understanding the importance of gifts and how they differ from bribes can be critical to international business relations.

Cultural theories that pertain to the discussion of an MNC's international dealings include the cultural cluster approach; Hall's distinction between low-context and high-context cultures; and Hofstede's five dimensions of culture. These theories all exhibit strengths and weaknesses in their attempts to categorize individuals and societies based on certain cultural beliefs.

The international organization must understand cultural differences when attempting to initiate change in a foreign location. Change prompted by an MNC must be carefully planned, and an MNC must clearly identify the costs and benefits of that change before proceeding.

DISCUSSION QUESTIONS

1. Define the term "sociocultural." Why should international business managers be aware of sociocultural elements when making their everyday decisions?
2. What are the elements of culture?
3. What is the typical American and European attitude toward work? Do you personally hold this attitude toward work?
4. How can religious beliefs affect international business decisions in the Middle East?
5. You have found out that your competitor is paying bribes to generate new business. Should you also pay them? Explain.
6. How can nonverbal communication affect a business relationship?
7. How might family groups and extended families affect the decisions of an international manager?
8. Why might multinational corporations act as agents of change? Provide some examples.
9. How can managers of a multinational firm get their local employees to accept new ideas?

NOTES

1. Murdock, "Common Denominator of Cultures."
2. Dienes, Hofstede, Kolman, and Noorderhaven, "Cross-Cultural Differences in Central Europe."
3. *Economist*, "Human Development Index," 30.

BIBLIOGRAPHY

Across the Board. "All in Favor of Bribery, Please Stand Up." June 1984, 3–5.
Business International. "Some Guidelines on Dealing with Graft in Korean Operations." February 25, 1983, 62.
Commission of the European Community. *The European Community and Education.* Brussels: Commission of the European Community, 1985.
Culture at Work. "High and Low Context." www.culture-at-work.com/highlow.html.
Dienes, Elizabeth, Geert Hofstede, Ludek Kolman, and Niels G. Noorderhaven. "Cross-Cultural Differences in Central Europe." *Journal of Managerial Psychology* 18 (January 2003): 76–88.
Economist. "Human Development Index." *Pocket World in Figures.* London: Profile Books, 2005.
———. "Islam for Beginners." March 18, 1989, 95–96.
———. "A People Problem." November 25, 1988, 49–50.
Fatemi, Khosrow. "Multinational Corporations, Developing Countries, and Transfer of Technology: A Cultural Perspective." *Issues in International Business* (Summer–Fall 1985): 1–6.
Hall, Edward T. *Beyond Culture*, New York: Anchor Books, 1976.

Hofstede, Geert. *Culture's Consequences: International Differences in Work Related Values*. New York: Sage Publications, 1980.

Huntington, Samuel. *The Clash of Civilizations and the Remaking of World Order*. New York: Touchstone, 1996.

Jacoby, Neil H., Peter Nehemkis, and Richard Eells. *Bribery and Extortion in World Business*. New York: Macmillan, 1977.

Kim, W. Chan, and Rene A. Mauborgne. "Cross-Cultural Strategies." *Journal of Business Strategy* (Spring 1987): 28–35.

Murdock, George P. "The Common Denominator of Cultures." In *The Science of Man in the World Crisis*, ed. Ralph Linton, pp. 123–142. New York: Columbia University Press, 1945.

Reardon, Kathleen. *International Business and Gift-Giving Customs*. Janesville, WI: Parker Pen, 1981.

Terpstra, Vern, and Kenneth David. *The Cultural Environment of International Business*. 2nd ed. Cincinnati: South-Western, 1985.

CASE STUDY 9.1

DELIS FOODS CORPORATION

The year 2010 was a very good one for Delis Foods Corporation, a San Francisco–based food conglomerate. Its domestic sales were $24 billion and its international sales were $7 billion, making it one of the largest companies in the processed-foods business. Innovative product development and strong marketing strategies are two of the main reasons for the company's success. Its international operations are directed out of San Francisco by William Schaefer, an executive with almost eighteen years of experience in international marketing, the last ten in the marketing of food products. Schaefer is proud of the 2010 performance, in which his division registered a world-wide sales increase of 12 percent over the previous year. Despite the overall results, however, he has to acknowledge one failure: the sale of iced tea in Dikorma.

Dikorma, a small country in Southeast Asia with a population of about 60 million, is a nation that is fast industrializing; the per capita GNP has risen to $6,600 per annum from a level of only $2,400 per annum twelve years ago. Dikorma is viewed by Delis Foods as an important target market that presents excellent opportunities. There is a large middle class that is fairly cosmopolitan and sophisticated. The country has a relatively free export-import market, and the balance of trade is maintained comfortably. Retail distribution is well developed and necessary ancillary services—transportation, banking, and telecommunications—are not a problem. The initial experience of Delis Foods with its large-scale marketing of instant noodles in Dikorma had been a great success. Delis soon became a household brand name, and the company was able to penetrate the market quite successfully with other products, such as ketchup, instant coffee, and nondairy creamers.

(continued)

Case Study 9.1 *(continued)*

Following up on its success, Delis Foods decided to make a bid for a segment of the huge cold-drink market. Dikorma is a tropical country where temperatures remain above 80 degrees for eleven months of the year. There is a large urban middle class, which provides a steady market for cold drinks. Delis Foods decided to introduce instant iced tea into this market. The product idea was fairly simple. The company would market iced tea in concentrated liquid form, and the consumer would only have to add water and ice to get a cool drink. There was no other iced tea brand available in Dikorma, and Delis Foods would have a monopoly. Moreover, Dikorma's middle class had proven receptive to new ideas in the past; the case of instant noodles was clear evidence.

The company decided on a hard-sell campaign across the country, utilizing all major media, including television, radio, newspapers, magazines, and roadside signs. The main theme was simple: "Beat the heat with Velima Iced Tea." A number of promotions were carried out, and the distributors and retailers were given attractive discounts to push the product.

Despite the initial effort, sales did not take off, and three months after the product launch, it became increasingly clear that the company had a loser on its hands. Extremely annoyed, Schaefer placed the blame on the marketing staff that designed and implemented the campaign. He asked them to find the reasons the product had not sold well and to modify the campaign accordingly.

The marketing group in Dikorma analyzed the entire project quite intensively, but it came up with little that could be called a mistake in the campaign. Moreover, there was apparently no dissatisfaction with the quality of the product. True, the coverage of the product had been limited to the urban centers, but that was because it was relatively highly priced and the rural market could not afford a sophisticated product such as instant iced tea. The product was retested, but it was found to conform to all standard requirements and there were no quality problems.

Confident that they had corrected the few errors in the campaign and assured that the product had no quality problems, the local marketing group of Delis Foods launched another, bigger campaign, promoting the product much more aggressively than in the previous campaign. This time attractive consumer incentives were offered, such as a free crystal glass with the purchase of every bottle of iced tea. The results were somewhat better. Attracted by the offer of free glasses and by the glittery campaign, consumers reacted positively and sales started to improve. The marketing group heaved a sigh of relief, but not for long.

Within the next six months, for what appeared to be completely inexplicable reasons, sales began to drop off again. The company had not increased its price, and no initial incentives were withdrawn, although maintaining these incentives was proving quite expensive to the company. The drop in sales became more accentuated each month. The marketing group and Schaefer were perplexed. After eight months of the second promotion, sales were so low that the company started to lose money on the product. The retailers also became nervous and stopped ordering. Some then complained that they were having trouble disposing of their inventories. Schaefer made a painful decision: admitting that the product had failed, he withdrew it from the market in July 2011, and Velima Iced Tea was taken off the shelves in Dikorma.

The chair of Delis Foods, Peter Sanderson, is quite philosophical about the failure and tells Schaefer to take things in context: "We all learn from our mistakes." Sanderson asks Schaefer to find out why the product had failed.

Schaefer realizes that it might be a good idea to get an external view of the problem. After all, in-company analysis, however sharp and intense, still has its limitations, and in this case the limitations were exposed beyond doubt. Delis Foods had tried to think of all the reasons its iced tea failed but did not come up with any that would explain, in concrete form, why an excellent product failed in an excellent market despite a great campaign and all other positive circumstances. Schaefer decides to call Gayle Johnston, the chief marketing consultant at MacArthur & Associates in Jakarta. Johnston is an expert on Southeast Asia markets. "He should be able to tell us what really went wrong," thinks Schaefer as he notes his appointment with Johnston for the following Thursday in San Francisco.

The meeting with Johnston is quite illuminating. Johnston suggests a whole new line of thinking. According to him, it was a sociocultural asymmetry that caused problems for Delis Foods in Dikorma. As Johnston explains, there was no way an iced tea product could have succeeded in Dikorma, because it clashed very strongly with ingrained sociocultural values. People in Dikorma, Johnston points out, do not drink tea without milk. In Dikorma iced tea, by definition, would be consumed with milk, but the entire campaign showed the beverage as being essentially sweetened black tea with ice. The other cultural barrier was that tea in Dikorma is viewed as a hot drink, not a cold one. Dikormans have been drinking hot tea for hundreds of years and are not likely to see it as a cold drink. They will drink cold milk, even perhaps cold coffee, but certainly not iced tea.

Schaefer protests that Dikormans had reacted positively to instant noodles, which they had never had before. They also had adopted several other new products: ready-baked cakes, frozen pizzas, and so on. Why this hostility toward iced tea? "That is simple," replies Johnston. Dikormans do not have pizza or cake ingrained in them as a part of their traditional culture. These are new products and they accepted them

(continued)

Case Study 9.1 *(continued)*

as such. But tea is not new in Dikorma; it is ingrained in the culture. Ingrained dietary habits are quite difficult to change, especially if the change is dramatically in opposition to the existing culture.

"Perhaps you are right," Schaefer admits. "At least the market has proved that you are. In the future we should do better. How about doing a study of the sociocultural traits of Dikorma and of our products to suggest which products we should try to keep out of this market?" "That's a useful idea," says Johnson, "but please make sure that you tie in the recommendations of my study with those of your marketing group."

DISCUSSION QUESTIONS

1. What primary errors did Delis make during the market feasibility study? What kind of strategy would you advise Delis to adopt to avoid this kind of situation in the future?
2. Analyze the sociocultural traits of a select country and devise a food product strategy that suits the cultural environment.
3. Suggest a list of typical processed food items that would not be successful in a country with a tropical climate and explain why.
4. Can cultural values be changed?

CASE STUDY 9.2

AIR AMERICA

Herbert Manning, general manager of Air America's Qamran office, has been with the company for twelve years. Manning had an undergraduate degree in economics and business and had worked for a leading travel agency in San Francisco before joining Air America as a sales executive. With his earlier experience and his enthusiasm and energy on the job, Manning made a favorable impression very quickly. Within two years he was promoted to the rank of area sales manager and elected vice president of Air America's worldwide sales club, having had the second highest level of sales among all of Air America's sales executives worldwide.

Manning continued to perform well as area sales manager, and three years later he was moved to the company's corporate headquarters in Dallas, Texas, as vice president of international marketing and sales with responsibility for planning and implementing the company's marketing and sales strategies in the Middle East, Africa, and southern Asia. Air America, though a major international airline, was not very strong in these markets, which it perceived would become increasingly important in the future. Manning took up the challenge with his well-known drive and energy, and during the next three years, Air America succeeded in negotiating air route agreements with four countries in North Africa, three in the Middle East, and three in southern Asia. Qamran, a small sheikdom in the Middle East, was designated as the regional base for this area and as a hub location for the airline. In these three years, Manning's region became an important source of revenue from international operations for Air America. Apart from an aggressive and well-targeted sales policy, overall increase in passenger traffic arising out of the oil price boom helped to boost ticket sales.

Toward the end of the third year, however, Air America, like many other airlines operating in the region, was suddenly hit with a sharp decline in demand as oil prices rose sharply and the world economy went into a deep recession. As the market shrank, competition intensified, and it became increasingly difficult to hold on to market share. Air America's share of the Persian Gulf market dropped by 7 percent. Combined with a sharp decline in overall market size, the drop led to a steep reduction in total revenues.

Concerned with the difficult situation in the region, Air America's senior management decided that an aggressive strategy had to be adopted to recapture market share and rebuild the airline's image as a dominant force in the region. A key element of the strategy was to appoint Manning as the regional manager of the Middle East and North Africa.

It was a big promotion for Manning. Regional managers were considered senior management in the company and were responsible for participating in the formulation of global strategy. Moreover, Air America's corporate policy emphasized considerable delegation and decentralization. Regional managers were, therefore, almost completely independent in their local operations and were primarily responsible for their own results. Manning was elated when his boss told him the news. He had wanted to go back to the field for some time now, and the position apparently offered all that he was looking for. In addition, relocation as a regional manager in Qamran meant that he would have several liberal fringe benefits given to Air America's expatriate managers: a large, furnished company house, a chauffeur-driven car, at least four servants, and additional allowances, including a large entertainment budget.

(continued)

Case Study 9.2 *(continued)*

Manning's first year was extremely successful. His drive and enthusiasm were infused throughout the local office, because he set a good example by his own untiring efforts. His years in the marketing division had provided him with considerable background knowledge of the operations, and he used that knowledge to seek and implement new ways to fight off Air America's competitors. Market share began to inch back upward and the revenue drop was reversed. Although the revenues were helped by a slight improvement in market conditions, there was no doubt that Manning's arrival was a key factor in the reversal of Air America's fortunes in the region.

The second year was good, too, although not as good as the first. Market share increased, as did the revenues by smaller degrees. One significant explanation for the slowing of increases offered by Manning was that other airlines had initiated equally aggressive counterstrategies, and it was not possible to improve the rate of Air America's gains without seriously compromising profitability.

Results started to decline in the third year, however. Market share gains slid back by 2 percent and revenues showed a slight decline. Manning seemed to have lost the drive and initiative that had characterized his work just a few months before, and some of Manning's subordinates seemed unhappy with his behavior and left the company. Gilbert Wyles, Air America's senior vice president of human resources, was quick to guess that the problem was Manning himself. Wyles decided that a meeting at corporate headquarters would be useful to discuss the whole issue. Manning was, after all, a star performer, and if he was facing any problems the company was fully prepared to help him.

The meeting lasted three hours. Initially hesitant to state the real problem, Manning finally admitted that his wife, Sandra, was having difficulties in adjusting to life in Qamran. Back in the United States, she had been a client relations executive in a small advertising company. It was not a very high position, but it allowed her to use her skills at dealing with people constructively. She had developed a fairly close network of good friends and a large circle of pleasant acquaintances through her job. Her decision to leave the job and accompany Manning to Qamran had not been easy, but she had decided to make the best of a new lifestyle that awaited her in their new overseas home. She did make a sincere effort at adjustment, but Qamran's society was governed by strict Islamic tenets, which meant that social freedoms for women were severely restricted. Although the Mannings enjoyed various social activities with diplomats and other expatriates, Mrs. Manning had little to do during the day. Women were not allowed to work in Qamran unless they were granted special work permits under exceptional circumstances. Even then women had to dress in a particular fashion prescribed by the authorities.

After the first year, Mrs. Manning grew increasingly restless about her new situation. Her problems were accentuated by the long absences of her husband, who went on frequent business trips that were essential to the success of his assignment. Mrs. Manning thought of various solutions and different ways in which her life could be made more interesting, but nothing worked, and her mental discomfort continued to increase. In the past few months, she had suffered long periods of depression and was not responding very well to treatment, which caused Mr. Manning tremendous anxiety and had adversely affected his professional performance.

Gilbert Wyles suggested that the Mannings take a vacation immediately, at the place of their choice, and that by the time they returned the company would have an answer to the problem. Manning was relieved, but at the same time he was skeptical of the company's intentions. As he walked out of the corporate headquarters to catch a cab for his hotel, he wondered whether he had done the right thing.

Meanwhile, Wyles, in his well-appointed office, put together a confidential memo to the international human resources policy group, a small set of top Air America executives in charge of framing company policies in international human resources management. The memo explained the background and circumstances of the situation and placed three options before the members:

1. The option suggested by Manning, to give his wife a job in his office in Qamran as a public relations officer. This would be possible if the company modified its personnel policy on employment of spouses and if enough pressure was exerted on the Qamran government.
2. Replace Manning with another expatriate executive, which could be easily done, but might lead to similar problems for the replacement.
3. Appoint a local national as regional manager or bring in a third-country national from Air America's other overseas offices.

DISCUSSION QUESTIONS

1. Which of the three options would you recommend to Air America and why? What would be the problems with the other options?
2. Is there a need for Air America to change its international staffing policies to avoid sending expatriate managers to overseas locations?

CHAPTER 10

Foreign Investment: Researching Risk

"The outcome of any serious research can only be to make two questions grow where only one grew before."
—Thorstein Veblen

CHAPTER OBJECTIVES

This chapter will:

- Look at the forces and opportunities that support foreign investment by multinational corporations
- Discuss the role political risk plays in counterbalancing the benefits or opportunities of investing abroad
- Describe the various ways host governments control foreign investment
- Present management techniques that can be used to reduce political risk when investing abroad

---

WHY INVEST ABROAD?

Every firm that considers investing abroad must weigh the potential advantages against the potential risks. To do that, in-house analysis must identify and evaluate key factors. There are several reasons to consider initially why firms should invest abroad, and a few general factors can be linked to the overall level of risk a particular host country holds for an MNC making a foreign direct investment. These factors include the attitude of the host country's government, the political system in place, the level of public discon-

Table 10.1 **Most Business-Friendly Environments**

1.	Singapore
2.	Switzerland
3.	Finland
4.	Canada/Hong Kong (tied)
6.	Australia/Denmark (tied)
8.	New Zealand/Sweden (tied)
10.	Netherlands
11.	Norway/Taiwan (tied)
13.	United States
14.	Germany
15.	Chile
16.	Belgium
17.	Ireland
18.	Qatar
19.	France
20.	Austria

Source: Economist, "Business Environment Rankings," 61.

tent or satisfaction, the unification or fragmentation of the local society on cultural and religious lines, the kind of internal and external pressures faced by the government, and the history of the country in the past few decades. In the pages that follow, we address each of these concerns in turn.

A recent publication by the *Economist* ranked the countries of the world according to the friendliness of the business environment. The rankings reflect the opportunities for, and the hindrances to, the conduct of business, as measured by the countries' rankings in ten categories, including market potential, tax and labor market policies, infrastructure, skills, and the political environment.[1] The top twenty countries are listed in Table 10.1.

BIGGER MARKETS

Many international firms decide to invest overseas to tap larger foreign markets. To keep growing, a firm must increase its sales, which may not be possible in the domestic market. Domestic markets, however large, are limited to a particular size and rate of growth and are the target of competition from other domestic firms with similar products and marketing capabilities. In such situations, a move overseas is a logical step for a company wanting to tap a larger market. Apart from the fact that the existence of a new, larger customer base would boost sales, overseas markets often confer additional advantages to the firm. For example, these markets may not have products that are similar to or of the same quality as those of the firm going overseas, and the competition from overseas markets may not be as strong as domestic competition.

HOST-NATION DEMANDS

Occasionally firms must invest overseas to tap international markets because host-country government restrictions require that the firm's products be manufactured locally. Such restrictions are generally imposed to boost the local economy and general domestic production and employment. Thus, the MNC that wants to tap an overseas market has to invest in overseas plants that are run by domestic managers, in local subordinates, or through some other arrangement.

ECONOMIES OF SCALE

A firm might want to invest in an overseas market because it is cheaper to manufacture goods locally rather than manufacturing them at home and exporting them. When the local market is large and the demand is consistent enough to justify investment in the plant and equipment needed to set up a manufacturing operation, production economies can occur through other factors. For example, the labor costs may be lower in the overseas location, the sources of raw materials may be closer to the plant in the overseas location, and the costs of shipping and marketing the products may be lower than those of home-based operations. Another important factor is the location of the firm. An overseas plant location may also be better suited to serve a third-country market.

COMPETITIVE MOTIVES

Often firms operate in head-on competition with other domestic and international firms. This type of competition is particularly severe in oligopolistic industries, where only a few large firms dominate the market. In such an environment, the moves of one firm are quickly duplicated and challenged by the others. Thus, if one firm moves abroad, its competitors make similar moves. One obvious motive for the move is to keep pace with the first firm in new markets and overall level of sales. The other motive is the need to match the overseas strategy of competitors, because if that is not done, the competition could acquire additional strength from its overseas operation, which could be leveraged in the domestic market, too. Competition often occurs between firms of different countries that dominate parts of the same industry (e.g., Caterpillar Company of the United States and Komatsu of Japan dominate the earth-moving machinery industry). If one company invades the home-country market of another, it is very likely that the competitor will be motivated to retaliate by accessing its competition's domestic market. For example, in the 1990s, Kodak decided to enter the Japanese market to counter Fuji's market share gains in the United States.

TECHNOLOGY AND QUALITY CONTROL

Many firms feel that if they license their technology to a company in the overseas location, their technology might be leaked to competitors. In fact, many companies, especially in the high-technology area, hold on to their know-how so closely that they do not license it as a matter of policy. The practice of retaining information within the company is often referred to as **internalization**. Some companies feel that licensing their technology may result in the licensee producing a product of inferior quality, which may be damaging to the product image. To obviate such possibilities, companies prefer to set up their own overseas manufacturing operations. Having their own operations also provides some companies with greater assurance of regular supply, better maintenance, and after-sales services for their products, which are crucial to retaining customer loyalty in a highly competitive international environment.

RAW MATERIALS

Many firms rely on raw materials imported from abroad, a reliance that can stem from both availability and cost considerations. The raw materials may not be available in the home country, or, alternatively, it may be more economical to access raw materials from overseas than domestically if the price differences exceed the additional transportation costs. If a firm decides to rely on overseas raw materials, it often becomes dependent on a regular supply at predictable and relatively stable prices. Long-term contracts with overseas suppliers are one way of achieving predictable and stable prices. In some cases, however, companies are unwilling to take the risk of the supplier's reneging on the contract so they decide to invest in extractive mining and other such raw materials sourcing operations overseas. Sometimes such investments are motivated by the consideration that the necessary technology is not available in the source country and therefore must be provided by the corporation interested in extracting the materials. Often permission from the governments of the countries where raw materials are available is centered on the type of technology the overseas corporation is able to bring to use in the extractive processes.

FORWARD INTEGRATION

Many companies wish to eliminate middlemen from their operations and forward integrate the different stages involved in the manufacture of their products and their sales to the consumer. For example, a firm may produce a soft-drink concentrate and sell it to a local bottler overseas who bottles and sells it in foreign markets. The profits from the revenues generated from the sales of the soft drink are shared by the company producing the soft drink concentrate and the local bottler. If the company selling the concentrate had its own bottling plant in the foreign country, it would be able to control the entire operation and eliminate sharing its profits with the intermediary agent. This motivation may prompt the company manufacturing the concentrate to set up its own bottling operation overseas.

TECHNOLOGY ACQUISITION

Multinational corporations often invest in other countries to gain access to new technologies that are not developed in the home country. Access to new technology is often sought by the outright acquisition of new firms possessing such knowledge. These new technologies are generally intended for integration with the entire global corporate strategy of the MNC that acquires them. Often, the company that acquires a new technology through an overseas acquisition sets up an overseas facility, which enhances the existing operations by adding the managerial, financial, and technological strengths of the parent company.

ASSESSING POLITICAL RISK

Political risk for multinational corporations includes adverse actions that may be taken by host-country governments against the firms. These actions can include changes in the operating conditions of foreign enterprises that arise out of the political process, either directly through war, insurrection, or political violence, or through changes in government that affect the behavior, ownership, physical assets, personnel, or operations of the firm.

Political risk does not necessarily arise out of an upheaval in the political climate of the host country. Perceptions often change within the same government, and, as a result, decisions detrimental to the interests of the firm can be made. Moreover, because policies can and do change, some degree of political risk is present in nearly all countries.

Factors responsible for political risk can be grouped into two categories: inherent and circumstantial. Inherent factors are conditions that are present constantly around the world that generate a certain danger of adverse action by host governments from the point of view of the multinational corporation (e.g., terrorism). Circumstantial factors are those conditions that can arise out of particular events in different countries.

INHERENT CAUSES OF POLITICAL RISK

Different Economic Objectives

The motivations and goals of a US MNC are often at variance with those of the host government (see Table 10.2). A primary example is in the area of balance of payments considerations. A host country that is facing difficulties with its balance of payments might seek to conserve its resources by maximizing the inflows and minimizing the outflows. It may also try to optimize the use of the available foreign exchange resources by placing restrictions on repatriation of profits, dividends, and royalties by a multinational corporation to its home country. The host government could also place restrictions on the time lag permitted for import and export payments, thus interfering with the MNC's internal leading and lagging strategy, which is devised to manage its finances and avoid exchange- and interest-rate risks.

Table 10.2 **Conflicting Objectives Between Developing Countries and Multinational Corporations**

Developing countries	Multinational corporations
Promote local ownership	Maintain global controls and efficiency
Increase local ownership and control	Minimize costs of technology and capital
Reduce duration of contracts and change payment	Receive reasonable returns for risk characteristics
Separate technology from private investment	Provide technology as part of long-term production and market development
Eliminate restrictive business clauses in technology and investment agreements	Maintain ability to affect the use of capital, technology, and associated products
Minimize proprietary rights of suppliers	Protect rights for profit from private investments
Reduce contract security	Use contracts to create stable business environment and to develop trust
Encourage technology and R&D transfer to host country	Maintain control of technology and R&D paid for by the company
Develop suitable products for host country	Gain global economies of scale to lower costs of products

In a leading and lagging strategy, firms decide which payables to pay early and which payables to pay late based on factors such as exchange rates, net receipts from their centralized cash management system, and the size or power of the company owed. Additionally, the leading and lagging can also pertain to the timing of collections of accounts receivable, for similar reasons.

Monetary and Fiscal Policies

The monetary and fiscal policies of a host government may be at variance with an MNC's desires. For example, a host country that is faced with impending inflationary conditions might want to raise the interest rates on bank lending, which may be detrimental to the interests of an MNC, whose costs of funds, and therefore of production, would go up correspondingly. The banks may also be directed to maintain quantitative ceilings on lending to prevent excessive increases in the money supply of the host country. The MNC, on the other hand, keen to retain its financing sources according to its own requirements, might attempt to circumvent these ceilings, further incurring the displeasure of the host government and raising a risk of further punitive action.

Similarly, fiscal policies followed by host governments may not be in the MNC's interests. The interest of the host government is invariably to maximize revenues, while that of the MNC is to minimize its tax liability. Increasing taxes is a major inherent risk that an MNC faces while operating overseas. Moreover, some countries levy a heavier tax on the repatriated portions of an MNC's profits, which is often in addition to the normal corporate taxes paid by a local company. Sometimes under these regimes, separate exchange rates are specified for different transactions. The goal of the host country might be to defend a particular level of the exchange rate that it deems appropriate in the pursuit of its best economic interest. For the MNC, however, this might mean that there is an artificial distortion in the amount of funds it is able to repatriate, which adversely affects its overall profitability.

Economic Development and Industrial Policies

The industrial and economic development policies of a host country can often pose a risk for an MNC. For example, countries may want to promote certain backward geographical regions where infrastructural facilities are low and might therefore require the expansion of MNCs to such regions even though investment there may not be economically feasible. Many host countries want to promote domestic industry and, particularly, small and medium-size enterprises. To do so, host countries tend to provide subsidies or other fiscal incentives or reserve the production of certain goods for such industries. Another promotion mechanism is the purchase policy of the government.

In many host countries, especially less-developed countries, the government is the largest buyer of goods and services. Exclusion from government contracts, therefore, affects the sales of an MNC's products significantly. Also, in many of the core and sensitive industries (e.g., defense and infrastructure-oriented industries), MNC participation may be prohibited. The risk arises from the possibility that some industries in which an MNC is active might be declared core industries or sensitive industries, and MNC operations may be expropriated or forcibly sold to local parties. The rationale behind the exclusion of MNCs from key industries is apparently apprehension in the minds of host governments that MNC control of key industries might endanger national security and hamper the ability of the government to conduct an independent foreign policy. Such policies are similar to what Vladimir Lenin referred to as the **commanding heights** of the economy. The commanding heights were key industries required to effectively control an economy. In the early 1900s, such industries included railroads, steel, and heavy industry. Based on many of the current barriers to foreign control, the modern-day commanding heights of the economy would appear to be banking, telecommunications, broadcasting, and other such service sector industries.

Colonial Heritage

Many host countries are former colonies that have gained their independence. The colonial era was marked by complete political domination by foreign powers and economic domination by foreign companies. Most of the foreign companies in that era used their privileged, often monopolistic positions to exploit local resources, markets, and labor to maximize their profits. As a result, they were seen to be a drain on the economies of the colonies, leaving a sense of distrust of MNCs in the minds of host-country governments, who fear that MNCs may still exploit their economies. As a result, they are extra careful in scrutinizing proposals for foreign direct investment by multinationals and monitor MNCs' activities closely. These concerns also explain to some extent why such stringent controls are placed on MNCs' activities. This fundamental apprehension does not permit MNCs to operate freely and creates a constant risk of adverse action by host governments.

Sociocultural Differences

To a degree, political risk arises out of the sociocultural differences between a host country and an MNC. Social codes of conduct in certain countries contrast sharply with those of the MNCs. While in a host country, an MNC's executives face the risk of offending local sensibilities over crucial sociocultural issues. Moreover, some basic behavioral trends and norms followed by an MNC as a part of its usual way of functioning may prove offensive to the government or the clientele. For example, Western companies often have female executives representing them in meetings and negotiations, which might offend host officials or clients in Middle Eastern countries because women there are not expected to play such roles. Even relatively simple things, such as greetings, gift-giving, and hospitality, can become serious issues if they offend a key government official or a client in a host country. An MNC must always do its homework and adapt itself to local culture if it wants to avoid political risk.

CIRCUMSTANTIAL CAUSES OF POLITICAL RISK

Change of Government

A change of government is a major political risk faced by MNCs. In many countries political opponents have economic policy positions different from those of the government in office, and a new government is often keen to reverse the policies of its predecessors. Thus, an MNC that has excellent relations with a host government may find its assets under the threat of expropriation because of a change in government. In addition to having a different economic policy, a new host government may be hostile toward an MNC if the company is perceived as a supporter of the new government's political opponents.

Political risk is particularly high in countries that are in the midst of a transition from one type of political system to another, such as from a capitalist to a socialist society. In the past, in many countries that shifted from capitalist to socialist systems, entire assets of MNCs were expropriated, some with compensation, but some without.

Political Difficulties of Host Governments

In many countries where economic and social conditions are fairly unstable, it is often difficult for a government to manage the resulting public discontent. Many governments, in an attempt to shift blame for economic ills, target MNCs as the cause of those problems. The politicians in power often play on the inherent mistrust that the general public has of these foreign, wealthy, and powerful firms.

Political Action by Other Groups

MNCs also face the risk of adverse political activity from opposition parties seeking an issue about which to criticize the government. A host government's support for an MNC provides opposition parties with an ideal issue to manipulate nationalist feelings by propagating the line that the country is exploited by the MNC and that this exploitation is supported by the incumbent party. Sociopolitical activists and environmental groups are another source of political risk. Many MNCs have large investments in factories and extractive industries, which easily attract attention. Therefore, many consumer, labor, and environmental groups can attack the safety and pollution standards of MNCs, even though those standards may be better than those of domestic corporations in the same industry. Moreover, such attacks are likely to evoke a more active response from host governments, such as penalizing the MNC more heavily than a domestic industry for similar offenses.

Bilateral Relations Between the Host and Home Governments

The attitude of a host government toward an MNC is dependent on the bilateral relations between the host government and the MNC's home government. If the MNC's home government comes into conflict with the host government, it is likely that the latter will take direct or indirect action against the MNC. In several instances, when hostilities have broken out between two countries, the assets of MNCs have been confiscated without compensation. Even when the conflict falls short of outright war, adverse action against MNCs can result. For example, if one country faces a ban on some of its exports to an MNC's home country, it may retaliate by blocking the repatriation of the MNC's profits. Occasionally, action has been taken against MNCs to settle political scores. For example, if an MNC's home country takes an opposing stance at international forums or indirectly supports the host country's enemies, the host country can retaliate by taking action against the MNC within its jurisdiction.

Local Vested Interests

MNCs also face the possibility of adverse action from the lobbying efforts of local vested interests (otherwise known as protectionist pressures). As a rule, MNCs have considerable competitive power because they enjoy many advantages. They introduce a dynamic competitive force into local economies that upsets the entrenched positions of local businesspeople by capturing market share and reducing local firms' ability to skim off the market by charging higher prices for their products. Moreover, by introducing new products of superior quality at relatively competitive prices, an MNC is often able to expose the weaknesses of local businesses and force them to improve their own economic and operating efficiencies to regain their competitiveness in the marketplace.

While some local businesses respond to the MNC challenge in this way, many do not. These businesses try to fight the MNC's intrusion by pressuring the government to impose restrictions on the MNC in order to increase its costs and reduce its ability to compete.

In some cases, local vested interests lobby the government to prohibit the MNC's entry into the country or attempt to have regulations introduced that prohibit the MNC from doing certain kinds of business. The local interest groups are thus a serious political risk in many countries. In the wake of the recent financial crisis, these pressures escalated in many markets given the economic uncertainty and the dearth of jobs.

Social Unrest and Disorder

Fundamental and deep-rooted tensions in some countries fragment the local social order. Either on their own or at the manipulation of political interests, these tensions can occasionally erupt into riots and other acts of public violence. In such situations, the law enforcement machinery of local governments may be inadequate to protect public property against destruction and looting. MNC assets have sometimes become the targets of arsonists and looters, especially if they are instigated by vested interests. As recent political uprisings in Syria and in Greece illustrate, political protest comes in many forms, both violent and nonviolent, but in either case, the rules of engagement for a multinational corporation could change very quickly.

TYPES OF HOST-NATION CONTROL

Host governments impose different types of controls on the activities of MNCs, ranging from limits on the repatriation of profits to labor controls.

LIMITS ON REPATRIATION OF PROFITS

Many host governments place limits and conditions on the repatriation of profits, dividends, royalties, technical know-how fees, and other such revenue. Some governments impose an absolute ceiling on the amount of dividends that can be repatriated each year, and in some cases, these ceilings are subject to additional conditions that stipulate a maximum percentage of profits that can be repatriated. Moreover, corporations may also be asked to meet certain financial standards, such as debt-equity ratios, before being permitted any repatriation of profits or dividends. Other countries have a hierarchal approval process. Remittances of small amounts of profits are allowed freely, but higher amounts need the approval of the authorities, which could be the central bank or the government itself.

Certain countries facing severe balance of payments problems place time restrictions on the repatriation of dividends and profits: corporations have to retain their entire earnings in the host country for a certain time period, which can vary from a few months to several years. In countries faced with a shortage of foreign exchange, a time constraint can appear without a specific regulation to this effect. This constraint occurs when each request for repatriation must be approved by the central bank and only a limited number of requests can be approved each year. As a result, requests are rated sequentially, and repatriation must wait, sometimes several years in countries in the midst of a serious and prolonged balance of payments crisis.

CURBING TRANSFER PRICING

Many host governments are alert to the practice of transfer pricing by MNCs. To eliminate the outflow of profits through this mechanism, they establish regulations that reduce the MNC's ability to move funds by manipulating the company pricing structure. Normally, such regulations enable host-country authorities to disregard the internal prices charged by the parent to the subsidiary and to assess the company using an independent calculation that is based on standard international prices for that commodity instead of the price shown on the books of the company. These regulations enable the host government to assess an MNC's tax and tariff liabilities independently and reduce the advantages that an MNC tries to achieve through transfer pricing.

PRICE CONTROLS

Some host governments still have highly controlled economies. One of the important features of such an economy is the presence of price controls. An MNC entering such a country may be forced to sell its goods at the controlled prices, even though they may be well below the planned prices. In some instances, host governments require specific margins over costs. Additional controls may also be imposed, usually in situations of shortages, impending inflation, or potential or active social discontent over prices.

OWNERSHIP RESTRICTIONS

Many governments restrict foreign ownership of MNCs to a certain percentage, which means that the remaining portion must be owned by local partners or offered as a public issue in the local stock market. In such situations, the company often cannot exercise total control over operations, and limits are placed on the amount of profits it can repatriate. When total ownership is in the hands of the company, a very high dividend can be declared to transfer profits and capital out of the country. If the company is partly owned by local partners, this manipulation is not possible because local shareholders can question company policies. Moreover, the company cannot declare an unduly high dividend because the same level of dividend would have to be paid to local shareholders. In addition, once ownership is diluted, an MNC faces a takeover threat, because local interests can hold enough shares to acquire the local subsidiary and oust the management.

JOINT VENTURES

Some countries require that MNCs come into the country only as a partner in a joint venture with a local company. The motive of the host government is to secure monitoring and control leverage over the MNC through its local joint-venture partner and to promote domestic industrial capabilities by associating local companies with international corporations. These joint ventures can sometimes work to an MNC's detriment, because a suitable joint-venture partner may not be available or the one chosen may not perform its share of obligations. Additionally, joint-venture partners may have differing goals, which hinders the success of the combined effort. Moreover, some MNCs are wary of joint ventures with local companies because they fear the leakage of closely held advanced technical knowledge.

Given these possibilities, joint ventures entered into by a multinational company with a host government or other entity should have clear goals, time constraints, and agreement on the limits of information sharing. All partnership eventually end, so the risk is to give up too much crucial information and, in effect, create a new competitor.

PERSONNEL RESTRICTIONS

Some host governments require that local citizens be placed on the board of directors of an MNC's local subsidiary. In many instances conditions of an MNC's entry into a foreign country stipulate that a certain number of top positions be filled by local citizens. Quite often this regulation is implemented by making a reverse condition, such as limiting the number of expatriate employees or managers a company can bring into its operations in the host country. These restrictions are made even more severe by stringent approval procedures for the issue of expatriate visas by home governments, and very often maximum salaries payable to overseas executives are subject to ceilings and higher tax rates.

IMPORT CONTENT

One of the primary concerns of many host governments is that MNCs are a drain on the foreign exchange resources of the country because they generate profits in local currencies and repatriate them in foreign currencies. To ensure that this foreign exchange drain is minimized, many host countries place restrictions on the amount of imports used for manufacturing products locally. The same objective is often achieved by specifying that a certain percentage of local inputs must be used in the MNC's product. Some MNCs that rely largely on imported inputs for the domestic market and, therefore, cannot meet the import content requirements must make up the foreign exchange loss by exporting either a certain percentage or a certain amount of their production. In other words, some sort of balance sheet of the foreign exchange inflows and outflows is drawn up and the size of the export obligation is decided on the basis of projected foreign exchange outflows of an MNC's operations. Such restrictions can pose difficult problems for MNCs whose strategy is to basically produce and sell in the domestic market of the host country and whose products are designed for this purpose.

DISCRIMINATION IN GOVERNMENT BUSINESS

Industrial policies followed by host governments are a major source of risk for MNCs. Discrimination in allocating government business is a major restriction on the scope and potential of MNC business opportunities in countries where the government plays a powerful economic role. Government purchases usually are made from domestic corporations. If such corporations happen to be the competitors of the MNC, then the former gains a major competitive edge through its access to an exclusive market. Moreover, government purchases are generally high in volume and result in substantial profits for companies who get that business.

LABOR CONTROLS

Some countries impose fairly comprehensive labor and social controls on MNCs. The stipulation may require that the labor for the firm will be recruited only through a government agency that screens all potential employees, enabling the government to influence the production of the company by controlling the supply of labor. The compensation paid to employees can be regulated by host governments. Some host governments stipulate that the wage rates of local employees be higher than the rates paid by domestic corporations to workers performing comparable tasks. The host governments also sometimes require additional benefits for local employees, such as health insurance, various allowances, and arbitrary levels of bonuses.

ASSESSING THE RISK

Assessing political risk is a two-stage process. In the first stage an assessment is made of the riskiness of the host country as a place to do business. In the second stage an MNC considers the risks involved in making a particular investment. An investment should be made only if the level of risk at both stages is found to be acceptable.

ASSESSING COUNTRY RISK

Country risk is a very broad measure that focuses on the riskiness of the country as a whole as a place for MNCs to conduct business. One prime consideration is the current and anticipated future level of political stability in the country. A stable country obviously provides a better investment climate. An assessment of political conditions is made by gathering relevant information from several sources: national and international media, diplomatic assessments, and professional agencies that specialize in monitoring developments in certain countries.

Some of these professionals develop their own ratings for the different degrees of risk in various countries with regard to foreign direct investment by MNCs. These ratings are developed by assigning weights to different political, social, and economic factors that could lead to political instability and disorder. These weights are then added and averaged according to a particular formula to arrive at a final rating of a country's level of risk. Because different factors are included and the exercise of assigning risk weights is arbitrary, there is a strong element of subjectivity in this analysis. In general, Western industrialized countries carry low levels of risk for MNCs. Risks seem to increase in inverse proportion to the income of the countries, with the low-income countries posing higher risk. There are, however, important exceptions, because some middle-income countries prone to sociopolitical turmoil carry an even greater risk than some of the lower-income countries.

ASSESSING INVESTMENT RISK

One starting point in assessing the risk attached to making investments is to investigate the attitude and actions of the host government with regard to similar investments made by other MNCs. The existence of local lobbies and the influence they exert on the government is also a useful indicator of investment-specific risk. Powerful local lobbies in a particular industry imply higher risk.

Tax structures, industry standards, government discrimination, ownership and management requirements, repatriation conditions, export obligations, and location constraints should also be considered.

MANAGING RISK

REJECTING INVESTMENT

Many MNCs find that the potential risks in certain countries are too great in comparison to the expected returns. Therefore, they reject the potential investment. Rejection may also occur when the initial negotiation of terms between the host country and the MNC does not result in an agreement. Because the host country is eager to attract overseas investment, the MNC rejection may sometimes prompt the host government to relax some of the conditions.

LONG-TERM AGREEMENTS

Many MNCs find that one way to reduce political risk is to negotiate long-term commitments from the host government on the regulation of the firm. Negotiating these safeguards requires skill and foresight. A balance must be struck between achieving the safest possible terms for the company and recognizing the current national policies of the host government. The limitation of these safeguards, however, is that there is no practical way to enforce them in the event that the host government reneges on its part of the contractual obligations. However, a government is less likely to take any adverse actions if it is bound by a written agreement not to do so, as compared to a situation in which it has not given any such assurances.

LOBBYING

Many MNCs resort to lobbying politicians and officials of host governments to influence the direction of policies and decisions that affect them, because much political risk arises from the potential actions that can be taken by host governments. Direct lobbying is done by establishing a liaison or representative office in the capital city of the host country. The representative of the company establishes direct contacts with local officials and politicians and lobbies them to maintain favorable policies for the MNC. At other times, a local liaison agent is used to lobby local officials, especially in those countries where the domestic political and official structure is complex and not easily understood by outsiders.

Indirect lobbying, or the use of news media or advertising to shape public opinion, is favored by many MNCs in countries where local officials are averse to dealing directly with foreigners. **Direct lobbying** involves the use of influence buying or bribing of officials and politicians who are important players in the shaping of official policy and attitudes of the home government toward MNCs. Although many multinationals do not admit offering such bribes, for obvious reasons, it is a common practice in many countries.

LEGAL ACTION

If threatened, MNCs can resort to legal action, but this approach is useful only in countries that have an efficient legal system and independent judiciary. Recourse to the law would be warranted when an MNC is of the opinion that a new decision or regulation of the host government is illegal under the laws of the country or violates any initial agreements made with the host government. Legal action, however, is a last resort, taken only when there is no other option. Such actions are usually taken only by those companies that have decided to divest their investments in the host countries, because bringing a legal suit against the host government is likely to bring forth retaliation.

HOME-COUNTRY PRESSURE

Many MNCs, when faced with an adverse position taken by the host government, seek the intervention of their home governments, generally through diplomatic channels. The foreign office of the home country generally exerts informal pressure on the government of the host country to alter its attitude toward the MNCs. If the issue is important, this intervention can take place at very high levels, such as heads of state. Apart from the general threat of deterioration of bilateral relations, home governments also occasionally hold out thinly veiled threats of retaliation against the corporations of the host country in the jurisdiction of the home country or threaten to erect trade or other barriers. This channel is effective when relations with the MNC's home country are particularly important to the host country.

JOINT VENTURES AND INCREASED SHAREHOLDING

Many MNCs decide to invest in host countries as joint-venture partners with local corporations; such ventures reduce the political risk. Once a local company is partnered with an MNC, any adverse government decision against the MNC also affects the local partner. A local partner would clearly exert a restraining influence on a government contemplating any such action. Moreover, the local partner, in all likelihood, would have significant contacts in the appropriate quarters of the host government that could be used for intensive lobbying on the MNC's behalf. Moreover, many host governments take a more indulgent approach to the MNC operating as a joint venture because it is perceived as sharing its profits and technical know-how with a local company, thus mitigating the traditional exploitative image of MNCs.

Many companies achieve similar objectives by using a slightly different route. Instead of taking on a local company as a joint-venture partner, they increase the level of local shareholding. In many instances the increase in local shareholding is instituted at the behest of the host government, which imposes the increase as a condition for the MNC's continued operation in its jurisdiction.

Increased local shareholding increases the benefits for the host country in many ways. The amount of profits to be repatriated abroad is immediately reduced when the local shareholders receive their dividends and other revenue in local currency. The foreign exchange liability arising out of share appreciation is also reduced because the basic foreign shareholding is replaced to some extent by domestic shareholding. With a large amount of local shareholding, the policies and operations of the corporation are more open to public and government scrutiny and, therefore, control. The possibility that the MNC can indulge in financial and business transactions detrimental to the country is also reduced.

PROMOTING THE HOST COUNTRY'S GOALS

To gain the host country's acceptance of its operations, an MNC may, as a strategic move, attempt to promote the host country's objectives, for example, by maximizing foreign exchange earnings. MNCs try to contribute to this objective by promoting exports of either their own products or the products of other local manufacturers. The action is strategic in that it is intended to prevent future problems and does not form a part of the normal business operations and objectives of the company. Once export earnings have been generated by the MNC for the host country, it becomes fairly difficult for the host government to justify adverse action, because the drain on foreign exchange resources is removed.

RISK INSURANCE

Many governments have agencies that offer insurance coverage against the political risks faced by MNCs operating in other countries. In the United States, the **Overseas Private Investment Corporation (OPIC)** guarantees risks faced by MNCs in developing countries. OPIC provides coverage against various eventualities that can adversely affect the MNC in a host country, such as expropriation, blocking of repatriation of funds by a host government, and problems created by the breakdown of law and order.

The World Bank, in an effort to promote private investment in developing countries, has an agency that protects corporations that invest in such countries from different forms of political risk. This agency, which began operation in 1988, is the Multilateral Investment Guarantee Agency (MIGA). Risk coverage through MIGA is intended to allay fears of political risk that prevent many MNCs from investing in developing countries, even if the latter are open to overseas investment. This agency is also discussed in Chapter 6.

CONTINGENCY PLANNING

Despite whatever measures a company may adopt and however good its relations with a host government might be, there always remains a definite element of political risk of national-ization, expropriation, or some other unacceptable form of regulatory imposition or control. To guard against such an eventuality, most MNCs have a contingency plan, which may or may not be in the form of a formal document. Some contingency planning is done when the investment is first made in the host country. If a country is considered risky in terms of possible expropriation, companies try to reduce the value of their physical investment and rely more on the supply of expertise and know-how that is paid for on a short-term basis. A country also may be considered dangerous because of technology leakage. In such a situation, the MNC would probably retain the know-how at its headquarters and supply intermediate products to its subsidiary for the final stages of processing or manufacturing.

SUMMARY

Investment in international business requires a cost-benefits analysis of the benefits gained versus the risks encountered by the investing firm. Influencing the decision to expand internationally are the opportunities to tap larger markets, host-country regulations requir-ing local production, achieving economies of scale, competition, implementing quality controls, raw materials sourcing, forward integration to eliminate middlemen, and the acquisition of new types of technologies.

Counterbalancing these factors are the political risks MNCs face from unilateral actions or expropriation by host-country governments. Political risks increase when the MNC and the host country have different economic objectives or conflicting fiscal and industrial policies. Circumstantial political risks may occur when the host government changes and the policies of the preceding government are reversed (in so-called bureaucratic govern-ments) or when the current government facing political difficulties or social unrest must amend its prior policies to the detriment of the MNC.

Host governments may also impose a variety of national controls on MNCs' activities, including limitation on the repatriation of profits and dividends, efforts to curb transfer pricing, implementation of price controls, restrictions on foreign ownership, local staffing and management requirements, import content rules, and labor and social controls.

Assessing political risk involves first assessing the riskiness of the host country as a place to conduct operations and then identifying the level of risk assumed by the MNC for making a particular investment. Political risk cannot be eliminated completely, but management techniques can reduce the level of political risk. Such techniques include not investing in particular countries, establishing long-term agreements with host-country governments, lobbying, legal action if the host country has a well-developed legal system, obtaining political pressure and assistance from the MNC's home-country government, providing for local ownership or joint venturing, promoting host-government objectives, developing contingency plans, and purchasing insurance coverage for political risk.

DISCUSSION QUESTIONS

1. Discuss the various factors that cause multinational firms to invest abroad.
2. What is the role of political risk assessment in shaping an MNC's foreign investment decisions?
3. Is political risk assessment an exact science? Explain.
4. How do host governments try to control the activities of MNCs within their own countries?
5. Which of the following businesses are most and least vulnerable to expropriation?

   - Accounting
   - Agriculture
   - Automobile manufacturing
   - Banks
   - Heavy equipment manufacturing
   - Hotels
   - Mining
   - Restaurants
   - Oil fields
   - Personal electronic goods manufacturing

6. Identify techniques that MNCs use to manage country risk.

NOTE

1. *Economist*, "Business Environment Rankings," 61.

BIBLIOGRAPHY

Austin, James E., and David B. Yoffie. "Political Forecasting as a Management Tool." *Journal of Forecasting* 3 (1984): 395–408.

Blanden, Michael. "Of Tin Hats and Crystal Balls." *Banker*, July 1988, 44, 46.

De La Torre, Jose, and David H. Neckar. "Forecasting Political Risk." In *The Handbook of Forecasting: A Manager's Guide*, ed. Sypors Makridakis and Steven C. Wheelwright. 2nd ed. New York: John Wiley, 1987.

Economist. "Business Environment Rankings." *Pocket World in Figures*. London: Profile Books, 2011.

Encarnation, Dennis J., and Sushil Vachani. "Foreign Ownership: When Hosts Change the Rules." *Harvard Business Review* (September–October 1985): 152–160.

Erol, Cengiz. "An Exploratory Model of Political Risk Assessment and the Decision Process of Foreign Direct Investment." *International Studies of Management and Organization* (Summer 1985): 75–79.

Fatehi-Sedah, Kamal, and M. Hossein Safizadeh. "The Association Between Political Instability and Flow of Foreign Direct Investment." *Management International Review* (Fourth Quarter 1989): 244.

Friedmann, Roberto, and Jonghoon Kim. "Political Risk and International Marketing." *Columbia Journal of World Business* (Winter 1988): 63–74.

Ghadar, Fariborz, and Theodore H. Moran, eds. *International Political Risk Management: New Dimensions.* Washington, DC: Ghadar and Associates, 1984.

Globerman, Steven. "Government Policies Toward Foreign Direct Investment: Has a New Era Dawned?" *Columbia Journal of World Business* (Fall 1988): 41–49.

Goddard, George Jason, and Marcum, Bill. 2012. "A World of Herf: The Importance of Market Concentration in CMBS Risk Assessment." *RMA Journal* (December 2012) pp. 36-42.

Goddard, Scott. "Political Risk in International Capital Budgeting." *Managerial Finance* 16 (1990): 7–12.

Herfindahl, Orris. 1950. *Concentration in the US Steel Industry.* Unpublished doctoral dissertation, Columbia University.

Hirschman, Albert Otto. 1945. *National Power and the Structure of Foreign Trade.* Berkley: University of California Press.

Lichfield, John. "Trans-Atlantic Company Acquisitions Gain Momentum." *Europe*, April 1989, 24–25.

Miller, Van V. "Managing in Volatile Environments." *Baylor Business Review* (Fall 1988): 12–15.

Perlitz, Manfred. "Country-Portfolio Analysis: Assessing Country Risk and Opportunity." *Long Range Planning* (August 1985): 11–26.

Rice, Gillian, and Essam Mahmoud. "A Managerial Procedure for Political Risk Forecasting." *Management International Review* (Fourth Quarter 1986): 12–21.

Schmidt, David A. "Analyzing Political Risk." *Business Horizons* (July–August 1986): 43–50.

Sethi, S. Prakesh, and Kan Luther. "Political Risk Analysis and Direct Foreign Investment: Some Problems of Definition and Measurement." *California Management Review* (Winter 1986): 57–68.

Stanley, Marjorie T. "Ethical Perspectives on the Foreign Direct Investment Decision." *Journal of Business Ethics* (January 1990): 1–10.

Terpstra, Vern, and Kenneth David. *The Cultural Environment of International Business.* 3rd ed. Cincinnati: South-Western, 1991.

GLOBALIZATION AT THE CROSSROADS: MARKET COMPETITION AND THE HHI

The level of competition in a given market is often crucial in determining the strategic actions of multinational firms. One method of estimating the competitiveness of a given industry is known as the Herfindahl-Hirschman Index (HHI), so named after two economists who independently devised the measure. The HHI is an economic measure that is commonly used by the Federal Reserve and the Department of Justice to investigate the level of market competition within an industry. In a market context, it is defined as the sum of squares of the market shares of firms within an industry, where the market shares are expressed as proportions. The measure takes into account the relative size distribution of the firms in a market. An HHI score can range between 0 and 10,000, increasing as the number of firms in a market declines and as disparity in the size between firms rises. A higher score indicates less competition in the market, with a 10,000 representing a pure monopoly. A market is considered to be less concentrated (i.e., highly competitive) when the HHI is less than 1,500, moderately concentrated when it is between 1,500 and 2,500 and highly concentrated (i.e., less competitive) at scores above 2,500. The US Department of Justice and Federal Trade Commission provide general guidelines related to HHI score increases related to merger activity.

Figure 10.1   **Example of HHI Calculations for Three Hypothetical Industries**

MNC	Industry One		Industry Two		Industry Three	
	Rev. $ Bill	Share %	Rev. $ Bill	Share %	Rev. $ Bill	Share %
Firm 1	250	10.00	850	68.00	500	100.00
Firm 2	250	10.00	125	10.00	0	-
Firm 3	250	10.00	75	6.00	0	-
Firm 4	250	10.00	50	4.00	0	-
Firm 5	250	10.00	25	2.00	0	-
Firm 6	250	10.00	25	2.00	0	-
Firm 7	250	10.00	25	2.00	0	-
Firm 8	250	10.00	25	2.00	0	-
Firm 9	250	10.00	25	2.00	0	-
Firm 10	250	10.00	25	2.00	0	-
Totals	**2,500**	**100.00**	**1,250**	**100.00**	**500**	**100.00**
HHI		**1,000**		**4,800**		**10,000**

If some of the market participants are unknown, it is often reasonable to assume that the remaining, unidentified portion of the market is divided among numerous firms. Typically, the highest market share assigned to the unknown players is assumed to be less than any of those with an identified share. For example, if the identified market represents 80 percent of the total, and the smallest share held by any one business is 5 percent, an analyst could assume that the remaining 20 percent of the market is divided among twenty firms (i.e., 1 percent each), or five firms (i.e., 4 percent each) or some similar multiple. Regardless, the assumption usually will have little impact on the final HHI score.

Figure 10.1 provides an example of the HHI calculation for three hypothetical industries of varying concentration. The HHI scores can display a wide range of values depending on the level of market competitiveness in a given industry.

QUESTIONS FOR DISCUSSION

1. Explain how the estimation of the HHI would aid a multinational firm's strategic decisions.
2. Develop an HHI for an industry of your choice and interpret the results.
3. The Herfindahl Index and the Lerner Index are close cousins of HHI. Research these two indexes and discuss their importance in assessing risk in today's global economy.
4. What other measures are available to the multinational firm to assess market competitiveness?

CASE STUDY 10.1

AMALGAMATED POLYMERS INC.

It is Friday afternoon, and James Hyman, an executive with Amalgamated Polymers Inc., is reviewing the briefing papers for next Monday's investment committee meeting. After all the hectic preparation and redrafting during the week that at times had threatened to spill over into Saturday, Hyman is growing increasingly tense. The briefs contain a proposal for Amalgamated Polymers to take an equity stake in Gulf Plastics, a medium-sized company producing a wide variety of plastics in Mazirban, a small but wealthy Arab country in the Persian Gulf. The proposal had been prepared by Hyman after almost six months of preliminary groundwork, and on Monday the members of the investment committee, which comprises the entire senior management of the company, will take their first look at it.

There are a number of reasons the proposal makes sense. Hyman's company, Amalgamated Polymers Inc., is a leader in the production of plastics and similar petrochemical by-products. It is based in Edinburgh, Scotland, and has plants in Great Britain, the Netherlands, and Turkey. The company has its own in-house R&D facility, which has helped Amalgamated become one of the important forces in plastics technology during the past fifteen years. Its patented product, Amalite, is in great demand by household goods manufacturers for making such kitchen items as storage jars and plastic cutlery. Much of the company's sales of Amalite are con-centrated in Europe and North America, but competition in these markets is growing, and there is a need to expand sales in other areas. While Amalgamated Polymers has considerable international marketing skills and sales contacts, it is essentially handicapped by a limited production capacity. To export to other markets, especially in developing countries, would require an expansion of production capacity in the existing plants or establishment of new plants. Expanding capacity in the existing plants would be difficult and expensive. The Netherlands and Edinburgh plants face severe environmental constraints and have come under pressure from local authori-ties, and particularly from environmental groups, because of their pollution-creating effects. The company has been forced to install very expensive equipment to reduce the harmful content of the emissions from its plants. Expanding capacity would no doubt give rise to pressures from local governments and other groups to install even stricter emissions-control equipment. Further, given the high labor and production costs in Edinburgh and the Netherlands, it does not make sense for the company to increase production at these plants in order to make sales in new markets, where prices have to be extremely competitive. Similar problems confront the company in connection with opening new plants in Edinburgh and the Netherlands. High costs, environmental concerns, and high wages rule out a move to invest in new plants. Further, the company is already highly leveraged and does not want to take on additional debt to finance new operations. There is an additional problem in Turkey. Ten years ago the company had received a license to establish and open one plant under a liberal foreign investment policy adopted by the government then in power, but another government has recently taken over and reversed that policy, and the chances of getting a license for a second plant are almost zero.

The difficulties of expanding operations at its existing facilities prompted Amalgamated Polymers to look for other options. One option is to establish a new plant in a low-cost location that is closer to potential markets. Several countries have offered themselves as potential sites for this option. The company has actively considered opening a new plant in a developing country because some of the constraints it faces in the developed countries are not present. The issue of overleveraging the firm, however, by taking on excessive debt to finance an entirely new operation continues to dog this option. Further, setting up a new plant in a developing country would require a time lag that is incompatible with the company's need to penetrate quickly into new markets and take advantage of its technological edge in certain areas. The issue of timing is particularly important because competitive companies also have major technological research plans and could catch up very soon, eliminating the advantage enjoyed by Amalgamated.

These considerations led to the idea of taking an equity participation in an ongoing company in a middle-income or low-income country. The strategy is to infuse new technical and management capability into the company to make it internationally competitive. Once this goal is achieved, its products could be exported to other, new markets.

Mazirban offers an ideal opportunity to implement the joint-venture approach. The country is a large producer and exporter of crude oil and natural gas, which are its main sources of revenue, but, like many other states in the Persian Gulf, the government is eager to diversify the economy and invest the surplus oil revenues in new industries employing high technology. Petrochemicals are a natural choice, because the raw materials, crude oil and natural gas, are plentiful and available at minimal cost. With the collaboration of major multinational firms, the government has established several petrochemical and oil-refining complexes. To attract additional foreign investments, it has established a liberal investment policy that places virtually no constraints on overseas parties to joint ventures in Mazirban. The only important conditions are that any overseas venture in Mazirban has to be established jointly with a local party and that the terms of this venture have to be approved by the government.

(continued)

Case Study 8.1 (*continued*)

Amalgamated Polymers found a potentially ideal partner in Gulf Plastics Ltd., a major plastics company owned by members of the ruling family and based in Ochran, the main port of Mazirban. Gulf Plastics was established in 2003 and for the past nine years has concentrated on the manufacture of basic plastic products, which it markets primarily within the country. Gulf Plastics was established with the help of a Japanese petrochemical company that also helped to run the company for the first five years. A few Japanese technicians still hold key positions in the manufacturing operations division of the company. Gulf Plastics has been looking for a technical and management partner to upgrade its technology and help it move overseas.

Gulf Plastics and Amalgamated Polymers, which have compatible interests and strategies, appear to be ideal partners. The terms of the collaboration would not present a problem; they are fairly standard in the petrochemical industry, and the details can be taken care of easily. For Amalgamated, the option of a joint venture with an ongoing company in plastics manufacturing seems to address all the fundamental concerns, at least in principle. To acquire an equity stake significant enough for the company to be able to influence the management of the joint venture, Amalgamated would not be pressed too hard financially. Further, since it would supply technology and management know-how, its contribution could be capitalized to offset a significant part of the total equity contribution it would make under the proposed joint venture. Because Gulf Plastics already has the basic infrastructure set up and would be sharing other costs, the total costs of capacity expansion would not be too high. There also would be no difficulty in directing some of Gulf's existing production capacity to the targeted markets, because the government of Mazirban is keen to earn foreign exchange. The costs would be further reduced because it would not be necessary, at least in the initial stages, to expand production capacity by too much.

Despite all these positives, there are a number of questions that Hyman thinks the executive committee will raise on Monday. He will have to spend the weekend in virtual self-isolation to think of what questions are likely to be raised and what responses he should have ready to justify this investment. After all, it is very important to him. If the project is approved, he will be placed in charge of his company's side of the venture, and eventually it would mean a senior position at the plant in Mazirban, boosting his career prospects. On the other hand, if the proposal is rejected by the committee, six months of work would be wasted, and he will face the additional embarrassment of giving the news to the Mazirban government and to Gulf Plastics, who are not likely to hide their feelings.

DISCUSSION QUESTION

1. Prepare a list of possible questions that the investment committee might raise about the proposal. What should James Hyman's responses be?

CHAPTER 11

Ethical Concerns: Multinationals and Sustainability

"You're living all over me."
—J. Mascis

CHAPTER OBJECTIVES

This chapter will:

- Review the major environmental concerns affecting the global community and the implications they have for multinational corporations at home and abroad
- Identify new challenges and opportunities that MNCs face as a result of growing environmental concerns

---

EMERGING ENVIRONMENTAL CONCERNS

National and international concerns about the environment have increased dramatically over the past decade. Although damage to the earth's environment has been an issue in development and industrial policies in many countries for the past several years, it has not been in the forefront of international attention; other issues, such as economic growth, industrialization, population growth, and poverty, have occupied center stage.

Concern for the environment has grown for several reasons. First, damage to the environment is becoming increasingly visible. A number of environmental and ecological disasters, including several involving large MNCs, have attracted worldwide attention. Second, environmental action groups have become more powerful. The ability of these groups to influence public policy has increased substantially following sustained support, both political and financial, from different sections of society that are more concerned with the environment than ever before. Third, a number of international bodies, such as the United Nations and the World Bank, and national governments have demonstrated their responsiveness to the issue by establishing environmental guidelines and, in the case of governments, by passing laws aimed at protecting the environment.

Concerns for the environment have wide-ranging implications for MNCs in both their home and host countries because not only are MNCs affected by general environmental guidelines but they are viewed as one of the prime sources of danger to the world's environment. This view is valid to a significant extent, given the fact that MNCs influence about 25 percent of the world's assets by their actions and affect, in one way or another, about 70 percent of internationally traded products and 80 percent of the world's land devoted to the cultivation of export-oriented crops. In many developing countries, MNCs are the prime source of industrial activity. Even where their share in total industrial activity is not large, they are the most visible and therefore the first focus of attention for environmentalist and similar groups.

These developments present both challenges and opportunities for MNCs. The challenges arise in the form of new considerations that MNCs must bear in mind while making investment and operating decisions and the additional costs they must incur to ensure that their operations are environmentally safe and comply with host-country regulations. In some instances, MNCs may be required to close or completely modify the production of certain plants for environmental reasons. Along with these challenges are new opportunities. Concern for the preservation of the environment calls for new types of products and new lines of business and, consequently, creates new markets. A final feature of environmentalism is sustainability. Sustainability concerns maintaining a level of production or harvesting that provides a reasonable supply for current consumption, but not so much today that tomorrow's supply will be in question.

SOCIAL RESPONSIBILITY OF BUSINESS

Economists have long debated what constitutes the social responsibility of business. Some believe that the primary purpose of any business is the maximization of corporate profits. Others believe that a business has an inherent responsibility to, for example, maintain an acceptable work environment for its employees, provide a living wage, provide adequate health benefits to its employees, and reduce the amount of pollutants that stem from the manufacturing of its products. Countries experiencing rapid industrialization, such as India and China, often experience deterioration in water- and air-quality levels as a by-product of the increase in the burning of fossil fuels such as coal, petroleum, and natural gas.

There are countless examples of corporations' ill effects on the environment, and there are almost as many responses to such problems. Some countries, such as those in the

European Union, believe in taking unilateral action to reduce their levels of pollution, while other countries, such as the United States and Australia, have expressed the desire to include the rapidly industrializing countries in any agreement regarding pollution control. While economists still debate whether a business has the moral responsibility to protect the environment, it seems that many nations of the world have already assigned this task to manufacturers the world over. Supranational organizations such as the WTO and NGOs such as Greenpeace have also entered the fray regarding environmental addendums to trade agreements and support of environmentally friendly causes.

Major Environmental Issues

Greenhouse Gases

Greenhouse gases contribute to global warming by trapping heat in the earth's atmosphere. It is predicted that if such gases continue to accumulate at the present rate, they will lead to an increase in global temperatures by 2°C to 3°C relative to preindustrial times. A 3° increase would melt the ice caps of Greenland, which would have a disastrous impact on the world's ecological systems, raising sea levels by as much as 20 feet (6 meters) and flooding low-lying coastal areas, many of which are industrial and urban centers with a high population concentration. To put things in historical perspective, the average global temperature in 1800 was 13.52°C (56.24°F), while today it is 14.48°C (58.06°F). Other worst-case scenarios predict temperature rises by 2°C by 2035, when the ice caps would start to melt. Some experts forecast a rise in average global temperatures to 16.5°C (61.7°F) by 2050 or even a rise to 18.6°C (65.5°F) by 2100.

The gases that contribute most to global warming and the **greenhouse effect** include carbon dioxide, methane, and nitrous oxide, with the first two accounting for about 75 percent of the warming effects. Presently, we are experiencing the highest level of carbon dioxide in the atmosphere in the last 800,000 years. A major source of carbon dioxide accumulation in the atmosphere is industrial combustion of fossil fuels. MNCs are major users of fossil fuels in a number of ways. They extract, refine, and transport much of the world's supply of fossil fuel and are significant consumers of such fuels, both as an intermediate and final source of energy. Table 11.1 illustrates the main economic activities that contribute to global warming. The production of greenhouse gases as a direct or indirect result of transnational corporations' operations is shown in Table 11.2.

Depletion of the Ozone Layer

The earth's environment is protected by a layer of ozone gas in the stratosphere that shields the earth's surface from potentially deadly ultraviolet radiation. In recent years the ozone layer has been seriously damaged by human-made chemicals, especially chlorofluorocarbons (CFCs). CFCs are used to lower temperatures in refrigerators and air conditioners and are utilized in making aerosol and foam propellants. Some CFCs also contribute to

Table 11.1 **Economic Activities and Global Warming**

Activity	Contribution to global warming (in percent)
Energy use and production of which	57
Industrial	22
Transportation	20
Residential/commercial	15
Use of chlorofluorocarbons	17
Agricultural practices	14
Deforestation and other modifications	9
Other industrial	3
Total	**100**

Source: US Environmental Protection Agency.

Table 11.2 **Greenhouse Gas Production**

Gas	Amount of gas generated by transnational corporations (approximate percentage of total amount generated)	Significant sources of greenhouse gases
CO_2	50	Emissions from automobiles 75 percent of oil and gas and 50 percent of coal use in OECD countries 50 percent of fossil fuel use in developing countries
Methane	10–20	50 percent from oil and gas production and use 50 percent from coal mine emissions
Chlorofluorocarbons	66	Use of aerosol sprays, car air conditioners, solvents, and refrigerators in OECD countries
Other (such as nitrogen oxides and ozone)	50	Emissions from automobiles 75 percent of oil and gas use in OECD countries 50 percent of coal use in OECD countries 50 percent of fossil fuel use in developing countries

Source: United Nations Economic and Social Council, Commission of Transnational Corporations.
Note: A designation of transnational corporation involvement is not meant to exclude involvement by others in the emissions of greenhouse gases, for instance, in their use of cars or other consumer goods. The estimates are designed to indicate an order of magnitude of emissions, which could be affected by measures taken by transnational corporations, whether self-initiated or government mandated.

global warming, and these and similar chemicals are projected to account for 10 to 15 percent of global warming between now and the middle of the twenty-first century. The depletion of stratospheric ozone leads to the accumulation of tropospheric ozone, which is a contributor to global warming through the greenhouse effect.

MNCs have been found responsible for a large proportion of this damage, because they were the main producers of products using and producing CFCs and other chemicals that damage the ozone layer. In fact, all major manufacturers of CFCs were multinational corporations, and the focus of world attention has been quite sharp on this aspect of their activity. In 1987, the Montreal Protocol banned the future production of CFCs. Much of the effect has already been experienced, however. Thus, the level of CFCs already released into the atmosphere will account for one-ninth of global warming over the next 100 years.

DEFORESTATION

The disappearance of the world's forests has had and is likely to continue to have extremely dangerous ecological consequences. The scale of the problem has already assumed alarming proportions. According to one source, every year 129,000 square kilometers (50,000 square miles) of forest is destroyed, while only 56,000 square kilometers (22,000 square meters) is replenished. This results in a net loss of between 73,000 square kilometers (28,000 square miles) and 84,000 square kilometers (32,000 square miles) each year, depending on the source of the estimates. The higher of these two net loss figures, 84,000 square kilometers (32,000 square miles), equates to an area approximately the size of Ireland.

Deforestation has a number of adverse global environmental effects. The loss of forest cover on mountains and hillsides decreases the soil retention capacity, which leads to rainwater washing valuable topsoil into rivers, reducing their depth and making them prone to flooding. The lack of forest cover reduces an area's potential rainfall and limits the supply of oxygen, which means that carbon dioxide increases proportionately and adds to global warming.

MNCs have been viewed as responsible for deforestation in many countries for a variety of reasons. Many MNCs are large producers and transporters of timber and timber products. Others have been associated with large industrial and civil construction projects that have been established on former forestlands. If deforestation ended entirely, manmade emissions of carbon dioxide would fall by seventy gigatons by 2050.

FISHING STOCKS

An additional environmental issue concerns the sustainability of the world supply of fishing stocks. In recent decades, the world's supply of various fishing stocks has deteriorated rapidly. Some species, such as the blue fin tuna, have seen stocks drop by 70 percent over the last fifty years. Reasons for overfishing are numerous, with blame spread among various governments, private fishermen, multinational corporations, and stock regulation agencies. Additionally, with the health benefits of fish consumption well-known, and with the rise in popularity of tuna and sashimi consumption, typical market mechanisms such as increased prices have not stemmed the rise in demand. Consumers appear willing to pay sometimes exorbitant prices in order to maintain current consumption levels of fish. Quotas set by international fish regulation agencies have continually been breached by

Table 11.3 **Industries Producing Hazardous Wastes**

Key manufacturing industries for industrializing nations	Hazardous wastes produced
Metal finishing, electroplating, etc.	Heavy metals, fluorides, cyanides, acid and alkaline cleaners, abrasives, plating salts, oils, phenols
Leather tanning	Heavy metals, organic solvents
Textiles	Heavy metals, toxic organic dyes, organic chlorine compounds, salts, acids, caustics
Pesticides	Organic chlorine compounds, organic phosphate compounds, heavy metals
Pharmaceuticals	Organic solvents and residues, heavy metals (especially mercury)
Plastics	Organic solvents and residues, organic pigments, heavy metals (especially lead and zinc)

Source: Leonard, "Hazardous Waste: The Crisis Spreads," 44.

illegal, unreported, or underreported fishing activities. The inability to achieve scientifically based quotas for fishing specific types of fish threatens the availability of these species for consumption in the future.

HAZARDOUS WASTE

The production, handling, transport, and disposal of hazardous industrial waste have become of serious concern in many countries, given the risks they carry both for the quality of the local environment and for general public health. According to the US Environmental Protection Agency, "Uncontrolled hazardous [waste] sites may present some of the most serious environmental and human health problems the nation has ever faced."[1] Concerns about hazardous industrial waste are now worldwide, the problem being equally serious in many less-developed countries, where regulations relating to the disposal and treatment of hazardous waste are not as well established. Hazardous wastes are generated by a wide variety of industries, in both developed and developing countries. Table 11.3 illustrates some of the key industries in industrializing nations that produce hazardous wastes.

Several ecological accidents and disasters involving hazardous industrial wastes have shown how serious this threat is becoming. For example, thirteen children died in 1981 from mercury poisoning in Indonesia after eating fish caught in a tributary of Jakarta Bay. Mercury levels in the water, polluted by chemical and heavy-metal wastes from nearby factories, were found to be more than sixty times those deemed safe by international standards. Similarly, a company in Mexico was forced to close after it was discovered to have been pumping highly toxic chromium wastes directly into the aquifer in the Mexico Valley area, threatening the water supply of nearly 20 million people. A critical issue in hazardous waste disposal is the transport of the waste. Companies in countries with heavily regulated hazardous waste disposal methods attempt to circumvent the regulations by transporting the wastes to other developing countries with little or no regulations.

Table 11.4   **Carbon Dioxide Emissions** (millions of tons annually)

1	China	6,099.1
2	United States	5,748.1
3	Russia	1,563.5
4	India	1,509.3
5	Japan	1,292.5
6	Germany	804.5
7	United Kingdom	568.1
8	Canada	544.3
9	South Korea	474.9
10	Italy	473.8

Source: Economist, Pocket World in Figures, 2011.

MNCs have been accused of not paying enough attention to the problems of hazardous waste in host countries that do not have well-developed environmental control regulatory frameworks. This issue has been brought into the spotlight by several ecological problems and disasters in developing countries that have occurred because of MNC laxity in observing environmentally safe procedures for the disposal and treatment of hazardous wastes generated by their overseas plants. Perhaps the most tragic environmental disaster was the leak of lethal methyl isocyanate gas from Union Carbide's pesticide plant in Bhopal, India, in 1984, which caused more than 2,500 deaths and serious impairment to several thousand more people.

Pollution

The problems of industrial pollution became increasingly serious in the late 1980s as industrialization expanded and intensified. Air pollution is caused primarily by emissions from factory chimneys, while water pollution is caused primarily by the discharge of industrial effluents into local bodies of water. In many countries the air has been so polluted at industrial centers that the local residents have increased incidence of respiratory and other diseases. In other countries, water pollution has ended the use of local rivers, lakes, and bays. Table 11.4 provides an estimate of the countries that emit the highest levels of carbon dioxide each year.

Kyoto Protocol

In an attempt to curb the collective emissions of greenhouse gases in order to achieve cleaner air worldwide, a multination agreement called the **Kyoto Protocol** was adopted in the third session of the Conference of Parties to the United Nations Framework Convention on Climate Change, in Kyoto, Japan, in 1997. The agreement required that fifty-five countries, which must represent at least 55 percent of the industrial world's greenhouse-gas emissions in 1990, must ratify the agreement for it to take effect. The goal of the Kyoto Protocol is to reduce the collective emissions of greenhouse gases by 5.2 percent from 1990 levels, while the European Union has agreed to reduce its carbon dioxide emissions by 20 percent relative to 1990 levels and to raise renewable energy to 20 percent of total energy consumption by 2020.

The European Union has been a strong proponent of the Kyoto Protocol, and the agreement has also been ratified by Japan and Canada, among other nations. The United States has not ratified the agreement, and India and China are not subject to reduced emission targets. Canada withdrew from the Kyoto Protocol in 2011, while Japan and Russia could not promise participation in further reduction targets.

Some experts have said that the Kyoto Protocol is doomed to failure, as non-Kyoto countries account for 70 percent of global carbon dioxide emissions. Some observers have also identified a **green paradox**: announced green policies by governments tend to increase global warming as more fossil fuels are brought to market before any intended sustainable alternatives materialize. The majority of government environmental policies focus on reducing demand, while the supply is left alone. Thus, reduced consumption of fossil fuels in Kyoto-participating nations is replaced with increased consumption elsewhere. A new Kyoto Agreement is planned by 2015, but if these major omissions are not corrected, future success is not assured.

MNC Responses

Multinational corporations, for valid reasons, have been held responsible for their contribution to the increased environmental problems the world faces today and are called on to adjust virtually every aspect of their activities.

Establishing In-House Environmental Ethics

MNCs' approach to battling environmental pollution and ecological degradation is dependent to a large degree on the corporation's ethical code. The corporation's response to these problems depends on what it perceives to be its responsibility. MNCs have tremendous political leverage, particularly in small LDCs, which need their technology, industrialization, and economic growth. Environmental laws are less developed in LDCs, while public awareness of environmental issues there is limited, and there are few channels for the effective and voluble expression of public opinion. The ruling powers in LDCs generally tend to have almost universal authority, and their decisions are difficult to challenge, which allows MNCs to establish environmentally unsound projects, should they decide to do so, as long as they have the confidence of the local authorities. Many prior studies have shown that MNCs tend to locate their more polluting plants in developing countries to escape the strict environmental standards and regulations imposed by developed countries. The inclusion of environmental initiatives in trade agreements could help to reduce the imbalance of enforcement of environmental improvement between the developed and developing worlds. Some developing countries have argued that developed countries have more historical and current culpability for environmental contamination then do the less-developed countries.

It is extremely important for MNCs to take a responsible approach to environmental issues. Many corporations have adopted such an approach, voluntarily restricting their environmentally unsound operations and even stopping production of environmentally unsafe products. Many others have not.

RELOCATION OF PRODUCTION

In the past, MNCs' location decisions were principally dependent on technical and economic criteria: raw material supply, infrastructural facilities, availability of a trained workforce, proximity to markets, availability of transportation, and so on. Now decisions to establish plants must evaluate potential effects on the environment. Not only must the economic consequences (such as feasibility and rate of return) be forecast, but plans must be made to protect the local environment. Thus, while permission from a government was sufficient in the past to establish a factory in a host country, MNCs are now likely to be required to discuss their site plans with local representatives and allay their concerns about a plant's actual and potential impact on the local environment and ecological balance.

MODIFICATION OF TECHNOLOGY

Traditionally, the main motivator of technological change was a search for more advanced and economically efficient technologies that would generate new and better products at lower costs. Recently, however, technology development has also focused on environmental safety. Technologies in development must be monitored in regard to their environmental consequences. So-called green technology applies to generating energy, creating nontoxic cleaning products, fostering sustainable development, and so on.

USE OF RAW MATERIALS

Raw material use is an important focus of technological modification. The raw materials currently in use may not be available in the future, principally for two reasons: they may be nonrenewable, as are fossil fuels, and their use may result in consequences that are harmful to the earth's environment. According to the **Hotelling rule**, the price of an extracted resource rises at a rate equal to the capital market interest rate. Thus, the smaller the remaining underground stock, the higher are the unit extraction costs. Unfortunately, if the expected profit is higher than the unit extraction cost, continued extraction is likely, in the absence of supply-based controls. As concerns with the environment grow, MNCs are called on to consider not only the monetary price of raw materials but their ecological consequences as well. Limitations imposed by these considerations exert pressure on MNCs to use technologies that reduce industrial waste, maximize consumption efficiency of raw materials, promote recycling of waste and used products, and concentrate on more durable and lasting products.

USE OF ENERGY

Energy use is another important area of concern in the general technological modifications that MNCs will have to continue to undertake as part of their response to environmental imperatives. Typical approaches in this area include gradual phasing out of energy-inefficient technologies and introduction of technologies based on clean, renewable, and environmentally safe sources of energy (e.g., solar power and hydrogen), as opposed to those based on polluting, nonrenewable sources, generally limited to fossil fuels. The problem has been complicated by nuclear accidents at Three Mile Island in the United States and Chernobyl in Ukraine, which have placed a major question mark over the future of nuclear energy as an alternative to conventional fossil fuels. The small nation of Iceland has been successful in the use of hydrogen power. Approximately 70 percent of Iceland's energy needs are met by geothermal and hydroelectric power. Iceland has a vast pool of geothermal energy beneath its surface, which allowed for the successful experimentation over the years with alternative sources of energy. All of Iceland's homes are heated via these clean energy sources, and only its transportation industry still requires oil and gas. In 2003, Shell opened a hydrogen station in the country, and buses that run on hydrogen power were also introduced. This early market entry was followed by demonstration hydrogen stations throughout the world in recent years.

Energy sources are likely to grow more expensive and scarce, while patterns of energy use are likely to be under increasing scrutiny from different quarters, including environmental groups and the media. MNCs must ensure that they use energy sources in an environmentally sound manner, which will require substantial investments in new or modified equipment, such as energy-efficient industrial furnaces, boilers, and exhausts, and new equipment to control atmospheric emissions, such as air filters and gas treatment chambers. Energy use will have to be modified not only in production, but also in all other facets of activity, including transportation.

ENVIRONMENTAL RESTORATION

The response to the environmental challenge cannot be limited to in-company modifications in production, technologies, energy, product mix, or location decisions. It must extend beyond the corporation, because the environmental impact of the operations of industrial concerns affects the local community and, in an aggregate sense, its home or host country. Company responses must be designed to compensate for aspects of environmental regeneration that are most directly and visibly linked to the areas of the corporation activities. For example, companies that use substantial quantities of wood would be called on to support local and national reforestation and social forestry programs. Companies that have had a role in adding to atmospheric pollution would have to support programs that attempt to remedy the consequences of such pollution, such as the cleanup of lakes and other fresh-water bodies damaged by acid rain, or international agreements such as the Kyoto Protocol. As discussed earlier, firms responsible for overfishing should have the responsibility of adhering to scientifically based quota limitations. More generally, it is becoming a growing responsibility of corporations to foster environmentally responsible behavior both among their employees and in the communities in which they are located.

POLLUTION DISCLOSURE

Environmental disclosure will be an important responsibility of MNCs in the future. MNCs will have to remain aware of and appropriately informed about the environmental impact of their activities through an efficient internal information system. These data would have to be shared with the outside world, both voluntarily and through mandatory reporting requirements and environmental audits. A touchy issue will be environmental compliance by an MNC's joint-venture partners or partly owned subsidiaries in host countries. While an MNC may prescribe a certain environmental standard for itself and wish to have it replicated by its joint-venture partners or overseas subsidiaries, that wish may not be reciprocal. Similarly, overseas partners may impose more stringent environmental constraints that an MNC may not wish to be bound by. The issue of environmental safety has become important in many negotiations for international joint ventures, and environmental responsibilities are often incorporated as fundamental provisions in the terms of agreement. MNCs have become particularly sensitive to this issue because of the dangers of environmentally unsound acts that their joint-venture partners might commit, for which they might have to take the blame in both their home and host countries, and which could damage their reputation for environmental responsibility in other countries.

It is extremely important that MNCs disseminate information on their own about the consequences, both favorable and unfavorable, of their operations on the environment. Proper disclosure of such information will be extremely important in maintaining the environmental image of a corporation and facilitating a feeling of confidence among different groups—local governments, creditors, consumers, suppliers, investors—in the firm's environmental soundness. Proper disclosure of the environmental status of a firm's activities also has an important damage-control role, inasmuch as it informs the public about possible dangers. Any harmful consequences for the environment emanating from MNC activity would be much more damaging to a firm if it became known that the MNC had chosen to suppress prior information it had about such a possibility.

IN-HOUSE ENVIRONMENTAL TRAINING

As a part of overall corporate planning, the environmental consequences of all future company activities should be assessed well in advance. A serious commitment to this type of oversight will enhance the corporate image.

One way of demonstrating this commitment is to include the corporation's environmental approach in its mission statement and corporate objectives. Any business plan intended for external audiences should include company-defined environmental goals, as well as specific plans for implementation. Planning for environmental safety must be comprehensive, covering future investments in plants and other physical facilities, use of natural resources, treatment of industrial wastes, prevention of environmental damage, protection of water resources, and prevention of accidents.

No plan can be successfully implemented if the operating-level staff is not actively educated. This is all the more true of plans for environmental soundness and safety because operating-level staff are likely to view the plans as peripheral to their central functions, not because of their antipathy to the environment, but simply because of their perception of its relative importance in the context of their work. MNCs must therefore engender a sense of commitment to environmental safety and responsibility among management and staff to elicit optimal cooperation in the achievement of the company's environmental objectives.

Personnel must also be informed about the nature of the environmental problems that confront the world, in general, and the environmental consequences of their activities as company workers, in particular. One way to give meaning to this exercise is to spell out ways in which employees could contribute to overall environmental safety in their own tasks. To ensure that these guidelines are taken seriously, firms must establish an incentive structure that encourages employees to monitor environmental standards and provide practical suggestions on how the company's environmental performance could be improved. A reward structure could also be established for groups or units, whereby the group could be rewarded on the basis of the environmental safety or standards it is able to maintain over a given period of time. It is essential to involve employees, at both management and staff levels, if any environmental safety program is to be successful.

MNC OPPORTUNITIES

While the environmental challenges facing MNCs are daunting, a number of opportunities have also arisen. Many MNCs have been quick to anticipate the trends in the world's regulatory, economic, political, and social environments and have been positioned to derive the maximum advantage from them.

NEW CONSUMER PRODUCTS

As the world grows more environmentally conscious, there is an increasing need for environmentally safe products. This demand points to the opening of new markets, first in developed and later in developing countries. Environmentally safe products have already made their appearance in many countries and embrace a wide range, from personal goods to consumer durables. Whole Foods Market is an upper-end grocery store that specializes in selling natural and organically grown food products. The company, which started in Austin, Texas, in 1980, now has more than 300 store locations throughout the United States, Canada, and the United Kingdom, and it proudly displays on its website that it has been ranked in the Fortune 100 Best Companies to Work For since 1998. Besides selling products free of preservatives, additives, and colorings, Whole Foods Market has also gone to great lengths to reduce the amount of energy consumption in its store locations, to promote recycling of paper, glass, and plastic, and to collect reusable items, such as batteries, light bulbs, and computer equipment, for recycling. As mentioned on the company's website, numerous store locations have utilized solar power for almost one-quarter of the store's energy needs.

NEW TECHNOLOGIES

Firms specializing in technology development are already receiving large orders for new, environmentally safe technologies in a wide range of industries. Environmental-control technologies are in particular demand. Cleaner and more efficient furnaces and technologies that treat toxic emissions and effluents are all in greater demand. Since 2000, automobile manufacturers have been selling hybrid automobiles, which run on a combination of gasoline and a rechargeable battery, a trend likely to continue given these vehicles' fuel efficiency. Lest we forget the green paradox, announced governmental policies promoting alternative sources of energy (often via new technologies) lead to increased consumption of current sources (and technologies) in the present.

NEW INDUSTRIAL PRODUCTS

Today's plants require a large number of mechanical modifications to meet environmental standards. Water-treatment plants, emission-control filters, waste-management systems, and the like represent new markets and opportunities that are going to expand across the world.

SUBSTITUTE PRODUCTS

A number of products that are in wide use but considered dangerous to the environment are likely to be phased out and replaced. Certain types of plastic products that were found to be resistant to biodegradation, for example, have been replaced with other polyurethane foam products, which either are biodegradable or can be recycled. In the words of comedian George Carlin, the plastic that mankind has created may be our true purpose on this planet, as without man there would be no plastics deposited in the ground.

NEW ENERGY SOURCES

A number of companies are intensively researching the development of new sources of energy for the future as well as new devices and products that run on such sources of energy. One of the most important of these new energy sources is solar power, which is clean, environmentally safe, and virtually unlimited. Working models of solar-powered automobiles have been developed and other solar-powered products have been in use for several years. As mentioned above, environmentally conscious companies such as Whole Foods Market use solar power in their stores in an attempt to save money while utilizing a clean source of energy. Additionally, oil giant Shell has embraced the concept of the hydrogen fuel cell enough to open a hydrogen station in Iceland.

ENVIRONMENTAL CONSULTING

Corporations specializing in environmental technology, design, and management and similar areas are already flooded with contracts and offers to develop environmental safety programs in several different countries. This area is likely to grow rapidly as industrial concerns, local and national governments, and communities attempt to upgrade the environmental quality of industries, neighborhoods, and other aspects of everyday activities. The growing support from the developed countries for such concerns has enabled the collection of substantial funds from various charitable and other foundations to be used to finance such services across a broad spectrum of countries.

THE ENVIRONMENT AT CENTER STAGE

The environmental issue has clearly moved from the periphery of MNC concerns to center stage. The environment now has to be factored into almost every decision, and top management can no longer simply delegate the responsibilities in this area. It is an issue for the headquarters of every MNC to consider when planning global and local strategies, whatever the internal organization structure of the business. MNCs that take an enlightened approach to this issue are quick to capitalize on opportunities while managing risks effectively and are likely to end up the winners. Unlike other forms of corporate activity, however, it is not enough if one corporation wins and another loses. Everyone must win if Earth's fragile and currently endangered environment is to be nurtured and sustained.

SUMMARY

Environmental concerns over greenhouse gases, depletion of the ozone layer, deforestation, overfishing, hazardous wastes, and industrial air pollution have moved to the forefront of international concern and attention. Because of the significant control and influence that MNCs have over world resources, they are being challenged to operate in more environmentally responsible ways. These challenges include conducting business ethically, conducting environmental impact studies before making plant location decisions, implementing technological modifications to reduce waste and increase environmental safety, developing environmentally safe energy sources, accepting social responsibilities for environmental regeneration, diversifying manufacturing, planning, educating, sharing information, and increasing investment in R&D. Environmental issues concern multinationals, national governments, NGOs, and supranational organizations. These varying interests often oppose each other, delaying improvement and increasing the tension concerning environmental matters.

New opportunities, however, are being created as new products and markets designed to meet environmental concerns become available.

DISCUSSION QUESTIONS

1. Why should MNCs be concerned with global environmental issues?
2. What are greenhouse gases?
3. What has been causing the depletion of the ozone layer? What role have MNCs played in this process?
4. What are hazardous wastes? Find some recent examples (from the *Wall Street Journal* or other periodicals) in which MNCs have been involved in either producing or cleaning up hazardous wastes.
5. What should be done to curtail overfishing in the future?
6. How can MNCs be more responsible for the global environment? Explain your answer.
7. What new opportunities will MNCs enjoy as a result of increased attention to environmental problems?

NOTE

1. US Environmental Protection Agency, "Policy Options for Stabilizing Global Climates."

BIBLIOGRAPHY

Bruce, Leigh. "How Green Is Your Company?" *International Management* (January 1989): 24–27.

Economist. Pocket World in Figures. London: Profile Books, 2005.

Hotelling, Harold. "The Economics of Exhaustible Resources," *Journal of Political Economy*, 39, no. 2 (April 1931), 137–175.

Jay, Leslie. "Green About the Tills: Markets Discover the Eco-Consumer." *Management Review*, 79, no. 6, (1990): 24–28.

Johnstone, Bob. "A Throw-Away Answer." *Far Eastern Economic Review* (February 1990): 62–65.

Leonard, H. Jeffrey. "Hazardous Waste: The Crisis Spreads." *National Development*, April 1986, 44.

Leonard, Richard. "After Bhopal: Multinationals and the Management of Hazardous Waste." *Multinational Business*, no. 2 (1986): 1–9.

Love, Patrick. "Fisheries: While Stocks Last." *OECD Insights*. Paris: OECD Publishing, 2010.

Mahon, John F., and Patricia C. Kelley. "Managing Toxic Wastes: After Bhopal and Sandoz." *Long Range Planning* 20, no. 4 (1987): 50–59.

Roberts, Gerald. "World Energy Outlook: What Managers Should Expect." *Multinational Business* (Spring 1989): 33–36.

Shell Hydrogen. "A Hydrogen Future for Iceland." www-static.shell.com/static/hydrogen-en/downloads/brochures/brochure.

Sinn, Hans-Werner. *The Green Paradox: A Supply-Side Approach to Global Warming*. Boston: MIT Press, 2012.

Smith, Douglas N. "EC Toughen Pollution Regulations." *Business Insurance*, March 5, 1990, 21.

Terpstra, Vern, and Kenneth David. *The Cultural Environment of International Business*. 3rd ed. Cincinnati: South-Western, 1991.

United Nations Framework Convention on Climate Change. "Kyoto Protocol." http://unfccc.int/resource/docs/convkp/kpeng.html.

US Environmental Protection Agency. "Policy Options for Stabilizing Global Climates." Draft Report to the US Congress. 1989.

Whole Foods Market. "Environmental Policy." www.wholefoodsmarket.com//issues/list_environment.html.

CASE STUDY 11.1

MILFORD PROCESSES INC.

Kenneth Briggs, general manager of the technical division of Milford Processes, has just finished reading a long, well-prepared brief written by a task force he had put together to report on the severe quality-control problems of the wholly owned subsidiary's plant in Matumba, East Africa. Reports of problems with the chemical-producing plant had been coming in for the last six months, becoming more serious in the last two months. Concerned with the future of the plant, Briggs had put together a small task force of head office and subsidiary technicians to investigate the problems and recommend solutions.

Their report is extremely direct. Quality at the plant is dropping and productivity has fallen. The defective rate of chemical batches has risen from 12 per thousand to 98 per thousand over the past six months. Productivity decreased by 16 percent in the past quarter.

These statistics trouble Briggs. The plant in Matumba had gone online only a year ago and was equipped with the latest equipment and machinery and the most advanced processing technology. The entire technical side of the operation was run by Milford's engineers, who had several years of experience. The first six months, in fact, had been a great success, and Matumba's productivity had matched Milford's worldwide standards in nearly every way.

After the first two quarters, however, things began to go wrong. One of the most difficult problems was electricity. When the plant was set up, the Matumba government had guaranteed an uninterrupted electricity supply to the plant as a part of the package of incentives it had offered to attract Milford into setting up an advanced-technology facility in the country. However, much of Matumba's electricity-generating capacity was based on hydroelectric projects, and these were dependent on the degree of rainfall that the country's catchment areas received during the rainy season, during the first four months of the year. This year the rains had failed to come, and water levels in the hydroelectric project reservoirs fell below operating levels. There was nothing the government or anyone else could do to generate power in adequate amounts to meet the country's needs. Bound by its promise and eager to maintain a hospitable environment for overseas investment, Matumba authorities had given high priority to the Milford plant's power needs. Despite their best efforts, however, the plant had no power for one day a week in the past four months, and in the past six weeks, production had to be shut down for two days a week. To keep up production volume and minimize production losses because of the plant shutdown, the production managers had reduced the number of quality-control checks both at the point of raw-material feeding and at final-production testing. The electricity shortage also resulted in the malfunctioning of the plant's temperature control systems at two stages of the production process, which was also affecting quality.

The task force had come up with two options, both of which assume that the electricity situation in Matumba is not likely to improve soon and that over the long term it could fluctuate considerably, depending on the pattern of annual rainfall. Moreover, if Matumba's drive to attract other overseas companies to the country meets with even moderate success, the demand for industrial consumption would go up sharply, and Milford would lose its most-favored status in this regard. The government is already under criticism from some quarters of the political opposition for bending over backward to please Milford. The opposition is actively calling for retracting Milford's privileged access to the country's generating capacity in times of scarcity.

The first option recommends that the company set up a captive power station, which, in effect, means the building of a complete power-generating facility to supply electricity exclusively to Milford's plant. The plant would cost an estimated $16 million to build and could be completed in about a year and a half. The facility would ensure that the chemicals factory would receive an uninterrupted supply of electricity, which would lead to consistent production performance and progressively higher productivity standards.

The other option is to modify the subsidiary's technological processes to be less dependent on electricity and to meet its energy needs from other sources, especially natural gas, which is readily available in Matumba at relatively inexpensive rates. Although using natural gas would be relatively cheaper, even after taking into account the costs involved in modifying some of the plant's technological processes and equipment, the option does pose some difficulties. The processes using natural gas are not as advanced as those using electricity, and there could be a marginal decline in product quality, even though the production volume could be maintained at the same level. Another issue is safety. Although Milford's safety standards are quite strict and well developed, it is possible that they could be compromised at the subsidiary level. The main problem is the safety orientation of local employees. Most had little experience in working in such a plant. A comprehensive safety training program and continued emphasis on safety consciousness could reduce the risks significantly but not eliminate them.

Briggs looks again at the report, which concisely puts together the main pros and cons of each option and closes with a clear, strong emphasis on the need for

(continued)

Case Study 11.1 *(continued)*

early action. "We'll have to decide within the next few weeks," he thinks. "Before the Germans and Italians come in and set up their operations, we have to dig in and dominate; it will be impossible to do it later." The next morning the members of the technical operations committee receive a notice of a policy meeting to be held Thursday in the main conference room to discuss the problems at the Matumba plant. Attached to the notice is a copy of the report with a request for each member to read it before the meeting.

DISCUSSION QUESTIONS

1. Assume that you are a member of the Milford technical operations committee. What questions would you raise at the meeting? Which of the options would you suggest? In your opinion, could Milford take other approaches to resolve these issues?
2. What environmental constraints are present with each of the possible options?

CASE STUDY 11.2

ALAPCO CHEMICALS LTD.

Wilbur Stevens looks in dismay at the mound of toxic waste piled high in a closed-off area near his factory as he drives past the dumping ground on his way to another busy day at his office in the Los Helios factory of Alapco Chemicals, where he is general manager. Los Helios is a major industrial location in the southern part of Valdina, a small country in Central America that has close ties with the United States and is heavily dependent on US aid for its continued survival. Alapco Chemicals had established its factory in Los Helios in 1934 and has since expanded its operations considerably. The main products of the Los Helios factory are pesticides and insecticides that are in great demand by Valdina farmers, whose crops are in danger from grave damage by weeds and pests that flourish in the hot and humid climate. Alapco is the only important producer of these products in the country and enjoys a monopoly over the market.

Although the company has shown consistent growth in both sales and profitability over the past decade, recently its environmental record has begun to be questioned by environmental groups, especially those based in the United States. The environmental problems of Valdina are undeniable. The air pollution in the country, especially in the area near Los Helios, is among the worst in the world. The country's forests have been almost completely decimated by indiscriminate logging both for revenue and for clearing land for new communities and industry in the small country. The nine main beaches of the country are so polluted by industrial and municipal waste that they have been declared unfit for swimming. One beach has been totally closed to the general public for the past five years.

A group of environmental activists has focused the blame on the government of Valdina and on local and foreign industry. Until two years ago there was no systematic legislation or even regulation of the environmental aspects of industrial and other forms of economic and development activities. The only regulation was in the form of some weak and often outdated factory codes, which were rarely enforced. Further, the government did not have a separate agency for environmental control; any issues raised were handled by the ministry concerned with a particular industry.

Growing international attention and the increasingly visible effects of the environmental deterioration in Valdina had ultimately goaded the government into action. In 2010, environmental legislation was passed that contained guidelines to be observed by both industry and agriculture. Globe-Watch, an active environmental action group in Washington, DC, had helped the government draft the legislation, which in its final form turned out to be fairly streamlined and quite stringent.

Enforcement of the legislation, however, was another matter. The government of Valdina, strapped for cash and deep in debt, did not have the resources to establish a system of periodic inspections and follow-ups to ensure that the guidelines were actually being followed. Moreover, being dependent on industry, especially the multinationals, to raise revenues, the government hardly had the political will to take stern measures to enforce its decree. As a result, much of the legislation remained merely on paper and any implementation was done voluntarily. Voluntary action was also limited because following the safeguards meant substantial capital outlay to purchase and install pollution-control equipment in factories or modify a plant or processes to ensure that they caused less environmental damage.

Alapco was one of the main polluters, partly because of the sheer size of its operation (it had the largest single plant in Valdina), partly because of the nature of the chemical-manufacturing process, and partly because some of its processes were quite old and had not been modified to control their effect on the environment. Again, because Alapco was the only producer of some of the chemicals needed by

(continued)

Case Study 11.2 *(continued)*

Valdina's farmers and because the company's top executives had extremely close connections with the government, no action was taken to enforce the new regulations, and things remained pretty much as they were for the next year, until Wilbur Stevens arrived in Los Helios as the new general manager of the plant.

Stevens was a brilliant engineer who held a master's degree in chemical engineering from Carnegie-Mellon University and an MBA from the Massachusetts Institute of Technology. He had worked with a tire company in Great Britain and with a chemical firm in Germany before returning to the United States as operations manager for Alapco's plant in Peoria, Illinois. In Peoria, Stevens had made an excellent impression on the senior management and workers. His management style and unique abilities had been major factors in turning around the plant's performance within three years from subpar productivity to one of the best among Alapco's fifteen plants. As a result, Stevens had been identified by top management as a potential candidate for the highest levels of the company hierarchy. As a part of the plan to groom him for senior management positions by giving him greater responsibilities and exposing him to an international situation, Stevens was appointed general manager and chief executive officer of the company's plant at Los Helios in Valdina.

On reaching Los Helios, Stevens was struck by the dominance Alapco enjoyed in the country. He was regularly invited to receptions given by senior government officials, and nearly every request he made on behalf of the company was quickly processed with a positive response. The plant was also operating with a reasonable degree of efficiency, considering its rather outmoded technology. Alapco's senior management had, as a matter of policy, continued to use this technology, taking the view that it was adequate to meet the current needs of the market in Valdina and that the introduction of new technology would result in high costs that the company would not be able to recover under the present conditions and market structure in Valdina.

Stevens soon began to feel quite comfortable in his new position. Valdina had an excellent school for the children of the many American expatriates, and his family had adjusted to the new conditions quite well. After a few months, however, he received a group of visitors from Washington who left him feeling uneasy. They were members of a delegation from Globe-Watch, and they informed Stevens that their group had helped the government of Valdina formulate the environmental policy and that they were, on their own, following up on that legislation. At first Stevens was annoyed and stated that this was a matter between his company and the government of Valdina and that if his plant was violating any of the regulations, it was for the government of Valdina to say so and not any third party. Further, he added, not a single letter or any other communication had been received from the government of Valdina on this issue, and he therefore believed that his plant was complying with all government requirements. The environmentalists were very direct. They showed Stevens a list of environmental violations that Alapco's plant in Los Helios was actually committing every day and compared the Los Helios operations to the operations of Alapco's plants in other areas, especially in the developed world. The presentation made clear that Alapco was following two different environmental standards: one in developed countries and one in developing countries. As far as Valdina was concerned, the reason for the double standard was the absence of the government's ability or willingness to enforce the legislation.

Stevens saw the point. He had been aware of this problem but he had not seen it in the same light as the environmental group; that is, as an ethical and moral responsibility of his company to their host country. Yes, there were toxic waste dumps just outside the plant and barely three miles from a densely populated residential area. A tropical storm could blow off the waste and cause serious damage. The emissions from the Alapco factory chimneys in Valdina were far higher in pollutants than those at any of the other Alapco plants. The Valdina plant had no effluent-treatment facility and all the chemical waste was routinely dumped into the sea. The problem was that, in Valdina, all this seemed natural. Everyone was doing it and no one complained. Nevertheless, Stevens realized that this casual neglect of environmental safeguards was fundamentally wrong and that the company should do something about it.

He called the company's headquarters in Lansing, Michigan, and suggested that Alapco should take unilateral action to improve the environmental standards of its Valdina plant and bring them into line with the company's other factories. He also submitted a cost estimate and pointed out that while there would be a slight erosion in the profits of the company, the benefits to the host country would be great. The head office, however, did not appear very enthusiastic. Although the members of the senior management team did not say so directly, the message seemed to be, "If we don't have to do it, why should we?"

Stevens was quite disappointed by this reaction. Maybe there is another way out of this mess, he thinks as he drives past the waste dump outside the factory.

DISCUSSION QUESTION

1. What would you do in this situation if you were:
   A. Wilbur Stevens?
   B. Director of Globe-Watch?
   C. Minister for industries of the government of Valdina?

CHAPTER 12

The Pathway Forward and Future Concerns

"The best way to predict your future is to create it."
—Abraham Lincoln

CHAPTER OBJECTIVES

This chapter will:

- Summarize the various forms of letters of credit in international trade
- Summarize the latest trends in international relations and trade
- Identify the role that technological innovation will have in creating greater efficiency and productivity
- Present a forecast of how multinational corporations will evolve in the areas of staffing, management style, and location of manufacturing facilities
- Offer other issues that will influence the MNC of the future

---

LETTERS OF CREDIT IN INTERNATIONAL TRADE

On the first night of our classes in international business and international finance, we typically ask our students what they want to get out of taking our course (other than an A or B!). Many students answer that they would like to better understand how to "do international business." The purpose of this beginning to the final chapter is to demystify options available to domestic business (i.e., the "good guys" of popular lore) from commercial banks (i.e., the "bad guys" of the popular press) in the hopes of experiencing what economist Jagdish Bhagwati calls the "Dracula effect": exposing a problem to light in the hopes that it shrivels up and goes away. Essentially, "doing" international business typically requires the use of a letter of credit or some variant thereof. The use of letters of credit demonstrates the essential role of commercial banks in international business.

Assume that you are the owner of a small to medium-sized business in the United States. You have found that you can reduce costs by purchasing products abroad that will serve as inputs to your domestic production. Or, alternatively, you have found a willing buyer for your end product in another country. Some pundits would decry the first alternative as unpatriotic, but cheer the second. In either case, the domestic business requires assistance in completing the international trade. Even more than with domestic trade, an international transaction typically involves two parties (a buyer and seller) who are unfamiliar with each other, at least at first. When you further complicate the issue with different currencies, unknown political and economic conditions, and diverse cultural outlooks, taking the chance to conduct business abroad can seem daunting. Given the lack of trust, it is highly unlikely that the seller would ship goods to the foreign jurisdiction prior to payment (i.e., via an **open account**). It is also equally unlikely that the buyer would agree to pay for the goods prior to receipt (i.e., via payment in advance). So goes the conundrum of international trade. The "good guys" are hampered with thoughts of what could go wrong. There would appear to be a need for financial services to facilitate this transaction.

Banker Acceptance Process

Depending on the size of the international transaction, some domestic businesses may opt to purchase the materials with their credit lines. This option is keen for small purchases, as it eliminates the need of foreign exchange for each party. As business transactions increase, this option is less viable, and in any case the basic conundrum of who pays and when is still present. Some innovative business owners can craft deals whereby both the buyer and seller trade goods rather than facilitating payment (i.e., counter trade), but these situations are not common and the basic conundrum is still there. So, in order to remove the fear of the unknown, some sort of intermediary is required. One option is the federal government via the **Export-Import Bank of the United States**. The Ex-Im Bank helped more than 3,200 small businesses expand their export sales in 2011. The Ex-Im Bank is not a direct lender, but provides insurance and guarantees of the lender's loans that fit into the Ex-Im Bank's program offerings. The Ex-Im Bank guarantees 90 percent of working capital loans made to US exporters by approved commercial lenders, as long as the company is located in the United States, has at least one year of positive operating history, has a positive net worth, and is exporting US-made products or services. The Ex-Im Bank also provides export credit insurance to qualified US exporters to eliminate uncertainty. This is all well and good, but the success of the Ex-Im Bank depends on commercial banks assessing the credit quality of the parties involved. Additionally, the budget of the Ex-Im Bank is limited relative to all companies currently active in the United States, and it appears that its mandate primarily concerns exporting of US goods

Figure 12.1 **Documentary Collection Process**

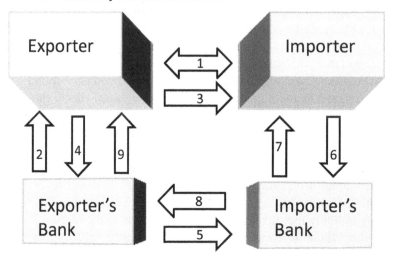

1. Exporter/Importer contract to buy/sell goods
2. Exporter's bank gives draft to exporter
3. Exporter ships goods to importer
4. Exporter delivers documents to its bank
5. Exporter's bank sends documents to importer's bank (or via correspondent bank)

6. Importer delivers payment to its bank
7. Exporter's bank pays for exporter goods
8. Importer's bank gives bill of lading to importer
9. Importer's bank pays exporters bank

(seen as the good side of international trade) versus imports. Since international transactions go both ways, in order to have a successful initiative, commercial banks must be involved in some way.

Depending on the level of familiarity that the exporter and importer have with each other, commercial banks offer products to facilitate an international (or domestic) transaction. In documentary collection, commercial banks serve as agents to facilitate payment. The exporter (or seller) draws up a draft, which is a demand for payment from the buyer at a specified time. The exporter's bank then contacts the importer's bank and authorizes the release of the **bill of lading** when the importer honors the terms of the deal. Figure 12.1 summarizes the steps involved in the documentary collection process.

Some of the terms in the prior paragraph require elaboration. Drafts, or demands for payment from a buyer at specified times, can be either sight drafts or time drafts. **Sight drafts** require payment upon transfer of the title of goods to the buyer. For time drafts, credit is extended to the buyer for thirty to sixty days. **Time drafts** can be classified as either "**trade acceptances**," where the draft is legally enforceable once "accepted" is written on the draft, or "**banker's acceptances**," whereby the bank accepts the time draft (and the associated risk of non-repayment) for a fee. In either case, the exporter holds the trade/banker acceptance until it comes due. Before acceptance, the draft is not an obligation of the bank; it is merely an order by the drawer to pay the bank a specified sum of money on a specified date to a named person or to the bearer of the draft. Upon acceptance, the draft becomes a liability of the bank. For very large banker acceptances with publicly traded companies as the buyer, banks can sell the time drafts as short-term investments to third parties. An American exporter may seek acceptance financing when it knows the buyer to be creditworthy and wants to extend it credit, but needs cash in the interim. Banks are willing to finance accounts receivable of exporters by purchasing time drafts, letters of credit, or via factoring open accounts at a discount from face value. The interest rate provided to the investor is a composite of the fee charged by the bank and the creditworthiness of the buyer. Further, time draft acceptances can be either with or without recourse. Time draft acceptances with recourse require that the exporter must reimburse the buyer of the acceptance if the importer fails to pay. Time draft acceptances without recourse leave the buyer of the acceptance stuck if the importer fails to pay. Thus, acceptances without recourse are more risky and are sold at steeper discounts to investors than trade acceptances with recourse.

Ideally, the tenor of the acceptance, the time from acceptance to maturity, will coincide with the length of the credit extended by the exporter so that the exporter will be able to pay the bank out of the proceeds from the sale (i.e., "self-liquidating"). Investors consider banker acceptances to be safe investments given that they are "two name" paper. Two parties, the accepting bank and the drawer, are obligated to pay the holder on maturity. As banker acceptances are generally created in amounts over $100,000, institutional investors dominate the market.

Regardless of the type of documentary collection, the bill of lading is a key document that facilitates the transfer of the goods being sold. The bill of lading is a receipt given by the carrier to the shipper acknowledging receipt of the goods being shipped and specifying the terms of delivery (included in steps 4 and 7 in Table 12.1). The bill of lading, which is a negotiable document, is also a document of title for the property and evidence of the contract of carriage. Approximately one-third of the problems associated with the transfer of goods come from discrepancies in this document. Items that must be listed in a bill of lading are shown in Table 12.1. The fourth and fifth items in Table 12.1 are important in order to establish where the items were made and where they are coming from. The sixth and seventh items are the primary things that we have discussed in this section. For the ninth item, there are typically three original bills of lading; when once one has been accomplished, the others stand void.

The earliest recorded bill of lading was in Florence, Italy, in 1526. Maritime shippers utilized the bill of lading as a means of tracking their shipments. One of the earliest usages of banker's acceptances was in Babylon, about 1600 BC. Traders would defer payment by making a promise to pay at a later date. Instruments more closely resembling modern banker's acceptances were used in Italy and Spain during the Middle Ages, while modern banker's acceptances gained their start more than 300 years ago in London.

Table 12.1 **Bill of Lading Requirements**

1	Name and address of carrier (shipping company)
2	Name and address of shipper (sender, consignor, or agent)
3	Name and address of consignee (buyer or agent)
4	Name and nationality of the ship
5	Port of loading and port of destination
6	Description of the goods shipped
7	Instructions on freight payment (prepaid or collect)
8	Place and date bill of lading issued
9	Number of originals of bill of lading

The benefits of the trade/banker acceptance process is that it simplifies the collection process, provides legal enforceability required by the seller of the goods, and allows the bank to obtain knowledge of international trade. Additionally, the bank fees charged for these services are usually reasonable given the relatively low risk, and the presence of such services makes it easier for a company to obtain factoring for its receivables. If the bank is involved in the process, the level of certainty of collection is seen as being increased. Additionally, the buyer (importer) will typically pay its outstanding orders via trade acceptance so as to not harm its reputation with its local bank, which often acts as the collector of the payment.

Even with these advantages, there are still disadvantages to the trade/banker acceptance process. The importer could still refuse shipment if it finds a better deal or finds a discrepancy in the goods provided. This refusal could run up the exporter's **demurrage fees**, which are fees associated with the storage of the exporter's goods at the foreign loading dock. Legal fees could also materialize as the seller pursues legal remedies available for the breach in contract. In order to solve the conundrum of the possibility of nonpayment, the letter of credit is often utilized by the "bad guys" to help out the "good guys."

LETTERS OF CREDIT PROCESS

The first letters of credit were used by the merchants and wealthy individuals promising payment based on their professional reputation in the twelfth century. The term "letter of credit" owes allegiance to *accréditation* in French (i.e., authorization), and *accreditivus* in Latin (i.e., trust). Indeed, authorization and trust are both necessary components of the letter of credit. The letter of credit differs from the banker's acceptance in that the importer's bank (the issuing bank) promises to pay the exporter's bank (the advising bank) when the exporter fulfills the terms of the letter of credit. The letter of credit process is detailed in Figure 12.2. Once the exporter (the seller or beneficiary) delivers the goods, the exporter presents documents to its bank requesting payment. Once payment has been made to the exporter, the exporter's bank then requests payment from the importer's bank, which then collects payment from the importer (the buyer or consignee). Given the promise made by the bank to pay the exporter once it has fulfilled its part of the bargain,

Figure 12.2 **Letter of Credit Process**

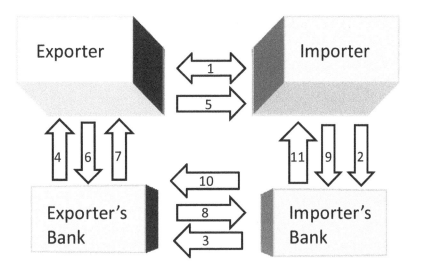

1. Exporter/Importer contract to buy/sell goods
2. Importer applies for a letter of credit
3. Importer's Bank issues a letter of credit to exporter's bank on importer's behalf
4. Exporter's bank informs exporter of level of credit
5. Exporter ships goods to importer
6. Exporter delivers documents to its bank
7. Exporter's bank checks documents and pays exporter
8. Exporter's bank delivers documents to importer's bank
9. Importer pays its bank for the value of the goods
10. Importer's bank sends payment to exporter's bank
11. Importer's bank delivers document to importer

the letter of credit solves the conundrum referred to earlier regarding nonpayment and generally provides less risk for the exporter than does documentary collection.

Typically, the documents required for payment include an invoice, customs forms, a packing list, proof of insurance, and the bill of lading. Banks will also typically require a copy of the export license, certification of product origin (to assess tariffs and quotas), and an inspection certificate to ensure that the goods meet domestic quality standards upon delivery. Prior to issuing the letter of credit (step 3 in Figure 12.2), the importer's bank will assess the creditworthiness of the importer, assess the timing of the transaction, and consider possible collateral options. Typically, the importer's bank will require a deposit equal to the amount of payment to ensure that the funds are available upon receipt of the documents as required in the letter of credit. It should be noted that in step 8 of Figure 12.2, the exporter's bank may opt to deliver documents to its correspondent bank in the importer's country, with the latter bank authorized to release the bill of lading.

Since the bank deals in documents and not goods, there is the potential for fraud on behalf of the exporter, when the goods specified in the invoice and bill of lading are not shipped to specification. Thus, even if the importer refuses shipment, the bank will pay the exporter as long as the exporter meets their requirements. In cases of forgery, the aggrieved bank can seek recourse against the exporter as well as the carrier that issued the bill of lading. Of course, the letter of credit does not guarantee payment to the exporter if the exporter does not comply explicitly with the terms of the letter of credit.

LETTERS OF CREDIT VARIETIES

Letters of credit come in many varieties. For starters, letters of credit can either be revocable or irrevocable. A revocable letter of credit can be modified (or revoked) by the issuer without notice to or consent from the beneficiary. An irrevocable letter of credit can only be modified or revoked with the consent of the beneficiary (seller), the **advising bank** (exporter's bank), and the issuing bank (importer's bank). All letters of credit should clearly indicate whether they are revocable or irrevocable. In the absence of such indication, the letter of credit shall be deemed irrevocable. Another feature of a letter of credit is confirmation. A letter of credit is confirmed when a bank other than the advising (exporter's) bank commits to irrevocably honor the payment of the credit, provided that the beneficiary (exporter) meets the terms and conditions of the credit. Confirmed letters of credit are particularly important from buyers in countries that are economically or politically unstable. An unconfirmed letter of credit is a credit guaranteed for payment by the issuing (importer's) bank. The safest form of letter of credit for an exporter is an irrevocable, confirmed arrangement. In this situation, the exporter is guaranteed to get its money from numerous parties to the letter of credit.

Another form is the transferable letter of credit. In this scenario, the **beneficiary** (seller or exporter) may request that the advising (exporter's) bank transfer the credit in whole or in part to a second beneficiary for execution. The first beneficiary has the right to change some of the terms and conditions of the original credit. The letter of credit must clearly state that it is transferable or it is not considered to be so. Another version of this is the back-to-back letter of credit, whereby the credit is established exactly as per the terms and conditions of the original letter of credit but with shorter time periods of shipment and negotiation to allow time for document substitution and negotiation of a second set of documents for the original letter of credit. Arrangements such as these are common when there is a middleman (i.e., a broker) involved in the transaction. In situations where the buyer requests partial deliveries of goods at predetermined intervals, payment can be made under a revolving letter of credit. In this situation, the bank is liable for the entirety of the value of all agreed partial deliveries, but is not required to effect payment for a given partial payment until the prior partial payment has been made. Another variation is a restricted negotiable letter of credit. In this arrangement, authorization from the issuing bank to pay the beneficiary is restricted to a specifically nominated bank. This arrangement would arise when the beneficiary requests to deal with a specific bank. In some situations, a red clause or green clause letter of credit can be negotiated between parties. These variations on the letter of credit design provide for advance payment under a documentary credit, which would seem to bring us full circle back to the bill of exchange (i.e., banker or trade acceptances). In the case of the red clause, payment is made in advance based on receipt of a written confirmation by the beneficiary to deliver the required documents by a specific date. The additional clause was originally written in red ink. In the case of a green clause, there is need of an additional document proving that the goods have been shipped to the designated warehouse by the seller or the seller's agent and held for storage in the name of the issuing bank. Given all the various types of letters of credit, we may all need a sanity clause if too many more are included!

A final form of letter of credit that we will discuss is the standby letter of credit. The standby letter of credit is different from the other variations discussed in that it is a security instrument as opposed to a payment instrument. In fact, the standby letter of credit is drawn upon only when one of the parties has not fulfilled its obligation. Additionally, the standby letter of credit is typically structured for a longer term than the documentary letters of credit previously discussed. Under the standby letter of credit, a request for payment has to be made by the beneficiary stating that payment (or performance) has not been effected by the principal. Standby letters of credit can be used in varying situations, whether it in support of international trade or to ensure fulfillment of a construction project.

The advantages of the standby letter of credit are that it can be used to cover many shipments and is typically cheaper given that utilization is the exception rather than the rule. Additionally, the standby letter of credit is typically payable on demand when accompanied by the beneficiary's statement that the buyer has failed to pay or perform as required. A disadvantage of the standby letter of credit is that the buyer (i.e., principal) is exposed to greater risks because the required documentation required by the seller (beneficiary) is ordinarily less comprehensive. For example, the standby letter of credit requires that goods be shipped in accordance with a sales agreement, versus the more comprehensive requirements for the documentary letter of credit as previously elucidated.

The Pathway Forward

The reported commercial letter of credit volume has run a ragged course since 2002, as is depicted in Figure 12.3 below. The numbers are based on SNL Financials call report database and are reported in thousands. We think it is time for a change of focus to improve performance.

In international affairs, there are often two sides to every story. As this section notes, the involvement of commercial banks is often crucial for successful international trade between firms. Given all the bad press that commercial banks have received in recent years, we think that it is time to shine light on the positive role that banks play in the facilitation of international trade. Our hope is that this discussion helps to reverse the habit of viewing commercial banks as bad guys and that Bhagwati's **Dracula effect** occurs such that international trade is increased via the financial products and other future-oriented mechanisms described in this final chapter.

Figure 12.3 **Commercial Letter of Credit Volume, 2002–2012**

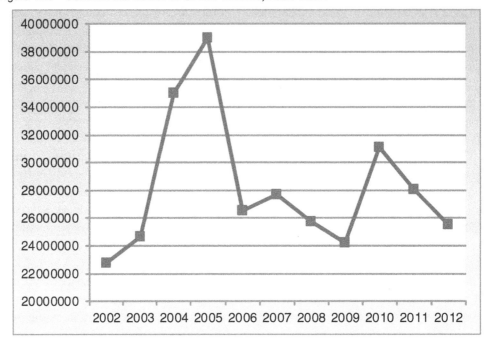

Source: Data from SNL Financial's Call Reports for Commercial LC's 2002–2012.

WHY STUDY THE FUTURE?

Besides managing their operations in the present, international business managers must also anticipate future changes. The need to assess future trends that are likely to impact business operations is obvious. If a business is able to accurately anticipate future trends, it has that much more time to adjust its own business practices and strategies, so when the expected changes actually occur, it will be in an excellent position to respond.

It is difficult to predict how and where changes will occur, but it is useful to assess future trends. Many firms develop sophisticated internal forecasting methods to generate possible scenarios in their areas of interest. Other firms use the services of specialized agencies or consulting firms that concentrate on future analysis.

There are, however, a few identifiable broad trends and resulting scenarios that are likely to have a major impact on the functioning and responses of international businesses.

FUTURE TRENDS AFFECTING INTERNATIONAL BUSINESS

EUROPEAN UNION INTEGRATION

As further discussed in Chapters 4 and 6, membership in the European Union increased to twenty-eight countries in July 2013 with the admission of Croatia. In the years to come, this expanding group of countries, which come with a variety of economic histories and cultural backgrounds, must figure out a way to succeed without infringing on the national sovereignty of the member states. Small nations such as Denmark have already expressed concern about being engulfed in a large bureaucratic organizational structure headquartered in Brussels, and there are other problems on the horizon. With the inclusion of Cyprus in the European Union in 2004, the problem of Turkey must be resolved. The northern portion of the island of Cyprus has been under Turkish control since the early 1970s, but this portion of the island was not admitted to the European Union when the southern portion was admitted. The Northern Turkish Republic of Cyprus is recognized as a sovereign nation only by Turkey itself, and Turkey has ambitions of joining the European Union in the near term. Originally, Turkey's application for admission to the European Union was stalled because the country is located primarily in Asia, but with the admission of Cyprus to the European Union, this geographic rationale is not as likely to thwart Turkey's desires. Turkey has also made numerous improvements domestically in human rights and in the performance of its economy, all with EU membership in mind. If Turkey is eventually admitted into the European Union, it would be the only member country with a Muslim majority. How the integration of Turkey into the European Union is handled could affect the union's relationship with other Islamic countries in the world, as well as the overall relationship between the European Union and the United States.

From an economic perspective, many of the current EU member states have had trouble meeting the convergence criteria as outlined in the Maastricht Treaty, with both Germany and France missing the deficit-to-GDP hurdle over the last few years. These missteps were a precursor to more severe problems in Greece, Italy, and Spain. These southern EU members sparked a sovereign debt crisis in the aftermath of the world recession in 2009. As with any policy, the failure to invoke punishment for exceeding the agreed fiscal constraints of the European Union will lead to the criteria themselves losing significance. Given the fiscal imbalances among countries in the Euro Area, there is discussion of semiautomatic enforcement mechanisms when nations fail to meet desired coverage criteria. In the aftermath of the Danish veto concerning adopting the euro as its currency, all future member states must adopt the euro eventually. Some countries, on admission, will require more time to meet the necessary requirements of euro adoption, but none have the ability to opt out of the currency union.

Another area of concern for the future of the European Union is the movement of Britain from its present common law system to the EU-mandated civil law system. As was discussed in an earlier chapter, civil law is more codified, while common law relies on the legal precedent of decisions to judge contemporary concerns. Should Britain move to the EU civil law system, it will find that its reliance on legal precedence is no longer acceptable and that some of the codified laws practiced in the European Union could in fact differ from what Britain has been used to for centuries.

A final area of concern for the European Union is how best to fund future bailouts of member nations should this be required in the future. Germany is opposed to the creation of pan-European bonds whereby the borrowing needs of all member states are backed by all other member states. France has supported the creation of a banking union, whereby all member nation banks are guaranteed future bailout, similar to the "too big to fail" policy of the United States. The creation of a guaranteed bailout fund is a first step toward a stronger fiscal union for the EU.

THE RISE OF BRICs AND MINTs

As has been discussed numerous times in this text, China and India have come a long way economically in the years since the first edition of this book was written. In recent years, the ascendency of Brazil, Russia, India, and China has brought a new acronym created from their initials: **BRIC**s. Brazil has seen much foreign direct investment (FDI) in both commodities and real estate. Russia has seen strong FDI related primarily to the energy industry. India, which has undergone much economic reform to reduce the level of protection from FDI, has become the recipient of many service-sector (especially technological) jobs from the United States and others in the Western world. Likewise, China has also seen huge growth in its annual GDP, which some forecast will be higher than that of the United States by the year 2050. Much of China's expansion has come in the manufacturing sector, in industries such as apparel, textiles, and furniture. Given the number of joint ventures currently undertaken between China and the Western world, China has been looking for a level of technology transfer from the West that would enable it to begin to manufacture products in the upper-end segments of industries where it is currently only the low-cost provider (such as apparel and furniture). China is looking to move from the role of copier to the role of innovator, a goal that the nation has in common with India. All of the BRIC nations have begun strategic alliances with one another in a further attempt at economic growth.

How long GDP expansion for the BRICs will continue is not known, but should these economies continue to successfully supplant much of the lower-cost jobs in both the service sector and the manufacturing sector in the Western world, there may be increased calls for protectionism in the West in the years to come. Even if the economic growth rates of the BRICs do not falter, the future should hold increased investment and economic growth for the so-called **MINT**s: Mexico, Indonesia, Nigeria, and Turkey. Besides being well positioned for capturing business from the BRICs should they slow down, the MINTs should benefit from increasing wages for the BRICs and increasing age in the Western world.

THE IMPORTANCE OF SOVEREIGN WEALTH FUNDS

Sovereign wealth funds (SWFs) are an increasing source of power for countries that run current account surpluses primarily owing to export of commodities. SWFs are government investment vehicles funded by foreign exchange assets that are managed separately from a given monetary authority's foreign exchange reserves.

Table 12.2   **World's Largest Sovereign Wealth Funds, 2013**

	Country	SWF Name	Assets	Inception
1	Norway	Government Pension Fund Global	$664.3 billion	1990
2	UAE-Abu Dhabi	Abu Dhabi Investment Authority	$627.0 billion	1976
3	China	SAFE Investment Company	$567.9 billion	1997
4	Saudi Arabia	SAMA Foreign Holdings	$532.8 billion	1952
5	China	China Investment Corporation	$482.0 billion	2007
6	China Hong Kong	Hong Kong Monetary Authority Investment Portfolio	$298.7 billion	1993
7	Kuwait	Kuwait Investment Authority	$296.0 billion	1953
8	Singapore	Government of Singapore Investment Corporation	$247.5 billion	1981
9	Singapore	Temasek Holdings	$157.5 billion	1974
10	Russia	National Welfare Fund	$149.7 billion	2008
11	China	National Social Security Fund	$134.5 billion	2000
12	Qatar	Qatar Investment Authority	$115.0 billion	2005

Source: SWF Institute, "Sovereign Wealth Fund Ranking," www.swfinstitute.org/fund-rankings/.

As of early 2013, there were more than sixty known SWFs totaling over $5 trillion in managed assets. While SWFs from Saudi Arabia and Abu Dhabi were established in the 1950s, the majority of these funds have been created throughout the world in the last decade. Some of these funds have a high level of transparency regarding their investment holdings, while others are not so forthcoming with information. The SWF Institute utilizes the **Linaburg-Maduell Transparency Index** to rank the relative transparency for each SWF, with a score of ten representing the highest level of transparency. One objective ranking measure is the reported size of the assets under management. Table 12.2 provides a ranking as of January 2013 for the twelve largest SWFs in existence.

PROTECTIONISM AND TRADE AGREEMENTS

The United States has signed numerous bilateral free-trade agreements (FTAs) over the last decade, and this trend should continue in the near term. Bilateral agreements such as the US-Singapore Free Trade Agreement, the US-Vietnam FTA, and the US-Korea FTA all promote the protection of certain industries that the United States still deems as strategic, such as agriculture and telecommunications. Over the last few years, there has been an increasing desire for the protection of various industries due to competition from Asia. Some industries, such as the furniture industry, are on opposite sides of the protectionism argument depending on which sector is being considered. Furniture manufacturers in the United States have lobbied Congress for the creation of protective barriers given the "unfair competition" coming from China, while furniture retailers, who profit from the lower-cost furniture coming from China, have lobbied against such protection.

Since the WTO supervised end to the textile quotas in 2004, nations with a high reliance on textile exports, such as Pakistan, have begun to orchestrate their own bilateral trade agreements with the developed world in an attempt to maintain high export levels. Thus, there will be a continued push from developing countries for the creation of more bilateral trade agreements; some economists have referred to a "spaghetti bowl" of world trade agreements, all having different preferential arrangements depending on what each signatory country has to offer.[1] As the number of bilateral trade agreements proliferates, the relevance of the World Trade Organization may be materially affected, as this organization does not have the ability to resolve disputes between countries that are not engaged in multilateral trade agreements. While we have discussed numerous multilateral trade associations in this text, such as NAFTA, ASEAN, and the European Union, the success of bilateral trade agreements could impede the progress of multilateral agreements. However, if bilateral agreements, such as the ones recently signed by the United States, account for a smaller percentage of world trade than the multilateral agreements, the influence of the WTO in trade policy will continue to be significant.

DEPRECIATION OF THE US DOLLAR

As discussed in earlier chapters, the US dollar has been of historical significance in international business. Over the last few years, the US dollar has experienced a significant deterioration when compared to the British pound, the euro, and the Canadian dollar. While this depreciation is good for US exporters in the short term, making their goods relatively less expensive when compared to the foreign goods priced in the foreign markets, the long-term effect of the depreciation of the dollar could begin to impact foreign portfolio and direct investment into the United States.

The US economy has certainly been an engine of the world economy over the last decade, and the US consumer's penchant for buying foreign imports has contributed to both the high level of consumer indebtedness and the negative current account balance in the United States since the 1980s. What is not clear, however, is the impact that continued current account deficits will have on the demand for US dollars in the future.

Some economists have predicted that the continued depreciation of the dollar will lead to many countries relying on an "index" approach to their foreign reserves. Rather than holding US dollars as the primary foreign reserve currency, some countries may opt to hold a portfolio of foreign currencies such as the yen, euro, and British pound, along with the US dollar. Given the problems recently with the euro, the lengthy stagnation of the Japanese economy, and the noted issues with the US dollar, there are few quality alternatives to the US dollar that are from sizable economies with a high volume of currency trade. To correct the downward movement of the US dollar, other economies such as India, China, Japan, and the European Union not only must become sources of imports to the United States but also must become consumers of US products and services in their own right. This will necessitate both effective world trade agreements and structural reforms in many of the aforementioned economies to increase the level of consumption and GDP growth over the next decade.

Table 12.3 **Oil Production and Consumption** (thousands of barrels per day)

Oil production		Oil consumption	
Saudi Arabia	11,545	United States	18,554
United States	11,133	China	10,232
Russia	10,397	Japan	4,728
China	4,416	India	3,417
Canada	3,868	Russia	3,250
Iran	3,538	Saudi Arabia	2,989
UAE	3,213	Brazil	2,759
Iraq	2,987	Germany	2,337
Mexico	2,936	Canada	2,292
Kuwait	2,797	South Korea	2,268

Source: Energy Information Administration 2012. www.eia.gov/cfapps/ipdbproject/IEDIndex3.cfm?tid=5&pid=53&aid=1.

ENERGY POLICY

The rise of China has brought with it an increased demand for oil over the last few years. As was discussed in Chapter 11, countries such as Iceland have successfully incorporated the use of alternative sources of energy, such as hydrogen, in their economies. For the foreseeable future, however, the continued use of fossil fuels such as oil, coal, and natural gas will dominate energy policy throughout the world. Table 12.3 provides a summary of the largest players in the oil consumption and production markets.[2]

As you can see, the United States is the world's largest consumer of oil, followed by China. Given the high level of industrialization in both China and India recently, and given that this process is expected to increase in the future, both of these countries should exhibit an increase in demand for oil in the coming years. It remains to be seen how the oil-producing countries will handle the increase in world oil demand. Saudi Arabia certainly has spare capacity from what it is currently producing, but many of the world's other primary sources of oil are producing at levels that are either at or approaching their national daily capacities.

GLOBAL RESOURCE DEPLETION

The next few decades are likely to be marked by rapid and far-reaching changes in the world economy that will influence international business in a variety of ways. The world's natural resources are likely to be depleted rapidly, and substitutes will have to be found. The depletion of such natural resources as oil, metallic ores, and minerals will weaken the economic position of those countries that rely almost solely on the export of such commodities for their foreign exchange earnings. On the other hand, exclusive monopoly over the technology used to manufacture substitutes could be acquired by large MNCs, which would increase their international economic dominance.

Environmental Degradation

At the dawn of the twenty-first century, the rapid and extensive deterioration of the world's environment had gained significant public attention, and environmental action groups had acquired considerable political influence in many countries, especially in the United States and Western Europe. Environmental groups were also active in many LDCs in Latin America, Asia, and Africa.

Much of the blame for the damage to the environment has been, and continues to be, placed on the MNCs. Concerns for the environment are particularly strong in certain areas of ecological damage: harm to the earth's ozone layer, atmospheric pollution, deforestation, pollution of inland freshwater resources and coastal waters, overfishing, and damage to the marine environment.

There is no doubt that pressures are likely to grow, and they may have several important consequences for MNCs. There is likely to be more stringent official regulation of the pollution and environmental effects of MNCs' manufacturing activities both at home and in host countries. A host country's greater awareness of the harmful effects of manufacturing activity on its local environment is likely to result in tougher environmental standards for MNCs setting up overseas operations. Further, MNCs may be required to reduce the environmentally adverse effects of their existing operations by installing more sophisticated pollution-control equipment or spending more on remedying existing environmental damage.

MNCs must also consider the possibility that environmental activists, who are increasingly influential in many developing countries, will take political action against them. It is indeed possible that while an MNC may meet the environmental standards laid down by the host government and have approval for its manufacturing operation, it may still face strong opposition from environmental activists who could attempt to stall actual implementation in a variety of ways. Such instances have occurred in a number of places around the world and it is possible that this tactic may mark a growing global trend.

For MNCs this scenario implies a need for greater investment in R&D for new environmentally safe production technologies and effective and economical pollution-control methods. Further, since public concern is so widespread, it is important for MNCs to increase their public relations efforts to convince governments and the general public that their operations are not harmful to the environment. Thus, in addition to product image, brand image, corporate image, and social image, the MNC of the future will have to be increasingly concerned with its environmental image.

Concern for the environment will also open new business opportunities for MNCs of the future. The development of pollution-control technologies and equipment by MNCs would put them in a position to market those to other MNCs and companies in host countries. Environmental concern will open up demands for new types of technologies aimed at solving some of the world's environmental problems and preventing further damage. Recycling, waste management, and reforestation are some of the things that are immediately important. In addition, there is likely to be considerable demand for environmentally sound products, such as biodegradable or recyclable materials. Many major corporations are now developing new products that address these concerns, and most of them are selling well.

INTERNATIONAL TERRORISM

In the aftermath of the events of September 11, 2001, the world must now deal with the threat of international terrorism, which has the potential to disrupt international business in the years to come. Aside from individual terrorist acts, which cause a temporary disruption in business, the Straits of Malacca, utilized by commercial shipping vessels on entry and exit from the port of Singapore, has seen a rapid increase in piracy, which could have a tremendous impact on international shipping if allowed to escalate. The existing international agreements concerning the security and utilization of international waters must be improved to allow for the prosecution of those that disrupt commercial shipping vessels in the area, and modernization must be brought to countries that currently harbor or support international terrorist groups.

THE DOHA AGENDA

One method for reducing the amount of terrorism in the world is increasing the level of modernity and the benefits of such modernity throughout the world. Many of the countries that support international terrorism are, in fact, failed states. Nations that are not poor but still support terrorism have yet to see the benefits of globalization reach their poorest citizens. The Doha Round of trade negotiations has the goal of improving the lives of those in the developing world ("the South") via increase in trade with the nations of the developed world ("the North"). Some economists, such as Jeffrey Sachs of Columbia University, believe that economic and social improvements in African nations will reduce the likelihood of failed states that would become havens for terrorists. One primary area of improvement in the **Doha agenda** would be the reduction of protection of the agriculture industries of the developed world. This is an industry in which many developing countries are able to produce products for export, but too often the wealthier countries have protectionist policies in place that do not allow LDCs to sell their products in international markets. Another area of improvement would be the reduction of trade barriers within the developing nations themselves, as these barriers often prevent the distribution of goods and services that could improve the quality of life for the citizens of LDCs. The French have a saying that it is better to remove the swamps than to swat at mosquitoes;[3] similarly, it would be better to improve the quality of life via increased trade than to deal with the likelihood of terrorist havens spreading throughout the developing world.

MIGRATION

Given the increased openness of many economies in the developed world, another issue that will require attention in the years to come is migration. With the aforementioned expansion of the European Union, the citizens of all these member states will eventually have the ability to migrate anywhere within the European Union in search of work. Germany, which is the closest geographically to many of the newest members, has gained a temporary restriction on the number of new immigrants from the east. In the United States, there have been calls for stricter border controls in both Mexico and Canada in the wake of the terrorist attacks of September 11, 2001. Parallel to the concern of too many immigrants in the near term is the potential problem of not enough immigrants into the Western world in the long run. Given current population trends, many of the developing economies of the European Union, the United States, Canada, and Japan will need new workers in the future. The aging of the citizens in the developed world will continue for the foreseeable future and will require either an increased level of job outsourcing to countries with very young populations (such as India) or an ease in immigration requirements to ensure that the necessary occupations are filled in the developed world. Some countries, such as Denmark, have begun to increase restrictions on the number of newcomers from other countries, while other countries, such as Canada, have increased the granting of citizenship to immigrants in an effort to increase the country's working population.

TECHNOLOGY EXPLOSION: THE INFORMATION ERA

Technology was certainly an important driving force behind the globalization of business in the twentieth century. In the twenty-first century, this trend is likely to be even stronger. Many major industrial corporations that have made large investments in technologies—lasers, fiber optics, superconductivity, digital and wireless electronics—are likely to find themselves at a significant competitive advantage vis-à-vis their competitors in their own and other countries. The depletion of natural resources and the growing consciousness about the threats to the environment are likely to spur new technological advances in safe and regenerative products.

Technology is also likely to make the working of international business more efficient and more competitive. The revolution in information and communications technology has already made it possible for a large MNC to monitor simultaneously from a single location the operation of hundreds of its facilities and offices spread across different countries and time zones. The expected increases in communications and computing power are likely to make this control even more efficient and economical and add significantly to MNCs' business capabilities. In fact, the types of communication and internal and external information services and systems available to a globally oriented company are likely to be an increasingly important factor in the firm's overall competitiveness. The edge provided by the access to advanced information technology will also expand the scope of international business because it will enable corporations to search, locate, analyze, evaluate, and choose new business opportunities and possibilities in different parts of the world with a facility that was not possible in the past.

THE INTERNET

Another area of increased future regulation will more than likely be the Internet. Communist countries, such as China, as well as theocratic governments, such as Iran, have already begun to censor Internet websites. Governments around the world will also increase the level of taxation of consumption on the Internet. It is apparent that the Internet will continue to bridge the gap of geographical distance between a given consumer and a given company, thus increasing the level of international trade. Numerous small businesses in the world are based on the Internet, which connects buyers and sellers throughout the world in a way before unimaginable.

IMPACT OF TRENDS ON MNCs

The multinational corporation is likely to remain the dominant form of corporate organization in international business for years to come. Its form and manner of operation, however, are likely to change substantially in response to changes and trends in the business environment. Multinational firms from emerging markets will continue their rise in global significance. These nascent competitors will forever change the landscape of western dominated firms seeking markets worldwide.

THE MEGACORPORATION

Developments in information, communications technologies, computers, and transportation are likely to shrink the world further and enable easier geographical expansion for major corporations. It is likely that today's corporations, seeking expansion, will utilize these opportunities to increase the size of their operations.

Although developments in technology are going to be rapid and far-reaching, they are also likely to be extremely expensive. Only very large corporations are going to be able to afford the expense of specialized and dedicated computer and communication networks, state-of-the-art manufacturing technologies, and the huge investments needed to build entirely new plants based on the new technologies. These firms will thus have a massive technological and competitive edge over their competitors.

Smaller companies may fall by the wayside, either going out of business or readjusting their operational focus. Mergers and acquisitions are going to continue to be common because major international corporations will attempt to either eliminate or join the competition. Strategic alliances may become more common because major corporations eye the same markets and work out relationships that share resources, strengths, and competitive advantages. Some of these trends are already beginning to surface. There has already been much consolidation of the banking industry in both the United States and in Europe.

GEOCENTRIC STAFFING

The personnel of MNCs are likely to become more geocentric than they are today. As the number of locations of operations increases, the parent office is likely to find it increasingly difficult to secure executives from the home country to fill positions in all locations. Moreover, as overseas personnel join MNCs in increasing numbers, a large pool of well-qualified local and third-country nationals is likely to emerge and be available for deployment in different operational locations of the globally oriented enterprise. In many developing countries, standards of technical and managerial education are rising rapidly. MNCs are finding it useful to recruit personnel locally for manning overseas operations, even at relatively senior levels. The geocentric corporation of the future is likely to have an internationally varied managerial executive cadre that is extremely mobile, regardless of individual nationality.

MULTICULTURAL MANAGEMENT

Management styles are likely to change considerably over the years, as global corporations respond to rapid changes. Corporations of the future are likely to incorporate management styles that will adapt to a host-country sociocultural environment instead of imposing home-country standards and practices. The experience gained managing in overseas locations, cultures, and environments is likely to generate a well-defined international management policy that will be based on a much better understanding of the different sociocultural environments of global corporation operations. Such a policy would definitely improve the interface with local governments, clients, and business associates and improve the efficiency and success rate of local operations.

MANAGERIAL TECHNOCRATS

Managers of the future must become technocrats, intimately familiar with the latest in communication and computer technologies, in order to operate in their high-tech office environments. There may be a lesser degree of physical effort required because improved communication facilities would cut down the need for the frequent traveling endured by today's international managers. Some indications of this scenario are already available in the form of videoconferencing facilities that are prevalent in many MNCs today. Increasing traffic congestion and rising problems of inner-city living will increase the development of the home office, which would enable a manager to work from home and be in constant touch with the office via advanced telecommunication facilities.

OVERSEAS MANUFACTURING FACILITIES

The growth of overseas manufacturing facilities is likely to continue due to the availability of lower labor costs in potential host countries, and MNCs are likely to be better served by this arrangement. As host governments mature, politically as well as economically, they are likely to prefer direct investment in their countries by MNCs, instead of receiving finished products in the form of imports. Foreign direct investment generally stimulates the local economy, and its benefits can be considerable if the local economy itself is well managed and balanced.

As the trend toward greater openness and market orientation takes root, many host countries are likely to seek direct investment by foreign firms, either by participation in privatization programs of existing state-owned enterprises or by takeovers of loss-making units in the private sector. The benefits of the infusion of new technology, managerial skills, and capital gained by the host countries will be recompensed by new business opportunities and a spread of the manufacturing base nearer the market for the MNCs.

Locating production overseas provides access to cheap labor and inexpensive inputs and reduces transit costs. Moreover, a more open and market-oriented government would be less prone to expropriate or nationalize an MNC's assets and, therefore, would not constitute a great political risk. This would provide a much better climate for foreign direct investment.

The one constraint that might inhibit rapid growth of foreign direct investment in many LDCs is the inability of the host countries to generate the foreign exchange resources necessary to enable a repatriation of profits by the foreign enterprises. One way out of this constraint is the linking of new investments by MNCs in foreign-exchange-strapped host countries to commensurate earnings by exports, either of the MNCs own products or those of other host country commodities or manufactures. Similarly, debt-equity swaps may result in additional investment, even in countries that are heavily burdened with external debt obligations.

FINANCIAL INTEGRATION

The 1990s saw several major changes in the fundamental relationships between the different international financial markets, changes that were reflected in new levels of integration, modernization, and globalization. Financial markets of the future are likely to be even more integrated, as existing barriers crumble and the free flow of funds across national borders becomes still easier. While integration and deregulation are characteristic of today's markets only in the industrialized world, the future may see the addition of new markets to the global financial network, as well as the resurgence of global regulation of financial markets.

The markets of the newly industrialized countries, and the more advanced developing countries, are likely to be increasingly integrated into the global economy. In this scenario, MNCs would have an opportunity for a truly global sourcing of funds. The foreign exchange markets would, of course, become much more liquid and complex, because there would be a large number of freely convertible currencies trading on international exchanges.

Concerns with exchange risks and destabilizing capital movements are likely to bring greater emphasis on international cooperation in the supervision of activities, both domestic and international, of financial institutions. The major industrial countries have already agreed on standards of capital adequacy to be observed by their banks via the **Basel Accord**. In the wake of the financial crisis, a new Basel Accord focused on increasing the capital that banks hold so that the need for bailout funds is less likely in the future. Some evidence of a greater opening up of the financial sector to external participation in the developing countries was provided by the Uruguay Round of GATT talks, in which many developing countries agreed to lower barriers to trade in financial services. The increasing openness of the financial sector has continued under the WTO, and many bilateral trade agreements, such as the US-Singapore FTA, also made advances to this end.

Rising Labor Unrest

MNCs are likely to meet with increasing demands for higher salaries and wages in most host-country operations as expectations rise along with costs of living. The trends in trade unionism, however, are likely to vary. With the collapse of the Soviet bloc, one of the main sources of ideological and political support for trade union movements in many countries is gone. Trade unions have become stronger in many third world countries however, especially as worsening living conditions have led to increasing demands for higher compensation levels, while difficult operating conditions have reduced MNC profitability.

MNCs may nevertheless have increasing leverage in dealing with trade unions through their capacity to shift production to different overseas locations. Further, greater use of automated manufacturing processes, especially through the use of industrial robots, may lead to less dependence on human labor on the production floor, which would reduce the bargaining power of trade unions. On the other hand, the developed world could see a rise in trade union membership should the level of job losses increase due to such outsourcing and automation.

In the aftermath of the recent financial crisis, many disenfranchised individuals have taken to the streets in protest of the perception that global capitalism is a zero-sum game. The "Occupy Wall Street" movement arose in the United States in response to government-backed bailouts of financial institutions deemed "too big to fail"; the bailouts were paid for largely by taxpayers known as the inhabitants of "Main Street." While the emotions are real, the solutions have proven to be scattered. Movements like this prove that the reputation of a multinational firm is pivotal for future success.

The Permanence of Change

Given all the future possibilities discussed in this chapter, the only thing that we can say will definitely happen is change. An increasing level of global competition will require many changes in the market dynamics in which today's corporations fight for survival. As countries such as India and China become more integrated with the developed world economies, these economies will have an impact on the future course of international business. Thus, more countries will be able to contribute to the progress of globalization, and the multinational corporation will be able to benefit from competing in a truly global market place now and in the years to come.

Summary

International business has changed dramatically in the past decade and will continue to change in the future. Responding to surging global democracy, diminishing natural resources, diverging economic conditions, and regional economic integration will require development of new roles and business practices. Global competition and international debt problems will also force change. Increased protectionism may result as the dialogue between the industrialized and the less-developed countries becomes more acute. Technology improvements, offering the opportunity to create more efficient enterprises, will continue to be the driving force of internationalization.

Mega-corporations will continue to emerge. Multinational corporations will be staffed geocentrically, and management practices will be adapted to incorporate host-country socio-cultural attitudes and beliefs. Managerial tasks will focus on high-technology communication and computer technologies and may promote the development of the home office. Overseas manufacturing facilities will become more common, and environmental issues will become more important as ecological effects become visible. Greater international cooperation will develop as financial markets integrate and modernize their global networks. Automation may lead to less dependence on human labor in manufacturing facilities. One thing is for certain: the only thing permanent in the global economy is change.

Discussion Questions

1. Why is the anticipation of future trends important to conducting business?
2. What are the major current international political trends, and how might they affect business relationships? How might they affect decision-making?
3. How will depletion of raw materials affect international business structures?
4. How does technology affect a corporation's ability to survive and compete in the world of the future?
5. What is a megacorporation?
6. Discuss geocentric staffing as it relates to future recruiting and hiring practices within a multinational corporation.

7. How might you better prepare yourself for the challenges of doing international business in the future?

NOTES

1. Bhagwati, *Free Trade Today*.
2. *US Energy Information Administration*.
3. Newsworld International, "Interview with Dominique Moisi."

BIBLIOGRAPHY

Ajami, Riad A., and G. Jason Goddard. "Give Banks Credit for Boosting International Trade." *RMA Journal* (May 2013): 10–15.

Behrman, Jack N. "The Future of International Business and the Distribution of Benefits." *Columbia Journal of World Business* 20 (1986): 15–22.

Bernum, Cynthia F. "The Making of a Global Business Diplomat." *Management Review* 78, no. 11, (1989): 59–60.

Bevans, Phillip G. "Canadian Banker's Acceptances." In *Current Issues in Canadian Business Law*, ed. R. Miner, 507. Toronto: Carswell, 1986.

Bhagwati, Jagdish. *Free Trade Today*. Princeton: Princeton University Press, 2003.

———. *The Wind of the Hundred Days: How Washington Mismanaged Globalization*. Boston: MIT Press, 2002.

Blocklyn, Paul L. "Developing the International Executive." *Personnel*, March 1989, 2–5.

Credit Suisse. Types of L/Cs. 2013. www.credit-suisse.com/ch/unternehmen/kmugrossunternehmen/en/import_export/akkreditive_dokinkassi/akkreditive/red_clause_green_clause.jsp.

Economist. Pocket World in Figures. London: Profile Books, 2011.

———. "Send Back Your Huddled Masses." December 16, 2004.

Export-Import Bank of the United States. "Global Access for Small Business." Last modified January 5, 2013. www.exim.gov/smallbusiness/global-access-for-small-business.cfm.

Gozlan, Audi. *Banker's Acceptances*. Montreal: Jewel, 2007.

Hayden, Spencer. "Execs Discuss Problems of International Business." *Management Review*, September 1989, 35–38.

International Chamber of Commerce. "Clean Bills of Lading." ICC Publication Document No. 283. 1980.

Knorr, Robert O. "Managing Resources for World-Class Performance." *Journal of Business Strategy* 11, no. 1 (1990): 48–50.

Laczniak, Gene R., and Jacob Naor. "Global Ethics: Wrestling with the Corporate Conscience." *Business* (July–September 1985): 3–9.

LaRoche, Robert K. "Banker Acceptances." *Economic Quarterly* 79, no. 1 (1993): 75–85.

Miller, Norman I. "Problems and Patterns of the Letter of Credit." In *Legal Problems of International Trade*, ed. P.O. Proehl. Urbana: University of Illinois Press, 1959.

Newsworld International. "Interview with Dominique Moisi, Deputy Director of the French Institute for International Relations." *Special Assignment with Bill Cunningham*, January 2005.

Sethi, S. Prakash. "The Multinational Challenge." *New Management* 4 (1987): 53–55.

SNL Financial. Commercial Letter of Credit Call Report Database, Holding Company Data. 2012.

Sovereign Wealth Fund Institute. SWF Fund Rankings. www.swfinstitute.org/fund-rankings/.

US Energy Information Administration, www.eia.gov/cfapps/ipdbproject/IEDIndex3.cfm?tid=5&pid=53&aid=1.

Wild, John J., Wild, Kenneth L., and Han, Jerry C.Y. *International Business: The Challenges of Globalization*. 3rd ed. Upper Saddle River, NJ: Pearson Education, 2006.

GLOBALIZATION AT THE CROSSROADS: SUSHI AND THE VEBLEN EFFECT

How much is that sushi in the window? This is a question that many consumers of sushi and sashimi products have been asking across the globe in recent years. Given the rise in popularity of the delicacy from the seas, the prices of raw fish have been on the rise exhibiting what is known in economics as the "Veblen Effect": an increase in demand associated with a rise in price for a product which is valued for its exclusivity. This effect is so named after Thorstein Veblen, who wrote the famous book "A Theory of the Leisure Class" which coined phrases such as "conspicuous consumption" and "conspicuous leisure." Both would seem to be at play here with the rise in consumption of sushi and sashimi products. Further complicating this apparent contrast to traditional economic theory is the vast decline in fish stocks over the last fifty years. For example, the International Commission for the Conservation of Atlantic Tunas (ICCAT) has estimated that the East Atlantic and Mediterranean spawning stock of blue fin tuna has declined by 70 percent over the last fifty years, while the West Atlantic spawning stock has declined by over 80 percent. The international trade of fish is not without a myriad of regulatory agencies which supervise the management of stock, the arrangement of tariffs, and the setting of quotas for the number of fish allowed to be caught each year. Even with the legal quota limits, the total fish which are caught each year far exceed these levels, with many being considered IIU catches (illegal, unregulated, and unreported). Given the health benefits of fish consumption and the rise in popularity of sushi and sashimi, the future looks bright for demand as long as the supply of fish exists.

The apparent breakdown of the pricing mechanism has continued unabated in recent years, even as environmental groups, governments, and businesses all voice opinions about the possible adverse impact on the environment, the declining levels of spawning stock, and the need to fulfill the wishes of customers seeking a healthier diet. National governments require exclusive economic zones of two hundred nautical miles off the coast for their exclusive sovereign usage, but still the IIU catches persist. Four million tons of all types of tuna are caught annually, with Japan being the largest consumer. The largest suppliers of tuna include Japan and most of southern Europe. Thailand is the world's largest canner of tuna with recent estimates at a 70 percent market share. Environmental groups claim that the quotas in place (which are vastly exceeded annually) are too high to maintain the species for future generations. This "Crossroads" issue includes the interests of national governments, businesses of all sizes, and environmental groups.

QUESTIONS FOR DISCUSSION

1. *Research stock levels and demand patterns for your favorite fish.*
2. *Itemize the research required to develop a plan of action to solve this "Crossroads" issue.*
3. *What might be a proposed solution for this problem?*
4. *Consider the dissenting opinions for your proposed solution. How might you overcome their arguments?*

CASE STUDY 12.1

REMAGEN BROTHERS LTD.

The protest meeting at the locked gates of Remagen Brothers Ltd. was getting increasingly turbulent. More than 2,000 unionized workers of the Weranpura factory were demanding a 26 percent increase in wages and an increase in the number of paid holidays from fifteen to twenty-one. The management's offer of a 9 percent pay increase led to a fairly quick breakdown in negotiations. The workers had gone on an indefinite strike that was now in its nineteenth day, with no chance of settlement.

Remagen's Weranpura plant had a history of troubled industrial relations from its outset. The plant was located in an industrial park set up by the government of Trivana, a small island country in South Asia. Remagen Brothers was a leading cosmetic, toiletries, and detergent manufacturer based in the Netherlands, with factories and other operations in eighty-two countries around the world. With sales revenues exceeding $2 billion annually, Remagen was a leading multinational in the industry, and its products had a well-differentiated brand image and enjoyed considerable brand loyalty worldwide. Remagen's decision to invest in Weranpura was motivated primarily by the attractive incentives offered by the Trivanian government in the special industrial zone. Remagen was allowed to import all its plant equipment as well as raw materials and intermediate products free of customs duties. The government provided excellent infrastructural facilities to the company, including banking and financial services within the industrial park zone. Remagen's income from its Weranpura factory also was free from Trivanian taxes for five years and then was to be taxed at a special rate. Profits and other remittances out of Trivana were freely allowed, although periodic reports had to be filed with the central bank.

Attracted by these incentives, Remagen's senior management had made the decision to establish a large plant to manufacture soaps and detergents to be marketed primarily in Southeast Asia. Trivana's labor costs were even lower than those of Southeast Asia, and Remagen's products were expected to have the edge needed to penetrate that highly competitive market.

Although Remagen's planners focused on the economic benefits provided by Trivana's low-cost labor force, other aspects of the local labor force were not studied in detail. Weranpura was located in the southeastern part of Trivana, which had a predominantly Marxist political orientation. All plants in the Weranpura industrial zone were unionized, and almost all the unions were affiliated with the People's Movement for Labor Rights (PMLR), an avowed Marxist labor federation that advocated militant action on the part of its affiliated unions to secure labor rights.

Remagen's managers began to sense the difficulties that lay ahead when the commissioning of the plant was delayed by a month because of a sudden strike by the workers of the plant's packaging unit. Top management, however, eager to start production, decided to lay off all the striking employees and hire new ones in their place. The view at that point was that the company should not be bullied by the union and should adopt a strong stance. This view was based on the fact that Remagen was paying at least 10 percent higher wages than any other employer in the Weranpura industrial zone and it could hire new workers whenever it wanted.

This view did not prove to be an effective strategy in dealing with labor issues. Once the workers were fully unionized, it became difficult to terminate the services of employees. The union provided excellent legal help for all its members, and an employee could involve the company in a long, fractious, and expensive litigation process. Labor laws in Trivana heavily favored employees over employers, and Remagen had no financial advantage it could leverage in the litigation process. Further, the workers were now governed more by the orders of union leaders than by the edicts of the personnel department. The union's management was prone to ordering strikes even if a single employee was to be replaced.

During its first two years, therefore, the company had adversarial industrial relations, and eighty-seven workdays were lost because of strikes. The management's policy continued to be based on maintaining a strong posture against the militant trade unions and refusing to give in on their demands. In the early strikes, although the company did lose workdays, the unions were not able to make much headway. The personnel department of Remagen's head office was pleased with the record of the Weranpura management, and the personnel manager had received two letters of commendation. This strike, however, was different. The workers and their leaders were apparently bent upon getting the company to agree to their demands. Further, it was also clear that the PMLR federation was providing financial support that would allow the striking employees to carry on the strike indefinitely.

The local manager of Remagen's personnel division, Mr. Ratnapure, was of the opinion that this time the company should negotiate with the striking workers and raise the level of compensation it was willing to offer in order to bring it nearer to union demands. He reasoned that the company's image in Weranpura was at stake, since the PMLR had successfully carried out a campaign against it by branding Remagen a "foreign exploiter." The government, although somewhat centrist in its political inclinations, was sensitive to the views of the PMLR, because the next provincial elections were in six months and there was talk of an alliance between the ruling party and the Marxists in this region. Therefore, if matters came to a head, Remagen could, at best, expect the government to be a mute bystander, caught

(continued)

Case Study 12.1 *(continued)*

between its political priorities and its eagerness to attract overseas investment in special industrial zones. Perhaps, argued Ratnapure, Remagen should involve the leaders of the PMLR in the talks, as the union leaders had been demanding. This would be viewed as a major concession and perhaps could lead to a moderation of the workers' demands on the compensation package.

Johann Michuft, the general manager of the plant, was initially taken aback by Ratnapure's suggestion, which seemed to go almost directly against the company's global industrial relations management policy. The company had a standard policy to make a firm and final offer of compensation in line with industry wages (or better). Further, the policy of the management was not to negotiate with any party other than the bona fide representatives of the plant's unions.

Talking to PMLR's representatives would clearly violate this policy. The company was doing quite well, and it could afford to give a raise to the workers that would be in line with what they were demanding, but that amount would be way ahead of the industry average in Weranpura (although much lower than wages paid to workers for similar jobs in the company's plants in Europe and North America). Further, dealing with the PMLR would be seen as a sign of weakness on the part of the company's management and could lead to another set of demands.

On the other hand, if the company did not negotiate with the unions and the representatives of the PMLR, it faced the possibility of a long-drawn-out strike that could result in the closure of this highly profitable plant. Moreover, the company's image as an employer would suffer in many countries of the region, where it was planning to establish other manufacturing facilities.

As he pondered these issues, Michuft typed a confidential memorandum to send to headquarters in the Netherlands, seeking instructions on whether company policy could be modified in Weranpura.

DISCUSSION QUESTION

1. What would be your instructions to Michuft if you were the director of international human resource management at Remagen's world headquarters in the Netherlands?

Glossary

absolute advantage—as stated by Adam Smith and David Ricardo, the specialization of each country in the goods that it can produce most efficiently

absolute uniformity—theory that proposes that accounting methods be standardized regardless of the different circumstances of different users

accounting exposure—degree to which the consolidated financial statements and balance sheets of a company can be affected by exchange rate fluctuations

acculturation—the process of not only understanding cultural differences, but modifying or adapting behavior to become more compatible with local culture

acquired group memberships—affiliations not determined by birth but based on such things as religious or political customs and practices

act of state doctrine—a legal principle that holds that sovereign nations can act within their authority considering assets or belongings taken by the state in public actions

ad valorem duty—determination of customs duties as a percentage of the value of the goods

advising bank—a bank in the country of the exporter that informs the exporter that letters of credit have been made available by foreign banks; an advising bank has no responsibility of payment associated with the letters of credit

African Development Bank (AFDB)—a development bank headquartered in Ivory Coast, with the objective of accelerating the development process in Africa

Agreement on Trade-Related Aspects of Intellectual Property Rights (TRIPS)—an agreement that allowed the creation of domestic laws concerning the protection of intellectual property rights

air waybill—a bill of lading accepted by the shipper, indicating that the shipper has received the goods and agrees to deliver the goods to the specified airport

alongside—upon delivery, placement of goods on a dock or a barge very close to the ship, so that the goods can be placed aboard the ship

American terms—prices of currencies quoted in terms of variable units of US dollars per unit of the foreign currency

Andean Community—a customs union among Latin American countries

antidumping laws—domestic laws that stipulate that a foreign country cannot sell a product at a cost below the cost of production (or less than fair value)

arbitrage—the process of buying goods in one market and selling them in another market; the profit is determined by the differential between the purchase price of the good and price at which the good is ultimately sold

arm's-length pricing—the same price for affiliates as is charged for unrelated third-party buyers

ascribed group memberships—affiliations determined by birth, based on such things as sex, family, age, or ethnicity

ASEAN Free Trade Area (AFTA)—free trade area formed by the Association of South East Asian Nations in 1992

Asian Development Bank (ADB)—a development bank that promotes economic growth and cooperation in Asia and the Far East

Asian financial crisis—1997–1998 economic collapse of many Southeast Asian nations due primarily to speculative bank lending in the region

autarky—an economy that does not trade with other nations; a closed economy

average cost pricing—using both fixed and variable costs in figuring the costs of production

back-to-back loans—arrangement for dealing with blocked funds whereby blocked funds are lent out to a local company, which then arranges for an equivalent loan to the parent company (also known as parallel loans)

backward-bending labor supply curve—phenomenon of a reduction in total labor hours due to higher salaries: the amount of income remains the same, but the number of hours worked actually decreases

balance of payments (BOP)—an accounting system that reflects one country's financial transactions with the rest of the world

balance of trade (BOT)—the difference between a country's total exports and its total imports

banker's acceptance—a draft drawn on a bank indicating that the bank agrees to pay according to the terms of the agreement

barter—the exchange of goods or services for other goods or services without using money

Basel Accords—system for quantifying loan portfolio risk for major international banks

beneficiary—the person in whose favor a letter of credit is issued or a draft is drawn

Berne Convention of 1886—international agreement protecting the copyrights of literary and artistic works

bid-offer spread—difference between the buying and selling price

bilateral agreements—trade agreements between two countries that are not under the influence of multilateral organizations such as the WTO

bill of exchange—a written order requiring the party to which it is addressed to pay the bearer or another named party a particular sum of money at a future date; banker's acceptance

bill of lading—a document that acts as both a receipt and a contract between a shipper and a carrier; it acts as a receipt that goods have been received by the shipper and as a contract indicating the terms of the delivery

bimetallism—situation when two metals (gold and silver) are used to determine the values of different currencies

boycott—the blanket prohibition on importation of all or some goods and services from a designated country

brain drain—a term describing the departure of a country's best-educated and most intelligent people in order to seek work abroad

branch offices—offices of a company at locations other than the headquarters

Bretton Woods—the location (in New Hampshire in the United States) where forty-four countries, including the United States, established the international monetary system that was introduced to stabilize the international flow of currencies; agreement led to Bretton Woods system

bribery—payments to government officials, politicians, and political parties to gain favors that are otherwise not allowed by law

BRIC—acronym denoting countries of Brazil, Russia, India, and China

brownfield strategy—the entering of a foreign market via the purchase of an existing company

bulldog bonds—foreign bonds sold in the United Kingdom

bundled technology—technology that the owner is willing to transfer only as a part of a package or system

bureaucratic law—system of laws that is set by the current leadership in a country and is subject to change when the government changes

call option—option that allows the purchaser to buy the underlying investment

Calvo doctrine—the theory that when foreign interests choose to enter a nation and conduct business there, they are implicitly agreeing to be treated as if they were nationals and are therefore subject to the laws and decisions of the sovereign nation and have no legal recourse outside of that nation

capital account—in a nation's balance of payments, account that measures the net changes in financial assets and liabilities abroad

cartel—a group of suppliers of a commodity who agree to limit the supply of the commodity and charge an agreed-on price

cash against documents (CAD)—a payment method in which an intermediary processes the title documentation upon receipt of a cash payment

cash conversion cycle—the length of time between the purchasing of raw materials and the receipt of cash after the finished goods have been sold; usually expressed in days and determined by adding inventory days on hand and accounts receivable days on hand, and subtracting accounts payable days on hand

cash in advance (CIA)—a payment method in which the full payment is made prior to the shipment of the goods

cash with order (CWO)—a payment method in which the payment is made when the order is placed

central banks—government institutions that control the growth of the money supply and regulate commercial banks

centrally planned economy—government-directed economic activity of a country through government ownership of the means of production

certificate of origin—a document that certifies the origin of a good

choice of forum—requirement of an international business contract that stipulates the relevant jurisdiction where potential disputes will be settled

circumstantial uniformity—the use of different methods of accounting standards depending on the variations in the economic conditions in a given country

civil law—codified system of laws in the form of statutes

Clayton Act—a US antitrust law that prohibits the acquisition of stock or assets of another firm if the purchase will reduce the competitiveness in the industry

clean letter of credit—letter of credit that requires only presentation of the bill of exchange to obtain payment

codetermination—a management method that includes representatives of labor in the decision-making process and on the boards of the companies

collective bargaining—the process by which management and labor discuss wages and working conditions

commanding heights—key industries required to effectively control an economy

common agricultural policy (CAP)—a policy of the European Union focused on price supports for existing agricultural programs

common law—a law established through precedents resulting from the cultural traditions of a country

common market—a customs union that also eliminates the barriers that inhibit the movement of the factors of production

comparative advantage—the theory, first introduced by David Ricardo, that even when one country has an absolute advantage in the production of two goods it can still benefit from trade if it trades with a country that has a relative advantage in the production of one good

compound tariff—combination of a specific and ad valorem tariff

confirmed letter of credit—a letter of credit confirmed by another bank that adds its guarantee

consignment—selling of goods by an agent representing the exporter; the agent delivers a payment, net of a commission, to the exporter

constant-dollar accounting—reporting assets, liabilities, expenses, and revenues in terms of the same purchasing power

contract manufacturing—the subcontracting by a multinational firm of the manufacturing operations to a local company via a specified contract

convergence criteria—specific targets of fiscal and monetary performance as specified in the Maastricht Treaty

convertible currency—currency that can be exchanged for another country's currency without the consent of the domestic government

copyrights—exclusive rights of authors, composers, singers, musicians, and artists to publish, dispose of, or release their work as they see fit for a specified period of time

correspondent bank—a bank that conducts business with foreign banks located in its country

cost and freight (C&F)—a term indicating that the cost and freight expense are included in the quoted price of the good; implies that the purchaser must secure insurance for the shipment of the goods

cost, insurance (CI)—a term indicating that the cost and insurance are included in the quoted price of the good; implies that the purchaser must secure shipment of the good

cost, insurance, freight (CIF)—a term that indicates that the cost, insurance, and freight are included in the quoted price of a good

cost method of accounting—an accounting method whereby the parent company reports income from a subsidiary only when the subsidiary declares a dividend to the parent (the parent values the subsidiary as an investment)

cost-plus pricing—an amount is added to the cost of production to determine appropriate pricing at the next level of distribution

counterfeiting—illegally using a well-known name on copies of a firm's goods

countertrade—a means of exchange by which one government attempts to limit the outflow of hard currency from the country by providing payment in the form of other goods

countervailing duty—an added tariff applied to goods that have benefited from an export subsidy

covered interest arbitrage—earning profits on interest-bearing instruments through differences in the spot and forward exchange rates

crawling peg—a foreign exchange relationship in which a country makes small periodic changes in the value of its currency with the intent to move it to a particular value relative to another currency over a period of time

credit risk insurance—a type of insurance that protects against nonpayment after the delivery of goods

cross-border supply—services supplied from one country to another

cross rate—the exchange rate between two countries based on the exchange rate of each currency against a third currency, usually the US dollar

cultural cluster approach—attempt to group cultures based on geographical similarities

cultural universals—similar elements that can be found in all cultures

culture—the learned beliefs and attitudes that characterize human populations, passed on from earlier generations

culture shock—the anxiety an individual experiences when introduced into an unfamiliar cultural situation

currency exchange controls—a government's means of determining how much foreign currency citizens or visitors can have and the exchange rate they must pay for it

currency swap—an agreement by which currency is exchanged at a specified rate only to be reversed at a future date

current account—part of the balance of payment account; measures the aggregate import and export of goods and services

current-cost accounting—an accounting system with the objective of accounting for the effects of inflation in the costs of assets

customs—(1) the process of collecting the duties on exports and imports; (2) the officials who collect the duties

customs union—an agreement between two countries that eliminates import restrictions between the member countries and establishes a common tariff for all other countries

date draft—a draft that matures a specified number of days after the date it is issued

deemed paid credit—an indirect foreign tax credit that can be taken in addition to the direct foreign tax credit to avoid double taxation

deferred payment credit—a letter of credit that specifies payment at some time following review of the exporter's shipping documentation

demurrage fees—costs for the storage of an exporter's goods at the foreign loading dock

depreciation of a currency—a reduction in the worth of a currency when compared to another currency or gold

devaluation—a government's decision to reduce the value of its country's currency by increasing the amount of local currency needed to buy foreign currencies

developed countries—countries that are advanced in GNP and living standards

developing countries—countries that are technologically less advanced than developed countries

development banks—institutions established in developing countries to foster economic development through investment or loans

direct investment—operation that has sufficient foreign ownership such that the firm's management decisions are influenced by the foreign interests

direct lobbying—influencing by establishing a liaison or representative office in the capital city and establishing direct contact with local officials and politicians

direct quote—the number of units of the home currency that are required to buy a foreign currency

disposable income—the portion of an individual's income available for consumption after taxes

distributor—an agent who maintains an inventory of the supplier's merchandise and sells directly to the consumer

documentary letter of credit—a letter of credit where a bank requires presentation of documentation in order to obtain payment

Doha Agenda—round of WTO trade discussions aimed at improving the performance of developing nations and reducing the remaining barriers to international trade (especially in agriculture)

domestic international sales corporation (DISC)—a subsidiary of a US firm established solely for exporting goods; receives special tax incentives to operate

double taxation avoidance treaty—agreement between nations whereby revenues of an MNC would not be taxed in the foreign country in return for the same treatment in the other country

Dracula effect—phenomenon of exposing a problem to light in the hope that it shrivels up and goes away; coined by economist Jagdish Bhagwati

draft (bill of exchange)—the order given by the drawer for the drawee to pay the payee a specified amount at a future date

drawback—the refund of duty on imported components used in the manufacture of goods that are exported on completion

drawee—the individual or firm responsible for payment of the indicated amount of a draft to the payee

drawer—the individual or firm that issues a draft

dual-equity issue—listing stock for sale on domestic and international stock exchanges simultaneously

dumping—selling goods in a country at a price below the cost of production and freight or, in some circumstances, selling goods in a foreign country at prices lower than those charged for the same good in the home country

duty—a tax one country must pay to sell its products in another country

economic exposure—the degree to which fluctuations in exchange rates will affect the net present value of the future cash flows of a company

embargo—a quota that prohibits all trade between countries

entry mode—the manner in which a firm chooses to enter a foreign market

equity method of accounting—reporting the value of equity shares (from 20 to 50 percent ownership interest) in a subsidiary on the parent company's consolidated financial statements

ethnocentric—having a strategy focused on the home market only

ethnocentric pricing strategy—a pricing policy in which a firm maintains the same prices that it charges in its home market in all the markets in which it operates

ethno-domination—situation when certain ethnic groups control the majority of business interests in a given market

euro—the official currency of the European Union

Euro area—the seventeen countries using the euro currency

Eurobonds—bonds traded primarily in Europe and in a currency different from the currency of the country in which they are sold

Eurocurrency—a currency in use in countries other than the nation of origin

Eurodollars—US dollars on deposit in banks outside the United States

Euro-equity issue—stocks sold on stock exchanges solely outside the home country of the issuing firm

Euronext—integrated stock market that consists of the stock exchanges in Paris, Amsterdam, Brussels, and others in Europe

European Bank for Reconstruction and Development (EBRD)—a bank that promotes the economic development of eastern and central Europe

European Central Bank (ECB)—central bank of the European Union

European Community—a common market formed in 1958 for its member nations; in 1991 there were twelve member countries: Belgium, Denmark, France, Germany, Greece, Ireland, Italy, Luxembourg, the Netherlands, Portugal, Spain, and the United Kingdom; later expanded into the European Union

European Court of Justice—court through which member states of the European Union can seek redress of disputes

European Economic Area (EEA)—common market that includes the members of the EU plus Iceland, Liechtenstein, and Norway

European Economic Community (EEC)—a common market for some nations not in the European Union, such as Iceland, Norway, and Switzerland

European Investment Bank (EIB)—a bank that pursues goals of regional development and economic and social cohesion within the European Union for current and upcoming members of the EU

European Monetary System (EMS)—system established in March 1979 in an effort to stabilize the currencies of European Community nations

European Monetary Union (EMU)—economic integration for most European Union member nations involving movement to the euro as currency for all members

European terms—foreign currency prices quoted in terms of one US dollar

European Union (EU)—group of twenty-eight economically integrated member states

exchange rate—a determination of value using only two currencies

exchange risk—the risk that one currency will be lower in value than it was previously

excise taxes—taxes levied on specific products or industries to achieve desired policy objectives by a host country's government (also known as sin taxes)

export broker—a firm or individual who locates and introduces buyers and sellers for a fee

Export-Import Bank of the United States (Ex-Im Bank)—bank that assists US exporting firms by issuing loans, guarantees, and insurance

export management company—a firm that acts as the export department for other firms; also known as export trading company

export processing zone—location where import duties are not levied because the goods are re-exported

exposure netting—the process of holding two currencies that are believed to be a hedge against each other

expropriation—seizure of property by a foreign government

extraction tax—tax that serves to reimburse a host country for the depletion of a natural resource

extraterritoriality—process by which a government attempts to apply its laws outside its geographic boundaries

factors of production—land, labor, capital, and technology

first to file—patent system in which the first to file a patent in a given country is awarded the patent without the need to prove that it is the inventor

first to invent—patent system in which patent protection is granted to the person or entity that first invented the technology or product

first world—the countries of the developed world, such as the United States, Canada, Japan, and the countries of western Europe

Fisher effect—the observation that in the long run, the real rates of return in countries that have no restrictions on the mobility of capital are the same, but the nominal rates vary in proportion to the expected rate of inflation in a particular currency

floating exchange rates—a process that allows for the valuation of currencies based on the supply and demand of the currencies

force majeure clause—a clause that excuses a party from fulfilling a contract because of conditions beyond its control

Foreign Corrupt Practices Act—legislation directed toward the elimination of bribery between US and foreign firms

foreign direct investment—foreign investment in a firm that constitutes effective control of the firm

foreign earned income—all monies employees receive as payment for services rendered in a foreign country; includes wages, salaries, and commissions

foreign exchange—transactions involving the exchange of one currency for another

foreign sales corporation (FSC)—a firm provided for in the tax code that permits US corporations to shelter income derived from exports

foreign tax credit—an income tax credit available to citizens or corporations that paid tax abroad on the same income

foreign trade organization (FTO)—an organization established in many ex-communist economies that is authorized to import and export goods of a particular industry

foreign trade zone—location determined by the government that does not need to pay tariffs or duties on imports, particularly goods that are assembled and re-exported

foreign unearned income—income that is derived from overseas investments

forward contract—a contract that establishes an exchange for a particular currency to be delivered at a future date

four tigers—Hong Kong, Singapore, South Korea, and Taiwan

fourth world—the least economically developed nations of the world

franchising—a licensing system in which a party is authorized to use the name and create the product of another firm for a fee

free alongside (FAS)—a term indicating that the quoted price includes the cost associated with delivering the goods to the desired vessel for shipment

free in (FI)—a term indicating that the cost of loading and unloading the vessel is the responsibility of the firm or individual who has hired the vessel

free on board (FOB)—a term indicating that the quoted price includes loading the goods onto a vehicle at some particular location

free out (FO)—a term indicating that the cost of loading the vessel is the responsibility of the firm or individual who has hired the vessel

free port—a port that does not require the payment of duties for use

free trade area—trade agreement that eliminates trade barriers among its members and allows them to set their own trade policies with nonmember states

free trade zone—government-established zones that permit free entry and storage of goods; duties do not need to be paid until the goods leave the zone

freight forwarder—a firm that transports goods for export

functional currency—the currency in which the cash flow of a company is generated

General Agreement on Tariffs and Trade (GATT)—a treaty intended to limit trade barriers and promote trade through the reduction of tariffs among the signatory nations

General Agreement on Trade in Services (GATS)—set of multilateral rules governing international trade in services

general export license—a license required to export goods not needing special authorization

geocentric—having an integrated world strategy that is best suited for the majority of markets where a company operates

globalization of markets—trend toward one huge global market through increasing volume and the variety of cross-border transactions in goods, services, capital, information, and labor force

GNI per capita—gross national income per capita; the amount of the nation's gross national product representing each individual of the total population (also known as GDP per capita)

gold exchange standard—a system established at Bretton Woods in which the United States agreed to exchange gold for US dollars at an agreed-on rate

gray-market exports—goods that are legally imported from the producing country into another country and then re-exported to a third country, where higher prices are then charged for the same goods

green paradox—situation where announced green policies by governments tend to increase global warming as more fossil fuels are brought to market before any intended sustainable alternatives materialize; phrase coined by Hans Werner Sinn, German economist.

greenfield strategy—entering a foreign market via starting up a new company

greenhouse effect—rise in global temperatures due to increase in greenhouse gases such as carbon dioxide, methane, and nitrous oxide

greenhouse gases—gases that contribute to global warming by trapping heat in Earth's atmosphere

gross domestic product (GDP)—the aggregate value of a nation's output based on factors of production located within the country but excluding exports and imports

gross national income (GNI)—the aggregate value of all goods and services produced by a country; also known as gross national product (GNP)

guest workers—authorized foreign labor

hard currency—currency that can be exchanged for other currencies quickly and without government permission

hard technology—physical hardware, capital goods, blueprints, and specifications

harmonization—the process of increasing the compatibility of accounting practices by setting limits on how much they can vary

hedging—using various instruments to protect against exchange-rate risk

high-context culture—culture in which a conversation's context is just as important as the words that are actually spoken

Hofstede's five dimensions of culture—theory that culture can best be described in terms of five primary areas: (1) social orientation (individual vs. collective), (2) power orientation (power tolerant vs. power respect), (3) uncertainty orientation (acceptance vs. avoidance), (4) goal orientation (aggressive vs. passive), and (5) time orientation (long-term vs. short-term)

home-country nationals—citizens of the country in which the headquarters of a firm is located

horizontal integration—business expansion into related product lines

host-country nationals—citizens of the country in which a subsidiary is located

Hotelling Rule—environmental economics rule whereby the price of an extracted resource rises at a rate equal to the capital market interest rate; rule by Harold Hotelling, economist.

hyperinflation—inflation that increases in hundreds or thousands of percent

import substitution—a policy of developing countries to promote the development of industries that are intended to replace the need for imports

indirect lobbying—a policy of influencing foreign governments with the use of news media and advertising to effect change in public opinion

indirect quote—rate quote in which the home currency is expressed as a unit and the price is shown by the number of units of a foreign currency that are required to purchase one unit of the home currency

infant-industry argument—the argument that an industry new to a country, especially a developing country, needs to be protected by tariff walls or risks being destroyed by larger foreign competition before it can grow and develop

inflation—increase in prices over time measured against a certain benchmark, typically known as the base year

Inter-American Development Bank (IADB)—a development bank located in Washington, DC, that is specifically geared toward the development of Latin America

interest-rate swap—exchanging fixed-interest-rate instruments for those with floating interest rates

internalization—a policy of retaining information within the company

International Accounting Standards Board (IASB)—a group whose aim is to harmonize the rules of accounting used in various countries

International Centre for Settlement of Investment Disputes (ICSID)—a group affiliated with the World Bank that provides a forum for resolving disputes between states and foreign investors

International Court of Justice—located in the Netherlands, the primary court of law for countries that have legal questions involving other countries

International Development Association (IDA)—affiliated with the World Bank Group, an association that was established in 1960 to provide long-term funds to the poorest member countries of the World Bank

International Federation of Accountants (IFAC)—a group whose aim is to harmonize international auditing principles and procedures

International Finance Corporation (IFC)—a part of the World Bank that loans money for private development in developing countries

International Labor Organization (ILO)—group affiliated with the United Nations that attempts to define and promote international standards regarding safety, health, and other working conditions

international law—rules that govern the activities and policies of nations with other countries; established between individual countries and apply only to countries that have entered into the agreements

International Monetary Fund (IMF)—Bretton Woods–created institution that promotes the expansion of balanced growth of international trade

international monetary system (IMS)—the structures and policies needed for the international transfer and exchange of funds

international trading companies—firms that supply most of the foreign goods to the markets in which they operate

intervention currency—a currency purchased by a government to affect the value of the government's currency

invisibles—services

irrevocable letter of credit—a letter of credit that is payable if all the conditions of the letter of credit are met

Japan Bank for International Cooperation (JBIC)—established and funded by the government of Japan; aim is to provide financial assistance to developing (primarily Asian) countries

J-curve effect—an effect associated with the devaluation of a currency in which the balance of payments actually worsens before it improves, thus the *J* shape of the curve

joint venture—*see* strategic alliance

jurisdiction—capacity of a nation to prescribe a course of conduct for its citizens and to enforce a rule of law on its citizens

just-in-time (JIT) inventory system—an inventory system in which deliveries are made as component parts are needed; a system created in an effort to reduce the costs associated with carrying inventory; also known as *kanban*

kanban—*see* just-in-time inventory system

Kyoto Protocol—international agreement to reduce the collective emissions of greenhouse gases in order achieve cleaner air in all parts of the world

lagging—creating deliberate delays with respect to the outflows or inflows (e.g., increasing the accounts payable days on hand)

laissez-faire—the concept of freedom of enterprise and freedom of commerce with minimal government intervention in a society's economic activity

leading—the early receipt of goods (e.g., reducing the accounts receivable days on hand for a firm)

Leontief paradox—a discovery by Wassily Leontief that US exports required less capital and more labor than US imports

letter of credit—a credit instrument that guarantees that the importer's bank will pay the exporter on receipt of certain documents

letters rogatory—the means by which courts from other countries request evidence from one country while in another country

licensing—a business arrangement that permits a firm or individual to use the patents, copyrights, and technology of another firm

lingua franca—a foreign language used as a common language in countries that have many languages

Linaburg-Maduell Transparency Index—ranking index for sovereign wealth funds based on transparency

lockouts—the closing or locking of the plant by an employer, and the barring of workers from entering the premises

London Court of International Arbitration—legal center that deals with disputes regarding private international commercial transactions

London Inter-Bank Offered Rate (LIBOR)—the interest rate used among large banks on large, overnight Eurocurrency loans

long position—a situation in which a firm makes a purchase of a currency or commodity in the expectation of a future appreciation in its value

Louvre Accord—international agreement made in Paris in 1987 by the G6 countries (United States, Canada, United Kingdom, France, West Germany, and Italy) to raise the value of the dollar on world markets

low-context culture—culture in which the words used by the speaker explicitly convey the speaker's message to the listener

Maastricht Treaty—agreement that provided the framework for the economic and political integration of the European Union; came into effect in November 1993 and set certain convergence criteria of monetary and fiscal performance that each member country would try to achieve for successful economic and political integration of the EU member states

Madrid Agreement of 1991—international agreement on the protection of trademarks

managed float—a term indicating government involvement in maintaining the exchange rate of a particular currency

management contract—an agreement in which one firm supplies managerial assistance to another for a fee

maquiladoras—in-bond export industry in which components produced in the United States are exported duty-free to Mexico for assembly and then exported duty-free back to the United States for completion

marine insurance—insurance that covers losses at sea that are not covered by the insurance of the carrier

market capitalization—the value of total stocks outstanding at a particular time (stock price multiplied by the number of shares outstanding)

marketing mix—a firm's process of addressing the marketing issues of price, promotion, distribution, and the product

marketing segmentation—the process of recognizing differences among consumers such that the firm can address those particular needs

marking identification—symbols used on cargo

Marshall Plan—program established by the US government after World War II to aid European countries

matrix organization—an organizational concept that superimposes one structure over another to gain both functional and creative expertise

mediation—a less formal third-party dispute resolution method than arbitration

mercantilism—an economic philosophy of the late seventeenth and early eighteenth centuries that encouraged the accumulation of gold and other precious metals

Mercosur Accord—customs union among South American nations

MINT—acronym denoting the countries of Mexico, Indonesia, Nigeria, and Turkey

Mittelstand—small to medium German enterprises with an export orientation

money laundering—the act of concealing the source of ill-gotten funds by changing them into legitimate business profits and bank deposits

moral hazard—a hidden reckless action of external partners who know they will be saved if things go wrong

most favored nation (MFN)—a clause in most treaties requiring that a trade concession that is given to one country be given to all other signature countries

multilateral agreements—trade agreements among three or more countries that are under the influence of multilateral organizations such as the WTO

Multilateral Investment Guarantee Agency (MIGA)—an agency affiliated with the World Bank Group that was established in 1988 to promote overseas direct investment flows into developing countries by providing guarantees against political risks

national competitive advantage theory—a theory by Michael Porter that states that successful international trade comes from the interaction of four country- and firm-specific elements: (1) factor conditions, (2) demand conditions, (3) related and supporting industries, and (4) the strategy, structure, and rivalry of a firm

nationalization—process in which a host government takes over an operation

net statistical discrepancy—errors and omissions in the balance of payments calculation for a given nation

newly industrialized countries (NICs)—*see* four tigers

nondiscrimination—treatment of foreign enterprises on the same basis as domestic enterprises

nontariff barriers—government policies that create restrictions on imports without the use of tariffs, for example, quotas, customs procedures, and safety and quality requirements

NOREX Alliance—integrated stock markets of Denmark, Iceland, Norway, Sweden, and a few other countries

North American Free Trade Agreement (NAFTA)—free trade agreement among Canada, Mexico, and the United States initiated in 1994

official reserves account—a nation's holdings of monetary gold and internationally accepted currencies

offshoring—outsourcing to overseas (or simply nondomestic) markets

oligopoly—a market with very few sellers

oligopsony—a market with very few buyers

one-step method—recording currency transaction using spot rate for the currency in effect on the day of the transaction

open account—a method of trade in which the exporter ships without guarantee of payment from the buyer

open insurance policy—an insurance policy that covers all shipments over a period of time

options—the right to purchase or sell before or on a given date

ordinary shares—shares that confer voting rights (on the London and Australian stock markets) and are similar to common stock in the United States

Organization for Economic Cooperation and Development (OECD)—group that publishes economic data, conducts research, and provides policy guidance for its member nations (primarily of the developed world)

Organization of Petroleum Exporting Countries (OPEC)—a cartel of twelve oil-producing nations

outsourcing—business decision to seek external firms for assistance in one or more nonessential operations

Overseas Private Investment Corporation (OPIC)—a corporation of the US government that insures US business interests overseas against such things as expropriation and the inconvertibility of currency

packing list—a list including quantities and identification of items being shipped

paper gold—*see* special drawing rights (SDRs)

parallel loans—*see* back-to-back loans

Paris Convention—international agreement that protects patents and trademarks

patents—rights granted by governments to the inventors of products or processes for exclusive manufacturing, production, sale, or use of those products or processes; the equivalent to a legal monopoly over the subject matter of the patent for a period of time

pegging—a fixed exchange relationship

perils of the sea—an insurance term used to denote marine occurrences such as stranding, lightning, collision, and seawater damage

petrodollars—name for the vast supply of loanable funds coming from oil-exporting countries, which led in part to the Latin American debt crisis of the 1980s

piracy—the use of illegal and unauthorized means to obtain goods, such as copying software

Plaza Accord—international agreement made at the Plaza Hotel in New York City in September 1985 that brought down the value of the US dollar

political risk—the risk associated with the political environment of a foreign country, such as social unrest within the country or government actions that alter a firm's ability to operate in the foreign country

polycentric—having strategies in multiple countries without integrating them

portfolio investment—investment for purposes other than control of a company; does not require the physical presence of a firm's personnel or products on foreign shores

predatory pricing—attempt to capture market share by cutting prices below the price charged in the home market

premium (in forward exchange)—a term indicating that the forward rate exceeds the spot rate

price fixing—collusion in the administration of prices

primary sector—traditional economic activities such as agriculture and mining

principle of comity—the principle by which each nation defers to another's sovereignty in the protection of rights of foreign citizens by showing reciprocal respect for other countries' laws and powers with respect to the acts of citizens abroad

Private Export Funding Corporation (PEFCO)—an organization that lends to foreign buyers in need of financing to purchase US exports

private law—law pertaining to individuals within nation-states, typically negotiated via a contract

process technology—knowledge used in the process of making a product or service

product adaptation—modification of the existing product line to take into account the cultural, legal, or economic differences between the domestic and foreign markets

product extension—marketing the same products abroad as are marketed at home, hoping that the foreign markets have tastes and preferences similar to those of the home market

product technology—knowledge used to make a product or service

production factor endowments—assets such as land, labor, capital, management and technological skills, specialized production facilities, and established distribution networks

productivity—the value of the output produced by a unit of labor or capital

progressive taxation—the system of taxation that holds that the more an individual or corporation earns, the higher the tax it pays

protectionism—government intervention in trade markets to protect specific industries in its economy

Protestant ethic—the view that work is a means of salvation, an attitude that has its roots in the Protestant Reformation

public law—the manner in which nations interact according to a legal framework

purchasing power parity (PPP)—a method of determining exchange rates between two currencies based on the purchasing power of similar goods

purposive uniformity—varying the determination of accounting standards according to the diversity of users and the circumstances of the users in a given country

put option—option that allows the buyer to sell the underlying investment

quota—a specified amount of a product that a government will permit to be imported

rationalization—a strategy to achieve economies of scale under which a subsidiary changes its purpose for production from manufacturing for its own market to manufacturing a limited number of component parts for use by several or all subsidiaries

reciprocity—*see* principle of comity

red-chip stocks—equities that are issued on the Hong Kong stock market but are controlled by mainland China

religious law—*see* theocracy

remitting bank—the bank that initiates payment of money

revaluation—an improvement of one currency in value in relation to another

revocable letter of credit—a letter of credit that the opening bank has the right to modify or cancel without notifying the beneficiary

rules of origin—specifications clarifying what actually constitutes member goods and services within a free trade area

samurai bonds—foreign bonds sold in Japan

Sarbanes-Oxley Act—legal requirements for increased financial reporting standards in the aftermath of numerous corporate fraud scandals in the United States

secondary sector—manufacturing and industrial activity

severance tax—*see* extraction tax

Sherman Act—US antitrust law that prohibits monopolistic activities in order to preserve competition in both US and foreign markets

short position—a situation in which a firm makes a purchase of currency or commodity in the expectation of a future depreciation in its value

shunto—spring wage offensive in Japan, when union wage negotiations take place

sight draft—a draft that is payable upon presentation to the payee

sin taxes—*see* excise taxes

Smithsonian Agreement—an agreement reached in December 1971 by the leading ten industrialized nations that established a new international monetary system

smuggling—the illegal trade and transportation of goods devised to circumvent customs duties, quotas, and other constraints on the movement of goods

society—a political and social entity that is geographically defined and is composed of people and their culture

sociocultural—factors that influence both society and culture

soft currency—a currency that cannot be easily converted

soft loans—loans that can be repaid with a soft currency and that charge a low interest rate

soft technology—management, marketing, financial organization, and administrative techniques that can be combined with hard technology to serve the needs of the user

sogo shosha—a Japanese general trading company

sovereign debt—the debt of a national government

sovereign immunity—the immunity of a government from the courts of its own country

sovereign wealth funds (SWF)—government investment vehicles funded by foreign exchange assets

sovereignty—the principle that individual nations have absolute power over the governing of their populace and the activities that occur within their borders

special drawing rights (SDRs)—also known as *paper gold*; rights created by the IMF that are essentially book entries that represent the right of the country holding them to access resources of equivalent value

specific duties—duties that are assessed based on a physical unit of measurement (per ton, per bushel, etc.) and are stipulated at a specific monetary value

spot exchange—the deliveries are completed within the same day that the deal is struck

spot rate—the exchange rate between two currencies used for immediate delivery

spread (in the forward market)—the difference between the spot rate and the forward rate

spread (in the spot market)—the difference between the quoted buy and sell rates of the foreign exchange trader

standard industrial code (SIC)—a coding system used by the US government to classify goods and services

standard international trade classification—a United Nations coding system used to classify commodities involved in international trade

steamship conference—steamship operators who agree to charge the same freight rate

straight bonds—debt issued with a fixed interest rate

strategic alliance—business arrangement in which two or more companies join together to form some sort of an operation; *see also* joint venture

strike—action that occurs when workers refuse to work and walk out of the place of employment

subsidiaries—companies that are owned by a parent company

subsidies—governmental (often monetary) support of specific industries to make them more competitive in international trade

switch trading—a type of countertrade in which a country unable to pay in a hard currency locates goods for exchange from a third country to pay its debt

tare weight—the weight of the container and packaging containing a good

target return levels—a method of price setting in which a fixed percentage or level of monetary return is added to the total costs of production

tariff—a tax assessed on goods that are imported or exported from a country

tariff quota—a tariff that requires a higher tax payment after a specified amount of the good has been imported or exported from the country

tax haven—a country with low or no required tax payments on income earned in other countries or on capital gains

tax incentive—a tax holiday or reduction of taxes due granted to a company making an investment

tax treaty—an agreement between two countries concerning the taxation of citizens and corporations of each country operating in the other

technology transfer—process by which knowledge is diffused through learning from its place of origin and introduction to other world markets

temporal method—method of accounting in which monetary items are translated at the current rate, while nonmonetary items are translated at the rates that preserve their original measurement bases

tenor—the time period allowed in a draft

terms of trade—ratio of export prices for a country in relation to its import prices

tertiary sector—services and related industries

theocracy—system of law based on religious beliefs that govern the behavior of a country's citizens

third-country national—citizens of neither the country of a subsidiary nor of the parent company

third world—less-developed countries (LDCs)

tied agent—independent intermediary who can only advise a customer on products offered by its firm, society, or insurer

time draft—draft that allows a certain period of time to elapse before payment is made

trade acceptance—draft which is legally enforceable once "accepted" is written on draft

trade creation—the resulting trading relationships once countries shift from a high-cost producer to a low-cost producer in the same customs union

trade deflection—process by which nonmember nations of a free trade area reroute their exports to member nations with the lowest external trade barriers in order to access the free trade area at the lowest possible cost

trade diversion—process by which member nations of a free trade area stop importing from lower-cost nonmember states in favor of member states

trade name—name used by manufacturers to differentiate their goods with customers

trademark—design or logo used by manufacturers to differentiate their goods with customers

transaction exposure—the calculation of the loss or gain associated with transferring currencies over national borders; also known as the impact of foreign exchange rates on a company's accounts receivable and accounts payable

transaction statement—a document that specifies the terms between an importer and an exporter

transaction taxes—taxes levied at the time a transaction or exchange occurs

transfer pricing—the price associated with the transfer or sale of goods between related companies or between a parent company and its subsidiaries

translation—the process by which financial statements are restated using a different currency

translation exposure—*see* accounting exposure

transparency—the requirement that governments should publish all laws and regulations

triangular arbitrage—taking profits from an imperfection in the exchange rates relating to three currencies; buying and selling the same currencies in different markets to make a profit from fractional differences in each market

Triffin paradox—during the gold standard, the more heavy the reliance by the rest of the world on US dollars for the expansion of world trade, the less confidence there would be in the United States' ability to honor its commitment of redeeming dollars for gold

TRIPS (Trade-Related Aspects Regarding Intellectual Property Rights)—an agreement created under the GATT

turnkey operation—a contract in which one firm constructs a facility and prepares it for operation and then relinquishes it to its new owners

turnover—an example of a term that has different meanings in different locations ("turnover" means sales in England, but means the replenishment of inventory stock in the United States)

two-step method—accounting for gains and losses for both the business activity and the currency exchange

unbundled technology—technology available separate from the total system of technology

unilateral transfers—flow of funds or goods for which nothing is expected in return

unitary taxes—taxes imposed by a specific state on the basis of a multinational's multistate or worldwide profits, rather than based on the profits generated from the host state

United Nations Conference on Trade and Development (UNCTAD)—conference established in 1964 to address concerns of developing nations on issues of international trade that affected their economic development

United Nations Educational, Scientific, and Cultural Organization (UNESCO)—specialized organization of the United Nations; its purpose is to contribute to peace and security by promoting international collaboration through education, science, and culture in order to further international respect for justice, the rule of law, and human rights along with fundamental freedoms proclaimed in the United Nations charter.

Universal Copyright Convention (UCC) of 1952—an international copyright protection agreement administered by UNESCO

utilitarianism—philosophy that states that moral values are reflected in policies that provide the greatest happiness to the greatest number of people

value-added tax (VAT)—a tax assessed based on an improvement made to the product that increases the value of the product

variable costs—costs that vary with the levels of production, such as labor or raw materials.

vertical integration—business expansion into areas within the same production chain

visibles—manufactured goods

voluntarism—principle that states that the workers alone will define and pursue their self-interest for the welfare of the enterprise

water's edge taxation—taxation that limits states in taxing the profits of a multinational firm that are generated in the United States, as opposed to worldwide profits

Webb-Pomerene Act—US law that allows for exemption from Sherman and Clayton antitrust laws if domestic firms join together for the purposes of gaining access to foreign markets

wharfage—the fee to use a pier or dock

wholly owned subsidiary—an entry mode in which the investing firm owns 100 percent of the new entity in a host country. *See also* brownfield strategy

wildcat strikes—strike by workers during an existing contract and with little or no notice to the employer

without reserve—a term indicating that an agent or representative is authorized to make decisions without consulting the group that he or she represents

World Bank—bank established initially to assist the countries of Europe following World War II; now assists in the development of developing countries

World Intellectual Property Organization (WIPO)—international signatory organization formed to protect intellectual property worldwide

World Trade Organization (WTO)—international forum formed in 1995 for resolving trade disputes

xenophobia—fear of the strange or foreign

yankee bonds—foreign bonds sold in the United States

zaibatsu—large Japanese conglomerates that also have trading companies as integral components

Index

About the Authors

**Riad A. Ajami** is currently professor of international business and global strategy and the director of the Center for Global Business at Wright State University, Dayton, Ohio. Professor Ajami previously held the position of professor of international business (with tenure) and director of the International Business Program at the Fisher College of Business at Ohio State University. Prior to joining Raj Soin College of Business, Professor Ajami was Charles A. Hayes Distinguished Professor of Business and director of the Center for Global Business Education and Research at the University of North Carolina, Greensboro (UNCG). Before joining UNCG, Professor Ajami held the position of Benjamin Forman Chair Professor of International Business and director of the Center for International Business and Economic Growth at the Rochester Institute of Technology. He has had visiting appointments as the Dr. M. Lee Pearce Distinguished Professor of International Business and Economic Cooperation, School of International Studies at the University of Miami; School of Business Administration at the University of California, Berkeley; the Wharton School, University of Pennsylvania; the Harvard Center for International Affairs at Harvard University; Hautes Etudes Commercials (Grande Ecole of Management), France; American University of Beirut; Istanbul University; and a distinguished faculty affiliate at Audencia (School of Management), France.

Dr. Ajami received his PhD from Pennsylvania State University in International Business, Strategic Management and Oil Economics.

Currently, Dr. Ajami is the editor in chief of the *Journal of Asia-Pacific Business* and serves as an editorial board member of *Competitiveness Review*, *Journal of Global Marketing*, *Journal of Transnational Management Development*, and other leading international, academic business journals.

Dr. Ajami is also the coauthor of *The Psychology of Marketing: Cross-Cultural Perspectives* (Gower Publishing, 2010); *Customer Relationship Management: A Global Perspective* (Gower Publishing, 2008); and *The Global Enterprise: Entrepreneurship and*

Value Creation (Haworth Press, 2007); and *International Business: Theory and Practice* (M.E. Sharpe 2006, second edition). He is also a frequent contributor to other books on the subject of international business. He has had articles on international business published in the *Wall Street Journal*, *Journal of International Business Studies*, *Management International Review*, *Strategic Management Journal*, *Journal of International Management*, and other leading international, academic business journals. Professor Ajami has appeared on national television and radio, including *Nightline*, PBS *News Hour*, *NBC News*, CNN, National Public Radio, and CBS Radio. Dr. Ajami was a principal and cofounder of the consulting firm Management International: Consultants and Advisors, based in Luxembourg and New York City.

G. Jason Goddard is currently vice president at Wells Fargo, where he has been a commercial lender for over fifteen years. Mr. Goddard is currently real estate risk advisor for income-producing investment real estate loans in the business and community banking segments, working in Winston-Salem, North Carolina. He obtained his MBA from the Bryan School at the University of North Carolina at Greensboro. Mr. Goddard is currently an instructor at the Bryan School at UNCG and the School of Business at Wake Forest University and is the assistant editor of the *Journal of Asia-Pacific Business*, where he has authored numerous articles. Mr. Goddard teaches the investment real estate course at both the undergraduate and master's level at Wake Forest University. Mr. Goddard also teaches the subject annually at the RMA-ECU Commercial Real Estate Lending School at East Carolina University in Greenville, North Carolina. He has also taught both an undergraduate and master's-level course in international business at UNCG, where he has coordinated the *America in the Global Economy* lecture series. Mr. Goddard has twice led a group of UNC-G MBA students on the study-abroad program in Paris, and teaches annually in Ludwigshafen, Germany, at the University of Applied Sciences. He has also taught the elective courses Customer Relationship Management, Financial Markets and Institutions, and International Finance at UNCG. Mr. Goddard has coauthored four books: *International Business: Theory and Practice* (M.E. Sharpe, 2006, second edition); *Customer Relationship Management: A Global Perspective* (Gower, 2008); *The Psychology of Marketing: Cross-Cultural Perspectives* (Gower, 2010); and *Real Estate Investment: A Value Based Approach* (Springer, 2012).